Theories of Journalism in a Digital Age

Given the interdisciplinary nature of digital journalism studies and the increasingly blurred boundaries of journalism, there is a need within the field of journalism studies to widen the scope of theoretical perspectives and approaches. *Theories of Journalism in a Digital Age* discusses new avenues in theorising journalism, and reassesses established theories.

Contributors to this volume describe fresh concepts such as de-differentiation, circulation, news networks, and spatiality to explain journalism in a digital age, and provide concepts which further theorise technology as a fundamental part of jour nalism, such as actants and materiality. Several chapters discuss the latitude of user positions in the digitalised domain of journalism, exploring maximal–minimal participation, routines–interpretation–agency, and mobility–cross-mediality–participation. Finally, the book provides theoretical tools with which to understand, in different social and cultural contexts, the evolving practices of journalism, including innovation, dispersed gatekeeping, and mediatized interdependency.

The chapters in this book were originally published in special issues of *Digital Journalism* and *Journalism Practice*.

Steen Steensen is Professor of Journalism and Head of the Department of Journalism and Media Studies at Oslo and Akershus University College of Applied Sciences, Norway. He has published numerous articles and book chapters on digitalization and journalism.

Laura Ahva is a Senior Research Fellow in the School of Communication, Media and Theatre at the University of Tampere, Finland. She has published articles in *Journalism Studies*, *Journalism* and *Digital Journalism*, and in various edited collections.

Journalism Studies: Theory and Practice

Series editor: *Bob Franklin*
Cardiff School of Journalism, Media and Cultural Studies, Cardiff University, UK

The journal *Journalism Studies* was established at the turn of the new millennium by Bob Franklin. It was launched in the context of a burgeoning interest in the scholarly study of journalism and an expansive global community of journalism scholars and researchers. The ambition was to provide a forum for the critical discussion and study of journalism as a subject of intellectual inquiry but also an arena of professional practice. Previously, the study of journalism in the UK and much of Europe was a fairly marginal branch of the larger disciplines of media, communication and cultural studies; only a handful of Universities offered degree programmes in the subject. *Journalism Studies* has flourished and succeeded in providing the intended public space for discussion of research on key issues within the field, to the point where in 2007 a sister journal, *Journalism Practice,* was launched to enable an enhanced focus on practice-based issues, as well as foregrounding studies of journalism education, training and professional concerns. Both journals are among the leading ranked journals within the field and publish six issues annually, in electronic and print formats. More recently, 2013 witnessed the launch of a further companion journal *Digital Journalism* to provide a site for scholarly discussion, analysis and responses to the wide ranging implications of digital technologies for the practice and study of journalism. From the outset, the publication of themed issues has been a commitment for all journals. Their purpose is first, to focus on highly significant or neglected areas of the field; second, to facilitate discussion and analysis of important and topical policy issues; and third, to offer readers an especially high quality and closely focused set of essays, analyses and discussions.

The *Journalism Studies: Theory and Practice* book series draws on a wide range of these themed issues from all journals and thereby extends the critical and public forum provided by them. The Editor of the journals works closely with guest editors to ensure that the books achieve relevance for readers and the highest standards of research rigour and academic excllence. The series makes a significant contribution to the field of journalism studies by inviting distinguished scholars, academics and journalism practitioners to discuss and debate the central concerns within the field. It also reaches a wider readership of scholars, students and practitioners across the social sciences, humanities and communication arts, encouraging them to engage critically with, but also to interrogate, the specialist scholarly studies of journalism which this series provides.

Recent titles in the series:

Theories of Journalism in a Digital Age

Edited by
Steen Steensen and Laura Ahva

Routledge
Taylor & Francis Group

LONDON AND NEW YORK

First published 2017 by Routledge

2 Park Square, Milton Park, Abingdon, Oxfordshire OX14 4RN
711 Third Avenue, New York, NY 10017

Routledge is an imprint of the Taylor & Francis Group, an informa business

First issued in paperback 2018

British Library Cataloguing in Publication Data
A catalogue record for this book is available from the British Library

ISBN 13: 978-1-138-68407-2 (hbk)
ISBN 13: 978-0-367-02945-6 (pbk)

Typeset in Myriad Pro
by RefineCatch Limited, Bungay, Suffolk

Publisher's Note
The publisher accepts responsibility for any inconsistencies that may have arisen during the conversion of this book from journal articles to book chapters, namely the possible inclusion of journal terminology.

Disclaimer
Every effort has been made to contact copyright holders for their permission to reprint material in this book. The publishers would be grateful to hear from any copyright holder who is not here acknowledged and will undertake to rectify any errors or omissions in future editions of this book.

Contents

CONTENTS

Citation Information

The following chapters were originally published in *Digital Journalism*, volume 3, issue 1 (February 2015). When citing this material, please use the original page numbering for each article, as follows:

Introduction
Theories of Journalism in a Digital Age: An exploration and introduction
Steen Steensen and Laura Ahva
Digital Journalism, volume 3, issue 1 (February 2015) pp. 1–18

Chapter 1
Actors, Actants, Audiences, and Activities in Cross-Media News Work: A matrix and a research agenda
Seth C. Lewis and Oscar Westlund
Digital Journalism, volume 3, issue 1 (February 2015) pp. 19–37

Chapter 2
Who and What do Journalism? An actor-network perspective
Alex Primo and Gabriela Zago
Digital Journalism, volume 3, issue 1 (February 2015) pp. 38–52

Chapter 3
Tracing Digital News Networks: Towards an integrated framework of the dynamics of news production, circulation and use
David Domingo, Pere Masip and Irene Costera Meijer
Digital Journalism, volume 3, issue 1 (February 2015) pp. 53–67

Chapter 4
The Notion of the "Blurring Boundaries": Journalism as a (de-)differentiated phenomenon
Wiebke Loosen
Digital Journalism, volume 3, issue 1 (February 2015) pp. 68–84

Chapter 5
The Material Traces of Journalism: A socio-historical approach to online journalism
Juliette De Maeyer and Florence Le Cam
Digital Journalism, volume 3, issue 1 (February 2015) pp. 85–100

Chapter 6
Journalism as Cultures of Circulation
Henrik Bødker
Digital Journalism, volume 3, issue 1 (February 2015) pp. 101–115

Chapter 7
Place-Based Knowledge in the Twenty-First Century: The creation of spatial journalism
Amy Schmitz Weiss
Digital Journalism, volume 3, issue 1 (February 2015) pp. 116–131

The following chapters were originally published in *Journalism Practice*, volume 9, issue 1 (February 2015). When citing this material, please use the original page numbering for each article, as follows:

Chapter 8
From Grand Narratives of Democracy to Small Expectations of Participation: Audiences, citizenship, and interactive tools in digital journalism
Chris Peters and Tamara Witschge
Journalism Practice, volume 9, issue 1 (February 2015) pp. 19–34

Chapter 9
When News is Everywhere: Understanding participation, cross-mediality and mobility in journalism from a radical user perspective
Ike Picone, Cédric Courtois, and Steve Paulussen
Journalism Practice, volume 9, issue 1 (February 2015) pp. 35–49

Chapter 10
The Relevance of Journalism: Studying news audiences in a digital era
Heikki Heikkilä and Laura Ahva
Journalism Practice, volume 9, issue 1 (February 2015) pp. 50–64

Chapter 11
Innovation through Practice: Journalism as a structure of public communication
Christoph Raetzsch
Journalism Practice, volume 9, issue 1 (February 2015) pp. 65–77

Chapter 12
Politicians as Media Producers: Current trajectories in the relation between journalists and politicians in the age of social media
Mattias Ekman and Andreas Widholm
Journalism Practice, volume 9, issue 1 (February 2015) pp. 78–91

Chapter 13
Gatekeeping in a Digital Era: Principles, practices and technological platforms
Peter Bro and Filip Wallberg
Journalism Practice, volume 9, issue 1 (February 2015) pp. 92–105

Chapter 14
Charting Theoretical Directions for Examining African Journalism in the "Digital Era"
Hayes Mawindi Mabweazara
Journalism Practice, volume 9, issue 1 (February 2015) pp. 106–122

For any permission-related enquiries please visit:
http://www.tandfonline.com/page/help/permissions

Notes on Contributors

Laura Ahva is a Senior Research Fellow in the School of Communication, Media and Theatre at the University of Tampere, Finland. She has published articles in *Journalism Studies*, *Journalism* and *Digital Journalism*, and in various edited collections.

Henrik Bødker is an Associate Professor in the Department of Communication and Culture at Aarhus University, Denmark. His research interests include art, culture and media, communication and digital design, and culture and society.

Peter Bro is Professor and Director of the Center for Journalism at the Syddansk Universitet, Denmark. His recent research has been published in *Journalism Practice*, *Digital Journalism*, and *Journalism Studies*.

Cédric Courtois is a Professor in the Faculty of Social Sciences at the Katholieke Universiteit Leuven, Belgium. His research focuses on (social) media-related audience practices and their consequences in a variety of contexts.

Juliette De Maeyer is an Assistant Professor at the Université de Montréal, Canada. She works at the intersection of journalism studies and digital technologies, with an emphasis on the materiality of newsmaking.

David Domingo is Associate Professor in the Department of Information and Communication Sciences at the Université libre de Bruxelles, Belgium. He is interested in the development of the journalism profession in the Internet age.

Mattias Ekman is a Senior Lecturer in Media and Communication Studies in the School of Humanities, Education and Social Sciences at Örebro University, Sweden.

Heikki Heikkilä is a Senior Researcher in the Department of Journalism, Communication and Media Research at the University of Tampere, Finland. His current research focuses on Wikileaks and journalism in an era of global leaks, and the legitimation challenges in a networked society.

Florence Le Cam is Chair of Journalism at the Department of Information and Communication Sciences at the Université libre de Bruxelles, Belgium. She researches the socialization of online journalists and the construction of their professional identities.

Seth C. Lewis is Shirley Papé Chair in Electronic and Emerging Media in the School of Journalism and Communication at the University of Oregon, USA. His research explores the digital transformation of journalism, human–technology interactions, and media innovation processes.

Wiebke Loosen is a Senior Researcher at the Hans Bredow Institute for Media Research, University of Hamburg, Germany. In her research, she focuses on the areas of journalism research, online communication, and methods of empirical communication research.

Hayes Mawindi Mabweazara is a Senior Lecturer in Journalism at Falmouth University, UK. He serves on the editorial board of *Digital Journalism*, is the co-editor of *Online Journalism in Africa* (2014), and is the author of *Africa's Mainstream Press in the Digital Era* that will be published in 2017.

Pere Masip is Professor in the School of Communication and International Relations Blanquerna at Ramon Llull University, Barcelona, Spain. His research focuses on the impact of technology in journalism practice.

Irene Costera Meijer is Professor of Journalism Studies at the Vrije Universiteit Amsterdam, The Netherlands. She manages several research projects which share a user/audience centred approach regarding news, coined 'Valuable Journalism'.

Steve Paulussen is an Assistant Professor in Media and Journalism Studies at the University of Antwerp, Belgium. His work focuses on different aspects of online journalism, participatory journalism, the professional profile of journalists, new media consumption, and newsroom convergence.

Chris Peters is Associate Professor of Media and Communication at Aalborg University's Copenhagen campus, Denmark. His research explores the ways people get and experience information in everyday life and the sociocultural impact of transformations in the digital era.

Ike Picone is an Assistant Professor at the Department of Communication Sciences at the Vrije Universiteit Brussels, Belgium. His research focuses on news and journalism studies and interactive and participatory news use, with a special interest in digital storytelling and self-publication.

Alex Primo is a Professor in the Department of Communication and Information at the Universidade Federal do Rio Grande do Sul, Brazil.

Christoph Raetzsch is a Postdoctoral Researcher in the Department of Journalism Studies at the Freie Universität Berlin, Germany. His research focus is on the intersections of the digital with the non-digital, and the practice and philosophy of metadata.

Amy Schmitz Weiss is Associate Professor in the School of Journalism and Media Studies at San Diego State University, California, USA. Her research interests include online journalism, media sociology, news production, multimedia journalism, and international communication.

Steen Steensen is Professor of Journalism and Head of the Department of Journalism and Media Studies at Oslo and Akershus University College of Applied Sciences, Norway. He has published numerous articles and book chapters on digitalization and journalism.

Filip Wallberg is a Lecturer in the Department of Political Science and Public Management, and the Centre for Journalism, at Syddansk Universitet, Denmark. His work has appeared in *Journalism Practice*.

Oscar Westlund is Associate Professor in the Department of Journalism, Media and

Communication at the University of Gothenburg, Sweden. He researches the evolving dynamics and interplay of journalism, ICTs, and crisis communications on an individual, generational, and societal level.

Andreas Widholm is a Senior Lecturer in Journalism at Södertörn University, Sweden. His research focuses on journalism, globalization, and the social and cultural consequences of new media technologies.

Tamara Witschge is Associate Professor and Rosalind Frank Fellow in the Faculty of Arts at the University of Groningen, The Netherlands. Her research focuses on entrepreneurial journalism, media and democracy, and media pluralism.

Gabriela Zago is an independent researcher in Vancouver, USA. Her research interests include online journalism, news circulation, and social media.

THEORIES OF JOURNALISM IN A DIGITAL AGE
An exploration and introduction

Steen Steensen and **Laura Ahva**

This special issue introductory article investigates contemporary notions of theory in journalism studies. Many scholars have argued that we need better ways of conceptualising what journalism is and how it develops in a digital age. There is, however, a lack of knowledge regarding what the theoretical trends within the interdisciplinary domain of journalism studies are today and to what extent contemporary inquiries into journalism are framed by emerging theories and perspectives. To fill this knowledge gap, we have conducted an analysis of more than 9000 metadata keywords and 195 abstracts found in the first 14 volumes (2000–2013) of the two most internationally acknowledged journals dedicated to journalism studies: Journalism —Theory, Practice and Criticism and Journalism Studies. The findings indicate that there has been a move towards greater theoretical awareness in journalism studies since 2000 and that the variety of theoretical approaches has increased.

Introduction

In the past 15 years or so, journalism research has paid much attention to how digitisation is changing journalistic practices, cultures and institutions. Early discussions revolved around the question of whether digitisation was bringing about radical changes or minor variations to journalism. However, recently there has been a move beyond discussing the symptoms of the alleged crisis of journalism towards more fundamental issues of digital journalism, such as what "the changing nature of the object itself" is (Broersma and Peters 2013, 2). Consequently, we see today the emergence of what we might call a "fourth wave" of research on digital journalism. This wave —succeeding the normative, empirical and constructivist waves (Domingo 2008) —theorises the field beyond the traditional institutions and understandings of journalism. It investigates, for instance, the "news ecosystem" (Anderson 2010), the "news landscape" (Peters and Broersma 2013), "ambient" (Hermida 2010) and "networked" (Heinrich 2011; Russell 2013) journalism—all of which have emerged because of practices predominantly related to social media.

What becomes evident in this fourth wave is that digitisation has brought a need to reassess the theories with which we make sense of journalism. Since the turn of the millennium, scholars have called for a wider range of theoretical perspectives in journalism studies (Zelizer 2000, 2004; Franklin et al. 2000; Löffelholz 2008; Mitchelstein and Boczkowski 2009). The fourth wave of digital journalism research has started to respond to that call, and this double special issue of *Digital Journalism* and *Journalism Practice* contributes with new answers—and new questions.

In this introductory article, we map out the landscape in which journalism has been theorised at the start of the twenty-first century. We do this by analysing the theoretical underpinnings of the articles published in the longest-running international journalism-centred journals of *Journalism Studies* and *Journalism—Theory, Practice and Criticism* from 2000 to 2013. Our approach can be regarded as an analytical exercise on the recent history of journalism research. We aim to examine notions of theory in journalism studies in the digital age—an examination that will offer a pathway into the articles of this double special issue.

The Growing Maturity of Journalism Studies

The phrase "theories of journalism" implicitly suggests that journalism studies is an academic discipline with a set of established theories that are recognised by a research community. However, such a presupposition can be contested. What constitutes an academic discipline can be evaluated in at least two ways, according to Becher and Trowler (2001, 47):

(1) The existence of a *structural framework* that identifies the discipline through manifestations in, for instance, the organisational components of higher education institutions; in scholarly organisations and conferences or designated divisions of such; and in academic journals dedicated to inquiries within the field.
(2) The existence of a *specific academic culture* with a shared set of theories and methodologies that are maintained through "traditions, customs and practices, transmitted knowledge, beliefs, morals and rules of conduct, as well as their linguistic and symbolic forms of communication and the meanings they share".

Journalism studies is ostensibly becoming an academic discipline in the first respect. Programmes in journalism studies have mushroomed at universities and colleges to such an extent that the field today is "one of the fastest growing areas of study within higher education" (Conboy 2013, xi). Divisions and sections for journalism studies have been established within major communication research organisations such as the International Communication Association (ICA), the International Association for Media and Communication Research (IAMCR) and the European Communication Research and Education Association (ECREA) since the turn of the millennium. Conferences solely dedicated to journalism studies—such as the biannual "Future of Journalism" at the University of Cardiff—have been established, and the beginning of the twenty-first century has seen the birth of several academic journals dedicated to the field, such as *Journalism—Theory, Practice and Criticism*, *Journalism Studies*, *Journalism Practice* and, most recently, *Digital Journalism*. Viewed through such a lens, journalism studies seems to move in the opposite direction compared to its object of inquiry: while journalism today is—not least due to digitisation—marked by the blurring of previously established boundaries and the consequent loss of autonomy as a profession, journalism studies is pushing for autonomy and demarcation from other disciplines.

However, if we consider the second point above, the picture becomes more complicated. Journalism studies is not marked by a specific and shared academic culture. As Zelizer (2004) notes, journalism studies is a highly interdisciplinary and thus diverse entity, shaped by national particularities, differences between journalism scholarship and journalism education, and by the fact that it has "borrowed unevenly from both the humanities and the social sciences" (19). Inquiries into journalism have drawn from a wide range of disciplines, predominantly political science, sociology, history, language and cultural studies. The result, according to Zelizer (2009, 34), "has been a terrain of journalism study at war with itself, with … a slew of independent academic efforts taking place in a variety of disciplines without the shared knowledge crucial to academic inquiry".

The recent emergence of the structural framework to support journalism studies as a possible discipline has, however, resulted in several attempts to stitch together the different pockets of scholarly inquiry into journalism, thus contributing to the coherence of the academic culture. Barbie Zelizer is, of course, a key contributor to this development, most notably through her published work but also as one of the founding editors of *Journalism*. In its first issue in 2000, she proclaimed the charter of the journal "to study journalism in all of its contexts and in so doing embrace a wider range of theoretical perspectives, cultural and historical circumstances, and research methodologies" (Zelizer 2000, 12). A similar agenda was launched the same year by the founding editors of *Journalism Studies*, who encouraged "contributions which represent the most diverse range of theoretical perspectives" (Franklin et al. 2000, 5). On the one hand, there is a wish to develop a shared understanding of journalism studies as a discipline, but on the other hand, the discipline is seen to be best served by a multitude of theoretical perspectives.

Furthermore, the last decade has seen the publication of several books bringing together the different approaches and perspectives related to the study of journalism: *Key Concepts in Journalism Studies* (Franklin et al. 2005); *The Handbook of Journalism Studies* (Wahl-Jorgensen and Hanitzsch 2009a), *Global Journalism Research* (Löffelholz, Weaver, and Schwarz 2008); *Journalism Studies: The Basics* (Conboy 2013); and *Journalism* (Tumber 2008)—a four-volume collection of the "canon" of journalism studies. This literature paints a picture of the theoretical evolution of journalism studies.

For example, Wahl-Jorgensen and Hanitzsch (2009b) divide the history of journalism research into four phases: the normative, empirical, sociological and global-comparative phases. These phases coexist and overlap, but their emergence can be traced chronologically. The normative phase marks the origin of journalism studies at the beginning of the twentieth century (even earlier in Germany), when scholars were concerned with what journalism ought to be and how journalists should do their job. It was a phase concerned mostly with the journalist as an individual, and the level of theoretical complexity was therefore low (Löffelholz 2008, 16).

The empirical phase finds its roots in the United States and the establishment of professional journalism education. The year 1924 saw the birth of *Journalism Bulletin* (later to become *Journalism & Mass Communication Quarterly*), which in its first issue contained a suggestion for empirical research on the form, content and effects of journalism (Singer 2008, 145). A strain of empirical research followed, which eventually led to the discovery of influential middle-range theories of journalism, such as White's "gatekeeper" theory in 1950 (Löffelholz 2008, 18; Wahl-Jorgensen and Hanitzsch 2009b,

6). This phase was influenced by the empirical turn in the social sciences at large and created a shift of attention from the individual to the organisational—a shift that was taken further in the sociological phase.

Two early examples of this shift are Breed's (1955) "Social Control in the Newsroom", which investigates newsroom policy in an ethnographic manner, and Galtung and Ruge's (1965) "The Structure of Foreign News", the "single piece of research that most cogently advanced a general understanding of news selection processes" (Zelizer 2004, 54). Furthermore, inquiries into the structures of news production boomed in the 1970s and 1980s, featuring critical examinations of the conventions, professional cultures and ideologies of journalism. Sociological approaches to journalism studies became more critical and diverse, as influences from cultural studies (in the United Kingdom and the United States) and systems theory (Germany) became significant. This diversity is identified by Schudson (2005) as four different approaches to the sociology of news: the economic organisation of news, the political context of news making, the social organisation of news work and cultural approaches.

The fourth phase of journalism studies as identified by Wahl-Jorgensen and Hanitzsch (2009b)—the global-comparative phase—is currently expanding the myriad of theoretical approaches to journalism studies. This phase is marked by increasing cooperation and networking among scholars with an ascending international research agenda reflecting the global and digital nature of information systems. The global-comparative phase is therefore closely tied to what we here define as "the digital age", in which theories taking established structures and practices of journalism for granted may lose their hold. This phase is marked by the dissolving of many borders: between nation states; national markets; the local and the global; the public and the private; mass communication and interactive communication; professionals and amateurs; production and consumption; and professions—to name a few.

These changes have created a need to rethink what journalism is and consequently to reassess theories of journalism. However, we must not jump to the conclusion that previously established theories are no longer valid in our digital and globalised age. Löffelholz (2008, 25) argues, on the one hand, that normative theories of the past "are not flexible enough to cope with the new media and communication world" because they are framed by political understandings that today are shrinking in relevance. An example of this is the normative relationship between journalism and democracy, which has dominated political science perspectives on journalism. Zelizer (2013) argues that democracy as a concept has over-extended its "shelf-life" in journalism studies and needs to be retired. On the other hand, systems theory, cultural theories (e.g. critical theory, materialism, theories of linguistics and semiotics) and what Löffelholz (2008) labels "integrative social theories" (e.g. structuration theory, field theory and the theory of communicative action) all have "considerable room for new ideas and the improvement of concepts; they are in no way finished business" (25). The progress of journalism studies should, therefore, not be based "on the substitution of 'outdated' theories, but on the gain in complexity through the emergence of new theories and modifications of older theories" (26).

There is, however, a lack of knowledge concerning the extent to which journalism studies today is framed, on the one hand, by emerging theories and perspectives and, on the other hand, by modifications or adoptions of old theories—but also what constitute the theoretical trends within the interdisciplinary domain. To fill this knowledge gap, we have conducted an analysis of all the volumes currently available of two internationally acknowledged journals dedicated to journalism studies: *Journalism—Theory, Practice and Criticism* (Sage) and *Journalism Studies* (Routledge/Taylor & Francis).[1] We must, however, note that this account of the recent history of journalism studies cannot fully grasp developments in different parts of the world, but it will, nevertheless, provide a portrayal of the field through two established publication routes.

The analysis is guided by the following research questions:

(1) What are the dominant disciplinary perspectives and theories articulated in these journals?
(2) Has there been any change from 2000 to 2013 in the theoretical framing of these inquiries into journalism?

Notions of Theory in Journalism Studies of the Twenty-first Century

To answer the research questions, we sampled (1) all metadata keywords from articles published in *Journalism* and *Journalism Studies* from 2000 to 2013 and (2) the abstracts of articles published in the volumes 2002, 2003 and 2012 of both journals.

Keywords and abstracts provide indicators of dominant themes and perspectives in publications and are therefore suited to trace possible theoretical trends within the field. Of course, there are no standardised procedures for article authors on what keywords to choose and what to include in an abstract. Nevertheless, abstracts and keywords represent well-known conventions or genres of academic writing. Abstracts are sites in which it is possible, even desirable, to make explicit the theoretical embedding and contribution of the work in a concise form (see, for instance, Day and Gastel 2012; Körner 2008).

The conventions pertaining to keywords, in turn, imply that the chosen words should (1) function as technical metadata identifiers for search engines and bibliometric classifications and (2) have a bearing on how we perceive keywords in a cultural sense. Concerning the latter, Williams (1985) notes that keywords are indicators of cultural change: keywords such as "culture" and "capitalism" acquire different meanings at different times across cultures. A keyword might therefore be defined as "a word or phrase, often mobilized by different groups of social actors for different purposes, whose meanings are contested during unsettled times" (Ghaziani and Ventresca 2005, 524). Keywords and abstracts in academic journals can thus indicate the discursive struggles and changes within a field.

We based our analysis on Zelizer's (2004) description of the dominant disciplinary perspectives in journalism studies:

- *Political science*: Research analysing the role of journalism and the media in different political systems, the relationship between politics and journalism, and sourcing patterns in journalism.
- *Sociology*: Research on the relationships, work routines and interactions among those who are involved in news production and the organisations, institutions and structures (including professional norms and values) that aid their work.
- *History*: Research that analyses past practices and structures of journalism, often to understand contemporary journalism.

- *Language*: Research that analyses journalistic texts, for instance by applying linguistic, semiotic, genre, discourse or framing theory. Included here are rhetoric, narrativity and literary theory.
- *Cultural analysis*: Research focusing on contextual factors that shape practices of journalism, the construction of news, the cultural symbol systems of the profession, journalistic self-reflection and identity, stereotypes, archetypes, myths, popular culture, and tabloid and mainstream journalism.

In addition, we included *economy*, *philosophy*, *law* and *technology* (cf. Zelizer 2004, 8) as disciplinary perspectives that influence journalism studies:

- *Economy*: Research on media management, business models, press subsidies, media conglomeration, etc.
- *Philosophy*: Research that focuses on the ethical, epistemological and ontological questions related to journalism.
- *Law*: Research analysing legal issues related to journalism, e.g. privacy law, freedom of information acts, etc.
- *Technology*: Research that takes technology as its starting point in the analysis of journalism, in either theoretical or practical terms, e.g. interactivity, multimedia, hypertext, etc.

This categorisation is, of course, debatable in that the borders are not always that clear, but we found it useful to anchor our analysis in an existing frame to avoid losing oneself in the interdisciplinary contours of the field. However, to maintain some flexibility, we also took into account the explicitly mentioned theories in the abstracts.

Keyword Analysis—Sample and Method

The aim of the keyword analysis was thus to map the theoretical perspectives and their possible fluctuation in the journal articles from 2000 to 2013. We extracted all keywords from the articles (excluding editorials, debate articles, book reviews, etc.) published in the 14 volumes of both journals from 2000 to 2013 from the journals' online archive (*Journalism*) and from the EBSCO database (*Journalism Studies*).[2] This resulted in a dataset as seen in Table 1.

There is a significant increase in the number of both articles and metadata keywords from the first to the second half of the period. In 2000, *Journalism* published three issues with five original articles per issue. This had increased to eight issues by 2013, with seven or eight original articles per issue. For *Journalism Studies*, the number

TABLE 1
Number of articles and metadata keywords in the dataset

| | 2000–2006 | | 2007–2013 | | 2000–2013 | |
	Articles	Keywords	Articles	Keywords	Articles	Keywords
Journalism Studies	252	2057[a]	359	4551[a]	611	6608[a]
Journalism	126	797	293	1769	419	2566
Both	378	2854	652	6320	1030	9174

[a]The number includes both the author- and database-provided keywords.

of issues increased from four to six during the same period, while the number of articles per issue stayed the same: eight or nine articles per issue.

Thus, the overall number of keywords in the journals had also more than doubled
from the first to the second period. However, quantitative comparison between keywords in the two journals should not be made, since the sample from *Journalism*
includes only the author-provided keywords, whereas the *Journalism Studies* sample
also includes database-provided keywords, or "subject terms" as they are referred to in
the EBSCO database. We were unable to separate the author-provided from the database-provided keywords in the extraction process. However, based on a manual reading
of a subset of *Journalism Studies* metadata keywords, we could not detect any significant semantic differences between author- and database-provided keywords, the differences pertained mostly to form of expression. Hence we maintain that the
dataset altogether represents the publications well, even if it does not provide possibilities for comparison between the journals.

The 9174 keywords in the dataset, as one might expect, contained many dupli-
cates. When we removed them, we were left with 4545 unique keywords. However,
due to the lack of standardised keywords, many of these were semantically similar
(e.g. "journalistic ethics", "ethics" and "journalism ethics"). We therefore grouped all
semantically similar keywords into clustered keywords, and thereby also reduced the
possible skewing effect of the two sets of keywords in *Journalism Studies*. Furthermore,
many keywords were not relevant for our analysis as indicators of theoretical perspectives. Among the most frequent keywords were general concepts such as "journalism"
and "news"; many were indicators of geographical belonging (e.g. "American journalism", "Greece"); and some were names (e.g. "George Orwell", *The New York Times*"). We
coded all such keywords as "not relevant". Finally, we were left with 826 clustered and
relevant keywords and were able to count their occurrence in the original set of 9174
keywords.

Keyword Analysis—Findings

Only 25 of the clustered and relevant keywords occurred more than 20 times in
the whole dataset, indicating that metadata keywords in journalism studies are very
much a story of the "long tail". More than half (445) of the clustered and relevant
keywords appeared only once. The most frequent keyword during the whole period
was "ethics", with a total of 149 occurrences, followed by "objectivity" (97 occurrences)
and "professionalism" (94 occurrences).

In Figures 1 and 2, we have the 20 most frequent clustered and relevant
keywords in the two periods 2000–2006 and 2007–2013. Thirteen of the keywords
appear in the top 20 list in both periods, indicating certain continuity. However, the
results also show that some themes and perspectives became less important and others
more so throughout the whole period.

If we look at the clustered keywords that appear in the first period (2000–2006)
but are *not* found in the most recent period—"campaign", "ideology",[3] "participation",
"propaganda", "public relations" and "sociology"—we see that many of them are connected to the field of political communication, which belong to the broader perspective
of political science (Zelizer 2004). This perspective is by far the most dominant in the

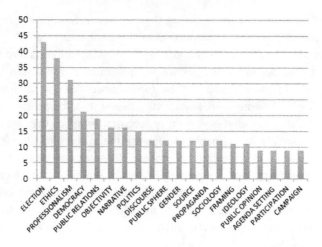

FIGURE 1

Occurrences of the 20 most frequent keywords, 2000–2006

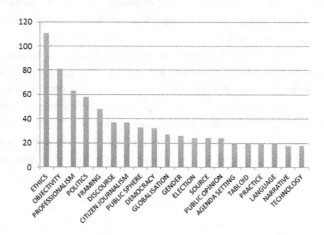

FIGURE 2

Occurrences of the 20 most frequent keywords, 2007–2013

first period. Twelve of the 20 most frequent keywords in Figure 1 can be categorised as belonging to the perspective of *political communication/political science* ("election", "democracy", "public relations", "politics", "public sphere", "source", "propaganda", "ideology", "public opinion", "agenda setting", "participation" and "campaign")—13 if we count "framing"[4] as belonging to the same perspective.

The next two most typical perspectives in the first period are *sociology* and *language*. According to our categories, both have (in Figure 1) three clustered keywords (*sociology*: "gender", "professionalism" and "sociology"; *language*: "discourse", "framing" and "narrativity"). The third perspective found among the top 20 clustered keywords in 2000–2006 is *philosophy*, with two clustered keywords: "ethics" and "objectivity".

However, it must be noted that many of these clustered keywords can belong to several perspectives depending on how they are framed within the articles, which is indeed a major limitation in this approach. Both "ethics" and "objectivity" can, for instance, be framed within a sociological perspective if these keywords are primarily understood as aspects related to the norms and values of professional practice. We have, however, tried to minimise such overlaps in our analysis by, for instance, coding keywords such as "professional ethics" as belonging to the clustered keyword "professionalism".

In the most recent period, as seen in Figure 2, *political communication/political science* is still the most dominant perspective, but now with only eight clustered keywords ("politics", "citizen journalism", "public sphere", "democracy", "election", "source", "public opinion" and "agenda setting"). Compared to the first period, the most frequent clustered keywords in 2007–2013 belong to a greater variety of perspectives: "tabloid" was coded as belonging to the perspective of *culture*, which was not found among the top 20 clustered keywords in 2000–2006, while "technology", of course, belongs to the perspective of *technology*, also not found in the first period. Four clustered keywords were here coded under *sociology* ("professionalism", "globalisation", "gender" and "practice") and four to *language* ("framing", "discourse", "language" and "narrativity") —slightly more than in the first period.

While our analysis is perhaps able to provide only tentative indications of the dominant perspectives, it clearly presents the trends in how the 20 most popular keywords developed throughout the period. Figure 3 shows the increased/decreased use of these keywords relative to the general increase in keywords between the two periods. "Objectivity" is the keyword with the highest increase in frequency from 2000–2006 to 2007–2013 relative to the general increase. "Citizen journalism" has the second highest increase, and is therefore an appropriate example of a single keyword that makes a dramatic entrance during the studied period. At the declining end of the figure, we find "public relations", which can be seen as a sign of demarcation within the entire domain of communication research.

Abstract Analysis—Sample and Method

To obtain a deeper understanding of the dominant perspectives and the role played by theory in the articles, we conducted a content analysis of metadata abstracts associated with each article published in the 2002, 2003 and 2012 volumes of both

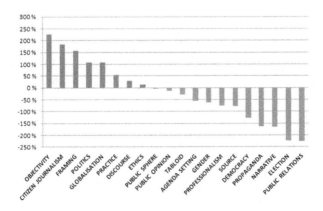

FIGURE 3
Trends among the 20 most frequent clustered keywords from 2000 to 2013, relative to the general increase in the number of keywords during the same period

journals. We chose 2012 instead of the perhaps more logical choice of 2013 since 2013 marked the launch of the new journal *Digital Journalism*, published by Routledge/Taylor & Francis. By choosing 2012, we were able to map the field as it was before the appearance of a journal distinctly dedicated to digital aspects of journalism. As we wanted to be able to map possible changes in the articulation of theory in the journals, we chose to have a point of comparison to the volume of 2012 from the start of the millennium. However, due to a significant difference in the number of articles published in the first two volumes of the journals, we chose to compare the later set with the volumes of 2002 and 2003. In 2002 the number of articles per issue increased from six to eight in *Journalism*, and in 2003 a fourth annual issue was added to *Journalism*, thus making the two journals more equal in size and together a more comparable set with the volume of 2012. A further reason for choosing two volumes from the early period was to reduce the possible impact of special issues with given topics.

All in all, we analysed 195 abstracts—90 from 2002/2003 (58 from *Journalism Studies* and 32 from *Journalism*) and 105 from 2012 (50 from *Journalism Studies* and 55 from *Journalism*).

All abstracts were carefully read and coded according to (1) what was regarded as the dominant disciplinary perspective; (2) the theoretical approach used (if any); and (3) whether a theoretical approach was explicitly stated or not. Each abstract was coded with only one perspective (according to the categorisation in Zelizer 2004), though many of them had elements from more than one perspective. Such abstracts were coded as belonging to the perspective that seemed most dominant. When in doubt, we consulted the original article.

No predefined categories were used for coding the theoretical approaches used in the studies. Here, each abstract was coded with all the theoretical approaches mentioned in the abstract. A test analysis of a subset of the abstracts revealed that many abstracts described an empirical article that built on previously established empirical knowledge without mentioning any specific theoretical approach. We therefore decided to code such abstracts under "grounded theory"—regardless of any explicit mentions of grounded theory in the abstract. Here, we understand grounded theory in a broad manner as a research stance that emphasises the role of empirical material as the basis for building theory.

Regarding the explicitness of the theoretical approaches, we coded each abstract with the variables "yes", "no" or "partly". "Partly" was used when the theoretical approach was visible without being explicit. Examples here include abstracts mentioning words such as "discourse", "frame" or "agenda" without stating that the article in question was based on discourse, framing or agenda theory. With this set of codes, we wanted to explore the role given to theory in abstracts.

Abstract Analysis—Findings

Figure 4 presents the distribution of dominant perspectives found in all abstracts: perspectives from *political science* and *sociology* dominate, while perspectives from *philosophy*, *economics* and *law* are barely present. The keyword analysis indicated the prevalence of keywords such as "ethics" and "objectivity", which we coded as belonging to *philosophy*. The abstract analysis, however, revealed that articles with such

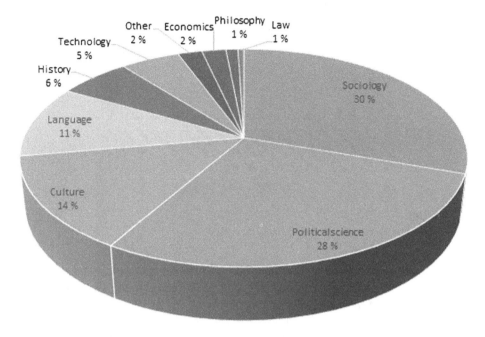

FIGURE 4
Dominant perspectives in abstracts in the 2002, 2003 and 2012 volumes ($N = 195$)

keywords are more likely to be embedded in a *sociological* framework, as such keywords are mentioned in reference to norms related to professional practice. The perspective of sociology with a focus on professionalism seems to have a firm position in the field.

The differences between the two periods regarding dominant perspectives in the abstracts are not as drastic as one might expect based on the keyword analysis. Perspectives from *political science* decreased from 32 per cent in 2002–2003 to 25 per cent in 2012, while perspectives from *sociology* increased from 26 to 34 per cent. *Culture* has decreased from 13 to 9 per cent, while *language* has increased from 8 to 13 per cent. Historical perspectives have decreased, while the booming perspectives are *technology* (from 3 to 7 per cent) and *economics* (from 0 to 4 per cent). All these findings are in line with the findings from the keyword analysis, but the image appears a bit more stable.

Looking at the most frequent theoretical approaches in the abstracts, we find that the grounded theory approach (as defined above) is by far the most popular. As Figure 5 shows, almost 20 per cent of all abstracts take such an approach in both periods on average. This indicates that journalism research is characterised by a perspective that constructs its object of study by drawing on empirical findings. There is, however, a significant decline in the grounded theory approach and an overall increase in other theoretical approaches from 2002–2003 to 2012, suggesting a move from empiricism to theoretical awareness—or at least a tendency to articulate theoretical orientations more explicitly.

Theories associated with *political science* ("democracy theory", "agenda setting", "media systems", "political economy" and "public sphere") and *sociology* ("professionalism", "field theory", "news values" and "gatekeeping") dominate the other most frequent theoretical approaches, but altogether the theoretical approaches—like the

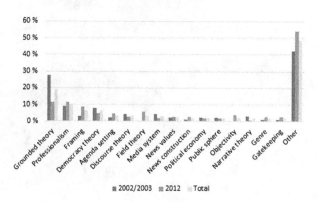

FIGURE 5
Theoretical approaches in the abstracts (*N* = 195)

keywords—are characterised by the "long tail". The "other" category in Figure 5 represents all the approaches that occurred only one or two times in the abstracts, ranging from "epistemology" to "orientalism".

The degree of theoretical explicitness in the abstracts differs slightly between the different perspectives. Abstracts with a political science, sociological and cultural perspective have a significant increase in theoretical awareness.[5] For instance, 61 per cent (22 out of 36) of all 2012 abstracts dealing with sociological perspectives specify the theoretical approach used, compared to only 26 per cent (6 out of 22) in 2002–2003. The move from empiricism to theoretical awareness is therefore most significant within sociological perspectives on journalism.

Altogether, in 2002–2003 only one-third of the abstracts explicitly name a theoretical approach, one-third mention an approach and one-third of the abstracts have no mention of any theories. However, in 2012, half of all abstracts explicitly mention a theoretical approach, and 34 per cent express a connection to a theoretical approach implicitly ("partly"), while 15 per cent have no mention of theories. The results thus suggest that there is an increase in explicit theoretical awareness, but the conventions of abstract writing also allow scholars to describe their research without references to theories.

Discussion of Findings

The findings of our analysis indicate that:

- There has been a broad paradigmatic change in journalism studies since 2000 from perspectives of political science to sociological perspectives.
- Journalism studies is dominated by an increasing variety of theoretical approaches. New approaches from technology and economics are influencing journalism studies, but in a limited manner.
- Aspects related to philosophical perspectives (e.g. ethics and objectivity) are becoming increasingly important for journalism studies. However, these aspects are not viewed through perspectives of philosophy but are analysed in a sociologically oriented framework, such as professionalism.

- There has been a move from empiricism to theoretical awareness in journalism studies since 2000, but (implicit) grounded theory is still the most dominant approach.

These generalised indications must, however, be balanced with the limitations of the dataset. First, the dataset consists only of abstracts and keywords from two journals. Even though they are the two most significant journals within journalism studies, many other journals within the broader field of media and communication studies publish studies on journalism. Furthermore, there has been an increase in the number of journals within the field at large and within journalism studies in particular since 2000. Of special significance here is the 2006 launch of the *Journalism Studies* "sister" journal *Journalism Practice*.

Second, journals might be more suited to empirically oriented publications than other means of publications, such as monographs. Given the limited word count, journal articles might favour presentations and discussions of empirical findings over elaborate theoretical discussions. This might explain the high degree of grounded theory empiricism found in our sample. However, it does not explain the increase in theoretical awareness that we found.

In spite of these limitations, we believe that our findings point to important trends in journalism studies, implying, at least in part, that the field is maturing and gaining increased autonomy as an academic discipline. As discussed above, a structural framework of a discipline has emerged since the turn of the millennium. It would therefore be nothing but expected that the theoretical awareness—perhaps also a more defined disciplinary identity—within the field has evolved during the same period.

However, the diversity of approaches and the interdisciplinary nature of journalism studies continue to thrive, which is indicated by the "long tails" of the keywords and theories. In the analysed abstracts, we found more than 100 different theories guiding the research, in spite of the fact that the vast majority of them were tied to the "old" perspectives of political science, sociology, language and cultural studies. This indicates that journalism studies still has not been able to "produce a coherent picture of what journalism is" (Zelizer 2009, 34). It is, however, debatable whether such coherence is a necessary or even possible aim in the digital era, where multiple journalisms coexist and the practice of journalism is dispersing. However, the first 14 volumes of *Journalism* and *Journalism Studies* have clearly achieved what the editors aimed for at the very beginning, to infuse the field with a wider range of theoretical perspectives (Zelizer 2000; Franklin et al. 2000).

Conclusions and Presentation of the Special Issue

Given the interdisciplinary nature of journalism studies (which we think is not weakened by the field's increased maturity and autonomy)—and given the increasingly blurred boundaries of journalism—we believe that there is a need within journalism studies to widen the scope of theoretical perspectives and approaches even further. A main aim of this special issue is therefore to contribute to such a change.

The spread of articles in this double special issue clearly points out that the research field is currently occupied with theorising the increasingly porous and enlarged domain of journalism. This "mind-blowing uncertainty in the evolution of journalism" in the digital era, as David Domingo, Pere Masip and Irene Costera Meijer put it in their article, seems to be a common denominator in the foundation of the contributions in the issue. The uncertainty, however, has not paralysed scholarship: it has invited researchers to assume new avenues to theorising journalism or inspired them to reassess old theories.

In this special issue, we find contributions that tackle this challenge in four main ways. First, the articles offer *conceptual configurations* with which to grasp the domain of journalism (e.g. de-differentiation, circulation, news network or spatiality). Second, the articles provide concepts with which to theorise further *technology as a fundamental part of journalism* (e.g. actants or materiality). These articles are all batched together in *Digital Journalism*.

Third, a group of papers discuss the *latitude of user positions* in the digitalised domain of journalism (e.g. maximal–minimal participation, routines–interpretation–agency and mobility–cross-mediality–participation). Fourth, contributors provide theoretically informed tools with which to understand the *evolving practice(s)* of journalism (e.g. innovation, dispersed gatekeeping and mediatised interdependency) in different cultural contexts. These articles are published in *Journalism Practice*.

Presenting the articles in Digital Journalism

The *Digital Journalism* issue is opened by Seth Lewis and Oscar Westlund, who argue that the study of digital journalism is in need of a sociotechnical framework that would provide a counterweight to the sociocultural emphasis of the earlier studies in digital journalism. Their suggested framework recognises human actors, technological actants, audience positions and the activities through which these interact.

Alex Primo and Gabriela Zago tap further into the role played by technology in understanding journalism and its boundaries. By drawing on actor-network theory (ANT), they make a case against social determinism in journalism theories. David Domingo, Pere Masip and Irene Costera Meijer continue with ANT by arguing that it is useful in letting researchers understand journalism through the idea of news networks.

Wiebke Loosen discusses the situation in which various agents are becoming involved in journalism, thus "blurring the boundaries" of the domain. Loosen's starting point is that the entire idea of de-boundedness can gain theoretical insight from systems theory.

Juliette De Maeyer and Florence Le Cam propose a methodological and theoretical stance that underlines the importance of mapping out the social history of digital journalism through the prism of materiality. Henrik Bødker identifies three main ways in which circulation has been and can be understood in the context of journalism: material dissemination, the dissemination of meaning and the reproduction of culture.

Amy Schmitz Weiss thereafter suggests that journalism practice as well as audiences' news experiences may be understood through the concept of "spatial journalism".

Presenting the articles in Journalism Practice

Chris ***Peters and Tamara Witschge propose a move from "grand narratives" towards "small expectations" in understanding the role of journalism in democratic participation. They argue for the necessity of an audience-inclusive aspect to theorising journalism and democracy. Ike Picone, Cédric Courtois and Steve Paulussen, in turn, suggest that journalism studies is in need of a "radical user perspective".

Heikki Heikkilä and Laura Ahva draw on practice theory to put forward a framework in which to study the construction of the relevance of news in the everyday practices of audiences. The legacy of practice theory to the study of journalism is further elaborated by Christoph Raetzsch. He advances an understanding of journalism as a structure of public communication enacted through practices by journalists and audiences alike.

Mattias Ekman and Andreas Widholm focus on the changing source relations in the digital environment related to social media, such as Twitter. They argue that a theoretical perspective that can best capture the current relationship between politicians and journalists is that of "mediatized interdependency".

This discussion of sources is broadened by Peter Bro and Filip Wallberg in their analysis of gatekeeping. They show that journalistic practice is currently captured by a model that emphasises the redistributed or eliminated nature of gatekeeping. In the final article, Hayes Mawindi Mabweazara presents a metatheoretical framework for the study of African journalism in the digital era that draws on sociology and a social construction of technology.

Blind Spots and Final Remarks

The articles in the special issue provide—at least—political, cultural, historical, sociological and technological perspectives for understanding journalism in the digital age. It also becomes very clear that the experiences and practices of users cannot be theorised separately from other aspects of journalism. The issue thus offers a rich pool of concepts to draw from and develop further.

Self-reflexively, it can also be noted that this special issue has some blind spots, which seem to be connected to the broader trends in which journalism is theorised. This selection of articles emphasises sociological perspectives and therefore falls in line with the main trend towards increased sociological inquiries found in the keyword and abstract analysis.

Furthermore, philosophical perspectives on digital journalism remain few. We believe that this is a blind spot not only of this special issue but of journalism studies at large. If we are to address the fundamental questions concerning the essential character of journalism, journalism studies should lean more heavily on perspectives such as ethics, ontology and epistemology. They liberate scholars from studying journalism only within the institutional framework.

We also believe that there is an increasing need to theorise the visual—and the entire blending of media modalities—in journalism. Digitisation brings forth many challenges to visual representations of reality. Such a discussion is opened by Henrik Bødker in this issue, but we believe this is an area that can gain from further theorising and tighter linkages with other research perspectives. Visual representations of reality in journalism tap into discussions of ontology and ethics and are therefore closely tied to philosophical perspectives. A forthcoming special issue of *Journalism Practice* on photojournalism edited by Stuart Allan will surely open up new perspectives on the increased significance of visual journalism.

In addition, the role of language as a theoretical perspective is not strong in this special issue. Even though our abstract analysis found a slight increase in language perspectives in journalism studies in the digital age, we believe that the field could benefit from an ever-greater inclusion of such perspectives in the future.

That being said, this special issue certainly contributes to the theoretical awareness for journalism studies in the digital age. The rapid technological development of the media landscape may sometimes seem like an impossible research context for scholars: the field is changing so fast that even empirical mapping seems to be lagging behind, not to mention theorisation. However, the contributions here indicate that it is possible and necessary to scrutinise digital journalism through a theoretical lens and that that lens can benefit from combining classical theories, explorative perspectives and empirical insight.

NOTES

1. *Journalism Studies* is the only international journal solely dedicated to journalism studies listed in the *ISI Web of Science Journal Citation Report* (JCR). In 2012, its impact factor (0.798) was ranked at 33 within communication studies. *Journalism* has been accepted for inclusion in JCR as of 2014. Both journals are associated with the journalism studies division of ICA.
2. The keywords and abstracts were extracted using the following procedure: the Firefox browser plug-in Zotero was used to download metadata for all articles published 2000–2013. When downloading metadata from the online archive of *Journalism*, the author-provided keywords were automatically downloaded as part of the metadata, but not from the online archive of *Journalism Studies*. For this journal, we therefore arranged a work-around involving the EBSCO database, from which keywords would download as part of the metadata. All the data was then exported from Zotero and imported into EndNote. We defined a tab-separated export style in EndNote where the journal name, article title, year and keywords (tags) were the only fields exported. This exported file was then imported into the Excel spreadsheet for analysis.
3. We clustered the keyword "ideology" as referring to ideology in a political sense. Keywords such as "professional ideology" were coded as belonging to the clustered keyword "professionalism". However, these choices, together with the nature of keywords as research data, may mask the influence of the cultural studies perspective (and the use of "ideology" in that context) on journalism research.
4. Frame analysis is a commonly used methodology in political communication, but as it deals with aspects of language, we have here chosen to categorise "framing" as a language perspective.
5. The sample is not large enough to show any reliable findings related to the other perspectives.

REFERENCES

Anderson, C. W. 2010. "Journalistic Networks and the Diffusion of Local News: The Brief, Happy News Life of the 'Francisville Four'." *Political Communication* 27 (3): 289–309.

Becher, Tony, and Paul Trowler. 2001. *Academic Tribes and Territories: Intellectual Enquiry and the Culture of Disciplines*. 2nd ed. Buckingham: Open University Press.

Breed, Warren. 1955. "Social Control in the Newsroom: A Functional Analysis." *Social Forces* 33 (4): 326–335.

Broersma, Marcel J., and Chris Peters. 2013. "Introduction. Rethinking Journalism: The Structural Transformation of a Public Good." In *Rethinking Journalism: Trust and Participation in a Transformed News Landscape*, edited by Chris Peters and Marcel J. Broersma, 1–12. Oxon: Routledge.

Conboy, Martin. 2013. *Journalism Studies: The Basics*. London: Routledge.

Day, Robert, and Barbara Gastel. 2012. *How to Write and Publish a Scientific Paper*. 4th ed. Cambridge: Cambridge University Press.

Domingo, David. 2008. "Inventing Online Journalism: A Constructivist Approach to the Development of Online News." In *Making Online News. The Ethnography of New Media Production*, edited by Chris Paterson and David Domingo, 15–28. New York: Peter Lang.

Franklin, Bob, Gerd G. Kopper, Elizabeth Toth, and Judy Van Slyke Turk. 2000. "Editorial." *Journalism Studies* 1 (1): 5–7.

Franklin, Bob, Martin Hamer, Mark Hanna, Marie Kinsey, and John E. Richardson. 2005. *Key Concepts in Journalism Studies*. London: Sage.

Galtung, Johan, and Mari Holmboe Ruge. 1965. "The Structure of Foreign News the Presentation of the Congo, Cuba and Cyprus Crises in Four Norwegian Newspapers." *Journal of Peace Research* 2 (1): 64–90.

Ghaziani, Amin, and Marc J. Ventresca. 2005. "Keywords and Cultural Change: Frame Analysis of Business Model Public Talk, 1975-2000." *Sociological Forum* 20 (4): 523–559.

Heinrich, Ansgard. 2011. *Network Journalism: Journalistic Practice in Interactive Spheres*. New York: Routledge.

Hermida, Alfred. 2010. "Twittering the News: The Emergence of Ambient Journalism." *Journalism Practice* 4 (3): 297–308.

Körner, Ann M. 2008. *Guide to Publishing a Scientific Paper*. Oxon: Routledge.

Löffelholz, Martin. 2008. "Heteregeneous—Multidimensional—Competing. Theoretical Approaches to Journalism: An Overview." In *Global Journalism Research: Theories, Methods, Findings, Future*, edited by David H. Weaver, Andreas Schwarz, and Martin Löffelholz, 15–27. Malden, MA: Blackwell.

Löffelholz, Martin, David H. Weaver, and Andreas Schwarz, eds. 2008. *Global Journalism Research: Theories, Methods, Findings, Future*. Malden, MA: Blackwell.

Mitchelstein, Eugenia, and Pablo J. Boczkowski. 2009. "Between Tradition and Change: A Review of Recent Research on Online News Production." *Journalism* 10 (5): 562–586.

Peters, Chris, and Marcel J. Broersma, eds. 2013. *Rethinking Journalism: Trust and Participation in a Transformed News Landscape*. Oxon: Routledge.

Russell, Adrienne. 2013. *Networked: A Contemporary History of News in Transition*. Cambridge: Polity Press.

Schudson, Michael. 2005. "Four Approaches to the Sociology of News." In *Mass Media and Society*, edited by James Curran and Michael Gurevitch, 4th ed., 172–197. London: Hodder Arnold.

Singer, Jane B. 2008. "Journalism Research in the United States. Paradigm Shift in a Networked World." In *Global Journalism Research: Theories, Methods, Findings, Future*, edited by Martin Löffelholz, David H. Weaver, and Andreas Schwarz, 145–157. Malden, MA: Blackwell.

Tumber, Howard, ed. 2008. *Journalism*. Oxon: Routledge.

Wahl-Jorgensen, Karin, and Thomas Hanitzsch, eds. 2009a. *Handbook of Journalism Studies*. Oxon: Routledge.

Wahl-Jorgensen, Karin, and Thomas Hanitzsch. 2009b. "Introduction: On Why and How We Should Do Journalism Studies." In *Handbook of Journalism Studies*, edited by Karin Wahl-Jorgensen and Thomas Hanitzsch, 3–16. Oxon: Routledge.

Williams, Raymond. 1985. *Keywords: A Vocabulary of Culture and Society*. Oxford University Press.

Zelizer, Barbie. 2000. "What is Journalism Studies?" *Journalism* 1 (1): 9–12.

Zelizer, Barbie. 2004. *Taking Journalism Seriously: News and the Academy*. Thousand Oaks, CA: Sage.

Zelizer, Barbie. 2009. "Journalism and the Academy." In *The Handbook of Journalism Studies*, edited by Karin Wahl-Jorgensen and Thomas Hanitzsch, 29–41. Oxon: Routledge.

Zelizer, Barbie. 2013. "On the Shelf Life of Democracy in Journalism Scholarship." *Journalism* 14 (4): 459–473.

ACTORS, ACTANTS, AUDIENCES, AND ACTIVITIES IN CROSS-MEDIA NEWS WORK
A matrix and a research agenda

Seth C. Lewis and **Oscar Westlund**

In contemporary journalism, there is a need for better conceptualizing the changing nature of human actors, nonhuman technological actants, and diverse representations of audiences— and the activities of news production, distribution, and interpretation through which actors, actants, and audiences are inter-related. This article explicates each of these elements—the Four A's—in the context of cross-media news work, a perspective that lends equal emphasis to editorial, business, and technology as key sites for studying the organizational influences shaping journalism. We argue for developing a sociotechnical emphasis for the study of institutional news production: a holistic framework through which to make sense of and conduct research about the full range of actors, actants, and audiences engaged in cross-media news work activities. This emphasis addresses two shortcomings in the journalism studies literature: a relative neglect about (1) the interplay of humans and technology, or manual and computational modes of orientation and operation, and (2) the interplay of editorial, business, and technology in news organizations. This article's ultimate contribution is a cross-media news work matrix that illustrates the interconnections among the Four A's and reveals where opportunities remain for empirical study.

Introduction

Amid the widespread diffusion of digital information technologies, the mediascape is changing in various ways. Perhaps most visibly among these changes, new configurations involving social *actors*, technological *actants*, work-practice *activities*, and different kinds of *audiences* have become interlinked in ways that confound boundaries between production and consumption, professional and nonprofessional, and intra- and extra-organizational domains. Thus, the nature of *who* or *what*—whether human actor or nonhuman technological actant—guides message formation and circulation, and *how* such media-shaping takes place in relation to *whom* (certain kinds of audiences) may require some rethinking.

For the study of institutional news production particularly and news work more generally, there is a scholarly need for theoretical frameworks that accommodate and account for the shifting character of these elements and the interconnections among them: human actors (e.g., journalists, technology specialists, and businesspeople); technological actants (e.g., algorithms, networks, and content management systems); and audiences (e.g., assemblages of audiences distinct to certain platforms, devices, or applications)—all potentially intertwined in the activities that constitute cross-media news work. The term *cross-media* refers to the integration of multiple media platforms. When combined with *news work*, the concept acknowledges the various forms of journalism within a holistic framework—including editorial as well as business and technology activities, thus rendering a more complete picture of news publishing at the organizational level (Westlund 2011).

In reviewing the literature on actors, actants, audiences, and activities, we argue that there is a lack of comprehensive theorizing that acknowledges these dimensions and their inter-relatedness in contemporary cross-media news work. This article's contribution is in explicating the "Four A's," introducing a matrix for visualizing their relationships, and proposing a research agenda for studying them in a more holistic fashion. Our overall purpose is to develop a heuristic for conceptualizing *news* production and distribution—and yet, the matrix we propose likewise could be applied to contexts of *media* creation and circulation more generally.

Toward a Sociotechnical Emphasis in Journalism Studies

During the past two decades, journalism studies scholars have paid special attention to the role of technology in news work (for reviews, see Domingo and Paterson 2011; Mitchelstein and Boczkowski 2009; Steensen 2011). This research has typically drawn upon established theories and concepts for explaining how various elements of technology have been incorporated into (or resisted by) the professional cultures and organizational contexts of journalism (Lewis 2012). These approaches have been helpful in clarifying the changing character of digital news production and the evolving relationship that journalists have with audiences (e.g., Singer et al. 2011). Yet, this line of research has given greater emphasis to human-centric considerations—such as individual role conceptions, organizational constraints, professional norms, national culture or ideology, and other socio-cultural factors—without sufficiently acknowledging the distinct role of technology and the inherent tension between human and machine approaches (exceptions include Anderson 2013; Boczkowski 2004). This human–technology tension is best understood as a continuum between manual and computational modes of orientation and output in contemporary cross-media news work—a way of perceiving the relative gravitational pull of each dimension in shaping news publishing (Westlund 2013).

Additionally, this vein of journalism studies has focused heavily, if not exclusively, on the editorial sides of news organizations. The result has been neglect in the literature for socio-technical objects and information technology specialists (exceptions include Ananny 2013; Nielsen 2012), particularly when such technologies and technologists operate beyond the boundaries of the organization. Even in recent studies of computer programmers and related technical specialists, scholars have prioritized the study of editorial implications *vis-à-vis* a broader reading of organizational change (e.g., Karlsen and Stavelin 2014; Lee-Wright 2008; Parasie and Dagiral 2013). This emphasis is understandable: editorial actors are most associated with shaping media content and its downstream impact on media audiences. Nevertheless, we argue alongside media management scholars that business elements are no less crucial to the overall framework of institutional news production.

Because of these blind spots in the literature—of failing to account more fully for the human–technology dynamic, on the one hand, as well as the organizational interplay of editorial, technology and business on the other—there is an opportunity for developing a *sociotechnical emphasis* in journalism studies. This emphasis is not a deterministic view that assumes technology is "changing" journalism; on the contrary, by bringing to the fore technologies and technologists as key aspects of study, this approach adds a sociotechnical focus to the ongoing sociocultural research being done about journalism, helping to reveal nuances in the relationships among human actors inside the organization, human audiences beyond it, and the nonhuman actants that cross-mediate their interplay. Additionally, this sociotechnical emphasis acknowledges the extent to which contemporary journalism is becoming interconnected with technological tools, processes, and ways of thinking as the new organizing logics of media work (Deuze 2007; Lewis 2012).[1]

Our point of departure is to clarify the larger set of dynamics operating in the human–technology and editorial–business–technology intersections to facilitate a matrix and a research agenda for cross-media news work. We do this by explicating actors, actants, audiences, and activities, in each case describing what we know from extant literature and thereafter suggesting how a sociotechnical emphasis might shed new light on these elements and their relationships.

Actors, Actants, Audiences, and Activities

Actors

Humans play a central part in shaping media. Sociologically minded scholars have emphasized the social construction of technology and user agency in assessing the "impact" of tools (Boczkowski 2004; Pinch and Bijker 1984). Nevertheless, scholars of communication and technology have concluded that in all but dismissing technological determinism entirely "we may have 'overcorrected'" (Neff et al. 2012, 300), privileging human power to the point of failing to account for the obvious in contemporary media life: "there are times and places when and where we are not fully in control of our machinescapes" (312). The upshot, Neff and colleagues suggest, is to acknowledge "technical agency," not in assigning consciousness to technology but in recognizing the constraints that humans may face in working within technical systems of ever-growing complexity and ubiquity.

How might this apply to a study of humans working within cross-media news work? For one, journalists have long worked with both machines (technology) and machine-operators (technicians) to accomplish journalism: from lithographs to typewriters to newspaper pagination to early online journalism to content management systems (CMS). There is nothing inherently new about what Powers (2012, 25) calls "technologically specific forms of work"—forms of news work that are inextricably tied to the technologies associated with them. What is important to recognize, however, is that such forms of work, from photojournalism of yore to programmer-journalism of today, carry certain assumptions about their journalistic legitimacy. To the extent that a news practice is distinctly connected to a technical affordance, it may struggle, at least in an early stage, to be recognized as "real" or simply "ordinary" journalism (Powers 2012). Perhaps journalists discount technically enabled forms of journalism because of their conviction that reporting—a most human endeavor—is central to their professional craft (Anderson 2013). Indeed, historically the broad work of news publishing—the content-centric work of editorial—has carried a manual orientation: journalists and editors manipulated comparatively "dumb" tools to manufacture news information. Digitization, however, has brought with it a variety of technologically specific forms of work, such as social media curation and online aggregation, as well as "smart" algorithms and automated processes that in some instances can replace activities previously performed by humans—typified by the emergence of "robot journalism" and its machine-written forms of news (van Dalen 2012). While many media scholars have directed attention to the increasingly precarious conditions of news workers because of institutional and organizational pressures, less research has focused squarely on the human–technology dimension as an organizing framework. Future research might therefore investigate how editorial workers are negotiating issues of authority, identity, and expertise in connection not only with technologically specific forms of work like programmer-journalism (Lewis and Usher 2013; Parasie and Dagiral 2013) but also with the machine-led processes assuming more responsibility for functions traditionally associated with professional control (Bakker 2012; Lewis 2012; Westlund 2011).

Beyond simply recognizing the interplay of journalists and technology on the editorial side, however, a sociotechnical emphasis would also address the roles of other actors, within and beyond the news organization. External to the firm, there are several actors that reasonably play a shaping role—from sources and advertisers, to policymakers and hardware/software providers. Here we wish to focus on two internally situated social groups that historically have been less visible to media researchers and yet are no less relevant in media organizations: technologists and businesspeople. It is crucially important to acknowledge these actors, in both theory and empirical practice, if we are to grasp contemporary changes in news media from an organizational perspective.

The first group of actors would include information technology (IT) specialists, systems designers, project managers, information architects, product developers, and other programming technicians—some working on editorial-facing news applications, some working on business-facing products and services, and others working across departments to support the overall systems of digital production and distribution. Looking at the editorial angle in particular, researchers are only beginning to account for the rise of computational journalism (Anderson 2012) and its diverse manifestations in form and content (Gynnild 2013), as programmers, hackers, and Web developers play an increasingly central role in new and legacy media organizations (Lewis and Usher 2013; Parasie and Dagiral 2013).

The second group of actors, businesspeople, would include marketers, sales associates, customer relationship managers, analysts specialized in big data and behavioral targeting, and others connected with supporting the bottom line of the cross-media enterprise. It likewise could include hybrid arrangements between business and technology, such as data science teams that analyze traffic patterns to help optimize the revenue potential of paywalls and mobile apps. Neither technologists nor businesspeople have received adequate attention in the literature on technological adoption, appropriation, and innovation in journalism. Journalism researchers typically have focused on journalists and their norms and practices (e.g., Domingo and Paterson 2011). Meanwhile, scholars of media management and economics have focused on commercial managers (e.g., Küng 2008). Technologists, in both streams of research, have been mostly "black-boxed" (Latour 1987)—disregarded as key objects of study because they reside so thoroughly in the background. A research opportunity lies in stitching these domains together in a more holistic study of cross-media news work, acknowledging the social construction of technology through the interplay of editorial, technological, and business interests, as Nielsen (2012) did in his study of blogging in legacy news organizations and Westlund (2011, 2012) demonstrated in his analyses of mobile news development.

Finally, this sociotechnical emphasis would also recognize the ways in which technologists are mediating growing forms of cross-awareness and coordination between the editorial and business sides, through the co-development of information products and services for multiple platforms. For example, in what sense have technologists facilitated, if not directed, different projects and outcomes, given their distinct communities of practice, cultural norms, and perceptions of the audience as active participants rather than as commodities or relatively passive recipients? (cf., Lewis and Usher 2013; Nielsen 2012). Additionally, at the intersection of these actors, what might contemporary research reveal about the social shaping of native advertising, branded content, and other experiments in new revenue streams to underwrite traditional news work? Situating human actors in relation to technological actants may help to ground such a research approach.

Actants

The term *actants*, as we define it, refers generally to material objects that are notable for their association with human actors and the activities they undertake in conjunction with such objects. We invoke the term carefully but purposefully. We recognize that in the context of actor-network theory (ANT), a sociological and methodological approach concerned with tracing associations ("following the actors to where they lead the researcher," in the common refrain), the term *actant* may refer to any actor, human or nonhuman, that is engaged in a networked system under scrutiny. Indeed, ANT adherents typically eschew most *a priori* categories altogether, allowing the determination of actors/actants and their relative influence in the network to emerge organically and situationally (Couldry 2008; Plesner 2009). ANT does not erase distinctions between human and nonhuman, but neither does it privilege one over the other in assessing the relative "force" through which the social or the technological determines outcomes. As Latour (2005, 71) notes, "the questions to ask about any [actant] are simply the following: Does it make a difference in the course of some agent's action or not?" Thus, in this discussion of *technological actants* in activities of cross-media news work, the question would become: Does a technological object like a CMS, application programming interface (API), or set of software code make a difference in the course of some actors' activities or not?

ANT therefore serves a key purpose in highlighting the relevance and role of non-human actors. Yet, even as we draw upon ANT, we also depart from it in articulating a sociotechnical emphasis that (1) acknowledges there are a variety of increasingly signifi-cant nonhuman actants distinct from human actors, here defined as *technological actants*, and (2) treats certain categorizations—such as journalism, technology, and busi-ness, and the Four A's themselves—as analytically useful and indeed necessary for the study of institutional news production. We take as a starting point that the *technologi-cal* actants described here are inscribed and instructed by humans, socially constructed to suit journalistic, commercial, and technological purposes within news organizations. It is in this social framing process, for instance, that CMS technology are encoded with journalistic news values in their DNA, determining how particular types of content are selected for publication across particular platforms; and that computational exploration in journalism—with its multifaceted interplay of data, social science, and storytelling—depends more on distinct human direction than the technology *per se* (Gynnild 2013). Such a perspective, borrowing from ANT but not necessarily being limited to it, may bring to the forefront those underlying technological actants and their networked rela-tionships with human actors—things that have long been missing in journalism and media studies literatures more focused on sociocultural explanations (Schmitz Weiss and Domingo 2010). Such a gaze, for example, brings forward an appreciation for new configurations of "newsware" (Ananny 2013): networks of technological actants like interfaces and algorithms, as well as cultural norms and practices connected to them.

Few studies have attempted to understand why some technological assets are embraced in journalism while others are not (Steensen 2011). To understand the "potential" for, and application of, such assets in journalism requires a more focused perspective on the technological actants that would facilitate them. Put another way: answering Latour's "does it make a difference?" question becomes difficult when the journalism studies literature has neither thoroughly identified the "it" (actant) in question nor the full array of contextual influences connected with its supposed differ-ence-making. While there is a vibrant subset of media studies that uses ANT to study journalistic change (e.g., Hemmingway 2008; Micó, Masip, and Domingo 2013; Plesner 2009; Schmitz Weiss and Domingo 2010; and in this special issue, Primo and Sago 2014 and Domingo, Masip, and Costera Meijer 2014), there remains an opportunity to better account for the particular place of technological actants *vis-à-vis* the entire organiza-tional assemblage of journalists, businesspeople, and technologists.

Moreover, a research approach that puts technological actants on a par with actors in cross-media news work would further our understanding about the relative influence of technology *vis-à-vis* humans (cf., Westlund 2013), whether internal or external to the news organization. The internal dimension is easy to imagine: e.g., the email (Plesner 2009), CMS (Schmitz Weiss and Domingo 2010), and related technologies that are inward-facing technological actants from the perspective of cross-media news workers. The exter-nal dimension might be understood as the growing variety of computational programs designed to capture and reconfigure information streams produced by news organiza-tions, re-presenting them for audiences. Examples of this would include mobile and tablet applications such as Flipboard, Zite, and Facebook Paper, driven by automated forms of personalized content packaging—as well as websites that specialize in digital aggrega-tion, incorporating a hybrid of actant- and human-led filtering and publishing, on sites like Techmeme and Mediagazer. Situated betwixt the internal–external dynamic are APIs, which function as go-between interfaces that, with permission, allow outside computer programmers to access and build upon the information resources from a provider. In the context of news work, researchers are only beginning to unpack how APIs might function as interstitial technological actants facilitating the likes of business model innovation (Aitamurto and Lewis 2013) or reconfigured relationships with the public sphere (Ananny 2013). Ultimately, future research should acknowledge the significance of actants and their functionalities, their organizational implications, and the consequences of their internal or external placement and purpose.

Audiences

The very notion of "audience" and the passivity associated with that term has long been a contested concept, with audiences variously imagined as commoditized recipients or active meaning-makers in the process of media consumption (Bolin 2012; Hagen and Wasko, 2000). Napoli (2010) argues that we are not witnessing the end of audiences, but rather an evolution in how they are understood by media institutions. In a "post-exposure audience marketplace," when metrics of audience exposure are being replaced by more fine-grained assessments of consumers' preferences, clicks, and engagement, audiences are being rationalized through massive data tracking (Napoli 2010)—and, at the same time, recognized for their increased autonomy and creative potential (Anderson 2011). Thus emerges certain tensions about how audiences are conceived from the standpoint of media organizations: as relatively passive *recipients* in the traditional mass media sense, as statistically aggregated *commodities* for media advertisers, or as *active participants* in cultural production. Within the media organization, these perceptions of the audience may be represented in distinct ways: journalists, known to care little about understanding the audience (Gans 1979), may be inclined to see them as (mostly passive) recipients of information professionally vetted for them. Businesspeople may predominantly take a commodity view, which goes hand-in-hand with tracing and capitalizing on digital footprints made readily available even while also recognizing the audience's utility in making media content viral and "spreadable" (Jenkins, Ford, and Green 2013)—and thereby more marketable. Technologists, meanwhile, may primarily see audiences as potentially active participants in the spirit of open source (Lewis and Usher 2013). These competing conceptualizations of the audience, while tentatively constructed here, can begin to illustrate not only how audiences are framed by different institutional actors, but also how certain framings may exert influence on others. For instance, if journalists begin minimizing their view of audiences as passive, they may do so in the direction of a market logic (e.g., commodities) and/or a participatory logic (e.g., active participants).[2]

The first of these perspectives—audiences as *recipients*—is both intuitively recognizable within traditional models of mass communication (e.g., Westley and MacLean 1957) but also thoroughly contested as a "historical fallacy" (e.g., van Dijck 2009). While the relative activity or passivity of such a receiving role is the subject of great debate (see Bolin 2012), the salience for this discussion is in representing audiences as publics intended to be informed through news. Such a conceptualization suits journalism's normative function as public monitor. As such, even while increasingly aware of the audience and its expressive capabilities online, journalists still find much of their professional purpose in imagining the audience as recipients who depend on them for news (Anderson 2013). Thus, "[audiences] are still, overall, receivers of information created and controlled by the journalist" (Singer et al. 2011, 189).

Seeing audiences as *recipients*, however, is not the same as seeing them as *commodities*, the second of the perspectives noted above. Political economists were early in arguing that mass media audiences were packaged as products sold to advertisers (Smythe 1977). Such discussions have gained traction again in the twenty-first century (Turow 2011), as cruder measures of media exposure give way to more sophisticated, data-intensive audience information systems that allow media firms and advertisers to determine not only who has consumed which pieces of content but also predict future content preferences, tailor content for particular individuals, and gather behavioral responses to content exposure (Napoli 2010). These approaches have raised concerns about privacy, particularly in light of revelations about institutionalized spying on individuals' digital traces. Of course, the business model behind many legacy news media relies on the commodification of audiences, and in the instance of newspapers, has also involved charging for content from these audiences. Picard and Westlund (2012) suggest that newspapers traditionally took a *producer-centric approach*, meaning that their actors predominantly relied on professional values for judgments, hardly bothering to understand their audiences. Such reliance on gut feelings about what audiences needed, rather than what they wanted, has been a consistent theme in the literature on journalists' relationship with audiences (Boczkowski and Mitchelstein 2013). However, and in conjunction with the trends in digital audience metrics noted above, news media have since developed a *consumer-centric approach* (Picard and Westlund 2012), one that more readily tries to understand and please audiences and advertisers, and thus treats audiences as commodities. Actors in news media organizations thus have mobilized more and more resources, including technological actants that enable continuous measurement, analysis, and commercialization of audiences.

Turning to research on audiences as *active participants*, the rise of interactive, user-directed, and social media has led to a paradigmatic shift in scholarly attention to audiences (Jenkins, Ford, and Green 2013; Loosen and Schmidt 2012). Emblematic of this turn, Bruns (2008, 2012) has introduced the concept of "produsers" to reflect how audiences play dual roles as producers and users of media. Exploring the relationship between journalism and active audiences, most research has suggested that legacy news media resist rather than embrace such participation. Journalists typically see users as "active recipients" who are encouraged to react to journalists' work but not contribute to the actual process of its creation (Singer et al. 2011). Nevertheless, some news media have taken a *participation-centric approach*, attempting to involve their audiences in activities of journalism as well as business and technological innovation (Picard and Westlund 2012). As technologists play a growing role in media organizations, some of this openness may be associated with the participatory logic of digital media (Lewis 2012) that is more readily embraced by technologists than journalists (Parasie and Dagiral 2013).

Audiences thus may be simultaneously treated as recipients, commodities, and active participants by news media, thereby serving normative, commercial, and cultural functions alike. In drawing out a multi-faceted perspective on audiences, Anderson (2011) argues that a distinction between "audience ignorance" and "audience responsiveness" on the part of journalists is a false one, complicated by the emerging role of *the algorithm*—an actant that plays a mediating role among journalists, news products, and audiences. Algorithmic journalism, he argues, diminishes distinctions between human and nonhuman forms of data and judgments, appropriating massive volumes of audience signals to steer content creation and circulation in the service of consumer preferences. The precise nature of the algorithms involved, and the implications for journalism and public knowledge that they entail, have yet to be examined.

More broadly, the role of actants at the intersection of actors and audiences in cross-media news work deserves greater scrutiny. Whether visible or invisible to end-users, technological actants intermediate relationships of production, distribution, and consumption—via systems for authentication, behavioral tracking, algorithmic personali-zation, APIs for content streams, social media platforms, and on and on. There are crucial matters of editorial, business, and technology practice connected to the pursuit of audiences through various technological actants: on the journalism side, the growth in job roles specifically focused on search engine optimization (SEO) and social media optimization (SMO); on the business side, the growth in capturing and crunching "big data" metrics on site visits, time-on-page, and drop-off rates—both to enhance advertis-ing muscle and improve return-on-investment (ROI), and to better predict the future news preferences of distinct audiences; and on the technology side, the growth in interactive applications that begin to shift the orientation from audience-as-recipient to audience-as-participant, consistent with technologists' preferred view (cf., Nielsen 2012). While having a relative competitive advantage in their access to data about people in the "offline" world, news media still remain far behind the visitor-tracking power of the likes of Google and Facebook—but the seemingly inexorable trend in that direction calls for research scrutiny that considers the entirety of actors and technological actants engaged in representing audiences in a cross-media context.

Activities

Media activities are synonymous with routinized practices that, in connection with social and material resources and contexts, give shape to media messages and their construction and subsequent circulation and reception (Couldry 2012). In the context of media organizations, such activities are the patterns of action through which an organi-zation's institutional logic is made manifest through media. Moreover, activities also include emerging and formative efforts toward media innovation (Westlund and Lewis 2014). In that light, this article has encouraged scholars to adopt a more holistic, socio-technical emphasis to cross-media news work activities.

Turning now to the specific activities in which actors, actants, and audiences are mutually engaged, Westlund's (2013) model of journalism provides a useful framework. It illustrates how various media activities—whether editorial or non-editorial, manual or computational, in orientation—fall on a continuum between repurposing and custom-ization (creation and/or adaptation). Attempting here to first contribute to the journal-ism studies literature, we give priority to exemplifying the dynamic interplay of actors, actants, and audiences in *journalistically oriented* activities.

Journalism has largely been treated as a routinized media practice, one with insti-tutionalized patterns of professional roles, working rules, and shared principles. While journalism has a distinct occupational ideology (Deuze 2005) and professional logic (Lewis 2012), its information processes are similar to communication practices that have long existed in complex societies, where the need to communicate across time and space, whether in a mass or interpersonal fashion, has been necessary for social function (Domingo et al. 2008). Nor are journalism's routines entirely static, as they evolve to accommodate new arrangements with actors and technological actants. Domingo et al. (2008) conceptualized these institutionalized communications functions in five stages of news production: access and observation, selection/filtering, processing/editing, distribution, and interpretation. They used that analytical framework to evaluate the relative openness of newspapers to citizen participation. Placing their findings in the context of this article, journalistic actors were found reluctant to relinquish their professional control to the audience, and technological actants—in this case, the structural components of news websites—offered little opportunity for audiences to contribute. Journalists remained in charge of decision-making along all five stages, and seemingly only invited audiences to participate in interpretation. This was facilitated by technological actants supporting online comments and forum discussions. Domingo et al. (2008) acknowledge that this likely has changed since their study in 2007.

The Cross-media News Work Matrix: Bringing Actors, Actants, and Audiences Together

The activities carried out in each of those five stages have an influence on the degree to which news is customized or repurposed. Attempting to explicate this further in light of the Four A's, we propose the Cross-media News Work Matrix (see Table 1), which synthesizes these five stages of journalistic activities in relation to actors, actants, and audiences. Following our previous discussions, actors are grouped into *journalists*, *technologists*, and *businesspeople*; actants are distinguished by their *internal* or *external* placement relative to the media firm; and audiences are classified as *recipients*, *active participants*, and *commodities*. For sake of clarity: activities are here represented by the five stages in the news production process.

The journalist actors naturally bear primary significance because this classification focuses on activities assumed to be mainly journalistic. Thus, our discussions will give emphasis here to how and why other actors, as well as actants and audiences, *might* be involved in these activities. Three criteria have been used for the assessment of each party's *potential* involvement in each respective stage: (1) their capability (i.e., competences and affordances), (2) their willingness (i.e., values and interests), and (3) their frequency of involvement (i.e., recurrent rather than sporadic).

Access/observation

Technologists and actants may be reasonably assumed to accompany journalists in gaining access to and making observations of events and information. Technologists assist journalists in adopting and modifying technological tools (actants) that serve purposes of securing source material or detecting patterns. For instance, computer scripts can help journalists scrape online information for data journalism, and increasingly precise tools facilitate the real-time analysis of audience sentiment across the Web and social media (cf., Godbole et al. 2007). The data retrieved and presented by technological actants to journalists may help identify potentially worthwhile topics for future stories, leading to the algorithmic journalism described by Anderson (2011). Even in a less

TABLE 1

The Cross-media News Work Matrix

	Actors			Actants		Audiences		
	Journalists	Technologists	Businesspeople	Internal	External	Recipients	Active participants	Commodities
Access/observation	Yes	Yes	No	Yes	Yes	No	Yes	No
Selection/filtering	Yes	Yes	No	Yes	Yes	No	Yes	No
Processing/editing	Yes	Yes	No	Yes	Yes	No	No	No
Distribution	Yes	Yes	Yes	Yes	Yes	No	Yes	Yes
Interpretation	Yes	Yes	No	Yes	Yes	Yes	Yes	No

On the left are listed institutionalized communication functions, or activities, traditionally associated with news production (based on Domingo et al. 2008). Where we have determined that such activities might reasonably involve certain actors, technological actants, or audiences in the contemporary media environment, based on literature and contacts in the industry, they have been marked with "Yes." When such involvements are judged as not likely, albeit possible, they have been marked with "No." Ultimately, the final determination of such classifications requires empirical research; this is merely a conceptual starting point toward that end.

quantitative sense, social media platforms, as key technological actants in news work, serve as "ambient" awareness systems (Hermida 2010), allowing publics to more readily observe the *zeitgeist* of a particular moment or event, and enabling more reciprocal forms of information exchange between journalists and audiences (Lewis, Holton, and Coddington 2014). By its very sociotechnical and sociocultural framework, Twitter has been found to facilitate the potential for new patterns in news sourcing as journalists use it to access, observe, and act upon the opinions not only of elites but also alternative actors engaged in public discussion (Hermida, Lewis, and Zamith 2014). News media may develop architectures that enable sophisticated measures of audience-tracking that feed into the access/observation stage of journalism. Besides these measurement-oriented technological actants residing inside of news media, external providers like Google Analytics or global data and insight consultancies like Kantar also provide relevant technological actants.

To date, however, most scholarly attention has been given to outlining the role of audiences as active participants in the *access/observation stage*—in the form of eyewitness accounts, photos/videos, source material, and so on (e.g., Singer et al. 2011). The development of technological actants has done much to facilitate journalistic interactions with audiences in this data-gathering phase. To cite just one example: *Aftonbladet*, the largest Swedish evening tabloid newspaper, launched new functionalities in 2012 for its mobile-based participatory journalism interface. Citizens have been recruited into a panel allowing *Aftonbladet* to trace their GPS-position around the clock, and also facilitate contact with them whenever desired. When journalists are notified about an ongoing event by their actants following news wires and police communication, such as an ongoing robbery in a suburb, they can ask their actant to identify which members of their active audience are within close proximity of the event. Moreover, the journalistic actors can exchange interpersonal messages with their active audience, who in turn can utilize their mobile device to take pictures, record videos, and immediately transmit this data to the journalists. With origins in telecommunications and computing, contemporary smartphones provide affordances for participation, seemingly without spatial and temporal limitations (cf., Westlund 2013).

Selection/filtering

Domingo et al. (2008) concluded that journalists were in exclusive control of this stage. Research has documented how newsrooms, with inherent hierarchies, have secured professional control of selection and filtering (Tuchman 1978). Technologists and businesspeople historically have not been welcome to exert much influence on the activities taking place in this stage. Nevertheless, as the editorial–business wall becomes more porous in a metric-driven environment, businesspeople presumably could have a say in the themes and topics their newsrooms address to attract audiences (as commodities)—though there is insufficient evidence that this is yet happening broadly. More likely is the influence that technologists may have when working in teams with journalists, proposing opportunities for developing news themes and topics as represented via digital technologies and interfaces—like the "Snow Fall" interactive feature co-developed by journalists and technologists at *The New York Times*. Technologists contributing to data journalism may thus have gained access to, and learned how to visualize, data on a specific topic. Following this, journalists may pursue narrative articles that complement that data visualization.

Both internally and externally placed technological actants have significance for the selection/filtering of news. Moreover, technological actants may also be programmed to allow for audiences to actively publish items themselves. Most research suggests that news media have done little to enable audiences to craft articles in their own right (Singer et al. 2011). A Swedish case study on the social shaping of a mobile news application found that journalists, supported by technologists, won ground for a traditional and producer-centric approach in which the technological actant mainly served the purpose of technology-led repurposing and customization. The proposal for a participation-centric application by the businesspeople, in which the actant would make it possible for active audiences to select/filter stories for publishing, was thus turned down (Westlund 2012).

Processing/editing

Manual modes of editing by journalists have dominated the routines of legacy news media, contributing to a path-dependent and institutionalized practice of manual re-mediation in digital journalism. This is a core stage of the news production process in which journalists typically do not allow audiences to take part. Moreover, little attention has been given to the fact that technology has become an ever-present part of processing/editing activities in journalism. Perhaps this is because the technological actants facilitating processing/editing, such as editorial CMS, have become institutionalized, naturalized, and even taken for granted. Similarly to electricity, time, and mobiles, such actants are largely invisible as long as they function as expected (Ling 2012). Internally situated actants facilitate interaction between humans and machines, through which journalists feed in news content for publishing. Many media companies, owning numerous newspaper titles, have in recent years invested in technologists and technological systems to facilitate the processing/editing of digital journalism through templates, reducing their need for human labor. Importantly, such technological actants are also being offered by external providers. Moreover, so-called responsive Web design (e.g., HTML5) has gained traction, whereby technological actants adapt content and visual elements to fit the affordances of mobile and desktop screens. Such strategies for technology-led activities that facilitate customization come with little need for intervention by human actors (cf., Westlund 2013).

Distribution

Distinct groups of digital publics are assembled according to human and algorithmic determinations: judgments, whether manual or computational in nature, about who receives what kind of information and through which modes of delivery. The issue of media distribution has often been lost amid scholarly emphases on production or consumption (Braun 2013). Journalism literature, however, has acknowledged the primacy that editors have in directing patterns of news distribution. Nevertheless, because distribution platforms are a strategic managerial issue, businesspeople are reasonably taking part in shaping the conditions for news distribution.

Building further on the above, we also argue that technologists and both internally and externally placed actants play a role in this stage of cross-media news work. Externally situated technological actants, such as Flipboard, Digg, Google News, and Facebook Paper, facilitate re-distribution or re-publishing of news. Social media likewise have gained a major role in the distribution and re-distribution of news, opening new ways for traffic in and out from the digital news platforms.

This has meant a loss of professional control over editorial content (Lewis 2012), as news information—and some of the discussion around it—becomes detached from its creator. It likewise has meant a commercial loss, as other stakeholders benefit from audience traffic and advertising revenue, in addition to the news media that invested in its production. Technologists may take part in the distribution stage by translating journalistic values into programming code—in a sense, directing technological actants to behave, to the extent possible, as if they were human journalists. Westlund (2011) found such processes taking place when technologists and journalists at *Göteborgs-Posten* determined how technological actants were to be employed for publishing across digital and mobile platforms. Packaging and presentation (e.g., location-sensitive or personalized news publishing) were seen as facilitating value-added and customized experiences for audiences. Finally, looking at the audience aspect of distribution, audience metrics allow for tracing audiences for different purposes. When using systems for authentication (personal login), news media can take advantage of greater awareness about individuals, their social connections online, and the audience collectively to redirect to distinct individuals a series of news recommendations. Such actants that support customization and personalization of news distribution carry the potential for making news a more enjoyable experience—and yet raise corresponding concerns about a loss of shared knowledge.

Interpretation

Interpretation is the only stage at which Domingo et al. (2008) found that news media were meaningfully allowing audiences to participate—namely by commenting on news stories and discussing public issues in forum spaces. The emphasis at this stage typically is about the relationship between journalists producing news and audiences actively responding to it (Singer et al. 2011). However, audiences as recipients may also take part in this stage, through their meaning-making (Bolin 2012) and socializing about the news, even when such engagement takes place through non-mediated conversations.

In the literature, businesspeople and technologists do not appear to play a significant part in this stage—though perhaps that is because their potential role in negotiating the interpretation of news has neither been clarified nor studied adequately. For example, a news innovation contest recently encouraged technologists to develop ideas for re-imagining dynamic spaces for online news discussion; the resulting entries suggested the potential for new tools (actants) that might facilitate a more civil, cohesive, and diverse discourse (Zamith and Lewis 2014). While the nature of interpretation by technological actants has received little attention in the literature, our matrix suggests that internal and external actants help shape the reception of media content simply by the way they shape initial and subsequent forms of (re)distribution to audiences across a proliferating range of mobile applications, aggregation websites, and customized email alerts (see above). Future research, however, is needed to assess the degree to which technological actants and their particular channels/platforms/algorithms are connected to particular interpretations of news by particular audiences.

Conclusion

The scholarly study of contemporary journalism, and cross-media news work specifically, is a complicated endeavor. The roles, boundaries, and processes of news work become increasingly hard to detect apart from other components in the same system. Traditional theories and concepts for unpacking journalism can take scholars only so far; what is still needed is a more comprehensive framework through which to account for the full array of actors, actants, audiences, and activities in cross-media news work. By adding a sociotechnical element to the sociocultural perspective of mainline research in journalism studies, this approach may help reveal new insights into the relationships among human actors inside the organization, human actors and audiences beyond it, and the nonhuman actants that cross-mediate their interplay. This approach better acknowledges how journalism is becoming interconnected with technological tools, processes, and ways of thinking.

In articulating what a sociotechnical emphasis might look like in future research, our key intervention has been to offer not only a conceptualization of the Four A's—actors, actants, audiences, and activities—but also a matrix through which to visualize their associations. This conceptual matrix can guide future empirical research, which in turn may reconfigure and/or strengthen the assessment of how actors, actants and audiences take part in journalistic activities. Preferably this would be done longitudinally, assessing not only actors' distinct practices but also their perceptions of one another as well as their complex perceptions of actants and audiences (as recipients, commodities, and active participants). While acknowledging that such an ambition may be hard to accomplish in a single study, we argue that the mere awareness of that wider view on cross-media news work would inform better-developed research questions, research designs, and ultimately contributions to the literature on journalism and technology. In relation to this, we propose that future research should conceptualize and study a sixth stage in news production called *analysis*, in addition to the five proposed by Domingo et al. (2008). Analysis would represent forms of feedback and organizational learning that loop back to the first stage, and involve actors, actants, and audiences in combination.

Future research might more thoroughly review, synthesize, and develop models for journalism, of which there are relatively few emphasizing the distinct interplay of and tension between human and technology, or manual and computational modes of orientation and output (see Westlund 2013). Finally, there are opportunities for informing news management and journalism education through a more comprehensive accounting of cross-media news work as a system of actors, actants, and audiences engaged in a complex set of media activities—each activity and ensemble of actors, actants, and audiences carrying with them key implications and concerns for business/commercial and professional/normative interests alike.

ACKNOWLEDGEMENTS

The authors gratefully acknowledge comments on this paper from Joshua Braun, Matt Powers, Jen Schradie, Rodrigo Zamith, anonymous review, and special issue editors Steen Steensen and Laura Ahva. Seth Lewis wishes to acknowledge the support of the Hubbard Faculty Fellowship at the University of Minnesota, and Oscar Westlund thanks the Wahlgrenska Foundation for its sponsorship of this article.

NOTES

1. Notably, in choosing *sociotechnical* as a framing, we acknowledge and yet depart from the sociotechnical systems perspective, which is more appropriate for studying field-level dynamics (Fortunati and Sarrica, 2010).
2. We are grateful to Matt Powers for helping us articulate this point.

REFERENCES

Aitamurto, Tanja, and Seth C. Lewis. 2013. "Open Innovation in Digital Journalism: Examining the Impact of Open APIs at Four News Organizations." *New Media & Society* 15 (2): 314–331. doi:10.1177/1461444812450682.

Ananny, Mike. 2013. "Press-public Collaboration as Infrastructure: Tracing News Organizations and Programming Publics in Application Programming Interfaces." *American Behavioral Scientist* 57 (5): 623–642. doi:10.1177/0002764212469363.

Anderson, C. W. 2011. "Deliberative, Agonistic, and Algorithmic Audiences: Journalism's Vision of Its Public in an Age of Audience Transparency." *International Journal of Communication* 5: 529–547. ISSN 1932-8036. http://ijoc.org/index.php/ijoc/article/view/884.

Anderson, C. W. 2013. "Towards a Sociology of Computational and Algorithmic Journalism." *New Media & Society* 15 (7): 1005–1021. doi:10.1177/1461444812465137.

Anderson, C. W. 2013. *Rebuilding the News: Metropolitan Journalism in the Digital Age.* Philadelphia, PA: Temple University Press.

Bakker, Piet. 2012. "Aggregation, Content Farms and Huffinization: The Rise of Low-pay and No-pay Journalism." *Journalism Practice* 6 (5–6): 627–637. doi:10.1080/17512786.2012. 667266.

Boczkowski, Pablo J. 2004. *Digitizing the News: Innovation in Online Newspapers.* Cambridge, MA: MIT Press.

Boczkowski, Pablo J., and Eugenia Mitchelstein. 2013. *The News Gap: When the Information Preferences of the Media and the Public Diverge.* Cambridge: The MIT Press.

Bolin, Göran. 2012. "The Labour of Media Use: The Two Active Audiences." *Information, Communication & Society* 15 (6): 796–814. doi:10.1080/1369118X.2012.677052.

Braun, Joshua. 2013. "Going over the Top: Online Television Distribution as Sociotechnical System." *Communication, Culture & Critique* 6 (3): 432–458. doi:10.1111/cccr.12015.

Bruns, Axel. 2008. *Blogs, Wikipedia, Second Life, and beyond: From Production to Produsage.* New York: Peter Lang.

Bruns, Axel. 2012. "Reconciling Community and Commerce? Collaboration between Produsage Communities and Commercial Operators." *Information, Communication & Society* 15 (6): 815–835.

Couldry, Nick. 2008. "Actor Network Theory and Media: Do They Connect and on What Terms?" In *Connectivity, Networks and Flows*, edited by Andreas Hepp, Friedrich Krotz, Shaun Moores, and Carsten Winter, 93–109. Cresskill, NJ: Hampton Press.

Couldry, Nick. 2012. *Media, Society, World: Social Theory and Digital Media Practice*. Cambridge: Polity.

van Dalen, Arjen. 2012. "The Algorithms behind the Headlines: How Machine-written News Redefines the Core Skills of Human Journalists." *Journalism Practice* 6 (5–6): 648–658. doi:10.1080/17512786.2012.667268.

Deuze, Mark. 2005. "What is Journalism? Professional Identity and Ideology of Journalists Reconsidered." *Journalism* 6 (4): 442–464. doi:10.1177/1464884905056815.

Deuze, Mark. 2007. *Media Work*. London: Polity Press.

van Dijck, José. 2009. "Users like You? Theorizing Agency in User-generated Content." *Media Culture Society* 31 (1): 41–58. doi:10.1177/016344370809824.

Domingo, David, and Chris Paterson, eds. 2011. *Making Online News: Newsroom Ethnographies in the Second Decade of Internet Journalism*. 2nd ed. New York: Peter Lang.

Domingo, David, Thorsten Quandt, Ari Heinonen, Steve Paulussen, Jane B. Singer, and Marina Vujnovic. 2008. "Participatory Journalism Practices in the Media and beyond: An International Comparative Study of Initiatives in Online Newspapers." *Journalism Practice* 2 (3): 326–342. doi:10.1080/17512780802281065.

Domingo, David, Pere Masip, and Irene Costera Meijer. 2014. "Tracing Digital News Networks: Towards an Integrated Framework of the Dynamics of News Production, Circulation and Use." *Digital Journalism*. doi:10.1080/21670811.2014.927996.

Fortunati, Leopoldina, and Mauro Sarrica. 2010. "The Future of the Press: Insights from the Sociotechnical Approach." *The Information Society: An International Journal* 26 (4): 247–255. doi:10.1080/01972243.2010.489500.

Gans, Herbert J. 1979. *Deciding What's News: A Study of CBS Evening News, NBC Nightly News, Newsweek, and TIME*. New York: Pantheon Books.

Godbole, Namrata, Manjunath, Srinivasaiah, and Steven Skiena. 2007. "Large-scale Sentiment Analysis for News and Blogs." *ICWSM*, 7.

Gynnild, Astrid. 2013. "Journalism Innovation Leads to Innovation Journalism: The Impact of Computational Exploration on Changing Mindsets." *Journalism*. doi:10.1177/1464884913486393.

Hagen, Ingunn, and Janet Wasko. 2000. *Consuming Audiences? Production and Reception in Media Research*. New York: Hampton Press.

Hemmingway, Emma. 2008. *Into the Newsroom: Exploring the Digital Production of Regional Television News*. London: Routledge.

Hermida, Alfred. 2010. "Twittering the News: The Emergence of Ambient Journalism." *Journalism Practice* 4 (3): 297–308. doi:10.1080/17512781003640703.

Hermida, Alfred, Seth C. Lewis, and Rodrigo Zamith. 2014. "Sourcing the Arab Spring: A Case Study of Andy Carvin's Sources on Twitter during the Tunisian and Egyptian Revolutions." *Journal of Computer-mediated Communication* 19 (3): 479–499. doi:10.1111/jcc4.12074.

Jenkins, Henry, Sam Ford, and Joshua Green. 2013. *Spreadable Media: Creating Value and Meaning in a Networked Culture*. New York: NYU Press.

Karlsen, Joakim, and Eirik Stavelin. 2014. "Computational Journalism in Norwegian Newsrooms." *Journalism Practice* 8 (1): 34–48. doi:10.1080/17512786.2013.813190.

Küng, Lucy. 2008. *Strategic Management in the Media*. London: Sage.

Latour, Bruno. 1987. *Science in Action*. Cambridge, MA: Harvard University Press.

Latour, Bruno. 2005. *Reassembling the Social: An Introduction to Actor-Network-Theory*. Oxford: Oxford University Press.

Lee-Wright, Peter. 2008. "Virtual News: BBC News at a 'Future Media and Technology' Crossroads." *Convergence: The International Journal of Research into New Media Technologies* 14 (3): 249–260. doi:10.1177/1354856508091079.

Lewis, Seth C. 2012. "The Tension between Professional Control and Open Participation: Journalism and Its Boundaries." *Information, Communication & Society* 15 (6): 836–866. doi:10.1080/1369118X.2012.674150.

Lewis, Seth C., and Nikki Usher. 2013. "Open Source and Journalism: Toward New Frameworks for Imagining News Innovation." *Media, Culture & Society* 35 (5): 602–619. doi:10.1177/0163443713485494.

Lewis, Seth C., Avery E. Holton, and Mark Coddington. 2014. "Reciprocal Journalism: A Concept of Mutual Exchange between Journalists and Audiences." *Journalism Practice* 8 (2): 229–241. doi:10.1080/17512786.2013.859840.

Ling, Richard. 2012. *Taken for Grantedness: The Embedding of Mobile Communication into Society*. Cambridge: MIT Press.

Loosen, Wiebke, and Jan-Hinrik Schmidt. 2012. "(Re-)Discovering the Audience: The Relationship between Journalism and Audience in Networked Digital Media." *Information, Communication & Society* 15 (6): 867–887. doi:10.1080/1369118X.2012.665467.

Micó, Josep L., Pere Masip, and David Domingo. 2013. "To Wish Impossible Things: Convergence as a Process of Diffusion of Innovations in an Actor-network." *International Communication Gazette* 75 (1): 118–137. doi:10.1177/1748048512461765.

Mitchelstein, Eugenia, and Pablo J. Boczkowski. 2009. "Between Tradition and Change: A Review of Recent Research on Online News Production." *Journalism* 10 (5): 562–586. doi:10.1177/1464884909106533.

Napoli, Philip M. 2010. *Audience Evolution: New Technologies and the Transformation of Media Audiences*. New York: Columbia University Press.

Neff, Gina, Tim Jordan, Joshua McVeigh-Schultz, and Tarleton Gillespie. 2012. "Affordances, Technical Agency, and the Politics of Technologies of Cultural Production." *Journal of Broadcasting & Electronic Media* 56 (2): 299–313. doi:10.1080/08838151.2012.678520.

Nielsen, Ramus K. 2012. "How Newspapers Began to Blog: Recognizing the Role of Technologists in Old Media Organizations' Development of New Media Technologies." *Information, Communication & Society* 15 (6): 959–978. doi:10.1080/1369118X.2012.694898.

Parasie, Sylvain, and Eric Dagiral. 2013. "Data-driven Journalism and the Public Good: 'Computer-assisted-Reporters' and 'Programmer-Journalists' in Chicago." *New Media & Society* 15 (6): 853–871. doi:10.1177/1461444812463345.

Picard, Robert G., and Oscar Westlund. 2012. "The Dynamic Innovation Learning Model: A Conceptualization of Media Innovation." Paper presented at the 10th World Media Economics and Management Conference, Thessaloniki, Greece, May 23–27.

Pinch, Trevor J., and Wiebe E. Bijker. 1984. "The Social Construction of Facts and Artefacts: Or How the Sociology of Science and the Sociology of Technology Might Benefit Each Other." *Social Studies of Science* 14 (3): 399–441. doi:10.2307/285355.

Plesner, Ursula. 2009. "An Actor-network Perspective on Changing Work Practices: Communication Technologies as Actants in Newswork." *Journalism* 10 (5): 604–626. doi:10.1177/1464884909106535.

Powers, Matthew. 2012. "'In Forms That Are Familiar and Yet-to-be Invented': American Journalism and the Discourse of Technologically Specific Work." *Journal of Communication Inquiry* 36 (1): 24–43. doi:10.1177/0196859911426009.

Primo, Alex, and Gabriela Zago. 2014. "Who and What Do Journalism? An Actor-network Perspective." *Digital Journalism*. doi:10.1080/21670811.2014.927987.

Schmitz Weiss, Amy, and David Domingo. 2010. "Innovation Processes in Online Newsrooms as Actor-networks and Communities of Practice." *New Media & Society* 12 (7): 1156–1171. doi:10.1177/1461444809360400.

Singer, Jane B., David Domingo, Ari Heinonen, Alfred Hermida, Steve Paulussen, Thorsten Quandt, Zvi Reich, and Marina Vujnovic. 2011. *Participatory Journalism: Guarding Open Gates at Online Newspapers*. Malden, MA: Wiley-Blackwell.

Smythe, Dallas W. 1977. "Communications: Blindspot of Western Marxism." *Canadian Journal of Political and Society Theory* 1 (3): 1–28.

Steensen, Steen. 2011. "Online Journalism and the Promises of New Technology: A Critical Review and Look Ahead." *Journalism Studies* 12 (3): 311–327. doi:10.1080/1461670X.2010.501151.

Tuchman, Gaye. 1978. *Making News: A Study in the Construction of Reality*. New York: Free Press.

Turow, Joseph. 2011. *The Daily You: How the New Advertising Industry is Defining Your Identity and Your Worth*. New Haven, CT: Yale University Press.

Westley, Bruce H., and Malcolm S. MacLean. 1957. "A Conceptual Model for Communications Research." *Journalism & Mass Communication Quarterly* 34 (1): 31–38. doi:10.1177/107769905703400103.

Westlund, Oscar. 2011. *Cross-media News Work: Sensemaking of the Mobile Media (R)Evolution*. Gothenburg: University of Gothenburg. https://gupea.ub.gu.se/bitstream/2077/28118/1/gupea_2077_28118_1.pdf.

Westlund, Oscar. 2012. "Producer-centric Vs. Participation-centric: On the Shaping of Mobile Media." *Northern Lights* 10 (1): 107–121.

Westlund, Oscar. 2013. "Mobile News: A Review and Model of Journalism in an Age of Mobile Media." *Digital Journalism* 1 (1): 6–26. doi:10.1080/21670811.2012.74027.

Westlund, Oscar, and Seth C. Lewis. 2014, Forthcoming. "The Agents of Media Innovation Activities: Actors, Actants, and Audiences." *Journal of Media Innovations* 1 (2).

Zamith, Rodrigo, and Seth C. Lewis. 2014. "From Public Spaces to Public Sphere: Rethinking Systems for Reader Comments on Online News Sites." *Digital Journalism*. doi:10.1080/21670811.2014.882066.

WHO AND WHAT DO JOURNALISM?
An actor-network perspective

Alex Primo and **Gabriela Zago**

Technology is typically seen as an instrument that aids journalistic processes. Digital artifacts, however, are seldom considered as active participants. Tautologically, journalism is defined as a practice of journalists. But journalism would not be the same without the role played by technological artifacts. To assess such a problem, this article discusses the ontological contributions from actor-network theory and how they may help to disclose the complex associations between a multiplicity of actors involved in journalism. Besides asking "who" does journalism, we argue that it is also necessary to assess "what" does journalism. We then show how technological actants transform journalistic practices in two recent processes: newsroom convergence and the creation of news by algorithms. Finally, we argue that this new ontology demands epistemological and methodological transformations in journalism studies.

Introduction

Journalism theories typically focus on the practices of journalists. However, journalism is more than what a journalist does. Moreover, ideologically driven theories adopt a deterministic perspective by describing what journalism should be. Rather, theories of journalism should allow scholars to interpret journalism the way it happens, instead of trying to determine what reality should look like.

Against those essentialist views, theoretical efforts that aim to consider the complexity of journalism need to consider the multiplicity of actors and the different associations that make it happen. From the computer to citizen journalists, a variety of participants may contribute to journalistic processes.

It is true that technology has always been discussed in journalism studies. Journalism itself is born and undergoes constant transformations because of technological developments (Pavlik 2001; Kovach and Rosenstiel 2011). However, analogical and digital artifacts are now as naturalized in newsrooms as the taxi is to the taxi driver (Plesner 2009). Accordingly, technology seems to disappear in journalistic practices, as it blends into everyday routines. Couldry (2008) notes that live coverage conveys the idea that the media provides direct connection to the events as they happen. That is, live media becomes a "black-box." But there are other actors that are hidden within. To assess such a problem, we will discuss the ontological contributions from actor-network theory (ANT) and how they may help disclose the complex hybrid networks that allow journalism to come about.

According to this perspective, associations involve human and non-human actors (or actants, in ANT's vocabulary). Therefore, the question "who does journalism?" now shows its limitations. Journalism in not produced solely by the "social relations" among editors, journalists, and sources, but also by non-human actants (such as computer networks), which participate in the process, transforming it (Plesner 2009). Hence, we argue that that question should be reformulated as such: "who and what do journalism?"

It is time to bring everyone and everything that is not a professional journalist back to the foreground. If these actors are lit again, the stage becomes crowded and a different scene may be viewed. As soon as they are all seen as participating actors of journalistic processes, new questions may be asked. Consequently, different conclusions may emerge and a different scenario becomes visible. This demands updates and new perspectives on journalism.

In this article, we concentrate our efforts on the discussion of journalism actors. As naming professionals or specific publics (reporters, editors, readers, etc.) may just result in a partial account, we focus on the role played by technological artifacts, understood as full-blown social actors, with transforming roles. Evidently, journalism would be different today without digital technologies. In fact, it would not even exist—at least as it is now known. Thus, journalism theories need to consider those artifacts as important as any other actant in the ongoing process of news production, circulation, and consumption.

Our aim is to promote a reflection on the ontology of journalism. Though necessary, it is not sufficient to refer to the intricate relation between digital technologies and journalists' practices, if the former is still thought of as a tool, playing no more than a supporting role. Even though their transforming presence may be recognized, an unbalanced relationship is portrayed. As soon as the agency of artifacts is recognized, as well as the transformations that it exerts over associations and other actants, the very definition of journalism needs to be reconsidered. Such an ontological turn certainly has important epistemological consequences, bringing what is thought to be under dispute.

Previous articles (Hemmingway 2007; Plesner 2009; Schmitz Weiss and Domingo 2010; Van Loon 2011; Micó, Masip, and Domingo 2013; Anderson 2013), within a still limited literature on ANT and journalism, have showed how digital artifacts should be treated as actants. We intend here to further the ontological debate on journalism and agency. As we will show, news outlets may publish articles produced entirely by algorithms. On the other hand, we argue that not every text written by professional journalists becomes journalism. Besides criticizing the anthropocentric traditions (e.g. humanistic, sociological) in journalism studies, we also question the partial perspectives that concentrate in just a fraction of the process, taking news production as journalism and newsrooms as its locus. These biased depictions are a recurrent symptom of theories dedicated to the practices of (human) professional journalists.

In order to achieve these goals, we begin by showing that the history of journalism develops with the history of technology. Then, we present the main premises of ANT and discuss how it can broaden the understanding of what journalism is. Later, we illustrate our points with two processes in which the agency of technological actants may be most clearly perceived: newsroom convergence and automated news production. Finally, we discuss how ANT may shed new light on the epistemology of journalism.

Technology and Journalism

The history of journalism is tied to the evolution of technology (Pavlik 2000; Deuze 2007; Briggs and Burke 2010; Heinrich 2011). Since the Roman official notes carved on stone to the latest news tweets posted live from an event through a smartphone, news production and circulation have developed side by side with communication technologies. This section intends to stress how technologies are inherent to journalism, not an accessory part. The importance of these artifacts in journalism is such that even its fields or genres (such as print journalism, broadcast journalism, and digital journalism) have been tied to a specific technology. Despite its brevity, the following historical review is important to highlight how this intimate relationship is later ignored, as soon as a definition of journalism is pronounced.

Print newspapers depend on the technology of print, which goes back to the invention of Gutenberg's printing press in 1447. Periodical newspapers appeared in the first half of the seventeenth century. Telegraph started to be used for the long-distance transmission of news in the 1850s (Heinrich 2011). Alexander Graham Bell's invention of telephone in 1876 not only transformed telecommunications but also how journalists gather news, such as in telephone interviews (Pavlik 2000). The invention of radio around the same period brought a new relationship between news organizations and its audiences. The emergence of broadcast journalism allowed people to hear news events directly. Later, in the 1950s, television provided a different experience: besides listening, the public could watch the news (Kovach and Rosenstiel 2011). The first use of a computer in journalism took place in 1952, but computers started to become commonplace in newsrooms only by the 1980s (Cox 2000). It was in the mid-1990s, with the commercial opening of the internet, that the computer started to be considered as a medium and the first attempts at digital journalism began (Pavlik 2001).

Early studies connecting information and communication technologies (ICTs) and journalism were linked to efficiency, exalting the potentials of new technologies for the development of "computer-assisted reporting" (Plesner 2009). The computer was seen as an aid for journalism, which could even replace traditional communication practices (such as face-to-face encounters or the telephone). Those approaches, hence, were limited to an instrumental view on digital artifacts.

But the relationship between technology and journalism goes beyond seeing the first as a substratum to the second. According to Pavlik (2000), technology influences journalism in four major areas: how journalists do their work, the content of news, the structure or organization of the newsroom, and the relationships among news organizations, journalists, and their many publics (audiences, sources, competitors, sponsors, controllers of the press). Yet, technology is portrayed as an external force (influence) that impacts humans and what humans produce. Such oppositions (inside/outside, humans/non-humans, cause/consequence), as well as other contrasts—such as micro/macro and professional/amateur—populate journalism theories. These binary strategies, however, artificially fragment journalism, reducing what is an entangled network to opposing poles.

What we defend is a perspective change. Looking through the lens of ANT, technology plays such a transforming role that we argue that it also *does* journalism. In order to develop this point, in the next section we turn our attention to ANT concepts and how they can be applied to the understanding of journalism.

Technological Artifacts as Actors in Journalism

What is journalism? Kruckeberg and Tsetsura (2004, 84) respond without any doubt: "we can be no more precise to argue that journalism is what journalists do." This tautological formula (Hanitzsch 2005) still needs to be overcome. Although several efforts try to recognize other social actors that directly or indirectly participate in the journalistic process (the cableman, the driver, the telephone operator, the reader that calls to report a problem, etc.), there are still many others that remain invisible. Even though this multiplicity of actors participates in diverse moments and modifies the process in an irreversible way, they are rarely considered or solely mentioned as external variables. This invisibility is not due to a potential transparency or intangibility. Their disappearance, as soon as one decides to list the participants of the journalistic process, begins with the limitation of what is considered an actor.

The redefinition of this concept by ANT is of particular interest to our later argument. As soon as one understands the real reach of the concept of an actor, how actors relate with other actors in a network, and how the network relates with each actor, it becomes possible to perceive the ontological limitations of the theories that try to explain social processes. The same is true with the study of journalism. After describing what ANT understands by "actants" and "social," we will then be able to discuss the agency of technological artifacts, how they act as mediators, co-producing journalism. Later, in future sections, we will use these concepts and premises to discuss the ontology, the epistemology, and the methodology of journalism studies.

According to ANT, the social is treated by traditional sociology as stuff, as a type of material. The latter, an essentialist perspective, views the social as a substance that qualifies something or a phenomenon *a priori*, and from which it is possible to derive conclusions and even predictions ("if that is social, thus..."). This is what Latour (2005) calls "social determinism." As we will show, this type of fatalistic force has historically misled journalism theories. While technological determinism is often observed and criticized in papers on digital journalism (Steensen 2011), the effects of social determinism in journalism theories needs to be definitely addressed.

The sociology of associations (an expression used by Latour as a synonym for Actor-Network Theory) addresses a sounding criticism to what it calls the sociology of the social. For Latour (2005, 8), traditional sociologists have "simply confused what they should explain with the explanation." ANT, however, does not believe in the possibility of a matter or a social force that backs phenomena and that might explain them. The social is a product of associations, but not an explanation. In other words, by negating the social as a leading force, ANT tries to observe the short-lived interactions that happen while the momentary associations occur. As Latour (2005, 65) explains, instead of a domain of reality, the social is a movement, a transformation (and thus the frequent use of the term "translation"): "It is an association between entities which are in no way recognizable as being social in the ordinary manner, except during the brief moment when they are reshuffled together."

Based on this view, ANT furthers the understanding of what an actor is. In short, an actor is whatever makes a difference in the ongoing action; it is what is made to act by many others (Latour 2005); or "any element in the network that acquires strength in association with others" (Hemmingway 2007, 24).

By deepening the comprehension of what actors are, and moving beyond the observation of humans interacting in an objectless world, Latour (2005, 5) states that the social should be thought of as "a trail of associations between heterogeneous elements." Everything that is not human, but participates in the emergence of the event, transforming it, cannot be taken just as context or background. More than a simple scenario, things allow that certain actions happen, besides constraining and influencing others.

In summary, moving away from deterministic frameworks, ANT seeks to assess the dynamics of heterogeneous associations while they occur. By revealing such complexity that seemed invisible until then (or observers preferred not to see), new descriptions and conclusions may emerge, as other questions may be asked.

While Silverstone (1994) and Couldry (2008) have previously discussed the pertinence of ANT to media studies, few efforts have been made to relate journalism and ANT (Hemmingway 2007; Plesner 2009; Schmitz Weiss and Domingo 2010; Van Loon 2011; Micó, Masip, and Domingo 2013; Anderson 2013). We believe that ANT's non-functionalist perspective and its skepticism about essentialized concepts (Couldry 2008) —"the social," "the technical," "the cultural"—may significantly contribute to further the understanding of how journalism happens.

Based on ANT's ontological propositions, we argue that journalism should not be seen through purist standpoints, which define characteristics it needs to have to honor its name. Journalism is not a tag that may be attributed to some texts and images. Instead, it is a momentary process that takes place while specific associations are maintained. In other words, nothing is journalism *per se*. Journalism happens. Journalism becomes.

The prescription of what is good journalism, how it needs to be, or who is authorized to work as a journalist are no more than social deterministic approaches. Yes, it is common for working fields to have their codes of excellence. Scholars, though, should not confuse these propositions of ideal conditions and routines with reality itself. Essentialist definitions of journalism function as if all actors were known, their behaviors could be foreseen, and all expected products were created in a vacuum, according to some standards. Any divergence would not be considered journalism.

We want to stress that journalism cannot be reduced to what a journalist does. Besides the problems of circular reasoning and self-referentiality, that simplistic postulate excludes everything that is not human. Technology is left outside, as something extraneous. Even though no practitioner or scholar would deny that journalism and technological artifacts have always been interconnected, when it comes to defining journalism those objects are set aside. On the other extreme, as soon as technology is understood to be the cause behind changes in the inverted pyramid style, the "multimedia journalist" or massive layoffs, for example, the debate dangerously approaches technological determinism.

However, as Couldry (2008) summarizes, for ANT "the social" is as technical as "the technical" is social. There is no pure social situation, no essential technical relation. Consequently, we might add, journalism is not made of a social substance, nor is it fundamentally a human process. It is, in fact, a hybrid complexity, as everything else.

A news story is not solely the result of social forces. Multiple actors are associated in a complex network, from the truck to the cable man, from the easy-access notepad to a correctly held camera. As Hemmingway (2007, 8) puts it, "we need to concentrate our efforts on understanding not just the role that technologies play, but more importantly, the *associations* that we discover between human and technological actors."

In order to deploy journalism processes from ANT's standpoint, it is necessary to follow all the actors and observe their actual contributions, instead of rushing to con-clusions—safely protected by sacred conceptions, such as ideology, truth, objectivity—or repeating the slogans of what journalism ought to be. It is time, then, to open the black box and look inside. Let all the actants be recognized, human and non-humans, their agencies, the associations they engage in, the traces they leave.

But actants are not all the same. According to Latour (2005, 39), an intermediary "is what transports meaning or force without transformation: defining its inputs is enough to define its outputs." On the other hand, a mediator is an actant that makes a difference in the ongoing processes, transforming and translating the meanings in con-struction.

Technological artifacts have been treated as intermediaries in journalism—carriers that can be used to enhance each step of journalistic routines. But, under certain cir-cumstances, technology can act as a mediator, transforming the news process. Plesner (2009) uses three examples to demonstrate the role of technological actants in news-work: e-mail communication between editors and collaborators, the use of search engines such as Google in order to find sources, and the telephone, allowing interviews in real time over large distances. These three common practices allow journalists to develop their own role and are fundamental to the resulting news piece. These instances, though, are not very far from the function of digital aids. In the next sections, we wish to go beyond these aspects, defending that a great number of non-humans are actually co-creators of journalism.

After criticizing the social and technological determinisms that undermine journal-ism theories and presenting why journalism is a creation of hybrid collectives, accord-ing to the contributions from ANT, we will now further our reflection on the ontology of journalism, discussing two settings in which the agency of digital artifacts is perhaps most noticeable.

Convergence and Automated Processes

The following discussion on media convergence and computational journalism (Karlsen and Stavelin 2014), even though their description will be rather brief, is intended to illustrate the concepts previously discussed and articulate them with recent phenomena (which will also complement our historical review). We will also debate the notion of network, which is central in digital journalism and convergence research, contrasting ANT's perspective with the concept of networked journalism (Bardoel and Deuze 2001; Heinrich 2011).

The term "convergence" was already being used in other contexts (Gordon 2003), but it was only in the 1990s that it started to be used to refer to technological devel-opments and to the integration of different languages and media (Belochio 2012). As Pavlik and McIntosh (2004, 19) define, "The coming together of computing, telecommu-nications, and media in a digital environment is known as convergence."

Viewing convergence in journalism as the reunion of technology devices in order to increase productivity, as Pavlik and MacIntosh (2004) do, is an oversimplification. In these cases, technology is once again observed merely as an intermediary.

For Van Loon (2011), perspectives that look at actual practices and consider convergence as steps towards greater integration in the newsroom (such as in García Áviles et al. 2009) show the potential of technology as an actant that helps shape journalism itself—as opposed to just enhancing how things are currently being made (Plesner's examples—e-mail and the telephone—might be a target of this last criticism if taken simply as aids for interviews). According to Van Loon, these perspectives on convergence could be complemented with ANT's framework in order to account for the complexity of the processes: "convergence is not one thing, but a label associated with a heterogeneity of practices" (Van Loon 2011, 13).

Other views identify multiple dimensions of journalism convergence. Domingo et al. (2007) see convergence as comprising four dimensions: integrated production, multiskilled professionals, multiplatform delivery, and active audience. This perspective goes a step further, but it stills considers convergence in a causal linearity, as something that adds greater workload to journalists (multiskilled professionals) and brings more technological devices to journalism practices (multiplatform delivery).

Later, Micó, Masip, and Domingo (2013) interviewed professionals in a newsroom moving toward convergence and identified a prevalence of the multiskilling dimension. The professionals saw it mostly as a negative thing and manifested their fear that convergence would lead to job cuts. We argue that the reported insecurity is a demonstration that technology is more than an intermediary. The transformations that the digital artifacts bring to the current associations show their active role as mediators.

It is important to note that ANT should not be treated as a convenient argument to highlight the importance of technology. The radicality of its ontological contributions encompasses epistemological and methodological consequences. Besides forcing the combination of two different theories (ANT and diffusion of innovations), Micó, Masip, and Domingo's research does not extend beyond the simple interview. Even though this is an important procedure, the authors oversaw ANT's methodological mantra: "follow the actors." The interviews with journalists maintain the focus on human agency, while other actants are kept "quiet." Several ethnographic methods, for example, have been used by ANT researchers to observe humans and non-humans while they associate and to collect the traces left in previous acts. If non-humans are at first described as actants, but the observation of their participation is later minimized or even ignored, the epistemological path arrives somewhere not far from departure, even though ANT was said to guide the exploration. Hence, while non-humans are kept as predicates, not as subjects, the anthropocentric tale of journalism will not be surpassed.

For Van Loon (2011), ANT's most important contribution is not the rediscovery of technology, but rather its methodology that allows the thorough description of the processes in which the social settings are shaped.

Yet, to "follow the actors" is not a simple procedure, as these associations are performed by a potential great number of humans and non-humans. As Latour (2005) explains, an ANT observer may not identify how all actants are connected, but knows that their associations make others do things. Because of this "principle of irreduction," actants are not differentiated hierarchically. Acting in a "flatland," all elements have the same weight.

Actually, this postulate leads us to another relevant concept in our discussion: the network. While media organizations have historically treated networks instrumentally (a broadcast infrastructure, for example), scholars have been recently debating the concept of network(ed) journalism.

Based on Castells' (1996) concept of network society, Heinrich (2011) proposes the model of network journalism to explain the complex relationship between different sources, producers, and news distributors in contemporary journalism. Even though her model considers the presence of more actors in the news process, it does not recognize technological artifacts as one of them (e.g. Facebook and Twitter). For example, after being published, a news piece can (re)circulate by being commented on and distributed by readers in social network sites (Zago 2011; Jenkins, Ford, and Green 2013).

In a similar direction, Bardoel and Deuze (2001, 92) use the expression of networked journalism to refer to "the convergence between the core competencies and functions of journalists and the civic potential of online journalism." To Russell (2011, 1), the concept should be understood as: "journalism that sees publics as creators, investigators, reactors, (re)makers, and (re)distributors of news and where all variety of media, amateurs, and professional, corporate and independent products and interests intersect at a new level." Although both views of networked journalism focus basically on human actors, they demonstrate an opening to encompass other practitioners besides journalists. However, technology is still not seen to have agency. It is portrayed as something that enables people to act.

In ANT's perspective, the term network has a specific meaning. It is not network in the technological or social sense, as networked journalism definitions seem to follow. Rather, it is understood as a "string of actions where each participant is treated as a full-blown mediator" (Latour 2005, 128). In fact, ANT makes no distinction between the individual and the whole. A network is defined by its actors as well as an actor is defined by its network (Latour et al. 2012). "Hence the term, actor-network—an actor is also, always, a network" (Law 1992, 384). What follows is that each actant, human or non-human, is a network within other networks.

Perhaps, the role of technological artifacts as an actant in journalistic networks is best perceived in what Träsel (2013) calls "post-human practices of journalism," such as in artificial intelligence journalism. From the creation of news by algorithms (Levy 2012; van Dalen 2012; Träsel 2013) to the use of algorithms for content curation (Rosenbaum 2011; Bakker 2012; Saad Corrêa and Bertocchi 2012), the presence of artificial intelligence in journalism is starting to become noticed. Since 2010, Narrative Science[1] automatically generates news from economic indicators and college league game reports (Levy 2012; van Dalen 2012).

Algorithms are used to deal with the profusion of information (Saad Corrêa and Bertocchi 2012). In journalism, this can be perceived in mobile apps such as Flipboard[2] and Facebook's Paper[3], which curate news content from various sites and social network services (Primo 2011; Saad Corrêa and Bertocchi 2012), or Google News, which uses Google Search algorithms in order to automatically aggregate news (Bakker 2012). Instead of eliminating the need for journalists, Saad Corrêa and Bertocchi (2012) suggest that these technologies demand more and more the presence of a human curator, who helps hierarchize and organize information gathered by automated software. Even artificial intelligence news demands someone to feed the machine with sentences and rules (Levy 2012). These relationships reinforce the associations between human and non-human actants in the co-creation of journalism.

The participation of algorithms in selecting and producing news can lead to radical transformations in newsrooms. When we look at these practices with ANT lenses, we can observe algorithms acting as mediators in hybrid networks. Algorithms can free journalists from having to write news pieces about extreme niche topics, so they can focus on more creative work (van Dalen 2012; Karlsen and Stavelin 2014). News consumption is also transformed by curation algorithms. Thus, the active participation of algorithms in journalism may affect all stages of news processes.

There is still debate, though, whether computational journalism is in fact journalism. While it is accepted that an algorithm may collect and process data better than a human, the translation of this information into a news piece by a robot is controversial. However, if the article fulfills its role in the news outlet and satisfies the reader, or even the blind review of a journalism scholar (an exercise similar to the Turing Test, used to evaluate an artificial intelligence system), would the fact that it was automatically produced disqualify the text as a news report? Once again we encounter the anthropocentric perspective denying any process that might challenge the human control over newsmaking.

All these sociotechnical collectives demonstrate the simultaneous presence of different kinds of agencies in journalistic processes. Such an understanding can help us observe more clearly who and what do journalism. Having reviewed and articulated the main concepts from ANT with recent news practices, we are now ready to revisit journalism theory traditions.

Rethinking Journalism Theories and Definitions

Applying ANT to journalism not only involves reevaluating the role of technology, but also reconceptualizing the sheer notion of journalism. Until now, we have focused on the inseparable relationship between humans and non-humans in journalistic practices. In this section we discuss how ANT's contributions impact theory construction in journalism. What follows the new perspective on journalism that we have been presenting is a need for significant epistemological revisions. Sure enough, this ontological turn will have repercussions on issues such as ethics, ideology, and value judgment, which have been traditionally inspired by essentialist premises.

A tension between the humanities and the social sciences has taken the definition of what journalism is into many directions. With this diagnosis, Zelizer (2004, 8) criticizes the limits of seeing journalism as an effect—according to her, a biased sociological view. Adopting a humanistic perspective, she opts for alternative ways to describe how journalism works, such as "performance, narrative, ritual and interpretive community."

Deuze (2005, 444) adds that journalism has been conceived as "a profession, an industry, a literary genre, a culture or a complex social system." The author then shows that the assessment of journalism as ideology is a significant one, as it may reveal how journalists and scholars view the profession (what it is and what it can be), according to shared ideal-typical values.

By adopting an ANT perspective, though, it is possible to observe that both the humanities and the sociological tradition lead to the same ontological mistake: the supposition that journalism is a practice restricted to humans; and according to ideological stances, of just certain humans: professional journalists. In fact, the dispute on the boundaries of who is a journalist remains (Zelizer 2004). The discussion on whether bloggers and other "amateurs" (Keen 2008) are part of the field, for example, has raised heated debates.

Professional self-definitions are found in the literature in a recipe style (Kovach and Rosenstiel 2001), most often narrated with imperative sentences. Deuze (2005) summarizes five ideal-typical values as follows: journalists provide a public service; journalists are neutral, objective, fair, and (thus) credible; journalists must enjoy editorial autonomy, freedom, and independence; journalists have a sense of immediacy; journalists have a sense of ethics and legitimacy. After analyzing each of these postulates, Deuze (2005, 458) concludes that

> any definition of journalism as a profession working truthfully, operating as a watchdog for the good of society as a whole and enabling citizens to be self-governing is not only naïve, but also one-dimensional and sometimes nostalgic for perhaps the wrong reasons.

After criticizing the literature that takes those idealistic values for granted and the utopian and anti-utopian discourses on "the impact of emerging sociocultural and socioeconomic issues on journalism," Deuze defends a holistic[4] argument that assumes that multimedia and multiculturalism are other "forces of change."

Anyhow, while it is still thought of in ideological terms, journalism will continue to be seen as guided by social forces. A professional ideology, though, is not a type of glue that brings journalists together and governs expected behaviors. In other words, journalism is not a substance, nor an idealistic essence. In fact, different professions have their manuals of procedures and codes of ethics. The same is true with the field of journalism. The problem arises when those texts are taken for granted, as the perfect description of what journalism is.

Based on a limited model of the social and on a normative professional perspective, journalism has been frequently assessed as it ought to be, not as it comes to be in each specific moment. What researchers observe, in these cases, is what their ideological models orient them to see. The profession's creed, however, is not what explains why journalism should be respected as a public service or the watchdog of democracy. Journalism is what needs to be explained, as it happens in democratic or dictatorial regimes, producing hard news or stories on celebrities.

More, the question "what is journalism?" should not be confused with "what is good journalism?" This type of value judgment might only make sense within certain groups that defend an explicit list of best practices, a rather arbitrary model with restricted validity. On the other hand, even what might be considered bad journalism, is journalism after all.

Not rarely, though, alternative forms of journalism (in relation to the normative standard) are labeled as deviations, yellow journalism or something outside the true journalistic realm.[5] First, participatory journalism projects and the articles supporting the movement seemed to put "good ol' journalism" at risk. As some milestone projects (e.g. *OhMy News International*, the global online participatory newspaper) later ceased to exist, critics that labeled activists and researchers of the movement as utopians might have felt vindicated. Now, the influence of ANT may be seen as a new threat to the stability of journalism. Actually, journalism continues to be enacted and reinvented every day. Journalism epistemology, on the other hand, is in fact being challenged by the ontological premises discussed in this paper.

Whenever other agencies are considered, the number of participating actants in journalistic processes greatly extrapolates the news organization's payroll. Hence, as the picture gets more and more populated, a demand for the actualization of journalism theories emerges. It is time then to reassemble journalism.[6]

As discussed in previous sections, the hybrid associations within sociotechnical collectives allow journalism to emerge. On the other hand, professional journalists and news organizations alone are not capable of "generating" journalism. The collection of theories united around the profession's ideology, that endlessly reiterate journalistic values and norms, cannot produce more than ostensive definitions. According to Latour (2005, 37), the object of this type of definition "remains there, whatever happens to the index of the onlooker." A performative definition, though, may only address what is in movement. As Latour illustrates, the dance is finished as soon as the dancers quit dancing. Seen from an ANT perspective, journalism does not correspond to a set of pure and mandatory qualities. Journalism exists just while it happens, and not as a transcendent essence.

Does an article, written by a newspaper journalist inside the media organization's building, that was not published but forgotten inside a drawer, constitute journalism? Or is it no more than an exemplar of what has been classified as a news genre? And if it was published momentarily on the website, but nobody read it while it was online? These provocative questions seek to challenge the clearly marked boundaries of ostensive definitions. They delimit what is in and what is out of journalism. The focus on newsmaking—particularly hard news—and the newsroom (Zelizer 2004), as well as on the professionals and their utopian self-descriptions (Deuze 2005), are seen as the "inside." Other people not related to the news organization, the audiences, and all objects (technological or not) are the "outside." The beginning and the end-point of journalism also seem to be easily described in the following linear progression: newsgathering, production, circulation. The distribution of news via some substratum delimits when the "inside" finishes and the "outside" starts. What happens after the news pieces are delivered—consumption and recirculation, or whatever names these associations receive—is frequently overlooked by journalism theories.

One interesting exercise is to abstractly delete some actors and their concatenations and ask if journalism would still emerge. For instance, would news production make sense without consumption? The same could be asked about the spontaneous movements of recirculation, which news organizations now eagerly try to promote.

Artifacts, we have shown, are traditionally not considered as an actor in journalism. But as soon as the internet connection breaks, for example, several associations would cease to exist, inside and outside the newsroom. Journalists would have difficulties relating to each other, assignment editors and the public would be separated, algorithms would not be able to curate data, factual images shot by citizens on site with their smartphones would not be received. With the absence of the internet, in this example, the multiplicity of silent digital actors suddenly becomes noticed.

Finally, it is important to recall that because of ANT's roots in semiotics, as Law (1999) observes, entities are not considered to carry inherent qualities. Rather, their attributes and forms emerge only while they are in relation with other entities. In the context of the discussion conducted in this article, we may conclude that nothing can be said to be journalism in itself.

Conclusion

After debating the anthropocentric perspectives in journalism studies, as well as social and technological determinisms, we addressed the problematic characteristics of dominant ostensive definitions. These normative descriptions of what journalism ought to be confuse the explanation with what should be explained. We have also discussed how the prevailing humanistic ontology of journalism ignores the active participation of non-humans.

Nevertheless, when an ANT researcher states that objects are not all intermediaries, that they may act as mediators that significantly transform associations and other participants, several voices rush to postulate: "without a journalist there would be no journalism." But, since there would not be journalism without non-human actants either, what follows is: technological artifacts and other objects also do journalism. Thus, besides "who," we also need to ask "what" does journalism. Besides the "hes" and the "shes," scholars should consider all the "its" that are active participants in associations, without which the processes would be radically different or not happen at all.

We have insisted that humans and non-humans constitute a hybrid collective. It is the concatenation of their associations that allows journalism to be enacted. What is urgent to recognize, hence, is that professional journalists are not alone and do not control journalism as they wish they could.

The new ontological premises that we have discussed here bring significant epistemological and methodological consequences. We are aware that this fact may undermine the adoption of this perspective, as it disturbs the stability of traditional theories and ideologically driven definitions. Yet, we are positive that because novel questions may be raised in journalism studies—as ANT premises widen the observation field, letting us see what was not before identifiable—new and innovative conclusions may be reached.

Yet, the attention that we advocate that has to be paid to the participation of objects in the co-creation of journalism should not culminate in some sort of fetishism of digital artifacts. Unfortunately, this would result in a new form of technological determinism, a problem that ANT intends to avoid.

FUNDING

This article was financed by the Conselho Nacional de Desenvolvimento Científico e Tecnológico (CNPq).

NOTES

1. See http://www.narrativescience.com/.
2. See https://flipboard.com/.
3. See https://www.facebook.com/paper.
4. Latour et al. (2012) criticize holistic perspectives as their arguments are based on the separation of two different levels: the micro and the macro. ANT, on the other hand, rejects that opposition and works with the leibnizian idea of monads. As we have shown before, ANT's metaphor of a "flatland" illustrates the existence of only one dimension, in which all actants have the same importance.

5. Curiously, definitions of alternative journalism (Atton 2003) and citizen/participatory journalism (Gillmor 2006) are also inspired by utopian discourses, with their own faith in what journalism should be.
6. This argument is a direct reference to Latour's (2005) book title: *Reassembling the Social: An Introduction to Actor-network-theory*.

REFERENCES

Anderson, C. W. 2013. *Rebuilding the News*. Philadelphia, PA: Temple University Press.

Atton, Chris. 2003. "What is 'Alternative' Journalism?" *Journalism* 4 (3): 267–272.

Bakker, Piet. 2012. "Aggregation, Content Farms and Huffinization." *Journalism Practice* 6 (5–6): 627–637.

Bardoel, Jo, and Mark Deuze. 2001. "Network Journalism: Converging Competences of Old and New Media Professionals." *Australian Journalism Review* 23 (2): 91–103.

Belochio, Vivian. 2012. *Jornalismo Em Contexto De Convergência: Implicações Da Distribuição Multiplataforma Na Ampliação Dos Contratos De Comunicação Dos Dispositivos De Zero Hora*. [Journalism in the Context of Convergence: Implications of Multiplatform Distribution in the Expansion of Communication Contracts of Zero Hora's Devices]. PhD diss., Universidade Federal do Rio Grande do Sul.

Briggs, Asa, and Peter Burke. 2010. *Social History of the Media*. New York: Polity.

Castells, Manuel. 1996. *The Rise of the Network Society*. Malden, MA: Blackwell Publishers.

Cox, Melissa. 2000. "The Development of Computer-assisted Reporting." Paper presented at the Newspaper Division, Association for Education in Journalism and Mass Communication, Southeast Colloquium, University of North Carolina, Chapell Hill, March 17–18.

Couldry, Nick. 2008. "Actor Network Theory and Media: Do They Connect and on What Terms?" In *Connectivity, Networks and Flows: Conceptualizing Contemporary Communications*, edited by A. Hepp, F. Krotz, S. Moores, and C. Winter, 93–111. Cresskill, NJ: Hampton Press.

Deuze, Mark. 2007. *Media Work*. Cambridge: Polity Press.

Deuze, Mark. 2005. "What is Journalism? Professional Identity and Ideology of Journalists Reconsidered." *Journalism* 6 (4): 442–464.

García Avilés, José, Klaus Meier, Andy Karltenbrunner, Miguel Carvajal, and Daniela Kraus. 2009. "Newsroom Integration in Austria, Spain and Germany." *Journalism Practice* 3 (3): 285–303.

Gillmor, Dan. 2006. *We the Media*. Sebastopol, CA: O'Reilly Media.

Gordon, Rich. 2003. "The Meanings and Implications of Convergence." In *Digital Journalism*, edited by Kevin Kawamoto, 31–55. Lanham, MD: The Rowman & Littlefield Publishers.

Hanitzsch, Thomas. 2005. "Journalists in Indonesia: Educated but Timid Watchdogs." *Journalism Studies* 6 (4): 493–508.

Heinrich, Ansgard. 2011. *Network Journalism*. London: Routledge.

Hemmingway, Emma. 2007. *Into the Newsroom: Exploring the Digital Production of Regional Television News*. London: Routledge.

Jenkins, Henry, Sam Ford, and Joshua Green. 2013. *Spreadable Media*. New York: NYU Press.

Karlsen, Joakim, and Eirik Stavelin. 2014. "Computational Journalism in Norwegian Newsrooms." *Journalism Practice* 8 (1): 34–48.

Keen, Andrew. 2008. *The Cult of the Amateur*. New York: Doubleday.

Kovach, Bill, and Tom Rosenstiel. 2001. *The Elements of Journalism*. New York: Three Rivers Press.

Kovach, Bill, and Tom Rosenstiel. 2011. *Blur*. New York: Bloomsbury.

Kruckeberg, Dean, and Katerina Tsetsura. 2004. "International Journalism Ethics." In *Global Journalism: Topical Issues and Media Systems*, edited by Arnold S. de Beer and John C. Merril, 84–92. Boston, MA: Pearson Education.

Latour, Bruno. 2005. *Reassembling the Social: An Introduction to Actor-network-theory*. New York: Oxford University Press.

Latour, Bruno, Pablo Jensen, Tommaso Venturini, Sébastian Grauwin, and Dominique Boullier. 2012. "The Whole is Always Smaller than Its Parts: A Digital Test of Gabriel Tardes' Monads." *The British Journal of Sociology* 63 (4): 590–615.

Law, John. 1992. "Notes on the Theory of the Actor-network: Ordering, Strategy, and Heterogeneity." *Systems Practice* 5 (4): 379–393.

Law, John. 1999. "After ANT: Complexity, Naming and Topology." In *Actor Network Theory and after*, edited by John Law and John Hassard, 1–14. Oxford: Blackwell.

Levy, Steven. 2012. "Can an Algorithm Write a Better News Story than a Human Reporter?" *Wired*, April 24. http://www.wired.com/gadgetlab/2012/04/can-an-algorithm-write-a-better-news-story-than-a-human-reporter/all/.

Mico, Josep, Pere Masip, and David Domingo. 2013. "To Wish Impossible Things: Convergence as a Process of Diffusion of Innovations in an Actor-network." *The International Communication Gazette* 75 (1): 118–137.

Pavlik, John. 2000. "The Impact of Technology on Journalism." *Journalism Studies* 1 (2): 229–237.

Pavlik, John. 2001. *Journalism and New Media*. New York: Columbia University Press.

Pavlik, John, and Shawn McIntosh. 2004. *Converging Media: An Introduction to Mass Communication*. Boston, MA: Pearson.

Plesner, Ursula. 2009. "An Actor-Network Perspective on Changing Work Practices: Communication Technologies as Actants in Newswork." *Journalism* 10 (5): 604–626.

Primo, Alex. 2011. "Transformações No Jornalismo Em Rede: Sobre Pessoas Comuns, Jornalistas E Organizações; Blogs, Twitter, Facebook E Flipboard [Transformations in Network Journalism: On Ordinary People, Journalists and Organizations; Blogs, Twitter, Facebook and Flipboard]." *Intexto* 2 (25): 130–146. http://seer.ufrgs.br/intexto/article/viewFile/24309/14486.

Rosenbaum, Steven. 2011. *Curation Nation*. New York: McGrawHill.

Russell, Adrienne. 2011. *Networked: A Contemporary History of News in Transition*. Cambridge: Polity Press.

Saad Corrêa, Elizabeth, and Daniela Bertocchi. 2012. "O Algoritmo Curador: O Papel Do Comunicador Num Cenário De Curadoria Algorítmica De Informação." [The Curator Algorithm: The Role of the Communicator in a Context of Algorithmic Curation of Information.] Paper presented at the XXI Encontro Anual da Compós, Juiz de Fora, Brazil, Compós.

Silverstone, Roger. 1994. *Television and Everyday Life*. London: Routledge.

Schmitz Weiss, A., and D. Domingo. 2010. "Innovation Processes in Online Newsrooms as Actor-networks and Communities of Practice." *New Media and Society* 12 (7): 1156–1171.

Steensen, Steen. 2011. "Online Journalism and the Promises of New Technology: A Critical Review and Look Ahead." *Journalism Studies* 12 (3): 311–327.

Träsel, Marcelo. 2013. "Toda Resistência é Fútil: O Jornalismo, Da Inteligência Coletiva à Inteligência Artificial [All Resistance is Futile: Journalism, from Collective Intelligence to Artificial Intelligence]." In *Interações Em Rede* [Networked Interactions], edited by Alex Primo. Porto Alegre, Brazil: Sulina.

Van Dalen, Arjen. 2012. "The Algorithms behind the Headlines." *Journalism Practice* 6 (5–6): 648–658.

Van Loon, J. 2011. "How to Be Mediatized? An Invitation to Metaphysics in Defense of Actor Network Theory." Paper presented at the International Communication Association's 2011 Virtual Conference.

Zago, Gabriela. 2011. "Recirculação Jornalística No Twitter: Filtro E Comentário De Notícias Por Interagentes Como Uma Forma De Potencialização Da Circulação [Journalistic Recirculation on Twitter: Filter and Commentary of News by Users as a Form of Potentiation of the Circulation.]." MSc thesis, Universidade Federal do Rio Grande do Sul.

Zelizer, Barbie. 2004. *Taking Journalism Seriously*. London: Sage.

TRACING DIGITAL NEWS NETWORKS
Towards an integrated framework of the dynamics of news production, circulation and use

David Domingo, Pere Masip and **Irene Costera Meijer**

Research on the evolution of journalism is still lacking appropriate theoretical tools to (re)conceptualise the blurring boundaries between professional news production in the media industry, the public actively engaged in using, circulating and producing information, and the diversity of social and material actors involved in these processes. This article suggests how actor-network theory (ANT) can contribute to overcome the limitations of existing paradigms in journalism studies through three complementary moves: dissociating news practices from specific theoretical categories, overcoming the disciplinary divide between the analysis of news production and news consumption, and problematising normative principles of journalism. The article concludes with a discussion of the practical challenges and methodological strategies researchers may need to address when using ANT to trace news networks: the practices performed by a remarkable diversity of actors for the production, circulation and use of news.

Introduction

As media scholars, our most pressing challenge is to provide comprehensive analyses of the current dynamics of news production, circulation and use in the digital public sphere. Journalism studies struggle to capture the diversity of actors, discourses and relationships, and evaluate their implications for the future of professional news production and the quality of public communication. Journalists have lost the (relative) monopoly of news gathering and distribution, but news media organisations are still producing most of the news we consume today, even those that circulate through social media and aggregators. Activists and public relations practitioners have not only professionalised their relationship with the media, but they also produce information using—in many cases—the formats and practices of professional journalism, and distribute it through the same online spaces. Citizens can feel more empowered than ever to select their sources of information and, at the same time, to become information sources themselves. All these trends, contradictory and convergent in many ways, challenge existing communication models and force us to reconsider the perspectives we use to understand the role of journalism in society (Chadwick 2011).

Rather than requiring new answers, journalism studies might be in need of asking new questions. What is *journalism*, or what is *news*, seem to be harder to define these days. Instead of focusing primarily on answering these questions, what could enrich most of the debates about the future of journalism would be to adopt as the central aim of our enquiry *how* journalism is constructed, maintained and eventually changed. In other words: what are the resources mobilised and activities performed by different actors in specific locations to shape something they call *journalism*. In this article we explore how actor-network theory (ANT) can be useful to open up these kinds of questions and problematise theoretical concepts usually taken for granted in our discipline.

Historically, journalism as an institution has shown a remarkable resilience to change; it still revolves around professional organisations that have a newsroom as their central workplace, with a set of practices, codes of ethics and business models that shape the kind of news they provide. We cannot zero out this configuration, because ethnographic data on newsroom practices (Costera Meijer 2005; Domingo and Paterson 2011) and on the relationship between journalists and their sources (Ryfe 2012, 24) suggest that the processes of socialisation reinforce the existing values and practices (Le Cam and Charbonneaux 2012). These shared norms act as a disincentive to adopt any innovation that may challenge the institutional configuration (Domingo 2008a; Micó, Masip, and Domingo 2013) and legitimate the role of professional media as the centre of the public sphere or the "news ecosystem" (Anderson 2010).

Nonetheless, continuity lives in permanent tension with change, and technological innovations are just one of the elements playing a part. Over the last three decades, corporatisation (Ryfe 2012, 14) has made newsrooms more vulnerable to business pressures (Heinonen and Luostarinen 2008, 235). The crisis of the revenue models of journalism has accelerated job cuts, precarious working conditions and a push for multi-skilling of professional news producers (Deuze 2007). In a digitally networked world, changes do not happen only within the institution of journalism, but also around it, and our theoretical baggage seems to be especially badly equipped to address the evolution and the diversity of news practices performed by those who used to be categorised as the sources and audiences of journalism (Costera Meijer 2013a). As researchers, we need a theoretical framework that enables us to problematise and trace the diversity of actors involved in changing news production and news use, people's expectations regarding what is news and who is entitled to produce it, their decisions regarding who they trust as news sources, their motivations and practices in the production of news, and their power relationships in the processes of the circulation of news.

In order to address all these aspects, it is necessary to have an approach that neutralises any apriorisms about the roles and practices of the multiplicity of actors. We believe that ANT (Latour 2005) can provide this approach. In the following sections we present key ontological and epistemological proposals of this research tradition, and discuss how they could open up relevant research questions in journalism studies. We first review the basic concepts of ANT and how they have been applied to the study of innovation in newsrooms. Then, we propose three strategic moves that ANT allows us to explore in order to address some of the current limitations of journalism studies when dealing with interrogating the continuities and changes in news production, circulation and use. The first move entails dissociating each of these practices from specific theoretical categories (such as *journalist* or *audience*). The second move takes the implications of the first in order to overcome the disciplinary divide between the analysis of news production and news consumption—or, more appropriately, "use" (Couldry 2004). The third move problematises the normative principles of journalism, transforming them from a benchmark for research into an element that in itself inter-acts with the rest of the actors engaged in news practices. The opportunities that each of these moves open for researchers are illustrated with examples taken from ongoing studies in the Netherlands undertaken by one of the co-authors. We finish the article with a discussion of the practical challenges and methodological strategies researchers may need to address to apply these three moves to empirical research.

Journalism as News Networks

For ANT, society is *performed* through relations, connections and associations; it is the outcome of daily interactions, rather than an abstract structure that organises those interactions and gives meaning to them: "a reality that is *done* and *enacted* rather than observed" (Mol 1999, 77). ANT invites the researcher to focus on the *actions* of the plu-rality of heterogeneous actors that participate in a social activity (Plesner 2009): people, ideals, symbolic constructions and material elements—including technology (see the article in this special issue by Primo and Zago 2014)—are seen as equally important ele-ments to analyse. ANT proposes the neutral concept *actant* to refer to the human and non-human participants that the researcher can trace through their actions, without prejudging their qualities (Latour 2005, 54). The main implication of this approach is that "everything is uncertain and reversible, at least in principle" (Law 1999, 4). This pre-pares the researcher to explore how change happens, and how stability is achieved and maintained: a specific arrangement to perform any social practice requires the "effort" (Latour 2005, 35) of actants to mobilise others and shape their actions, and ANT is well equipped to trace these dynamics.

Coherent with a research tradition that was born to untangle scientific and tech-nological innovations, so far ANT has mainly been applied in journalism studies to study the adoption of digitisation in newsrooms and how it interplays with journalistic professional identities and practices (Hemmingway 2008; Micó, Masip, and Domingo 2013; Plesner 2009; Schmidt Weiss and Domingo 2010; Spyridou et al. 2013). These studies, in the context of a broader collection of constructivist approaches to the evolu-tion of journalism (Domingo 2008b), demonstrate how change is a process of constant negotiation between the journalists, the tools they use and other members of news or-ganisations in charge of strategic decisions (the marketing department, the IT depart-ment), through everyday interactions and practices. The relationship between human and non-human actants has been at the centre of these studies: Schmitz Weiss and Do-mingo (2010) found that content management systems designed by the IT team of media companies had a complicated relationship with the journalists using it, who sometimes boycotted the practices prescribed by the software because they did not align with their existing news practices. In a regional BBC newsroom, Hemmingway (2008) explored how personal digital production equipment enabled journalists to produce more human-interest stories as they had more flexibility in dealing with the deadlines of hard news.

In the newsrooms, researchers have used ANT to trace *networks* of the associations between actants and the processes of *translation* that arranged them into the set of practices they perform (Latour 2005, 108). Innovations are the unpredictable outcome of these processes. We believe that we can take ANT a step further in our exploration of how *journalism as a practice* is (re)configured. If we trace the actions of the diversity of actants involved in news production, circulation and use, we will quickly be tracing "a network that extends from the machinery of the newsroom, through its personnel, its news technologies, skills and working practices, beyond the newsroom and out into the messy world beyond" (Hemmingway 2008, 27). As we analyse *news*, or what counts as news in particular circumstances and under certain conditions, through tracing the network of how it is produced, circulated and used, we propose to label our object of study as *news networks*, as initially suggested by Hemmingway:

> The news network incorporates all of the traditionally defined internal and external realities [to a newsroom], and dismantles the concept of internal and external substituting these for a network of translations, practices and actors that in and by itself constitutes the *reality* of news. (Hemmingway 2008, 27)

Who or what is part of a news network may not be restricted to familiar *loci* (Heinonen and Luostarinen 2008). Outside the newsrooms, political organisations, commercial companies and activist movements are becoming increasingly organised in the ways they produce and distribute information and opinion to the rest of society. Newsrooms, then, are not the centre of specific news networks, but just one of the places where it is reasonable to start tracing how news is collectively used.

News network is a notion that attempts to embrace the practices and discourses that people (journalists, managers, activists, public relations practitioners, citizens) perform to produce, circulate and use news (collections of ideas, facts and points of reference about matters of common concern in society such as reportages, articles, comments, pictures, etc.), considering professional ideals (autonomy, quality, transparency, democracy, public sphere, etc.), symbolic constructions (newsworthiness, shares, ratings, etc.) and material artefacts (technologies, tweets, newspapers, newsrooms, etc.) as elements that are all important in the process. Taking as epistemological standpoint the concepts and protocols of ANT, we understand a news network as a dynamic set of relationships between (human and non-human) actants for the production, use and circulation of news. The concept of news network, in its literality, connects with "networked journalism" (Jarvis 2006; Heinrich 2011). Yet, ANT uses the word *network* not to describe a particular technological configuration (e.g. the internet) or the dispersed nature of news production (e.g. citizen journalism), but "to designate a mode of inquiry that learns to list, at the occasion of a trial, the unexpected beings necessary for any entity to exist" (Latour 2011, 799). For news to exist, it should be tried and traced. What does news need to subsist through a complex network of allies, accomplices and competitors? It is the researcher who will trace each specific news network by following the actants (Latour 2005, 12).

Latour has repeatedly regretted the label of *actor-network theory* for being too open to misinterpretations, and has argued that it should rather be seen as an ontology, or "a very crude method to learn from the actors without imposing on them an *a priori* definition" (Latour 1999, 20). We think that in this moment of mind-blowing uncertainty in the evolution of journalism, it is worthwhile embracing the attitude that

ANT promotes and exploring how it enables us to ask more appropriate research questions than currently existing theoretical paradigms in journalism studies. Instead of putting the focus on what is journalism and where are its boundaries, ANT may let us trace how it is constructed, who (and what) participates in constructing it (see Primo and Zago 2014), and how they change it or perpetuate it.

First Move: From Categories to Practices

Couldry (2008, 100) considers that the most powerful contribution of ANT to media studies is "its anti-functionalism and its general scepticism about essentialised notions of 'the social', 'the technical', 'the cultural' and so on": no social or institutional configuration is taken for granted, but rather it is understood as the result of the relationships between actants in a localised setting. Instead of making assumptions or defining dozens of ambiguous criteria to determine the differences between what is and what is not "media" (Council of Europe 2011) or *journalism*, ANT proposes to step out of theoretical categorisations: "divisions or distinctions are understood as effects or outcomes. Attributes come from relations with other entities" (Law 1999, 1). Focusing on the (inter)actions of the actants, on what they do, rather than trying to fit them in categories based on what they are (or what they are supposed to be) can be a productive approach to grasp the diversity and particularity of actants implicated in a news network.

ANT deactivates the dichotomy producers–consumers that lies at the core of theories of journalism studies by erasing the *a priori* assumptions that specific human and non-human actors are expected to perform specific actions based on predefined categories such as *journalist* or *audience*. Instead of essaying the coinage of new hybrid concepts (*produser, citizen journalist*) that convey the inefficacy of the existing models to explain what actants are doing in the digital era, an anti-functionalist approach makes it easier to acknowledge that professional journalists actually *use* themselves a lot of news in order to be able to produce their own news stories, or that certain citizens that do not work for media organisations may be very efficient at circulating some news on Twitter and making them *trending topics* before professional newsrooms take them to produce their own account of the story. In these two illustrations we are still consciously using the concepts of "professional journalists" and "professional newsrooms", taking them as the broad terms whose meaning and function should be deconstructed. In this particular case, the opposition between *professional* and *citizen* might be meaningful because it denaturalises that news is something which comes from and is published only on professional platforms. The use of the term *professional* as adjective was not necessary for many decades, because the notion of *journalist* self-evidently referred to a professional; and vice versa, *citizens* have always been active in producing and distributing news, but until recently they were called PR practitioners, activists, sources or experts before the term *citizen journalists* tried to transfer to them the normative ideals of the profession (Borger et al. 2013; see the third move). The crucial step provided by ANT is that these concepts are no longer loaded with *a priori* expectations of what a (professional) journalist is supposed to do. Instead of taking as starting point the existing categories and their predictable positions, and eventually studying from there how many actors do or do not fit in those categories, an ANT perspective proposes to focus on the connections between actants through their inter-actions in order to understand how they become what they are, or better, why do they do what they do (Latour 2005, 217). That is what we can call an *actor-network*: the actant being defined by the network of relationships—or *translations*, in ANT terms—that can be traced. Actants can only be tracked down if their trail becomes visible by performing actions in interaction with other actants: they may enable others to do something, force them to do it, or stop them from doing it.

Let us consider an example where the disparity of connections mobilised by two different actants end up revealing how a professional journalist stops an activist from becoming a legitimate source. Abma (2013) meticulously traced the various ways trans-lation between professional journalists and citizen reporters failed in a participatory journalism project started by a Dutch regional broadcaster. The story illustrates how lots of things can go wrong when people step out of their conventional roles and do not conform to particular expectations. First of all, the protagonist of the traced prac-tice, a citizen journalist called Harm, wanted to connect with a reporter to provide a video he had made about an elderman's changing views about admitting new energy-generation windmills. The receptionist he got on the phone when calling the general number of the regional newscaster misinterpreted his request to discuss the video with the newsroom as a request to engage a reporter to cover the story, and redirected the call to a freelance documentary maker (Patrick). Patrick also associated Harm's request with in-depth investigative reporting, a genre that takes a lot of time and thus money to produce, and did not understand Harm's offer: the citizen was eager to take up the reporting role for free and Patrick would only have to supervise the project as is com-mon in crowdsourcing or networked journalism projects (cf. Schaffer 2012). Patrick was unable to translate his conventional ideas and expectations about the relation between citizens and journalists (or between a professional and an activist) into a relationship between two equals who could benefit from co-creation. On top of that, Patrick, as a freelancer, was not in the position of seriously discussing the project with the news-caster. In the end, he advised Harm to send the video interview to the newscaster's general mailbox for news tips. Harm took his advise and used the popular file-sharing software WeTransfer to send the news video he had made to the newscaster, mobilis-ing his technological expertise:

> It is an easy to use medium. You send it via WeTransfer … and you come directly in contact with the people who are dealing with those things … That way you can achieve a lot … Because if you tell them through the phone, the response is: yes inter-esting. But if that kind of people can check it quickly on their left screen, then they think: yes, that video item we need to have. (Abma 2013, 35)

This third translation did not work out either. Even after some weeks, Harm was not called back and finally he lost his appetite for co-creation and put his energy into working with a national newscaster who was willing to broadcast the video. To under-stand why Harm was not called back by the regional newscaster, the researcher rechecked the whole process and tried to trace all the relevant actants. He asked a pro-fessional reporter to explain why Harm's WeTransfer message had not been noticed. One explanation was that the regional newscaster had difficulties downloading it because it used Lotus Notes as a mail system. But even if some editor would have been able to download the message he or she might not have been able to translate the message into something he or she could make sense of. According to the consulted editor the message could not be read as a press release and did not contain a clear reference to a sender (the return address was noreply@wetransfer.com). And these were a *conditio sine qua non* for the regional newscaster to recognise news pitches by sources. "If someone sends a press release about a big happening, I would have known what to do with it. In this case I had to find out for myself."

This story of a "participatory journalist" illustrates how ANT stimulated the researcher to trace alternative ways in which professional journalists seem to be reluctant to change. It is not because they lack good intentions, but because they are literally unable to come to terms with citizen journalism. The example portrays the active role of technology and professional conventions in preventing translation and thus preventing a news network. It also illustrates how ANT deals with power differences. The theory has been fiercely criticised for being "just descriptive" (Couldry 2008; Latour 2005, 256) and not being sensitive to power relationships. As an analytical principle, ANT purposefully *flattens* the landscape to give actors the opportunity to show how they shape each other, but "this flattening does not mean that the world of the actors themselves has been flattened out" (Latour 2005, 220). However, instead of taking power for granted, the anti-functionalist approach claims that "power is not something that one can merely possess" (Hemmingway 2008, 34). Power can only be traced when actants, in this case the receptionist, different professional journalists, conventions about journalism and information technology, "exert" it to make others do something or prevent them from doing something. If we understand power as a trail to discover, we may not only be able to explore how journalism as a practice is maintained with the repartition of roles that professionals strive to keep, but we also open the door "to explore what is possible" (Latour 2005, 261): to trace new actants entering the scene and the new associations they establish, to follow how actants struggle to assemble themselves in ways that challenge the existing configurations of the news network.

An important, numerous and diverse set of actants that might become part of the news network is "the people formerly known as the audience" (Rosen 2006). In this case we come back to this catchy periphrasis because it magnificently captures the spirit of the ANT perspective. Rather than labelling them *a priori* as an audience—an aggregated mass of recipients of news products, as users—actively engaging with the content or as citizens—political subjects making decisions based on their interpretations of news, we are on firmer ground if we merely make the effort of including them in our efforts to trace the news network. Following Nick Couldry (2004), we propose to explore what range of media practices are oriented to journalism and what is the role of journalism-oriented practices in ordering, anchoring, controlling and organising other practices. The value of such an approach could be that it opens up questions about what people are actually doing when they *use*, *produce* or *circulate* news and how they categorise what they are doing. This approach avoids again "the disciplinary or other preconceptions that would automatically read their actions as, say, 'consumption' or 'being an audience', whether or not that is how the actants see their actions" (Couldry 2004, 125). It also avoids labelling *a priori* particular production activities outside the newsrooms as *citizen journalism*, *activism* or *public relations*.

The digitisation of journalism enables new practices of news use such as regularly *checking* (Costera Meijer 2013b), *secondary gatekeeping* (Singer 2013) or *produsing* (Bruns and Highfield 2012) the news. In this context of apparently drastic change, Groot

Kormelink and Costera Meijer (2013) found that old news habits are also maintained with new media technologies: Bram (28) claims that watching the news of the Dutch public broadcaster on his laptop gives him more freedom: "You no longer have to sit down at a specific time". However, despite enjoying being able to decide when to watch the news, Bram still likes to stick to the live broadcast of the 8 o'clock news to structure his evening. Therefore he often watches its live streams on his laptop. This specific example can illustrate the richness of exploring news practices with an approach that focuses on following the actions of actants, sensitive to what a rigid theoretical framework would judge as contradictory decisions.

With the first move, ANT takes off the shelf of the researcher the pressure of defining beforehand what is journalism today, who produces the news and how. The answer to what counts as journalism becomes the output of our empirical enquiries. Instead of devoting our efforts to build a theoretical model that predicts what journalism looks like in the digital age, ANT provides us with analytical tools that may help us gather empirical evidence about what is actually going on when news (or what counts as news) is being produced, circulated or used.

Second Move: Bridging Disciplinary Gaps

The ontological consequences of the first move enable us to revisit journalism with fresh, new analytical eyes. Most importantly, it may enable us to bridge the gap between three main research traditions that have addressed the evolution of journalism: the sociology of newswork, with a focus on professional work practices; the paradigm of literary criticism, with its emphasis on news texts; and reception studies' explorations of media consumption patterns and habits. Each of these research traditions addresses the historical construction of online communication from different standpoints, and their efforts to reach out towards each other leave a grey area of conflicting concepts and paradigms. Tracing news networks with a focus on practices can help researchers follow the whole process of news making in all its ramifications and multidirectional trajectories, capturing the contributions of the diversity of actants involved: witnesses, aggregators, social media platforms, activists, politicians, involved citizens, journalists, content management systems, journalistic principles, casual readers of journalistic products or receptionists. How pieces of content become news (or not, as we saw in the example in the first move) happens in very subtle and interrelated ways. ANT obliges us to abandon for good the obsolete linear model where the source is on one end and the journalist as a gatekeeper mediates the message to a public.

The exercise of following the actants that form a news network may foster research questions that problematise the definition of journalism as an institution and its role in the everyday life of our societies. It definitely invites us to explore, through the eyes of the variety of actants, the boundaries of journalism as an occupation, and the difference between information and news. Researchers have advocated to trace the processes "through which journalists struggle to claim professional status" (Schudson and Anderson 2008, 90) and to "track the contours of this nascent boundary work" done by professional journalists and other actors performing journalism (Lewis 2012, 852). We think this cannot be done without dismantling the automatic focus on institutions, categories and structures; the "media-centrism" (Schlesinger 1990) dominating journalism studies. Lewis (2012) agrees with Anderson (2011) about the need to "blow up" the newsroom as an isolated object of study, suggesting ANT as one of the key tools for researchers. Approaching journalistic institutions from an ANT perspective will not automatically weaken these institutions, but will actually enable us to understand better their vulnerability, their value and their contingency, and to provide arguments for the social debate about the future of journalism and the collective exploration of new ways to improve their chances of survival. We will discuss the normative implications of this approach in the third move.

Research that does not explicitly draw from ANT already showcases the advantages of moving beyond the newsroom (Anderson 2010; Ryfe 2012), and relativises the signs of a loss of hegemony of journalistic institutions as the legitimate producers of the main news narratives. In the first case, by taking as the object of study the city of Philadelphia, instead of specific newsrooms, Anderson was able to reconstruct the circulation of news between different social actors actively involved in the production of information, and concluded that activists and bloggers tended to legitimise professional media as the hegemonic producer of the news narrative by seeking the attention of the journalists to report on their claims. Each of the actors "categorised and recategorised" the others "depending on their own position within the media system" (Anderson 2010, 306), interacting with them based on the perceptions and expectations they had regarding their roles: journalists treated bloggers as sources and never saw them as competitors. We believe taking the ANT challenge and tracing the actions of all actants involved is not only necessary to construct and track down a specific news network, but also may have relevant consequences for the problematisation of journalism and its *black box* status for many members of society (Hemmingway 2008, 24). An ANT approach invites the researcher to humbly reconsider the importance and the meaning of journalism and news in the wider context of everyday life to understand how news practices *order* or *anchor* other practices. Most digital news users check news sites and apps throughout the day, whenever it is convenient, often when users have little time. This means news is anchoring everyday activities like visiting the toilet or waiting in line at the supermarket. News is also ordering practices of preparing and eating food. Some examples come from interviews with a variety of people about their personal news use (Groot Kormelink and Costera Meijer 2013). Jantien turns on the news while she is preparing dinner. It moves to the foreground when she is cutting her vegetables, but it is just as easily relegated to being a background noise when she walks into the kitchen:

> Jantien (28): "I walk on and off between the kitchen and the TV, but I also cut my vegetables in front of the TV … I'm not like, 'Oh it's 6 pm, I'm going to watch the news'. It's more that it coincides with, I'll go cut the vegetables and … I'll turn on the TV with it, because I just think that's nice."

Jantien is not in the first place interested in the content of the news; instead, the news structures her evening as a "behavioral regulator" (Lull 1990, 36). Time to cook is time to watch the news. While cooking, the news also offers "a flow of constant background noise [and] a companion for accomplishing household chores and routines" (Lull 1990, 36). Practices like watching the news order other practices like having breakfast or preparing dinner or starting one's workday. A journalism studies approach that takes as departure point just the texts, the reception or the production of news might miss the point.

Third Move: Problematising Normativity

The process of tracing news networks opens up yet another opportunity to journalism studies. Focusing on practices rather than on predefined categories, positions and structures, and tracing news networks in order to discover the dynamics of continuity and change in journalism, enables us to problematise normativity and become self-reflexive about our relationship as researchers with the phenomenon we study. Normative ideals of what journalism should be, in terms of quality and in terms of its role in democratic societies, may be traced as actants in the news network when they shape the practices of news production, circulation and use. Instead of taking normativity for granted, as the benchmark to criticise the shortcomings of contemporary journalism, ANT suggests focusing on how normativity is performed and constructed. From this perspective, principles are not abstract concepts; when interacting with journalists, these ideals sometimes hinder potential news stories from being produced, and at other times it stimulates their production or selection. Costera Meijer's (2003, 2005) ethnography of the Dutch public newscasters' newsroom showed how journalists' operationalisation of their key professional value *independence* enabled them to produce important news items they did not think their audience "liked", but at the same time hindered them from inventing more enthralling ways to narrate the news: "unlike the commercial newscaster, we don't have to think about our audience" (Costera Meijer 2003, 18). Not only journalists make normative claims about their work: citizens also have normative expectations, as when bloggers demand journalists to fulfil their commitment to accuracy (Vos, Craft, and Ashley 2012) or citizens assess news and reference information as more credible than other types of online information, because they expect news organisations to apply some editorial rigour and fact-checking procedures to the information that they provide (Flanagin and Metzger 2000). What counts as a *news*, therefore, is the result of complex interactions in constant flux, composed of and enabled by multiple communication acts. There is empirical evidence that the norms and values by which we recognised journalism for some time may be changing. The rituals of objectivity seem to be losing ground among online journalists, substituted by new rituals of transparency (Karlsson 2010). In the meantime, news users put "reliability" or "trust" at the top of their list when it comes to valuable journalism (Costera Meijer 2013a; Doeve and Costera Meijer 2013). Objectivity seems to be perceived by more and more participants in news networks as a myth. Problematising normativity means to include it in the process of tracing the news network, to see how it shapes practices, but also how it is (re)created in the daily interactions between actants. At the same time, normativity is invoked in attempts to delineate the boundaries of who can be considered a journalist; norms "are put to use as a way to decide, in part, who they are and to which sort of group they pertain" (Latour 2005, 182). Furthermore, with an ANT perspective, the "dispersion" of journalism as a practice (Ringoot and Utard 2005) becomes a fascinating challenge to be traced empirically, rather than a problem that does not fit within theoretical categories: there may be many different normativities, different definitions of what journalism should be. They could be competing, or have completely autonomous lives in separately traced news networks in different countries, different journalistic beats, different newsrooms, different communities.

The other consequence is that researchers can engage in critical reflections upon their own use of these normative ideals (see Blumler and Cushion 2013). Tracking down normative definitions problematises the research questions we ask and the categories we use. Surveys in which journalists are asked to check how much they agree with a set of ideals and news articles that are scrutinised to assess balance and accuracy are not innocent investigations but are informed by and are part of the normativity that might be better traced as a node or actant in the news network. In fact, as researchers we are also part of the network we trace, because the sole way to trace it is by inter-acting with the actants we find in the process (Latour 2005, 259). ANT proposes to take a reflective distance from our own convictions during the tracing of the actions of the rest of the news network, letting them define themselves instead of imposing our cate-gories. But it also invites us to include scientific discourses into the object of study, share our provisional results with them and discuss our ideals, to give back to the news networks through our scientific production "an arena, a forum, a space, a representa-tion" (Latour 2005, 256) of how news is produced, circulated and used that could be used as a tool to foster decisions, changes that may take journalism closer to the ideals, now open to a critical discussion among actors. This could contribute worthwhile input to the call of Blumler and Cushion (2013, 8) for a "dialogue with practitioners" that should overcome the "defensiveness and denial" with which journalists often receive critical research results.

Research Strategies to Trace News Networks

Tracing news networks can be exhausting, but we agree with Latour (2005) that it will be worth the effort. The insights we can achieve by denaturalising the sociologi-cal concepts we take for granted in journalism studies and patiently following the actants to reconstruct how news is produced, circulated and used in a specific context can help us reassess the role of journalism in our contemporary societies and render visible its diversity. From a pragmatic point of view, the task may seem overwhelming. The only way to reassure ourselves that it is worth starting to trace news networks is to acknowledge that there is not only one news network to map, but a multitude of them, to some extent interconnected, but reasonably autonomous. Each researcher can aspire to trace a specific news network at a time and by sharing the results with others, the mosaic of the *journalisms* that are being practised today would start to emerge. News networks are bound to communities, be they geographical or topical. They over-lap, and they shift continuously. Our intuition is that the most feasible way to enter the field to trace a specific news network is to identify a controversy (Callon 1981), a spe-cific circumstance when actors are struggling over the definition of a social issue such as the prohibition of the use of veils in public spaces (Domingo and Le Cam 2013). These moments are precious opportunities for the researcher to see some parts of the black box of public communication becoming visible as some actants challenge the existing obligatory points of passage. The other ideal moment to enter the field is the appearance of a new actor in the news production scene, or a drastic redesign of the organisation of an established actor, such as the newsroom or the products of a media organisation. Controversies and innovations oblige actors to (re)act and those actions are the core material for an ANT study.

Latour (2005) has repeatedly argued that ANT is not a theory in the traditional sense of the word, but rather a protocol or a guide about how to avoid imposing our scientific apriorisms on to our object of study. In this, it is not bound to a specific methodology, even if most ANT studies could be described as ethnographies. In the digital era, being true to the aim of following the actants requires the combination of a wide array of online and offline methods. The advantage of digital communication technologies for ANT is that they leave much clearer traces of the connections between actants than other forms of communication (Latour et al. 2012). Methods to test and explore may include computerised big data analysis (Lewis, Zamith, and Hermida 2013) to identify (online) content related to a specific news event or controversy and identify news producers (An et al. 2011; Kwak et al. 2010) and how news narratives circulate (Leskovec, Backstrom, and Kleinberg 2009); network analysis (Anderson 2013) of the explicit and implicit links between actants through the published content; discourse analysis of news products to assess the evolution of sources and narratives over time; online (Hine 2008) and offline ethnographies (Anderson 2013) to trace the practices of identified actants, and find new ones; reconstruction interviews (Reich 2009) to explore their attitudes and perspectives on the news network; media diaries and think-aloud protocols with the people formerly known as the audience to reach out explicitly to their side of the network (Costera Meijer 2013a; Groot Kormelink and Costera Meijer 2013); action research (Reason and Bradbury 2007) to explore ways to change the exist-ing relationships in the network, etc. As new questions arise in the process of tracing the news network, we are sure researchers will have the challenge of exploring new methodological strategies.

Ultimately, tracing the news network, putting the emphasis on practices rather than on institutions, will open the black boxes of normative definitions of journalism and democracy. We feel there is a dire need of distancing research from the strong normative tradition that has guided journalism studies for decades, as that can deliver us the opportunity to rethink normativity together.

REFERENCES

Abma, Carst. 2013. "Tussen Formeel En Informeel; Genetwerkte Journalistiek Met RTV N-H En Lokale Communities in Noord-Holland [Between Formal and Informal; Networked Jour-nalism with RTV N-H and Local Communities in North-Holland.]." Master thesis Journal-ism Studies VU.

An, Jisun, Meeyoung Chay, Krishna Gummadi, and Jon Crowcroft. 2011. "Media Landscape in Twitter: A World of New Conventions and Political Diversity." Paper presented at the International AAAI Conference on Weblogs and Social Media, Barcelona, July, 17–21.

Anderson, C. W. 2013. "What Aggregators Do: Towards a Networked Concept of Journalistic Expertise in the Digital Age." *Journalism*. Published online before print June 25, 2013, doi:10.1177/1464884913492460.

Anderson, C. W. 2011. "Blowing up the Newsroom: Ethnography in the Age of Distributed Journalism." In *Making Online News—Volume 2: Newsroom Ethnography in the Second Decade of Internet Journalism*, edited by David Domingo and Chis Paterson, 151–160. New York: Peter Lang.

Anderson, C. W. 2010. "Journalistic Networks and the Diffusion of Local News: The Brief, Happy News Life of the Francisville Four." *Political Communication* 27 (3): 289–309.

Blumler, Jay G., and Stephen Cushion. 2013. "Normative Perspectives on Journalism Studies: Stock-taking and Future Directions." *Journalism*. doi:10.1177/1464884913498689.

Borger, Merel, Anita van Hoof, Irene Costera Meijer, and José Sanders. 2013. "Constructing Participatory Journalism as a Scholarly Object. A Genealogical Analysis." *Digital Journalism* 1 (1): 117–134.

Bruns, Axel, and Tim Highfield. 2012. "Blogs, Twitter, and Breaking News: The Produse of Citizen Journalism." In *Produsing Theory in a Digital World: The Intersection of Audiences and Production in Contemporary Theory*, edited by Rebecca Ann Lind, 15–32. New York: Peter Lang.

Callon, Michel. 1981. "Pour Une Sociologie Des Controverses Technologiques [For a Sociology of Technological Controversies]." *Fundamenta Scientiae* 2 (3/4): 381–399.

Chadwick, Andrew. 2011. *The Hybrid Media System*. Oxford: Oxford University Press.

Costera Meijer, Irene. 2013a. "Valuable Journalism: The Search for Quality from the Vantage Point of the User." *Journalism* 14 (6): 754–770.

Costera Meijer, Irene. 2013b. "When News Hurts. the Promise of Participatory Storytelling for Urban Problem Neighbourhoods." *Journalism Studies* 14 (1): 13–28.

Costera Meijer, Irene. 2005. "Impact or Content? Ratings versus Quality in Public Broadcasting." *European Journal of Communication* 20 (1): 27–53.

Costera Meijer, Irene. 2003. "What is Quality Television News? A Plea for Extending the Professional Repertoire of Newsmakers." *Journalism Studies* 4 (1): 15–29.

Couldry, Nick. 2008. "Actor Network Theory and Media: Do They Connect and on What Terms?" In *Connectivity, Networks and Flows: Conceptualizing Contemporary Communications*, edited by Andreas Hepp, Friedrich Krotz, Shaun Moores, and Carsten Winter, 93–108. Mahwah, NJ: Hampton Press.

Couldry, Nick. 2004. *MediaSpace: Place, Scale, and Culture in a Media Age*. London: Routledge.

Council of Europe. 2011. "Recommendation CM/Rec(2011)7 of the Committee of Ministers to Member States on a New Notion of Media." http://wcd.coe.int/ViewDoc.jsp?id= 1835645&Site=CM.

Deuze, Mark. 2007. *Media Work*. Cambridge: Polity.

Doeve, Martje, and Irene Costera Meijer. 2013. "The Value of Transparency in Journalism for Audiences and (Public) Media Organizations." Paper presented at the conference Future of Journalism, Cardiff, September 12–13.

Domingo, David. 2008a. "Interactivity in the Daily Routines of Online Newsrooms: Dealing with an Uncomfortable Myth." *Journal of Computer-mediated Communication* 13 (3): 680–704.

Domingo, David. 2008b. "Inventing Online Journalism: A Constructive Approach to the Development of Online News." In *Making Online News: The Ethnography of New Media Production*, edited by Chris Paterson and David Domingo, 15–28. New York: Peter Lang.

Domingo, David, and Chris Paterson, eds. 2011. *Making Online News—Volume 2: Newsroom Ethnography in the Second Decade of Internet Journalism*. New York: Peter Lang.

Domingo, David, and Florence Le Cam. 2013. "Journalism in Dispersion: Exploring the Blurring Boundaries of Newsmaking through a Controversy." Paper presented at the conference Future of Journalism, Cardiff, September 12–13.

Flanagin, Andrew J., and Miriam J. Metzger. 2000. "Perceptions of Internet Information Credibility." *Journalism and Mass Communication Quarterly* 77 (3): 515–540.

Groot Kormelink, Tim, and Irene Costera Meijer. 2013. "Tailor-made News: Meeting the Demands of News Users on Mobile and Social Media." Paper presented at the conference Future of Journalism, Cardiff, September 12–13.

Heinonen, Ari, and Heikki Luostarinen, 2008. "Reconsidering 'Journalism' for Journalism Research." In: *Global Journalism Research: Theories, Methods, Findings, Future*, edited by Martin Löffelholz and David Weaver, 227–239. Cambridge: Blackwell.

Heinrich, Ansgard. 2011. *Network Journalism: Journalistic Practice in Interactive Spheres*. London: Routledge.

Hemmingway, Emma. 2008. *Into the Newsroom: Exploring the Digital Production of Regional Television News*. London: Routledge.

Hine, Christine. 2008. "Virtual Ethnography: Modes, Varieties, Affordances." In *The SAGE Handbook of Online Research Methods*, edited by Nigel G. Fielding, Raymond M. Lee, and Grant Blank, 257–270. Thousand Oaks, CA: Sage.

Jarvis, Jeff. 2006. "Networked Journalism." *Buzzmachine*, July 5. http://buzzmachine.com/2006/07/05/networked-journalism/.

Karlsson, Michael. 2010. "Flourishing but Restrained." *Journalism Practice* 5 (1): 68–84.

Kwak, Haewoon, Changhyun Lee, Hosung Park, and Sue Moon. 2010. "What is Twitter, a Social Network or a News Media?" Proceedings of the 19th International Conference on World wide web. ACM.

Latour, Bruno. 2011. "Networks, Societies, Spheres: Reflections of an Actor-network Theorist." *International Journal of Communication* 5: 796–810.

Latour, Bruno. 2005. *Reassembling the Social: An Introduction to Actor-network-theory*. New York: Oxford University Press.

Latour, Bruno. 1999. "On Recalling ANT." In *Actor Network Theory and after*, edited by John Law and John Hassard, 15–25, Oxford: Blackwell.

Latour, Bruno, Pablo Jensen, Tommaso Venturini, Sébastian Grauwin, and Dominique Boullier. 2012. "The Whole is Always Smaller than Its Parts' – A Digital Test of Gabriel Tardes' Monads." *The British Journal of Sociology* 63 (4): 590–615.

Law, John. 1999. "After ANT: Complexity, Naming and Topology." In *Actor Network Theory and after*, edited by John Law and John Hassard, 1–14. Oxford: Blackwell.

Le Cam, Florence, and Juliette Charbonneaux. 2012. "Pratiques Managériales Et Socialisation Des Journalistes En Ligne [Management Practices and the Socialisation of Online Journalists]." In *Le Numérique En Sociétés* [Digitization in Society], edited by Godefroy Dang Nguyen and Priscilla Créach, 131–156. Paris: L'Harmattan.

Leskovec, Jure, Lars Backstrom, and Jon Kleinberg. 2009. "Meme-tracking and the Dynamics of the News Cycle." Proceedings of the 15th ACM SIGKDD International Conference On Knowledge Discovery And Data Mining. Paris, June, 28-July, 1.

Lewis, Seth C. 2012. "The Tensions between Professional Control and Open Participation." *Information, Communication and Society* 15 (6): 836–866.

Lewis, Seth C., Rodrigo Zamith, and Alfred Hermida. 2013. "Content Analysis in an Era of Big Data: A Hybrid Approach to Computational and Manual Methods." *Journal of Broadcasting & Electronic Media* 57 (1): 34–52.

Lull, James. 1990. *Inside Family Viewing: Ethnographic Research on Television's Audiences*. London: Routledge.

Micó, Josep Lluís, Pere Masip, and David Domingo. 2013. "To Wish Impossible Things: Convergence as a Process of Diffusion of Innovations in an Actor-network." *International Communication Gazette* 75 (1): 118–137.

Mol, Annemarie. 1999. "Ontological Politics. A Word and Some Questions." In *Actor Network Theory and after*, edited by John Law and John Hassard, 74–89. Oxford: Blackwell.

Plesner, Ursula. 2009. "An Actor-network Perspective on Changing Work Practices. Communication Technologies as Actants in Newswork." *Journalism* 10 (5): 604–626.

Primo, Alex, and Gabriela Zago. 2014. "Who and What Do Journalism? An Actor-network Perspective." *Digital Journalism*. doi:10.1080/21670811.2014.927987.

Reason, Peter, and Hilary Bradbury, eds. 2007. *The SAGE Handbook of Action Research: Participative Inquiry and Practice*. Thousand Oaks, CA: Sage.

Reich, Zvi. 2009. *Sourcing the News: Key Issues in Journalism. an Innovative Study of the Israeli Press*. Cresskill, NJ: Hampton Press.

Ringoot, Roselyne, and Jean-Michel Utard. 2005. *Le Journalisme en Invention: Nouvelles Practiques, Nouveaux Actants* [The Reinvention of Journalism: New Practices, New Actants]. Rennes: Presses Universitaires de Rennes.

Rosen, Jay. 2006. "The People Formerly Known as the Audience." *Press Think*. June 27. http://archive.pressthink.org/2006/06/27/ppl_frmr.html.

Ryfe, David. 2012. *Can Journalism Survive: An inside Look at American Newsrooms*. Cambridge: Polity Books.

Schaffer, Jan. 2012. *Networked Journalism: What Works*. Washington, DC: J-Lab. http://www.j-lab.org/publications/net-j/overview/.

Schlesinger, Philip. 1990. "Rethinking the Sociology of Journalism: Source Strategies and the Limits of Media Centrism." In *Public Communication: The New Imperatives*, edited by Margorie Fergusson, 61–83. Thousand Oaks, CA: Sage.

Schmitz Weiss, Amy, and David Domingo. 2010. "Communities of Practice Innovation Processes in Online Newsroomsas Actor-networks and Communities of Practice." *New Media and Society* 12 (7): 1156–1171.

Schudson, Michael, and Chris Anderson. 2008. "Objectivity Professionalism and Truth Seeking in Journalism." In *The Handbook of Journalism Studies*, edited by Karin Wahl-Jorgensen and Thomas Hanitzsch, 88–101. New York: Routledge.

Singer, Jane B. 2013. "User-generated Visibility: Secondary Gatekeeping in a Shared Media Space." *New Media & Society* 16 (1): 55–73.

Spyridou, Lia Paschalia, Maria Matsiola, Andreas Veglis, George Kalliris, and Charalambos Dimoulas. 2013. "Journalism in a State of Flux: Journalists as Agents of Technology Innovation and Emerging News Practices." *International Communication Gazette* 75 (1): 76–98.

Vos, Tim P., Stephanie Craft, and Seth Ashley. 2012. "New Media, Old Criticism: Bloggers Press Criticism and the Journalistic Field." *Journalism* 13 (7): 850–868.

THE NOTION OF THE "BLURRING BOUNDARIES"
Journalism as a (de-)differentiated phenomenon

Wiebke Loosen

The notion of the "blurring boundaries" has become a flashy label to characterize the way journalism is manifestly changing in the age of the internet. This article explores this idea of de-boundedness and discusses the question whether there is anything more behind it than a catch-all diagnosis for the processes of change and transformation in the circumstances of communication in society, in general, and for journalism, in particular. To this end, de-boundedness as a proposition initially receives a more concrete definition. Its foundations in theories of differentiation and especially in the theory of social systems by the German sociologist Niklas Luhmann will be discussed, where differentiation, that is, drawing lines of demarcation, is the essential factor. It is shown that systems theory provides different possibilities for characterizing forms of de-differentiation or "blurring boundaries". Within systems theory they can be interpreted in terms of the evolutionary emergence of new forms of journalism, the co-evolutionary processes between journalism and its environment and/or as interpenetrations of journalism with other societal systems. It is demonstrated that changes in journalism oscillate between differentiation and de-differentiation, so that it can be described as a (de-)differentiated phenomenon.

Introduction: The "Blurring Boundaries" of Journalism

The notion of the "blurring boundaries" has become a flashy label to characterize the way journalism is manifestly changing in the age of the internet. Meanwhile, such labelling crops up in journalists' description of themselves: for example, the editor-in-chief of the British *Guardian*, Alan Rusbridger, indicates how exploring "digital space" has led to a completely new notion of what journalism is: "It brings with it an entirely new idea of what journalism is—indeed, for some, it calls into question whether there is any such distinct thing as 'journalism'" (Rusbridger 2011).

Scholl and Weischenberg (1998) had already come to a similar conclusion at the end of the 1990s. On the basis of their representative survey of journalists, "Journalismus in Deutschland" [Journalism in Germany], they conclude that journalism, as a clearly demarcated, identifiable context displaying meaning and enabling action, was clearly losing its contours and could scarcely be described or observed as an entity any more (273).

Since then, empirical findings and (everyday) observations have mounted up and testify to journalism's problem with demarcation and identity:

> The system of "journalism" is increasingly losing any boundaries separating it, in terms of contents and topics, from entertainment and PR, organisationally from management, marketing and technology, and as regards society as a whole, from the global entertainment industry … Entertainment, advertising, PR and politics have taken over the steering wheel … Spin-doctors, "editorial marketing", infotainment, news shows, sensationalist television and daily talk shows are just a few indices of this change. (Weber 2000, 9, own translation)

Eight years later, Deuze (2008, 4) comes to similar conclusion, also acknowledging the by then much stronger influence of the internet:

> The boundaries between journalism and other forms of public communication—ranging from public relations or advertorials to weblogs and podcasts—are vanishing, the internet makes all other types of news media rather obsolete (especially for young adults and teenagers), commercialization and cross-media mergers have gradually eroded the distinct professional identities of newsrooms and their publications (whether in print or broadcast), and by insisting on a traditional orientation towards the nation, journalists are losing touch with a society that is global as well as local, yet anything but national.

The aspects named above touch on various levels of journalism (see Loosen and Scholl 2002; Scholl and Weischenberg 1998, 273): the technology of the mass media and their organization, as well as the process of news production and consumption.

When we consider journalism, it is clear how this situation has gained momentum, above all through (technological) expansion into online media. For many years now, the major challenge confronting journalism—and for research into it—has been seen in the developments around the internet and online communication (Mitchelstein and Boczkowski 2009; Neverla 1998). That is because the introduction and increasing entrenchment of the internet—the *unbounded medium par excellence*—has triggered a global change in the structure of the mass media (Bruns 2008; Castells 2007). In recent times, what was originally a peripheral medium has expanded at a pace never before seen and taken on a central importance for information and interaction, blurring the boundary between individual and mass communication (Bruns 2005). This development is promoting, not least, an extensification of economic influences on media and journalism, because the internet, by its very nature, facilitates various synergies between broadcasting and online media (see Loosen 2005), but also leads to new struggles over market-share.

In the course of this development, *de-boundedness* is a sort of catch-all diagnosis for the processes of change and transformation in the circumstances of communication in society. Journalism research's programme of work thus consists increasingly of engaging with phenomena of blurring boundaries—*in* journalism and *between* journalism and other forms of communication. In this process, journalism's case history is, by and large, not disputed: a "built-in schizophrenia" (Weischenberg 2004, 171, own translation) shapes the journalism of western media systems anyway, existentially determines the way journalists work between social responsibility and profit orientedness, governs the central *paradoxes of journalism* (Pörksen, Loosen, and Scholl 2008, own translation) and now seems to be moving to a new level as online conditions dissolve customary lines of demarcation.

What follows primarily intends to discuss the question of whether there is anything more behind the diagnosis of blurring boundaries or a concept of de-boundedness than a catch-all diagnosis and a flashy label. To this end, de-boundedness as a proposition will initially receive a more concrete definition. Its foundations in theories of differentiation and especially in the theory of social systems by the German sociologist Niklas Luhmann (1997, 2013) will be discussed, where (viewed, in the first instance and in terms of time, *before* any observation of de-boundedness) differentiation, that is, drawing lines of demarcation, is the essential factor. Such an approach is not chosen accidentally, but refers to the fact that German journalism research is (some say: was) to a notable extent informed by systems theory based on the theoretical framework of Luhmann (Görke and Scholl 2006; Löffelholz 2008; Rühl 2008; Weischenberg and Malik 2008). However, the discussion on "blurring boundaries"/de-boundedness is also seen as useful outside this theoretical approach as the drawing of boundaries or the making of distinctions is fundamental to all kinds of (scientific) observation.

In this paper, "journalism" is (mainly) referred to from a system theoretical perspective, which at the societal level defines journalism "as a social system that enables society to observe itself, as it provides the public independently and periodically with information and issues that are considered newsworthy, relevant, and fact-based" (Weischenberg, Malik, and Scholl 2012, 207). That is, of course, only one possible understanding of journalism, as theoretical approaches to journalism are "heterogeneous, multidimensional and competing" (Löffelholz 2008), ranging from middle-range theories to social theories. However, the notion of "blurring boundaries" is also relevant for other macro conceptions on journalism and its function in society (as well as for meso and micro conceptions, of course), such as the normative or cultural perspective—if only to compare different approaches of drawing boundaries (e.g. to separate journalism from other forms of communication, journalists from other communicators) or call them into question.

The aim of the paper is to demonstrate that change in journalism oscillates between differentiation and de-differentiation, so that it can be described as a (de-)differentiated phenomenon. A conclusion and some reflections on the potential for further development of de-boundedness as a proposition will close this consideration of it. In doing so, this article neither offers an introduction into Luhmann's theory of social systems (for a brief and comprehensible introduction, see Borch 2011), nor a theoretically comparative approach (something which, nevertheless, would be promising), nor an historical approach (Birkner 2012). What it offers, instead, is a theoretically driven discussion of the question as to what the diagnosis of blurring boundaries means for a theory, which is based on drawing boundaries. The intention is to obtain further theoretical insights derived from the widespread notion of the "blurring boundaries" in the field of journalism to understand better the underlying transformation processes—and research into them.

Evidence for the Proposition of De-boundedness of Journalism

Research into journalism uses the notion of the "blurring boundaries"—to which reference here is made by using the term *de-boundedness*—to collate quite different phenomena, which all point to changes, to a shift in journalism, and to touch on all of its contexts (see Blöbaum 2005; Borger et al. 2013; Mitchelstein and Boczkowski 2009). They can tend to indicate cases of de-boundedness which are inherent in systems and in structures, as, for instance, between journalistic sub-systems/types of media and between areas within journalism, as well as indicating cases of *functional de-boundedness* between journalism and other systems of functioning, or respectively, forms of communication (see Lünenborg 2009, 60–63; Meier 2013, 265, tab. 7.6; Neuberger 2004, 97), examples being here the opening-up of journalism:

- towards *public relations* in the sense of a professional de-bounding;
- towards *technology*, which promotes online journalism and, with that, de-bounding between individual types of media;
- towards *advertising*, where the boundary to the editorial function is in play, and thus, in the last analysis, the autonomy of journalism too; and
- towards *entertainment*, which, in turn, brings with it de-bounding both in form and in content and, with that, hybrid genres like infotainment and edutainment.

In general terms, these developments derive from processes of globalization of national systems of journalism (Cottle 2009), of the *economization* of media institutions (Loosen and Scholl 2002; Weber 2000, 21–24), as well as quintessentially from the technologically driven digitalization of data, leading to technological, functional, economic, regulatory and receptive convergences (Jenkins 2008; Latzer 1997; Meikle and Young 2012).

Additionally, there is, both within and outside journalism research—and frequently in connection with online communication—discussion of various (supposed) dichotomies, which are becoming increasingly less precise by dint of de-bounding processes; particularly prominent here are, for example, the fact/fiction (Baum and Schmidt 2002) as well as the private–public distinction (Ford 2011; Jurgenson and Rey 2012; Loosen 2011; Rössler 2005; Thompson 2011). Especially the internet and social media—and their steady incorporation into the societal communication environment—seem to force us to rethink fundamental categories, often leading to hybrid terms to characterize the de-bounding of spheres, e.g. "mass self-communication" (Castells 2009, 58–70), "produsage" (Bruns 2008) as well as "personal publics" (Schmidt 2014). They are all pointing to the porous boundary between communicator and recipient, between a few senders and a large dispersed audience of receivers. The latter is probably the most often mentioned phenomenon of de-bounding connected to online circumstances. It impinges on professional journalism and its relationship to its audiences in a quite particular way, because the technical and participatory mechanisms of the interconnectivity enabled by the internet have a lasting effect on this fundamental relationship (Lewis 2012; Loosen and Schmidt 2012; Ostertag and Tuchman 2012; Neuberger 2009).

At this point, it becomes clear that the term *de-boundedness* does not necessarily apply only to journalism, but also to the proposition that all of society's variegated systems of functioning are confronting wide-reaching transformations: "Systems are increasingly de-differentiating themselves, are linking up more intensively with their environments, are becoming unbounded and are unravelling" (Weber 2000, 9, own translation). Such a diagnosis has to perturb approaches based on the theory of differentiation—like the theory of systems—which take the "lack of homogeneity among the components of modern society" (Schimank 2007, 11, own translation) as their point of departure.

Pörksen and Scholl (2011, 27) point out that cases of de-bounding do mostly come in for catch-all diagnosis but that they are frequently validated (empirically) through examples or peripheral phenomena. It does, therefore, make sense to work with a *multi-level model*, as developed by Weber (2000, 22–23). It differentiates (see Pörksen and Scholl 2011, 27)

- between the *macro level of social affairs* (cases of de-bounding, for instance, through increasing concentration of the press; a growing dictate from business);
- the *meso level of individual organizations* (cases of de-bounding, for instance, between editorial desks and marketing departments);
- the *micro level of direct interactions* (cases of de-bounding, for instance, between core journalistic activities and non-journalistic ones), as well as those cutting across the micro–macro divide;
- *level of journalistic coverage/output* (cases of de-bounding, for instance, elements and forms of presentation which inform, comment and entertain, respectively).

As plausible and widely disseminated as the proposition of de-boundedness indeed is, the above presentation makes it clear, however, that it relates to considerable terminological inaccuracies, but also to a succession of (consequential) theoretical and methodological problems (Neuberger 2004): what is the nature of the *viewpoint* determining the perspective used as a point of departure for describing something as de-bounded? How is the *time-period* defined, during which a phenomenon of de-bounding can/should/must be observed? What *degree of de-bounding* has to be demonstrated here, in order then to be able actually to talk about de-boundedness? What is the *relation* between structural and functional (diagnoses) of de-boundedness?

These questions indicate that de-boundedness involves a *process* and one with a point of departure where—if considered chronologically—previously something must have stood that was not de-bounded, and was, therefore, differentiated, or respectively, was viewed as such. That means the description of de-boundedness provided by research confronts the same problems as, for instance, the description of *change*, which also has to develop with due regard to a time-period still to be determined (Blöbaum 2008). However, change can encompass other forms of transformation and does not so clearly denote a developmental direction. It is

> not to be understood deterministically as a result of environmental influences, as adaptation to the surroundings, but, above all, as a process of self-transformation within a system (where, however, we should also look for impulses from the system's surroundings). Therefore, change in the system of journalism comes across as a normal process and should not be regarded as the end or as the destruction of journalism, as long as the system's autopoeisis, its self-production on the basis of its own elements, is not endangered. (Blöbaum 2008, 120, own translation)

By contrast, in most cases de-boundedness is not characterized as a "normal process", but it frequently carries negative connotations and is interpreted as a regression or as a functional threat—even if that is not necessarily inherent in the concept.

Convergence and *hybridization* (Chadwick 2013; Jenkins 2008) emphasize, on the contrary, much rather the coalescing, the merging of previously observed boundaries, and these two terms mostly maintain a sharper focus on what is new as it emerges from the coalescing of what have been up to now separate areas (e.g. in relation to media markets or media formats)—without the originally posited differentiation being, therefore, dissolved or otherwise disappearing.

With reference to journalism, the proposition of de-boundedness provides a counter case, as it is, in its essence, tied up with the question as to how far the social function of journalism is endangered by other forms of public communication or, however, secured by (the above-delineated) processes of de-bounding in a changed society (Lewis 2012; Loosen and Scholl 2002). Various facets of this question determine a large part of the research into journalism (culminating in the question: "Can Journalism Survive?"; Ryfe 2012), and so it does also revolve around—more or less explicitly—the normatively relevant (and, for journalism, existential) dread of journalism being exposed to a creeping loss of function by dint of losing its monopoly (on the internet).

There is, however, no reason for deeming processes of de-bounding—as shown by the examples outlined and the different levels on which they are observed—automatically *threatening to functions*. Examples of de-bounding frequently do not apply to journalism overall and not so much to the core (e.q. news journalism); much rather they apply to special areas and the periphery (e.g. entertainment journalism or citizen participation)—even if (or indeed: precisely because) interactions between the core and the periphery are thus not excluded (Görke 2009).

(Systems) Theoretical Grounding of the Proposition of De-boundedness

The diagnosis of the blurring boundaries, or to put it more abstractly, the proposition of de-boundedness, is indeed prominent in research (into journalism), but does not have, however, either a *disciplinary homebase* or anything similar to that, or a grounding in theory (Neuberger 2004); in fact, the notion of "blurring boundaries" lacks theoretical underpinning—or better: is initially "theoretically agnostic".

However, a theoretical grounding can be manufactured, because the proposition of journalism's de-boundedness can certainly be related to research into journalism using systems theory—by acknowledging that this is only one of various possible theoretical approaches on journalism (Löffelholz 2008). Following this (roundabout) pathway, we can then—that is what this article seeks—also obtain theoretical insights taking us further. In the first instance, however, the *empirically down-to-earth diagnosis of de-boundedness* does shake theory up. Such disruption happens because the theory of systems (research into journalism here refers, above all, to Niklas Luhmann's theory of social systems; see for an introduction Görke and Scholl 2006) is a theory of differentiation, and, as such, it operates with a differentiating logic, that is, starts with drawing dividing lines and, in the process, tends rarely, if at all, to look at de-boundedness (Loosen 2007; Pörksen and Scholl 2011).

If we are so inclined, then the search for the theoretical roots to the understanding of *journalism as a (de-)differentiated phenomenon* means "back to start" for any approach to journalism through the theory of differentiation. Without this (or that) theoretical grounding, the proposition of de-boundedness very quickly becomes exhausted in a relatively mundane listing of phenomena considered de-bounded. At this point, we can establish the differences between de-boundedness and de-differentiation: we tend to talk about *de-boundedness* (or blurring boundaries) in connection with (everyday) empirically observed phenomena and about *de-differentiation* much rather in connection with questions of theory; this applies particularly to sociology, and here it applies with reference to criticism of the theory of functional differentiation and in connection with its ambivalent effects.[1]

That should not amount to saying that theoretical insights derived from the proposition of de-boundedness, and taking us further on from it, can only be gained by recourse to systems theory, which can readily be accused of drawing lines of demarcation too rigidly (see, on this, the criticism from Görke 2009). Another fruitful recourse could be found, for example, with respect to the sociology of professions and its application in journalism studies, where the emphasis also is on boundaries, boundary work and boundary maintenance—and all of this with respect to journalism as an already "very permeable occupation" (Abbott 1988, 225) (Lewis 2012; Schudson and Anderson 2009).

All the same, it is obvious that the proposition of de-boundedness (in Germany) has developed (particularly) from the centre of systems theoretical research into journalism and that this latter should link its empirical observations *somehow* to this theory and ideally apply them to the development of theory. To this extent, the proposition of de-boundedness is, in a certain way, a homegrown problem, which *has to* shake up systems theoretical research into journalism, because the point of departure of every systems theoretical analysis is the difference between the system and its environment, and drawing lines of demarcation is its basic operation. What is central to this perspective, indeed downright constituent of it, is the question as to *what* is differentiating itself and so lending itself—on the level of social subsystems—to dividing off, as a social system, from other ones. The start always involves drawing lines of demarcation.

The (theoretical and methodological) consequences of such an approach become apparent by describing systems theoretical research into journalism from a meta perspective as a *"differentiation/de-differentiation cycle"* separated into the following briefly described four phases (set out in more detail in Loosen 2007): in its function, this research has followed the logic of the theory of differentiation and did at the outset attend, above all, to the difference between system and environment. That is, to demarcating journalism, or other alternatively suggested systems like *mass media, the public sphere* or *publishing* (for an overview, see Scholl and Weischenberg 1998, 63–71). These different definitions of systems should all be understood as "suggestions for the observation of systems" (Pörksen and Scholl 2011, 35, own translation) and can only come about when separated off from the environment, to which other entities are attributed according to particular demarcations (*first phase: focus on differentiation*).

Consequently, for journalism (research) the question does repeatedly come up as to its structural couplings and interrelations with other systems, also including the performance that is the specific contribution journalism provides for other social systems. This perspective marks, for example, various studies on the relationship of journalism with public relations, politics and the economy (*second phase: focus on structural couplings*). Overall, indications of an "unravelling at the edges" of journalism here show up at various points (Scholl and Weischenberg 1998, 270), such as increasing reliance on public relations and an extensification of economic influence. These observations, in turn, have encouraged the tackling of phenomena of de-boundedness and the dissolving of boundaries between areas once clearly outlined, for instance between different media types such as print and TV and their increasing interrelations due to the integration of online newsrooms and cross-media strategies (*third phase: focus on de-differentiation*). Subsequent empirical studies, conceived under these premises, then showed, in turn, that journalism can still be separated off functionally against the background of various processes of de-bounding as well (Loosen 2005), and that, as a whole, we can much rather talk about a "functional stabilization" (Weischenberg, Malik, and Scholl 2006, 191, own translation) of journalism:

> Taking all results together we observe a decrease of professionalism in the *structure* of German journalism (regarding the number of journalists and non-professional freelancers) but a stabilization regarding the *function* of journalism for society (role perceptions and perceived autonomy). (Weischenberg, Malik, and Scholl 2012, 218)

Against this background (until further notice), the conclusion, therefore, ran: journalism is "unravelling" around the *edges* (Scholl and Weischenberg 1998, 270), but is hardening (itself) up at the *core* (Weischenberg, Malik, and Scholl 2006, 201–203) (*fourth phase: indicators for a [de-]de-differentiation?*). From this meta perspective (which would still merit more precise investigation and serves as an illustration here), a *circular process* appears between differentiation and de-differentiation as an oscillation between theory (describing boundaries) and empiricism (observations of de-boundedness). Such a process also illustrates the power of theoretical assumptions to steer empiricism (definition of boundaries) and the empirical evidence's power to cause disruption (diagnosis of de-boundedness), and it can thus be interpreted as a reciprocal reaction between theory and empiricism: clearly, a perspective drawn from the theory of differentiation (on journalism) is not impermeable to empirically observed cases of de-boundedness—possibly also creating an actual initial sensitivity to the latter.

To determine the relationship between differentiation and de-differentiation/de-boundedness yet more closely, it makes sense to differentiate the concepts still further, because it has already become clear that they are used in quite different contexts, which address both functional and structural levels. The sociologist Jürgen Gerhards (1993) regards de-differentiation, for example, as strictly analogous to functional differentiation and only existing with the "removal of a long-term difference between system and environment" (271, own translation)—that would be the case if journalism cannot be separated from other forms of public communication any longer.

As already sketched out above, research into journalism developments, however, come in for characterization as de-boundedness/de-differentiation beyond this social macro level too. Such developments are the ones operating on the meso level (organizations/editorial desks), the micro level (journalistic activities and roles) or on the level of coverage/media output. So they concern, on the one hand, the function of journalism and, on the other, its structures.

Part of the confusion surrounding the concept of de-boundedness—and its theoretical counterpart, de-differentiation—accordingly refers to the separation made, or respectively, the separation not always made, between functional and structural differentiation and de-differentiation. This latter contention is also illustrated by systems theory's (few) statements on de-differentiation, which Niklas Luhmann (2004, 99) describes as paradoxical because it proceeds from what it purports to eliminate:

> But dedifferentiation cannot mean that one can forget differentiations, for the "de" prefix would then be meaningless. If dedifferentiation presupposes memory, this proposal amounts to preserving differences. (Luhmann 2013, 349)

This aspect also draws our attention to the necessary balance or the tension of stability and change (in journalism's evolution). It is not only that we can identify "change" only against the background of "stability", the discussion around "blurring boundaries" also indicates that the underlying differences are still important: as long as we discuss/care about/observe "blurring boundaries", the underlying boundaries are still a relevant object of matter.

What we must also bear in mind is that the capacity for change and the capacity for de-bounding both make systems dynamic and capable of learning (e.g. the integration of online media and the emergence of online journalism) and thus contribute to preserving their functions (extending journalistic performances on the internet). Furthermore, maintaining stability (in times of highly dynamic changes in our communicative environment) requires significant resources. Thus, in journalism, change necessarily happens within the "tension between tradition and change" (Mitchelstein and Boczkowski 2009)—and namely in the field of journalism itself as well as in its academic investigation, where "the modes of inquiry oscillate between using existing concepts to look at new phenomena and taking advantage of these phenomena to rethink these concepts and come up with new ones" (562).

Viewing de-boundedness empirically, we can examine it theoretically as to whether it is a matter of:

- *changed structures* (on the level of journalistic organizations, working routines, roles);
- *changed performance relations to other systems* (e.g. journalism and its performance for politics, sports, economy, etc.);
- *changed structural linkages/interdependencies between systems* (e.g. between journalism and public relations);
- *new forms of differentiation, or respectively, re-differentiation* (e.g. on the level of structures); or even of
- *functional de-differentiation*, which does indeed denote a system's (partial or temporary) loss of function.

As empirical observations have to be made on the micro or meso level, it becomes obvious that these analytical types cut across the levels differentiated in the multi-level model in the previous section. This circumstance also implies the theoretical challenge of drawing conclusions for the macro, the societal level (Pörksen and Scholl 2011, 28). If the theoretical interpretation of empirical observations is to be at least internally valid, then, in each case, it has to involve observing *changes*, because de-bounding can only be discerned against the background of previously drawn boundaries.

Differentiation can, therefore, also be based on structural de-differentiation—that is something Luhmann (1997, 615) unequivocally indicates. In addition, the phenomena of de-boundedness we have examined show they are brought about, above all, in liminal locations, on peripheries, in zones of interdependence and with reference to innovations—first and foremost, the developments around online communication, as these are relevant to journalism. We have, therefore, to assume that it is precisely these phenomena which have not yet been completely integrated into routines (Powers 2012). It is precisely in the online area that developments are so headlong and the changes so dynamic, that de-bounding (or respectively, what is taken to be that) can be observed quasi *live* (and by a generation of researchers socialized by certain (media) boundaries and equipped with specific theoretical and methodological instruments for observation). That these phenomena (e.g. with reference to the separation of publicly relevant data/information off from that which is to be protected as private) are also being intensively discussed in the public sphere shows that society's involvement in them is also something which still has to be negotiated.

With various cases of de-bounding, it is possibly a matter of transitional phenomena leading to the drawing of new boundaries and new contours for journalism (Neuberger 2004, 107)—this may be, for example, changes in structure or differentiations and re-differentiations. One example for these changes in structure is probably "the disappearance of the newsroom" (Wahl-Jorgensen 2010, 33), as news production in "interpenetrating communication environments"—according to an observation by Cottle (2009)—no longer "takes place within any one organizational centre of production". In any case, it is obvious that journalism is not just becoming unbounded, but is also differentiating itself into further categories, for instance, in the direction of online journalism and social media journalism (Braun and Gillespie 2011). That means these differentiations are also based on a structural de-differentiation from a technical viewpoint (e.g. the overcoming of media barriers through the digitalization of data), or respectively, "adopt" these de-differentiations to achieving differentiation. This state of affairs describes, if we are so inclined, a general principle of the structure of online communication: everywhere de-differentiations occur in one place, (re-)differentiations occur in another.

At this point, it has repeatedly become obvious that unboundedness/de-differentiation can only be identified with reference to something initially regarded as differentiated; and there can indeed be differences of opinion about this—they point out that diagnoses of de-boundedness fundamentally *depend on observers* (Pörksen and Scholl 2011). This is particularly exemplified by the discussion on de-bounding between entertainment and journalism, inclusive of the differently evaluated problems ensuing (Görke 2009). When detecting de-boundedness, it is always tied up with the question as to which are the previously defined boundaries forming the basis. That is to say, how closely—and if indeed at all—the boundaries of what is now ostensibly de- or unbounded were previously drawn.

De-Boundedness 2.0 and the Further Development of the Proposition of Blurring Boundaries

De-boundedness has become a catch-all diagnosis for processes of change and transformation in the way society communicates. At the same time, in particular the oft-cited dissolving of boundaries between communicators and recipients has become a *leitmotif*. It figures particularly in research into journalism and the media, which deals with the "redrawing of the boundaries between the spheres of production and consumption" (Mitchelstein and Boczkowski 2009, 577) in various ways. In many respects, these developments appear in journalism as if seen under a magnifying glass. In this way, journalism serves—within and beyond its boundaries—as a *key system* for observing central developments in online communication (as, for example, the rise of "social media" or content production driven by data and based on algorithms).

For journalism, the customary relationship to its audience, between communicators and recipients, between professional and non-professional utterance, is also changing. Germane studies are, however, also showing that journalism knows very well how to co-opt user activities for its own purposes (e.g. for researching and distributing journalistic contents), and that the traditional boundaries between the roles of communicator and recipient have not really been overcome around the editorial desks (Borger et al. 2013; Singer et al. 2011) but that "audience material" is serving, above all, "as one more news source among many" (Williams, Wardle, and Wahl-Jorgensen 2011, 94).

There is a valid reason for journalism's resistance to change—or better: its balance between change and persistence (not only) when it comes to audience participation. The fundamental difference between journalists' professional roles and those of their audience is a substantial one in journalism/the system of journalism; the end of this difference would also signal the end of journalism as a system with particular functions. At the same time, social media, however, show that the relation between professional and audience roles—as well as the respective definition of these roles (in terms of self-conceptions, routines, etc.)—can be subject to changes (Loosen and Schmidt 2012). These lower the technical hurdles to making all sorts of content accessible online, to filtering, moulding and distributing it further, and in this way a range of relationships and network forms develop between journalism and social media (Braun and Gillespie 2011; Neuberger, vom Hofe, and Nuernbergk 2010). They point out that, in the course of these developments too, de-bounding (between professional and audience roles, journalistic and user-generated contents, production and reception) involves forms of differentiation (e.g. in the form by which the new role of the social media editor is delineated), or respectively, these latter forms are merged with such de-bounding and, taken altogether, lead to altered forms of audience-inclusion in journalism (Heise et al. 2013). Therefore, this development too oscillates between differentiation and de-differentiation.

De-boundedness is, then, on the one side not initially a very precise concept, and is one which can characterize many different developments and changes in journalism. It certainly owes its popularity to being plausible in a downright graphic way. That makes it also relevant for journalistic praxis, media ethics and for criticism of the media, as it designates concrete and palpable phenomena, which are indeed capable of essentially threatening the boundaries of journalism—to public relations, for instance.

This concept turns out to be (on second glance) uniquely awkward for researchers' pronouncements: that is because the discussion about (empirically) observed phenomena of de-differentiation and their (systems) theoretical explicability has the disadvantage of practically requiring the entire systems theoretical research into journalism be worked through—but it also has the significant advantage that this work can be used for developing theory (Pörksen and Scholl 2011). To this end, laboriously drawn boundaries (established through various suggestions existing not by chance or at a whim) must be subject to new discussion under the changed relations of communication in society too and are also, in part, re-defined. In this way, it might also be partially possible to alleviate a deficit in (systems theoretical) research into journalism: it does indeed work with the instruments of a theory of society which it bases on differentiation theory, but it uses these predominantly with a viewpoint focused on a social subsystem. The comparison between differing social subsystems is largely missing, which—something Niklas Luhmann's work on various social systems of functioning shows—provides important insights via the ways of establishing common factors and differences between the systems and refines the investigative instruments. Without a comparative perspective of this sort, however, we can hardly survey the very "space of communication" represented by the internet, where journalism does fulfil a central function, on the one hand, and on the other, other providers (can), however, represent functional equivalents (Neuberger 2009).

Nevertheless, everything described as de-differentiation does not involve journalism's function and threaten its existence: journalism *does* exist "since, and as long as, society has been wanting it as such, goes on wanting it, demands it or simply scrutinizes it" (Pörksen and Scholl 2011, 36, own translation). The notion of the "blurring boundaries" illustrates that in a particular way: as long as we discuss/care about/ observe "blurring boundaries", the underlying boundaries are still relevant. The various discussions on them are part of societal, academic and journalistic (self-)reflection and, as such, an indicator for the fact that journalism is still a distinct social institution—even though one in constant flux. Actually, we (as society, journalists, audience members, journalism researchers) seem to be in the middle of a process of figuring out what we regard as "journalism"—and its function for society. Journalism research should observe how this is "manufactured"; possible research strategies, which take "blurring boundaries"/(de-)differentiation processes in journalism as a starting point, could be:

- comparing the "centre" (e.g. news journalism) with the "periphery" (innovative fields such as "data journalism" or "collaborative journalism") in terms of roles, routines, self-conception, etc.;
- analysing what "the audience" use and regard as journalism and news;
- analysing what different actors (in and outside newsrooms) and organizations produce and regard as journalism and news;
- analysing how, and to what extent, productive actors interact with their audiences—and what their understanding of "audiences" is.

Nevertheless, the question of whether journalism is still observable/identifiable with such a differentiation theoretical approach remains crucial. What it requires—but that is also true for different approaches to journalism—is that research into journalism needs to come up with an at least "vague definition" of what it wants to investigate as "journalism"—and remains sensitive to the observation of "blurring boundaries".

Obviously, in the online age, journalism's greatest challenge lies in employing all the forms of de-bounding for the maintenance of its own boundary with other forms of communication. Research into journalism helps to examine how it does this; setting out the difference between differentiation and de-differentiation is one way to do it.

ACKNOWLEDGEMENTS

I would like to thank the translators Dr Stan Jones and Anja Welle.

NOTE

1. There are various "theories of social differentiation". The sociologist, Uwe Schimank (2007), points to the long tradition behind the perspective taken by such theories and, in his textbook, manufactures, for example, a systematics which both makes connections and sets boundaries between the ideas of classical figures in sociology (Durkheim, Simmel, Weber, Marx), on the theory of differentiation, as well as between Talcott Parsons' view of social differentiation via systems and environment, and Niklas Luhmann's view of social differentiation, together with approaches to social differentiation via the theory of actors.

REFERENCES

Abbott, Andrew. 1988. *The System of Professions: An Essay on the Division of Expert Labor.* Chicago: University of Chicago Press.

Baum, Achim, and Siegfried Schmidt, J., eds. 2002. *Fakten Und Fiktionen. Über Den Umgang Mit Medienwirklichkeiten* [Facts and Fictions. On Dealing with Media Realities]. Konstanz: UVK.

Birkner, Thomas. 2012. *Das Selbstgespräch Der Zeit. Die Geschichte Des Journalismus in Deutschland 1605–1914* [The Times Talking to Themselves. The History of Journalism in Germany 1605–1914]. Köln: von Halem.

Blöbaum, Bernd. 2005. "Wandel Und Journalismus—Vorschlag Für Einen Analytischen Rahmen [Change and Journalism—A Suggestion for an Analytical Framework]." In *Journalismus Und Wandel. Analysedimensionen, Konzepte, Fallstudien* [Journalism and Change. Dimensions of the Analysis, Concepts and Case Studies], edited by Markus Behmer, 41–60. Wiesbaden: VS Verlag für Sozialwissenschaften.

Blöbaum, Bernd. 2008. "Wandel Redaktioneller Strukturen Und Entscheidungsprozesse [The Change in Editorial Structures and Decision Processes]." In *Seismographische Funktion Von Öffentlichkeit Im Wandel* [The Seismographic Function of the Changing Public Sphere], edited by Heinz Bonfadelli, Kurt Imhof, Roger Blum, and Otfried Jarren, 119–129. Wiesbaden: VS Verlag für Sozialwissenschaften.

Borch, Christian. 2011. *Niklas Luhmann.* London: Routledge.

Borger, Merel, Anita van Hoof, Irene Costera Meijer, and José Sanders. 2013. "Constructing Participatory Journalism as a Scholarly Object." *Digital Journalism* 1 (1): 117–134.

Braun, Joshua, and Tarleton Gillespie. 2011. "Hosting the Public Discourse, Hosting the Public: When Online News and Social Media Converge." *Journalism Practice* 5 (4): 383–398.

Bruns, Axel. 2005. *Gatewatching: Collaborative Online News Production.* New York: Peter Lang.

Bruns, Axel. 2008. *Blogs, Wikipedia, Second Life, and beyond: From Production to Produsage.* New York: Peter Lang.

Castells, Manuel. 2007. "Communication, Power and Counter-power in the Network Society." *International Journal of Communication* 1: 238–266.

Castells, Manuel. 2009. *Communication Power.* Oxford: Oxford University Press.

Chadwick, Andrew. 2013. *The Hybrid Media System: Politics and Power.* Oxford: University Press.

Cottle, Simon. 2009. "Journalism and Globalization." In *The Handbook of Journalism Studies*, edited by Karin Wahl-Jorgensen and Thomas Hanitzsch, 341–356. New York: Routledge.

Deuze, Mark. 2008. "Understanding Journalism as Newswork. How It Changes, and How It Remains the Same." *Westminister Papers in Communication and Culture* 5 (2): 4–23.

Ford, Sarah Michele. 2011. "Reconceptualizing the Public/Private Distinction in the Age of Information Technology." *Information, Communication & Society* 14 (4): 550–567. doi:10.1080/1369118X.2011.562220.

Gerhards, Jürgen. 1993. "Funktionale Differenzierung Der Gesellschaft Und Prozesse Der Entdifferenzierung [The Functional Differentiation of Society and Processes of De-differentiation]." In *Autopoiesis. Eine Theorie Im Brennpunkt Der Kritik* [Autopoiesis. A Theory in Critical Focus], edited by Hans Rudi Fischer, 263–280. Heidelberg: Carl-Auer-Systeme.

Görke, Alexander. 2009. "Untergang Oder Neuschöpfung Des Journalismus? Theori-eperspektiven Und Theorieprobleme Der Hybridisierungsdebatte [The Downfall or Rec-reation of Journalism? Theoretical Perspectives and Problems in the Hybridization Debate]." In *Spezialisierung Im Journalismus* [Specialization in Journalism], edited by Beatrice Dernbach, and Thorsten Quandt, 73–93. Wiesbaden: VS Verlag für Sozialwis-senschaften.

Görke, Alexander, and Armin Scholl. 2006. "Niklas Luhmann's Theory of Social Systems and Journalism Research." *Journalism Studies* 7 (4): 644–655. doi:10.1080/1416700600758066.

Heise, Nele, Wiebke Loosen, Julius Reimer, and Jan Schmidt. 2013. "Including the Audience. Comparing the Attitudes and Expectations of Journalists and Users towards Participation in German TV News Journalism." *Journalism Studies.* doi:10.1080/1461670X.2013.831232.

Jenkins, Henry. 2008. *Convergence Culture. Where Old and New Media Collide.* New York: New York University Press.

Jurgenson, Nathan, and P. J. Rey. 2012. "Comment on Sarah Ford's 'Reconceptualization of Privacy and Publicity'." *Information, Communication & Society* 15 (2): 287–293. doi:10.1080/1369118X.2011.619552.

Latzer, Michael. 1997. *Mediamatik—Die Konvergenz von Telekommunikation, Computer und Rundfunk* [Mediamatik—The Convergence of Telecommunication, Computers and Broadcasting]. Opladen: Westdeutscher Verlag.

Lewis, Seth C. 2012. "The Tension between Professional Control and Open Participation. Journalism and Its Boundaries." *Information, Communication & Society* 15 (6): 836–866.

Löffelholz, Martin. 2008. "Heterogeneous—Multidimensional—Competing: Theoretical Approaches to Journalism—An Overview." In *Global Journalism Research*, edited by Martin Löffelholz and David Weaver, 15–27. Hoboken, NJ: John Wiley & Sons.

Loosen, Wiebke. 2005. "Entgrenzungsphänomene im Journalismus: Entwurf einer theoretis-chen Konzeption und empirischer Fallstudien [On the 'Medial Capacity for De-bound-ing' of Journalistic Working Processes]." *Publizistik* 50 (3): 304–319.

Loosen, Wiebke. 2007. "Entgrenzung des Journalismus: Empirische Evidenzen Ohne Theoreti-sche Basis? [The De-bounding of Journalism: Empirical Evidence Without a Theoretical Basis?]" *Publizistik* 52 (1): 63–79.

Loosen, Wiebke. 2011. "Online Privacy as a News Factor in Journalism." In *Privacy Online: Perspectives on Privacy and Self-disclosure in the Social Web*, edited by Sabine Trepte and Leonard Reinecke, 205–218. Heidelberg: Springer.

Loosen, Wiebke, and Jan-Hinrik Schmidt. 2012. "(Re-)Discovering the Audience. The Relation-ship between Journalism and Audience in Networked Digital Media." *Information, Communication & Society* 15 (6): 867–887.

Loosen, Wiebke, and Armin Scholl. 2002. "Entgrenzungsphänomene Im Journalismus: Entwurf Einer Theoretischen Konzeption Und Empirischer Fallstudien [Phenomena of De-bounding in Journalism: Design for a Theoretical Conception and Empirical Case Studies]." In *Fakten Und Fiktionen. Über Den Umgang Mit Medienwirklichkeiten* [Facts and Fictions. On Dealing with Media Realities], edited by Achim Baum and J. Siegfried Schmidt, 139–151. Konstanz: UVK.

Luhmann, Niklas. 1997. *Die Gesellschaft Der Gesellschaft* [The Society of Society]. Frankfurt am Main: Suhrkamp.

Luhmann, Niklas. 2004. *Ökologische Kommunikation. Kann Die Moderne Gesellschaft Sich Auf ökologische Gefährdungen Einstellen?* [Ecological Communication. Can Modern Society Adapt Itself to Ecological Dangers?] Wiesbaden: Westdeutscher Verlag (first published in 1986).

Luhmann, Niklas. 2013. *Theory of Society*. Vol. 2. Translated by Rhodes Barrett. Stanford: Stanford University Press.

Lünenborg, Margreth. 2009. "Spezialisierung *Und* Entdifferenzierung Im Journalismus. Eine Theoretische Systematisierung [Specialization and De-differentiation in Journalism. A Theoretical Systematization]." In *Spezialisierung Im Journalismus* [Specialization in Journalism], edited by Beatrice Dernbach, and Thorsten Quandt, 59–72. Wiesbaden: VS Verlag für Sozialwissenschaften.

Meier, Klaus. 2013. *Journalistik* [Journalism Studies]. Konstanz: UVK.

Meikle, Graham, and Sherman Young. 2012. *Media Convergence. Networked Digital Media in Everyday Life*. Basingstoke: Palgrave Macmillan.

Mitchelstein, Eugenia, and Pablo J. Boczkowski. 2009. "Between Tradition and Change. A Review of recent Research on Online News Production." *Journalism* 10 (5): 562–586.

Neuberger, Christoph. 2004. "Lösen Sich Die Grenzen Des Journalismus Auf? Dimensionen Und Defizite Der Entgrenzungsthese [Are the Boundaries of Journalism Dissolving? The Dimensions and Deficits of the Concept of Unbounding]." In *Zukunft Der Medien —Medienzukunft* [The Future of the Media—The Media Future], edited by Gunnar Roters, Walter Klingler, and Maria Gerhards, 95–112. Baden-Baden: Nomos.

Neuberger, Christoph. 2009. "Internet, Journalismus Und Öffentlichkeit. Analyse Des Medienumbruchs [The Internet, Journalism and the Public Sphere. An Analysis of the Upheaval in the Media]." In *Journalismus Im Internet. Profession—Partizipation—Technisierung* [Journalism in the Internet. Profession—Participation—Technologization], edited by Christoph Neuberger, Christian Nuernbergk, and Melanie Rischke, 19–105. Wiesbaden: VS Verlag für Sozialwissenschaften.

Neuberger, Christoph, Hanna Jo vom Hofe, and Christian Christian Nuernbergk. 2010. *Twitter Und Journalismus. Der Einfluss Des 'Social Web' Auf Die Nachrichten* [Twitter and Journalism. The Influence of the 'Social Web' on the News]. Düsseldorf: Lfm-Dokumentation no. 38.

Neverla, Irene, ed. 1998. *Das Netz-medium. Kommunikationswissenschaftliche Aspekte Eines Mediums in Entwicklung* [The Net-medium. the Aspects of a Developing Medium in Communication Studies]. Opladen: Westdeutscher Verlag.

Ostertag, Stephen F., and Gaye Tuchman. 2012. "When Innovation Meets Legacy." *Information, Communication & Society* 15 (6): 909–931. doi:10.1080/1369118X.2012.676057.

Pörksen, Bernhard, and Armin Scholl. 2011. "Die Entgrenzung Des Journalismus. Analysen Eines Mikro-Meso-Makro-Problems Aus Der Perspektive Der Konstruktivistischen Systemtheorie [The Unbounding of Journalism. Analyses of a Micro-Meso-Macro Problem from the Perspective of the Constructivist Systems Theory]." In *Ebenen Der Kommuni-kation. Mikro-Meso-Makro-Links in Der Kommunikationswissenschaft* [Levels of Commu-nication. Micro-Meso-Macro Links in Communication Studies], edited by Thorsten Quandt, and Bertram Scheufele, 25–53. Wiesbaden: VS Verlag für Sozialwissenschaften.

Pörksen, Bernhard, Wiebke Loosen, and Armin Scholl, eds. 2008. *Paradoxien Des Journalismus: Theorie—Empirie—Praxis* [Paradoxes of Journalism: Theory—Empiricism—Praxis]. Wie-sbaden: VS Verlag für Sozialwissenschaften.

Powers, Matthew. 2012. "'In Forms that are familiar and yet-to-be Invented': American Jour-nalism and the Discourse of Technologically Specific Work." *Journal of Communication Inquiry* 36 (1): 24–43.

Rössler, Beate. 2005. *The Value of Privacy*. Cambridge: Polity Press.

Rühl, Manfred. 2008. Journalism in a Globalizing World Society. A Societal Approach to Jour-nalism Research. In *Global Journalism Research*, edited by Martin Löffelholz and David Weaver, 28–38. Hoboken, NJ: John Wiley & Sons.

Rusbridger, Alan. 2011. "The Splintering of the Fourth Estate." *The Sydney Morning Herald*, November 22. http://www.smh.com.au/federal-politics/society-and-culture/the-splinter ing-of-the-fourth-estate-20101122-182yf.html.

Ryfe, David M. 2012. *Can Journalism Survive? An inside Look at American Newsrooms*. Cam-bridge: Polity.

Schimank, Uwe. 2007. *Theorien Gesellschaftlicher Differenzierung* [Theories of Social Differenti-ation]. Wiesbaden: VS Verlag für Sozialwissenschaften.

Schmidt, Jan-Hinrik. 2014. "Twitter and the Rise of Personal Publics." In *Twitter and Society*, edited by Karin Weller, Axel Bruns, Jean Burgess, Merja Mahrt, and Cornelius Pusch-mann, 3–14. New York: Peter Lang.

Scholl, Armin, and Siegfried Weischenberg. 1998. *Journalismus in Der Gesellschaft: Theorie, Methodologie Und Empirie* [Journalism in Society: Theory, Methodology and Empiri-cism]. Opladen, Wiesbaden: Westdeutscher Verlag.

Schudson, Michael, and Chris Anderson. 2009. "Objectivity, Professionalism, and Truth-Seeking in Journalism." In *The Handbook of Journalism Studies*, edited by Karin Wahl-Jorgensen and Thomas Hanitzsch, 88–101. New York: Routledge.

Singer, Jane B., David Domingo, Ari Heinonen, Alfred Hermida, Steve Paulussen, Thorsten Quandt, Zvi Reich, and Marina Vujnovic. 2011. *Participatory Journalism: Guarding Open Gates at Online Newspapers*. Malden, MA: Wiley-Blackwell.

Thompson, John B. 2011. "Shifting Boundaries of Public and Private Life." *Theory, Culture and Society* 28 (4): 49–70.

Wahl-Jorgensen, Karin. 2010. "News Production, Ethnography, and Power: On the Challenges of Newsroom-centricity." In *The Anthropology of News and Journalism: Global Perspec-tives*, edited by S. Elizabeth Bird, 21–35. Bloomington: Indiana University Press.

Weber, Stefan. 2000. *Was Steuert Journalismus? Ein System Zwischen Selbstreferenz Und Fremdsteuerung* [What Guides Journalism? A System between Self-reference and Remote Determination]. Konstanz: UVK.

Weischenberg, Siegfried. 2004. *Journalistik. Medienkommunikation: Theorie Und Praxis, Vol. 1: Mediensysteme—Medienethik—Medieninstitutionen* [Journalism Studies. Media Commu-nication: Theory and Praxis Vol. 1: Media Systems—Media Ethics—Media Institutions]. 3rd ed. Wiesbaden: VS Verlag für Sozialwissenschaften.

Weischenberg, Siegfried, and Maja Malik. 2008. "Journalism Research in Germany: Evolution and Central Research Interests." In *Global Journalism Research*, edited by Martin Löffelholz and David Weaver, 158–171. Hoboken, NJ: John Wiley & Sons.

Weischenberg, Siegfried, Maja Malik, and Armin Scholl. 2006. *Die Souffleure Der Mediengesellschaft. Report über Die Journalisten in Deutschland* [Society's Souffleurs. A Report on Journalists in Germany]. Konstanz: UVK.

Weischenberg, Siegfried, Maja Malik, and Armin Scholl. 2012. "Journalism in Germany in the 21st Century." In *The Global Journalist in the 21st Century*, edited by David H. Weaver and Lars Willnat, 205–219. New York: Routledge.

Williams, Andy, Claire Wardle, and Karin Wahl-Jorgensen. 2011. "Have they Got News for Us? Audience Revolution or Business as usual at the BBC?" *Journalism Practice* 5 (1): 85–99.

THE MATERIAL TRACES OF JOURNALISM
A socio-historical approach to online journalism

Juliette De Maeyer and **Florence Le Cam**

This paper explores how the study of objects of journalism, retraced through the material traces left in metajournalistic discourses, might constitute a robust basis to investigate change and permanence in contemporary journalism. We delineate a research program focusing on materiality that requires foremost that objects should not be taken for granted and, therefore, that each object's social history be minutely retraced. Stemming from two specific objects (the blog and the hyperlink), the paper argues that beyond their idiosyncrasies, both follow a similar rationale that could be extrapolated to other objects and lead to a materially focused social history of journalism in a digital age. The paper first clarifies how we approached the notion of "objects of journalism" and which objects we chose to study. Then, we show how different theoretical frameworks led us to adopt a similar research stance and a shared hypothetico-inductive path: determining how objects are parts of a series and analyzing metajournalistic discourses to retrace each object's history on an empirically grounded basis. The resulting attention to filiations and context ultimately produces a contextualized socio-history of objects.

Introduction

Studying online journalism reveals a number of inconsistencies in the traditional concepts and frames of reference of journalism studies. The categories traditionally used and analyzed by journalism scholars have shown their limitations. Professional journalists are no longer—if they ever were—the central and sole actors producing the news. They now share the stage with institutions, citizens, companies, experts, or "infomediaries" (Rebillard 2010; Spano 2011) who can—to a certain extent—directly communicate with the public (Matheson 2004; Lowrey 2006; Reese et al. 2007; Domingo and Heinonen 2008). The roles assumed by these different actors are fuzzy, dispersed (Ringoot and Utard 2005), and sometimes intertwined. Boundaries separating professional journalists from other news producers retain their relevance to understand the concerns of professional journalists working in traditional media (Aubert 2008; Coddington 2012; Eldridge 2014), but large parts of the news now emanate from other groups of actors, rendering the boundary metaphor inadequate in many cases.

The same could be said about the very notion of news media. How can we define the news media? How can we draw the contours of media outlets? The plurality of formats, the diverse conditions of production and means of news dissemination confuse researchers, forced to draw imaginary and arbitrary lines between news sites, blogs, aggregators, etc. Because our traditional categories are challenged, the core notions guiding the study of journalism—analyzing journalistic identities or ideology, media content and context, news production processes and reception—become dubious and difficult to grasp theoretically as well as methodologically.

Going beyond the usual litany on the changing nature of journalism, when weighing the question of transformation and permanence, one must wonder whether journalism is changing that much, or if it is our perspective that is being decentered, forcing us to take into account the entire field.

What is it exactly that we study, and how? Studies of journalism in a digital age often emphasize change, which is extensively and well described when analyzing the content produced, the journalistic practices, the reaction of audiences, the managerial discourses, etc. Each of these topics is unquestionably relevant to understand journalism. But decontextualizing our observations from history supports a rhetoric of disruption that describes the changes as unprecedented, unheard of. As if the past was irrelevant and could be discarded. A second drawback is the direct use of indigenous discourses coming from the industry, journalists themselves or the vague nebulae of experts in online news. Often these indigenous discourses permeate academic research as an illustration of the arguments made by researchers and not as data that need to be analyzed (Brousteau et al. 2012). Finally, technical objects are not necessarily problematized as such. They are considered as tools, likely to have an effect on the practice of journalism, to be adopted or not (with various levels of socio- or techno-determinism). They are naturalized as something unique—i.e. different from other, earlier tools—by the actors using them as well by the scholars investigating them. Yet they belong to a broader category, that of the objects of journalism.

This paper intends to deconstruct this rhetoric of novelty and argues for a social history of "things that exist". Studying *objects of journalism* constitutes a sound perspective to cope with the fundamental *dispersion* of journalism (Ringoot and Utard 2005). In recent years, we have had the opportunity to examine closely two specific objects: the hyperlink and the blog. These explorations led us to deal with a *tangible material* that can be traced and followed through discourses and history, avoiding artificial, *a priori* boundaries between who is a journalist and who is not, what counts as news media or the definition of the public. Though the theoretical frameworks for both objects were distinct, a shared urge to explore the social history of objects in journalism became obvious. It allowed us to track down the objects and reconstruct their history, territory, and evolution. It tried to contextually define journalism by analyzing the "things" that actually populate it.

The present paper draws on our two case studies to argue that beyond their idiosyncrasies, they act according to a similar rationale that could be extended to other objects and lead to a materially focused social history of journalism in a digital age. The following sections first clarify how we approached the notion of "objects of journalism" and which objects we chose to study. Then, we show how different theoretical frameworks led us to adopt a similar research stance and a shared hypothetical-inductive path which is developed in the next sections: determining how objects are parts of a series and analyzing metajournalistic discourses to retrace each object's history on an empirically grounded basis. This attention to filiations and context ultimately produces a contextualized social history of objects.

Two Objects of Journalism: The Blog and the Hyperlink

Analyzing the materiality of the discursive traces left by objects of (online) journalism requires examining what these "things", these objects are. Many disciplines, having undergone a "material turn", came up with sophisticated definitions of objects and materiality (e.g. Dolphijn and Tuin 2012; Carlile et al. 2013). We can, however, start with a very mundane definition: an *object* in journalism studies is something that can be seen and touched. It can be named and materially defined, it is often perceived as a tool, a device, or an artifact. It might resemble other things in the media world, and it is neither necessarily new nor impressive. A list of such objects would include: a pair of scissors, a pen, a typewriter, a desk, a computer, a press card, a database, a quote, a particular piece of software, but also broader sets of objects that constitute infrastructure, such as the newsroom, the building of media companies, or the CMS (Content Management System) used for their website. Journalism scholars have recently expressed an interest in objects and materiality that emerges from the study of digital phenomena but embrace a broader point of view, for example with Anderson (2013, 1010) arguing that "the traceability of action afforded by digital tools" draws our attention to the long-term material operation of newsmaking.

Following the material traces left in successive discourses by a specific object enables us to trace its *concrete material* in the collective and changing news production process: how do news producers use the object, how is it incorporated in their routines, how do they talk about it? Focusing on a concrete material means that this specific object is relevant as an expressive tool *in itself*. This standpoint is the result of a hypothetico-inductive perspective which expresses a somewhat radical stance: among the many objects that populate journalism, the challenge is to extract one. Having selected one (for many different reasons), a complex process of discovering traces of construction and evolution occurs. When we chose to study the blog (Le Cam 2010) and the hyperlink (De Maeyer 2012, 2013), we chose to focus on each object *in itself* and to adopt a hypothetico-inductive stance to determine—gradually and iteratively —the broader phenomena that the objects could embody or be the symptom of. Both objects had notable qualities to help us understand change and permanence in online news production: they corresponded to the mundane definition of *objects of journalism*, they had become common in many parts of journalistic production but had given or still gave rise to heated controversies, and they had a technical dimension but could not solely be reduced to it.

Our shared approach pays attention to filiations, i.e. how linking and blogging are constructed in journalistic discourses and practices, in reference to others and how they evolve over time. The social-historical approach accounts for the genesis of phenomena. It contends that social situations, actors, and context cannot be isolated from their historical context. Discourses, practices, and objects are part of series. They belong to a larger history which is not always obvious at first sight. The research about the history of the term "weblog" at the time it first spread, between 1992 and 2003, was conducted through the analysis of the previous filiations of this practice, trying to find out who named, promoted, and defended it, and by collecting discourse about the practice through time. This social-historical approach highlighted the plural origins of the practice, the discursive conflicts between actors that were trying to "invent" a social practice on to the Web and the fragility of the discourses about innovation (Le Cam 2010). The research on hyperlinks needed, before undertaking content analysis or ethnographic inquiries, to disentangle the different meanings and representations that journalists associate with the idea of linking. As a result, a discourse analysis was conducted on a set of metajournalistic texts ranging from 1999 to 2013. Beside the clarification of the thematic arguments in which the hyperlink was enmeshed, it showed the non-linear nature of journalistic (technical) imaginaries that do not embrace a sequential evolution toward a consensual synthesis but rather see conflicting arguments co-existing in loops. It also showed the array of social worlds with which journalism overlaps. The following sections explain why and how we explored these filiations.

From Distinct Theoretical Backgrounds to a Shared Hypothetico-inductive Stance

Our intuition that objects are not isolated and that they needed to be replaced in their own social-history came from different theoretical backgrounds.

The study of the hyperlink was largely shaped by the perspective of actor-network theory (ANT) and Bruno Latour's sociology of association (Latour 2005) which advocates the need to follow the actors themselves and reminds us that objects cannot be reduced to an *a priori* definition but depend on "concrete assemblages". The concrete assemblages have to be traced to understand the complexity of associations and translations between actors (including non-human actors such as objects). This approach led to studies that focus on innovation as the main site where the social becomes visible—ANT has mostly been applied along these lines by journalism scholars (see e.g. Hemmingway 2008; Weiss and Domingo 2010; and the articles in this special issue by Primo and Sago (2014) and Domingo, Masip, and Costera Meijer (2014))—but Latour also acknowledges that historical investigations can produce "good accounts": even when "objects have receded into the background for good, it is always possible —but more difficult—to bring them back to light by using archives, documents, memories, museum collections" (Latour 2005, 81).

The study of the blog, on the other hand, was inspired by the conception of dialogism. For Mikhail Bakhtin, words "have always already been used, and carry, in themselves, traces of their previous uses; but the 'things' are also affected, if only in one of their previous states, by other discourses" (Todorov 1981, 98–99). The French tradition of discourse analysis[1] (Kristeva 1967; Maingueneau 1984; Chareaudeau 1995) argues that there is a literal presence (more or less literal, complete or not) of a text in other texts, and more importantly, that each discourse carries references to other previous or contemporary discourses (different in time and space). Analyzing the dialogism in speeches, in action, and sometimes in objects (and the discourse they produce) reveals the traces of the social-historical construction of practices and discourses. This perspective is relevant for journalism studies as it makes some permanencies understandable and traceable.

The will to explore online journalism's relatively recent history also exists in other theoretical traditions, notably those inspired by Michel Foucault's "archeology" and "genealogy". For instance, the project of media archeology (which is not limited to news media but encompasses "media" more broadly) "sees media cultures as sedimented and layered, a fold of time and materiality where the past might be suddenly discovered anew, and the new technologies grow obsolete increasingly fast" (Parikka 2012, 192). As a result, media archeology scholars suggest that we explore the entanglement of past and present (Huhtamo 2011; Parikka 2012). Foucault's perspective was also directly applied to online journalism studies by Borger et al. (2013), who have explored the genealogy of "participatory journalism" as a scholarly object and aimed to retrace its "discursive formation" in scholarly discourse about journalism. Foucault was also at the heart of the edited book *Le journalisme en invention* (Ringoot and Utard 2005) to explain the constant and historical invention of journalism through the dispersed discourses and the polyphonic nature of journalism as a social practice.

Although these theoretical frames are very different, we argue that they produce a similar research stance that seeks to investigate the discursive social-historical layers of an object. This is achieved by (1) replacing the object in a series of previous objects and (2) starting to reconstruct the history of each object by exploring metajournalistic discourses about it.

Objects Are Parts of Series

Our first step was to determine how each object can be compared to others in time and space. For instance, the way hyperlinks are used in news items echoes the use of other (discursive) devices such as the quote: it is a connecting apparatus that links the journalistic text with other texts, that potentially embodies the external voice within a news item. The use of reported speech—signaled with quotes—is not an immanent feature of news: it is the product of the historical evolution of journalism (Tuchman 1972; Schudson 1982; Charron 2002), profoundly marked by its context and shaped by its environment. Just as there is more to the footnote than mere referencing, the use of quotes in news production does not solely serve communicative purposes (i.e. reporting what others have said) but also has important social functions. Scholarship on the quoting practices of journalists suggests that "quotes are not only a tool for citing another's words but they fulfill a ritual or communal function by helping to consolidate the authority of the speakers who use them" (Zelizer 1995, 34). As a way of connecting documents and ideas, the hyperlink relates to other cross-reference systems such as footnotes or citations. Inquiries in these systems have shown that they are not mere functional tools for those who use them. They actually reflect many layers of social and contextual meaning (Grafton 1997; Scharnhorst and Thelwall 2005; Landau 2006; Zimmer 2009).

A similar comparison can be made about blogs. The ability to self-publish is not new: from the 1930s until the 1970s, old *samizdat* (texts from dissidents in the USSR and the Eastern bloc) or fanzines paved the way for self-publication. Published by individuals or small groups, fanzines about science fiction, rock-and-roll, feminism, or comics were one of the results of a rather irreverent posture and were rooted in themes usually neglected by mainstream media (Wright 2001). Self-publication was then an alternative way of expressing cultural interest, trying to reach or build a community. Those magazines look like amateur publications, printed on paper of poor quality, and often distributed from hand to hand. With the ability to create websites, some fanzines evolved and became *e-zines*, then *webzines*—keeping their editorial identity, but taking advantage of the features of online publication (Rebillard 2002). Following the idea of self-publication, blogs emerged from that tradition (even if it is not their sole source). Just like fanzines, some blogs were supposed to produce an alternative discourse, allowing individuals to express themselves outside the mainstream media. Other blogs are rooted in different practices: they were launched as an evolution of their owner's personal and static homepage, or were seen as the direct continuity of personal, written diaries (Jeanne-Perrier, Le Cam, and Pélissier 2005). Moreover, according to the Web's indigenous history, there is another forefather to blogs: Tim Berners-Lee's "What's new?" pages. At the beginning of the 1990s, Berners-Lee, best known as the inventor of the World Wide Web, began to publish the newest information on the Web, constantly updating the page with new links. All those pre-existing objects (fanzines, webzines, diaries, or "What's new" pages) show a format constantly evolving, but also constantly echoing past embodiments. The comparison with pre-existing objects helps us understand the way these objects have gradually shaped the emergence and our understanding of what we now call "blogs".

When comparing our digital objects of interest (the hyperlink, the blog) with previous, related devices, we were forced to admit that they are neither completely new nor are they merely technical. If we were to reduce them to a technology, we would study (and measure) their "adoption" level and qualify their absence or presence in news media, in order to measure the level with which they embrace technological innovation—along the lines of early waves of online news research, influenced by technical determinism and online "utopias" (Domingo 2006; Weiss and Domingo 2010; Steensen 2011) that aimed to gauge if news site "lived up to the potential" (Tankard and Ban 1998) of new technologies. On the contrary, our approach posits that technical objects are not to be seen as a straightforward dichotomy—they are either adopted or fail to be adopted—but rather that they are inhabited by a series of meanings, discourses, and social influences that need to be historicized and contextualized.

Accessing the Histories of Objects via Metajournalistic Discourses

By comparing our objects with previous objects we established that our objects were probably not merely technical and that they were likely to be shaped by layers of social context that need to be empirically investigated. This was achieved by following the material traces that the objects left in metajournalistic discourses, that is, the discourses produced by journalists about journalism or themselves. By following the metajournalistic discourses, we can unearth the origins of an object, its diverse filiations, the different ways in which actors frame it, understand it, and make sense of it in relation to their practices of journalism and the practices of adjacent social worlds. The following section describes how we gathered relevant corpuses of metajournalistic discourses. We then discuss how this relates to the tradition of discourse analysis, while adding an original focus on the material traces of interdiscursivity (embodied in hyperlinks).

Which material can we use to retrace the contextual histories of objects? Research dealing with metajournalistic discourses usually relies on trade journals (Touboul 2010; Powers 2012; Philibert 2014), news media coverage (Carlson 2014), or even books and memoirs written by journalists (Hampton 2012). One could easily imagine other fertile sources of metajournalistic discourses that occur "in many public sites inside and outside of journalism" (Carlson 2009, 2014, 34): in most countries and media cultures, journalists' unions, regulators, press councils, educators or handbooks all produce discourses about journalism that could be analyzed as "a perpetual stream of interpretive activity intent on defining the shifting amalgam known as journalism" (Carlson 2014, 33) and also as a way to construct or imagine a professional and collective journalistic identity (Le Cam 2009; Ruellan 2011). But in the case of online journalism and its specific objects, there is no obvious, institutionalized source of specific metajournalistic discourse—at least in the cultural area that we primarily investigated for our research on blogs and links, that is, French-speaking journalists: memoirs still need to be written, unions and regulators remain more interested in traditional media than in online news, handbooks only briefly touch upon the topic of blogs and hyperlinks. This scarcity does not mean that there is no metajournalistic discourse about our objects of interest, but rather that there is no such discourse produced by the institutionalized, traditional metajournalistic sources.

Metajournalistic discourses about linking and blogging do, however, exist in alternative spaces: on Twitter, in the media criticism blogosphere, in specialized news sites, in the comments of all those publications, etc. They are produced by many actors with different, sometimes overlapping roles: they are bloggers, educators, journalists, activists, entrepreneurs, etc. All are interested in producing comments and discourses about online journalism that "set out to define good and bad journalism, good and bad journalists, and what ought to be done with the news" (Haas 2006, quoted in Carlson 2014). Therefore, we needed to broaden the scope and we did so in two ways: by—at least provisionally—dropping the limit of national borders (hence looking at discourses that primarily come from other media cultures) and by including as many different actors as necessary instead of trying to determine *a priori* which relevant institutions to focus on. The former argument seeks to embrace the fact that ideas, discourses, and cultures circulate across national borders—an assumption rooted in our fieldwork (Le Cam 2012; De Maeyer 2013): when we asked journalists to explain how they knew what they knew about online journalism, they often quoted US media gurus just as much as national figures.

The multiplicity of actors does not facilitate the work of identification of collective and dominant discourses. Blogs, collective websites, tweets, columns, etc., have produced an impressive flow of discourses, which are often quite hard to manage, to distinguish one from the other, and even to discover. Yet, these sources are most relevant to understand the histories of our objects. Such a multiplicity of voices implies, especially on the Web, that some discourses are much more visible than others. They concentrate collective attention because of the status of actors, their page rank, the media coverage they have obtained, or even the sheer volume of comments and discourses that they produce. When looking for metajournalistic discourses about online news objects, some actors appear unavoidable: well-established trade journals such as *Columbia Journalism Review* or *Online Journalism Review*, well-known bloggers, scholars, journalists, entrepreneurs, or educators (sometimes combining these roles). Some media outlets also play a prominent role due to their capacity to promote their own innovation, their innovative strategies (such as the BBC or *The New York Times*). They produce discourses that are visible and highly structured. These leading actors can initiate conversations, they can set the agenda. Their positions reflect their visibility in the field of online journalism, and they are therefore valuable for grasping the mainstream flow of discourses. They act as "first observation lenses" but must be used to reveal "how dispersed discourses are woven into articulated literatures" (Venturini 2010, 265). These actors are hiding others that seem less visible at first sight. But the diversity of discourses, the connections between actors and their speeches can be revealed. Hyperlinks, cross-references, and the meshing of voices can help to find those connections. Sometimes, a simple link can help us to discover a new world of discourses, and previously inconspicuous actors. There is no easy methodological solution to avoid the trap of centrality: we need the central actors because we need to start somewhere—they are often the only thread we can pull. Hence, we must document the role and position of every actor in context so as to appraise their relative importance. By rigorously following the cross-references they make, the links they produce, we can progressively discover other actors, back in time but also speaking from less central positions—effectively multiplying the points of observation (Venturini 2010, 259).

Retracing the discourses does not only imply looking at what is being said, but also determining by whom. Most of the actors that we encountered in our explorations had multiple and fluctuating identities: one can be a journalist, a blogger, and an educator at the same time. Entrepreneurs launch successful start-ups then are hired by media companies. Bloggers also tweet, open new blogs, and occasionally write a column for a mainstream news media. As our commitment to context urges us to always explicitly define every actor's role and position, it is not sufficient to do so once and for all. People's identities evolve over time, and it implies that each actor's biography should be minutely retraced in parallel with the histories of the objects.

To reconstruct the social history of our objects, we needed to systematize our approaches and navigations on the Web. In both our studies, we followed the same logic: a systematic monitoring of connections created by hyperlinks. In corpuses of discourses published on the Web, hyperlinks are the most obvious material sign of cross-references. The hyperlink is perhaps the most material trace to reassemble online discourses. It allows reconstruction of a series of conversations, navigating from link to link—a process that can be called serendipity, or the exploration of "topical localities" (Davison 2000)—in attempts to materialize their interdiscursivity. Links between discourses are obviously those shown in texts that have been chosen by actors. We do not have access to other, hidden, references. Nevertheless, they represent a thread to follow. This commitment to follow hyperlinks gives us the opportunity to look at the interrelationships between actors of the Web. It allows us (by comparing the dates of publication, for example) to understand in which direction ideas and discourses flow. We can observe mimetic practices ("I quote the same thing as you do") and we are able to analyze the discourse at a given time in specific situations. Hyperlinks also help us to reconstruct the "worlds" of actors on the Web; and, most importantly, they give us access to controversies (Venturini 2010, 2012). The use of hyperlinks between documents and actors is not just a process of exchange-gift. It is also a way for players to blame and contest some practices—in line with traditional metajournalistic discourse that often takes shape as criticism (Haas 2006; Carlson 2009).

The systematic exploration of hyperlinks to identify series of metajournalistic discourses has a concrete result: it highlights intersections with other types of discourses and exhibits their cross-fertilization. It shows that the metajournalistic discourse does not exist as such, isolated. Our research on blogs highlighted several affiliations coming from other worlds: journalists, researchers, writers (diarists), IT specialists or librarians. Similarly, discourses on hyperlinks show that the online journalism community quotes and takes over elements from others communities and their rhetoric: search engine optimization (SEO) experts, bloggers, founders of the Web, librarians, usability experts, etc. Sometimes these intersections are staged. Some direct references highlight the links that actors themselves want to promote. But they also use discourses stemming from other contexts without explicitly embedding cross-references: discourses flow, they are dispersed and sometimes reused. The circulation masks how actors are borrowing opinions one from another. These adjustments can then (to some extent) be traced through the interdiscursivity materialized in hyperlinks.

From Interdiscursive Materiality to a Social History of Objects

The analysis of interdiscursive traces left in metajournalistic discourses allowed us to retrace each object's social history in a way that is empirically grounded. Objects are not only inscribed in series including pre-existing objects that the researcher can examine. They also fundamentally belong to various socio-historical contexts, in relation to political, economic, cultural, and organizational concerns—and these contexts are partly accessible in the discovery of interdiscursive traces.

As a cultural and a political practice, blogs have been used—if only rhetorically—as an excuse to disseminate and reinforce the idea of participatory journalism at the beginning of the 2000s. The growth and development of blogs, and the growing media attention they attracted, correspond to what is called the "informational shock" from the terror attack on the United States on September 11, 2001. At that time, many actors expressed the will to disseminate their own ideas and opinions in relation to current events. Impactful international events strongly encouraged actors to create what has been called *current events blogs* (Mayfield 2004; Bahnisch 2006; Trammell 2006): the Iraq War, the 2004 US Presidential campaign, the South Asian Tsunami of 2004, the London and Madrid bombings, etc. Blogs were then presented as a way to facilitate the participation of the public, as a tool to encourage freedom of expression. Such arguments are voiced by a range of actors—journalists, academics, entrepreneurs—for whom the defense of the freedom of expression is not always the sole motivation. They also defend an ideology that bets on the importance of audiences in the public sphere, and on the obligation, for media as well as politicians, to be transparent and efficient as they are overseen by the public.

Using a link in a news story is not only a question of complying with simple rules of Web writing, journalistic style, or adding a new layer of information. Many other constraints weigh on the apparently harmless link. For instance, links are at the core of the link economy which structures the Web and its economic flows (Turow and Tsui 2008). Such convoluted economic interests may lead news producers to adopt seemingly counterintuitive behaviors, such as generously linking to direct competitors, or avoiding to do so even if it would have been the best "journalistic" choice. Conversely, one could argue that the link is not a pure economic object and that it is fundamentally social. The link is, for example, at the core of symbolic dynamics interconnecting online content producers and reducing the act of linking to a rational, economic incentive would hide its deep social qualities. All these issues are repeatedly enmeshed and actualized in the way news producers routinely create links.

Focusing on objects allows us to unravel the ins and outs of the dynamics shaping news production: it provides direct insights into economic, ideological, organizational concerns. Even if an object can be considered "as a tool only", it constitutes an observable phenomenon for scholars. Objects are shaped by the context and the actors —and this is exactly why they are of interest to the researcher. They are the product of a history, of a representation which gives them birth, of a set of discourses which have shaped the tool. Exploring objects requires us to adopt a dialectical perspective, to account for the process of mutual shaping that ties objects to contexts, practices, and discourses. Adopting this perspective, the sociology of objects becomes primarily a social history of objects in discourses, which constitutes an essential prerequisite to study changes and permanence.

Conclusion: Retracing Change and Permanence

Defending a material and social historical approach in journalism studies is an attempt to move away from a proneness to infer change on the sole basis of observing the contemporary. Our proposal argues for an empirical and pragmatic stance of the researcher. Looking for traces that can be collected and ordered opens the way to a much clearer understanding of our cases. This approach is both a methodological and a theoretical proposal—as every approach should be. On the one hand, it encourages corpuses of traces, both contemporary and historical, to be constituted. On the other hand, it aims to re-contextualize journalism in its concrete and pragmatic environment, tools, and practices through the analysis of materiality.

Three important limitations should nevertheless be mentioned. First, the study of how metajournalistic discourses are intertwined confronts us with the problem of non-observables. Not only because some of the links and documents no longer exist, but also because the ways some discourses borrow from others are not materially embedded in hyperlinks. Our approach has to deal with "empty discourses", blanks and blind spots. Secondly, the language has not been a central concern, but it should be explored as a main limit of our studies. The publications we chose as gateways are mainly written in English. They quote very few texts in other languages, and it distorts the vision of the importance of certain actors, discourses, or practices. Thirdly, we have to deal with the vaporous nature, the volatility of discourses published online. Websites tend to rapidly disappear or their content can be modified, posing numerous archiving problems to librarians (Anderson 2005) and social scientists eager to use online material (Gill and Elder 2012), highlighting the need for shared principles for Web historiography (Brügger 2012). Tools such as the Wayback Machine from Internet Archives come in handy, but their limits and biases (Thelwall and Vaughan 2004; Howell 2006) must be taken into account.

Our approach was inspired by our distinct theoretical backgrounds that pleaded for an exploration of the material traces that form an object's social history. However, as researchers mainly using sociological, empirically grounded approaches, we were confronted with the problematic deduction of the meanings of texts. We could not simply rely on explanations constructed by the readers—in that case, by us. In order to find empirically grounded meaning, our hypothesis was that every practice or discourse carries traces of its history, of the previous actors, contexts, local environments in which they occurred. The progressive maturation of things leaves traces in discourses and practices and these traces become material. Consequently, they can be collected, selected, ordered. The ambition was to trace not only the direct references to other discourses or practices, but also the re-use and echo of anterior discourses produced in other spaces, discourses which circulate, are adopted or adapted by others. In other words, it is a focus on the materiality of the discursive traces.

To do so, we used hyperlinks as the most evident discursive traces. Hyperlinks enable scholars to reconstruct the order of discourses about an object of journalism. As we have tried to explain in this article, hyperlinks are the material traces of the intertextuality that characterizes metajournalistic discourses (just as any other type of discourse). Metajournalistic discourses about a specific object of journalism are full of references to other texts, and retracing them allows us to dig into their social history and context.

In one of our case studies, this principle works as nested dolls: using hyperlinks as material traces of metajournalistic interdiscourses about hyperlinks, as a way to untangle the social history of the link as an object of journalism. Such a convoluted process, that we similarly applied to the blog, helps us achieve our objectives: understand how these objects inscribe themselves in a diachrony, how they exist in specific contexts, and how the metajournalistic discourses about them evolve. It results in a mapping of controversies, over the past 20 years, that describes the positions of actors, the choices that have been made, the *leitmotiv* or the redundancies in the debates about journalism. Hyperlinks were very useful as they embody references to actors, to other practices. They reveal the circulation of discourses about a practice, taking into account the diversity of actors and social worlds involved. By following hyperlinks, we acquire a panoptic view of the diversity of actors who have played a role (minor or major) in the structuration of a practice. It helped to consider the dispersion of actors. In our two cases, hyperlinks are the materialization of the interdiscursivity shaping journalism. Such an approach can of course be applied to any other object of journalism —be they digital or not, obvious or more discrete: the pair of scissors, the typewriter, the CMS, the comment, etc. The reference to materiality implies not only the role of objects within the environment (see Paveau 2012), but also, in a very pragmatic way, to look at every tool—be they obvious or not—that helps journalists do their work (Colson, De Maeyer, and Le Cam 2013). That includes the newsroom as an organizational territory, the smartphone, the computer, the pen, the notebook, the camera, but also tiny elements such as the mention of the date on websites or newspapers, or broader materiality such as the ways in which news is intertwined in cultures of circulation (see the article in this special issue by Bødker (2014)). In that sense, objects do not refer to the "objects of study", as evoked in methodological textbooks. Objects have to do with the fact that they can be described, recognized, and most importantly, that they leave traces in their environment. Traces then refer to the fact that they are visible in the newsroom or in the daily life of journalists or others newsmakers, that they mean something unequivocal for those producing the news. Objects have an existence, they are elements that act as a way of mediation to produce journalism. In doing so, they can be traced—notably within (inter)discourses. Studying all these objects by following their material, interdiscursive traces would form a detailed view of contemporary news-making firmly rooted in nuanced accounts of the socio-historical context.

Defining objects of online journalism and retracing their social histories is only the first step of a materially focused research stance. It needs to be complemented with a thorough discussion on how a materially informed point of view can be applied to the study of news contents and the news production processes themselves, i.e. studies of the objects *in action*.

NOTE

1. The French school of discourse analysis differs from the Anglo-Saxon tradition of "discourse theory", which has been applied to media studies by scholars such as Carpentier and De Cleen (2007).

REFERENCES

Anderson, Byron. 2005. "Archiving the Internet." *Behavioral & Social Sciences Librarian* 23 (2): 113–117. doi:10.1300/J103v23n02_07.

Anderson, C. W. 2013. "What Aggregators Do: Towards a Networked Concept of Journalistic Expertise in the Digital Age." *Journalism* 14 (8): 1008–1023. doi:10.1177/1464884913492460.

Aubert, Aurélie. 2008. "Rue 89: Un Modèle Horizontal De La Production D'information? [Rue 89: A Horizontal Model of News Production?]" *Médiamorphoses* 10: 99–104.

Bahnisch, Mark. 2006. "The Political Uses of Blogs." In *Uses of Blogs*, edited by Axel Bruns and Joanne Jacobs, 139–149. New York: Peter Lang.

Bødker, Henrik. 2014. "Journalism as Cultures of Circulation." *Digital Journalism*. doi:10.1080/21670811.2014.928106.

Borger, Merel, Anita van Hoof, Irene Costera Meijer, and José Sanders. 2013. "Constructing Participatory Journalism as a Scholarly Object." *Digital Journalism* 1 (1): 117–134. doi:10.1080/21670811.2012.740267.

Brousteau, Nadège, Valérie Jeanne-Perrier, Florence Le Cam, and Fabio Pereira. 2012. "L'entretien De Recherche Avec Des Journalistes. Propos Introductifs [The Research Interview with Journalists. An Introduction]." *Sur Le Journalisme-about Journalism-Sobre Jornalismo* 1 (1): 6–12.

Brügger, Niels. 2012. "When the Present Web Is Later the Past: Web Historiography, Digital History, and Internet Studies." *Historical Social Research/Historische Sozialforschung* 37 (4): 102–117.

Carlile, Paul R., Davide Nicolini, Ann Langley, and Haridimos Tsoukas. 2013. *How Matter Matters: Objects, Artifacts, and Materiality in Organization Studies*. Oxford: Oxford University Press.

Carlson, Matt. 2009. "Media Criticism as Competitive Discourse Defining Reportage of the Abu Ghraib Scandal." *Journal of Communication Inquiry* 33 (3): 258–277. doi:10.1177/0196859909333693.

Carlson, Matt. 2014. "Gone, but Not Forgotten." *Journalism Studies* 15 (1): 33–47. doi:10.1080/1461670X.2013.790620.

Carpentier, Nico, and Benjamin De Cleen. 2007. "Bringing Discourse Theory into Media Studies: The Applicability of Discourse Theoretical Analysis (DTA) for the Study of Media Practises and Discourses." *Journal of Language and Politics* 6 (2): 265–293.

Charaudeau, Patrick. 1995. "Une analyse sémiolinguistique du discours [A Semiolinguistic Analysis of Discourse]." *Langages* 29 (117): 96–111.

Charron, Jean. 2002. "Parler De Soi En Faisant Parler Les Autres: Identités Journalistiques Et Discours Rapportés [Talking about Oneself While Making others Talk: Journalistic Identities and Reported Speech]." In *Les Mutations Du Journalisme En France Et Au Québec* [Mutations of Journalism in France and Québec], edited by Rémy Rieffel and Thierry Watine, 83–100. Paris: Panthéon-Assas.

Coddington, Mark. 2012. "Building Frames Link by Link: The Linking Practices of Blogs and News Sites." *International Journal of Communication* 6: 2007–2026.

Colson, Vinciane, Juliette De Maeyer, and Florence Le Cam. 2013. *Du Pigeon Voyageur À Twitter: Histoires Matérielles Du Journalisme* [From the Carrier Pigeon to Twitter: Material Histories of Journalism]. Bruxelles: Centre d'Action Laïque.

Davison, Brian D. 2000. "Topical Locality in the Web." In *Proceedings of the 23rd Annual International ACM SIGIR Conference on Research and Development in Information Retrieval*, 272–279. Athens, Greece: ACM. doi:10.1145/345508.345597.

De Maeyer, Juliette. 2012. "The Journalistic Hyperlink." *Journalism Practice* 6 (5–6): 692–701. doi:10.1080/17512786.2012.667273.

De Maeyer, Juliette. 2013. "L'usage Journalistique Des Liens Hypertextes. Étude Des Représentations, Contenus Et Pratiques À Partir Des Sites D'information De La Presse Belge Francophone [The Journalistic use of Hyperlinks. A Study of Representations, Contents and Practices Starting from the Websites of the Belgian Francophone Daily Press]." PhD diss., U libre de Bruxelles.

Dolphijn, Rick, and Iris van der Tuin. 2012. *New Materialism Interviews & Cartographies*. Ann Arbor: Open Humanities Press.

Domingo, David. 2006. *Inventing Online Journalism. Development of the Internet as a News Medium in Four Catalan Online Newsrooms*. Phd diss., Universita Rovira i Virgili.

Domingo, David, and Ari Heinonen. 2008. "Weblogs and Journalism. A Typology to Explore the Blurring Boundaries." *Nordicom Review* 29 (1): 3–15.

Domingo, David, Pere Masip, and Irene Costera Meijer. 2014. "Tracing Digital News Networks: Towards an Integrated Framework of the Dynamics of News Production, Circulation and Use." *Digital Journalism*. doi:10.1080/21670811.2014.927996.

Eldridge, Scott A. 2014. "Boundary Maintenance and Interloper Media Reaction." *Journalism Studies* 15 (1): 1–16. doi:10.1080/1461670X.2013.791077.

Gill, Fiona, and Catriona Elder. 2012. "Data and Archives: The Internet as Site and Subject." *International Journal of Social Research Methodology* 15 (4): 271–279. doi:10.1080/13645579.2012.687595.

Grafton, Anthony. 1997. *The Footnote: A Curious History*. Rev. ed. Cambridge Mass: Harvard University Press.

Haas, Tanni. 2006. "Mainstream News Media Self-criticism: A Proposal for Future Research." *Critical Studies in Media Communication* 23 (4): 350–355. doi:10.1080/07393180600933196.

Hampton, Mark. 2012. "'Journalists' Histories of Journalism." *Media History* 18 (3-4): 327–340. doi:10.1080/13688804.2012.722272.

Hemmingway, Emma. 2008. *Into the Newsroom: Exploring the Digital Production of Regional Television News*. London: Routledge.

Howell, Beryl A. 2006. "Proving Web History: How to Use the Internet Archive." *Journal of Internet Law* 9 (8): 3–9.

Huhtamo, Erkki. 2011. *Media Archaeology Approaches, Applications, and Implications*. Berkeley: University of California Press. http://www.SLQ.eblib.com.au/patron/FullRecord.aspx?p= 769730.

Jeanne-Perrier, Valérie, Florence Le Cam, and Nicolas Pélissier. 2005. "Les Sites Web D'auto-Publication: Observatoires Privilégiés Des Effervescences Et Des Débordements Journalistiques En Tous Genres [Self-publication Websites: A Privileged Observatory for Turmoil and Journalistic Misbehaviors]." In *Le Journalisme En Invention. Nouvelles Pratiques, Nouveaux Acteurs* [Journalism in Invention: New Practices, New Actors], edited by Roselyne Ringoot and Jean-Michel Utard, 161–202. Rennes: Presses universitaires de Rennes.

Kristeva, Julia. 1967. "Bakhtine, Le Mot, Le Dialogue Et Le Roman." *Critique* 239: 438–465.

Landau, Jack L. 2006. "Footnote Folly. A History of Citation Creep in the Law." *Oregon State Bar Bulletin*. http://www.osbar.org/publications/bulletin/06nov/footnote.html.

Latour, Bruno. 2005. *Reassembling the Social: An Introduction to Actor-Network-Theory*. Oxford: Oxford University Press.

Le Cam, Florence. 2009. *Le Journalisme Imaginé. Histoire D'un Projet Professionnel Au Québec* [Imagined Journalism. History of a Professional Project]. Montréal: Lémeac.

Le Cam, Florence. 2010. "Histoires Et Filiations Du Terme 'Weblog' (1992–2003). Perspectives Pour Penser L'histoire De Certaines Pratiques Sociales Sur Le Web [History and Filiation of the Word 'Weblog' (1992–2003)]." *Les Enjeux De L'information Et De La Communication*, http://w3.u-grenoble3.fr/les_enjeux/2010/LeCam/index.html.

Le Cam, Florence. 2012. "Une Identité Transnationale Des Journalistes En Ligne? [A Transnational Identity of Online Journalists?]." In *Journalisme En Ligne: Pratiques Et Recherches* [Online Journalism: Practice and Research], edited by Amandine Degand and Benoît Grevisse, 61–86. Bruxelles: De Boeck.

Lowrey, Wilson. 2006. "Mapping the Journalism-Blogging Relationship." *Journalism* 7 (4): 477–500. doi:10.1177/1464884906068363.

Maingueneau, Dominique. 1984. *Genèses Du Discours* [Origins of Discourse]. Bruxelles: Ed. Pierre Mardaga.

Matheson, Donald. 2004. "Weblogs and the Epistemology of the News: Some Trends in Online Journalism." *New Media & Society* 6 (4): 443–468. doi:10.1177/14614480404 4329.

Mayfield, Ross. 2004. "The Political Effects of Blogging: Call for Indicators." *Many 2 Many*, February 9. http://many.corante.com/archives/2004/02/09/the_political_effects_of_blog ging_call_for_indicators.php.

Parikka, Jussi. 2012. *What is Media Archaeology?* Cambridge: Polity Press.

Paveau, Marie-Anne. 2012. "'Ce Que Disent Les Objets. Sens, Affordance, Cognition' [What Objects Say: Meaning, Affordance, Cognition]." *Synergies. Pays Riverains De La Baltique* 9: 53–65.

Philibert, Jean-René. 2014. "Discours Sur La Presse écrite Nord-Américaine De La Fin Du XIXème Siècle Et Implantation Du Journalisme D'information [Discourses on the North American Written Press in the Late 19th Century and the Establishment of News Reporting]." In *Changements Et Permanences Du Journalisme* [Change and Permanence of Journalism], edited by Florence Le Cam and Denis Ruellan, 21–39. Paris: L'Harmattan.

Powers, Matthew. 2012. "In Forms That Are Familiar and Yet-to-Be Invented." *Journal of Communication Inquiry* 36 (1): 24–43. doi:10.1177/0196859911426009.

Primo, Alex, and Gabriela Zago. 2014. "Who and What Do Journalism? An Actor-network Perspective." *Digital Journalism*. doi:10.1080/21670811.2014.927987.

Rebillard, Frank. 2002. "Webzines, E-Zines: Quels Nouveaux Médias? [Webzines, E-Zines, Which New Media?]" *Médiamorphoses* 4: 57–62.

Rebillard, Franck. 2010. "The Intermediaries of Online Information." *INA Global*, September 24. http://www.inaglobal.fr/en/numerique/article/intermediaries-online-information.

Reese, Stephen D., Lou Rutigliano, Kideuk Hyun, and Jaekwan Jeong. 2007. "Mapping the Blogosphere: Professional and Citizen-based Media in the Global News Arena." *Journalism* 8 (3): 235–261. doi:10.1177/1464884907076459.

Ringoot, Roselyne, and Jean-Michel Utard. 2005. "Genre Journalistique Et 'Dispersion' Du Journalisme [Journalistic Genres and the 'dispersion' of Journalism]." In *Le Journalisme En Invention: Nouvelles Pratiques, Nouveaux Acteurs* [Journalism in Invention: New Practices, New Actors], edited by Roselyne Ringoot and Jean-Michel Utard, 21–47. Rennes: Presses universitaires de Rennes.

Ruellan, Denis. 2011. *Nous, Journalistes: Déontologie Et Identité* [We, Journalists: Deontology and Identity]. Grenoble: Presses Universitaires de Grenoble.

Scharnhorst, Andrea, and Mike Thelwall. 2005. "Citation and Hyperlink Networks." *Current Science* 89 (9): 1518–1524.

Schudson, Michael. 1982. "The Politics of Narrative Form: The Emergence of News Conventions in Print and Television." *Daedalus* 111 (4): 97–112.

Spano, William. 2011. "L'agenda D'une Rédaction De Presse écrite: Contribution à La Mise Au Jour Des écritures Du Journalisme [A Newsroom's Datebook: Contribution to Unveil Journalistic Writing]." *Communication & Langages* 170: 23–42. doi:10.4074/S033615 001101402.

Steensen, Steen. 2011. "Online Journalism and the Promises of New Technology." *Journalism Studies* 12 (3): 311–327. doi:10.1080/1461670X.2010.501151.

Tankard, James W., and Hyun, Ban. 1998. "Online Newspapers: Living up to the Potential?" Presented at the annual conference of the AEJMC, Baltimore.

Thelwall, Mike, and Liwen Vaughan. 2004. "A Fair History of the Web? Examining Country Balance in the Internet Archive." *Library & Information Science Research* 26 (2): 162–176. doi:10.1016/j.lisr.2003.12.009.

Todorov, Tzvetan. 1981. *Mikhaïl Bakhtine: Le Principe Dialogique. Suivi De Ecrits Du Cercle De Bakhtine* [Mikhaïl Bakhtine: The Dialogic Principle]. Paris: Seuil.

Touboul, Annelise. 2010. "Journalistes Et Publics, L'annonce D'un Mariage De Raison [Journalists and the Public, a Marriage of Convenience]." *Communication & Langages* 165: 19–30.

Trammell, Kaye D. 2006. "The Blogging of the President." In *The Internet Election: Perspectives on the Web in Campaign 2006*, edited by Andrew Paul Williams and John C Tedesco, 133–146. Lanham: Rowman & Littlefield.

Tuchman, Gaye. 1972. "Objectivity as Strategic Ritual: An Examination of Newsmen's Notions of Objectivity." *American Journal of Sociology* 77 (4): 660–679.

Turow, Joseph, and Lokman Tsui. 2008. *The Hyperlinked Society: Questioning Connections in the Digital Age*. Ann Arbor: University of Michigan Press.

Venturini, Tommaso. 2010. "Diving in Magma: How to Explore Controversies with Actor-network Theory." *Public Understanding of Science* 19 (3): 258–273. doi:10.1177/0963662509102694.

Venturini, Tommaso. 2012. "Building on Faults: How to Represent Controversies with Digital Methods." *Public Understanding of Science* 21 (7): 796–812. doi:10.1177/0963662510387558.

Weiss, Amy Schmitz, and David Domingo. 2010. "Innovation Processes in Online Newsrooms as Actor-networks and Communities of Practice." *New Media & Society* 12 (7): 1156–1171. doi:10.1177/1461444809360400.

Wright, Frederick A. 2001. "From Zines to Ezines: Electronic Publishing and the Literary Underground." Thesis (PhD)., Kent State University.

Zelizer, Barbie. 1995. "Text, Talk, and Journalistic Quoting Practices*." *The Communication Review* 1 (1): 33–51. doi:10.1080/10714429509388250.

Zimmer, Michael. 2009. "Renvois of the Past, Present and Future: Hyperlinks and the Structuring of Knowledge from the Encyclopedie to Web 2.0." *New Media & Society* 11 (1–2): 95–113. doi:10.1177/1461444808099573.

JOURNALISM AS CULTURES OF CIRCULATION

Henrik Bødker

The universe of journalism has always consisted of interspersed texts, practices and meanings. Yet, much journalism research has often isolated either texts and/or contexts and thus assumed relations between professional practices, informed (rational) readers and (conceived) core texts. It is, however, more important than ever to shift attention away from texts to the processes through which they are circulated. This is partly because the many cultural forms of journalism (textual, institutional, technological, material, behavioural and imagined) are undergoing significant changes, one of which is being interrelated in new and increasingly complex ways. To understand some of the related processes, this article proposes a notion of circulation that implies a close attention to the ways in which the various forms of this landscape travel, intertwine and connect and, in particular, to the ways in which these forms construct and maintain what is termed cultures of circulation. In order to approach such processes, this article traces the photographic mediation of a specific event with the overall aim of beginning a theorization of the landscape of journalism as interrelated cultures of circulation.

Introduction

April 9, 2013, marked the 10-year anniversary of the toppling of Saddam Hussein's statue in Baghdad's Firdos Square. The many re-circulations of some of the iconic images from this event were accompanied by discussions of developments in Iraq after its "liberation". An early example of this was an article in the *International Herald Tribune* on March 9, where the headline "10 Years After the Invasion of Iraq, a World of Hurt" appeared over the image in Figure 1.

This and other images (both live and still) from that day in Firdos Square have appeared in a myriad of media both off- and online since 2003 and are—as iconic images—different from everyday press photos, e.g. photos of known politicians in non-extraordinary situations. Iconic images have become situated at important political, social and cultural fault lines and therefore mark or embody specific, "enhanced" moments in history. This involves, says Lucaites and Hariman (2001, 37), being "regularly reproduced and copied across a range of media, genres and topics". Processes of iconicity are therefore important avenues for understanding the logics of journalism and mediation at any given time. In a more general sense, however, news photographs can be argued to be condensed narratives that often constitute the kernel of larger public discussions in the sense that news photography usually is embedded in written journalism. As the smallest narrative unit in journalism, the photograph constitutes a

FIGURE 1
The toppling of the statue in Firdos Square (from the *International Herald Tribune*)

cultural form that is deeply woven into the wider processes of journalism. Following photos may thus point to more general relations within the landscape of journalism.

The processes leading up to the toppling, their timing and unfolding are very hard to disentangle from processes of mediation. The range of live and still images at the time developed within and in relation to a media landscape hungry for highly symbolic and condensed imagery. Across major networks and publications, well-chosen images embodied headlines such as "Baghdad Falls to US as Regime Collapses" followed up by "BAGHDAD was finally liberated this afternoon as a 20ft statue of Saddam Hussein was brought crashing to the ground in the city centre in front of crowds of jubilant Iraqis" (*The Evening Standard*, April 9, 2003). One way of getting a sense of the dispersal of imagery since 2003 is through a Google images search for "Saddam Hussein statue pulled down". This produces the opening screen in Figure 2 (in which the photos are sorted by "relevance").

The 15 images seen here are the first out of approximately 600. As far as sources are concerned, roughly half of the first 15 images are from regular news sites (*The Guardian*, *New York Daily News*, BBC and CBC), one is from a highly specialized news site (*Military Times*), two are from a professional organization (The American Enterprise Institute), one from an independent journalist, two are from personal blogs and two are from smaller interest groups: Pentax (camera) users and a hobby site which discusses the vehicle used to pull down the statue. Among the 15 is also the Wikipedia entry on Firdos Square. In terms of temporality, the postings range from 2003 to 2013. On almost all the sites one can see that the images and related text have been shared and/or commented.

The view produced by such a search is arguably a somewhat random and tiny slice of the incredible maze of interlinked images and texts that make up the textual aftermath of the highly symbolic act of tearing down the statue. A number of important issues, however, can be drawn from this example. What is highlighted, firstly, is the simple but important point that such a slice is so easily available. And, secondly, that this availability underlines and complicates aspects of temporality within the

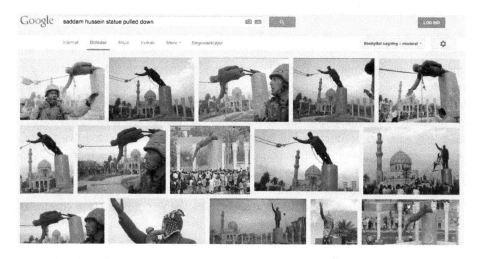

FIGURE 2
Google search, May 10, 2013

journalistic realm. Thirdly, this example emphasizes the different contexts or cultures in which specific news images or items have been circulated and, linked to this, the movement of such images into and out of commodity form. Lastly, it points towards the increasingly complex processes of circulation.

These issues will be discussed below through a progression towards a theoretical frame for studying journalism not as a demarcated culture of production disseminating texts but as interspersed cultures of circulation, which preliminarily can be defined as cultures that are "created and animated by the cultural forms that circulate through them" (Lee and LiPuma 2002, 192). Taking my cue from the paper by Lee and LiPuma (2002), which informs the title of this article, I am following in the footsteps of an inter-disciplinary group of researchers, who convened a workshop in 2011 to explore the application of the term "cultures of circulation". In the introduction to the ensuing special issue of *Poetics* Aronczyk and Craig (2012, 93) aptly argue that:

> Lee and LiPuma set out to dislodge the concept of circulation from its traditional ana-lytic frame as a form of transmission or delivery between unidirectional phases of pro-duction and consumption in order to recognize it as a dynamic cultural phenomenon in its own right. Rather than conceiving of circulation in terms of the movement of discrete objects, images and people between defined points in space and time, we are encouraged to acknowledge its performative character, its active role in constituting objects and identities and spatiotemporal environments.

Before getting to what that means in relation to the landscape of journalism, some of the overall ways in which the concept of circulation has been applied to journalism will be outlined.

Journalism and Circulation

Within journalism, circulation has traditionally referred to the distribution and/or dissemination of discrete containers of meaning (e.g. newspapers or TV programmes).

In this most basic sense, it is a material process governed by specific infrastructures. Circulation may, however, also refer to the dissemination of meaning, e.g. how specific messages travel and spread via but also beyond the material carriers of text. And, rather than the distribution of already contained meaning, the notion of circulation may refer to processes underlying the (on-going) production of meaning and cultures. Circulation in relation to journalism is thus at the same time material dissemination, the dissemination of meaning, and the (re)production of culture (as seen by for instance Stuart Hall, who will be discussed in more detail below). This last perspective points in the direction of a cultures-of-circulation perspective. Yet, there is an important distinction of emphasis in that the cultures-of-circulation perspective is interested in understanding how the circulation of certain forms establish and maintain certain practices/actions/cultures rather than in understanding how the meaning of texts are constructed through circulation. This is the distinction I make between the circulation of meaning and the meaning of circulation. Both perspectives can, however, be seen within a broad definition of journalism "as a complex network of participatory practices" (Goode 2009, 1288). In order to underline the "the performativity of circulation" (Aronczyk and Craig 2012, 96), the notion of participation should *not* be limited to non-professionals.

In relation to this one might (somewhat teasingly) argue that new media practices, e.g. social media and other cultures of circulation, have included professional journalism rather than the more conventional view that journalism increasingly has included the audience—a view underlying the focus on "participation". Rather than an inclusion from above, the range of new media practices drawing professional journalism closer (or down, as some would argue) can be seen, as Miller (2012) argues, as a reassertion of the vernacular that the professionalization of journalism pushed to the very edges of the analogue media system. But whereas Miller is mainly concerned with style, the reassertion in focus here should rather be seen as a re-emergence of vernacular modes of (re-) circulation. Seen from such a perspective, a range of new media practices have allowed professionals a glimpse into the processes through which news circulates and through which cultures are constituted. "[N]ews tends to circulate over an ever widening area, as means of communication multiply", Park (1940, 684) noted decades ago. Although Park focused on the physical dissemination of newspapers in an urban setting, he was well aware that the construction of meaning linked to circulation was more much complex than what could be depicted as circles on an urban map. But, he says, for "a report of events current may have the quality of news, it should not merely circulate—possibly in circuitous underground channels—but should be published, if need be by the town crier or the public press". "Such publication", he continues,

> tends to give news something of the character of a public document. News is more or less authenticated by the fact that it has been exposed to the critical examination of the public to which it is addressed and with whose interests it is concerned. (Park 1940, 679)

The possibilities of giving something the character of a public document has indeed multiplied; and with that, the status of publication has become increasingly contested. Identifying the "varied forms through which journalism makes its name" (Zelizer 2008, 86) has thus become a more complex task. One should, therefore, not talk about journalism but rather of communicational landscapes of journalism that comprise ranges of somewhat hybrid meditated forms and cultures dispersed in complex global settings.

Thus, as Valaskivi and Sumiala (2013, 2) argue: "it is the intensification of 'mediated public forms' in mediatized societies that make circulation [a] particularly relevant approach in [the] study of contemporary society".

Mapping Circulation. In the analogue landscape the geography of circulation could be based on the reach of radio and TV broadcasting or the addresses of newspaper subscribers. An early instance of this can be seen in Park (1929). "Newspaper circulation", he says, "may be represented schematically in a succession of concentric circles ... [in which] circulation, like land values, tends to decline from the city center to its circumference" (62). Yet, what such analogue maps cannot reveal are all the meetings between texts and readers not taking place in the homes on the address list. For most publications, however, readership has outnumbered subscribers, which means that publications are lying around, picked up and passed on. Yet, such movements and meetings—e.g. on the street, at the café, at the hairdresser, on the train, at the breakfast table, in the living room, in the toilet, etc.—have rarely been conceived as important in themselves. Rather, the actual processes resulting in the meetings of text and reader have often been assumed and/or neglected. This is partly because meaning often has been assumed to be (self-)contained within the text and thus (objectively) unpacked no matter how the text was obtained and where the reading took place.

What the Firdos Square example demonstrates is that tracking and conceptualizing the mediated life of a specific happening have become both easier and more difficult: easier, because such mediations increasingly leave more lasting and easily available digital traces; more difficult, because mediations multiply, interlink and layer across the almost endless and complicated interstices making up the increasingly global digital landscape. Following the digital traces produces a rudimentary digital geography in which meetings between specific content and constituencies have taken place.

While a mapping of the digital circulation geography may be easily available and (perhaps) relatively extensive, it is also very different from what it may have been possible to retrieve in an analogue landscape. In the digital news landscape, almost any substantial piece of news is, right from its digital publication, drawn into a progressive layering. This is firstly so because digital news stories "do not have a specific periodicity ... and [thus] apply [divergent notions of] newsworthiness and updating criteria (Ureta 2011, 191). Within breaking news, at least, this means that the iteration of the writing process has become partly public, something which also may be used as a collective correction device. In addition to this, stories may link backwards to earlier versions or related issues; and beyond the sequential build-up of stories and their progressive layering within a certain Web domain, texts are layered as interlinked mediations across the digital expanse through circulation.

With digitalization, the increased dispersal and fragmentation of news consumption over place, platforms and time is, however, beginning to draw scholarly attention (see among others Newman and Levy 2013; Westlund 2013). Yet, with regard to processes of circulation, the neglect seems to persist. Anderson (2010, 291, emphasis in the original) noted about "new journalism literature" that "[r]esearch on changing patterns of newswork, in short, has focused on *news production* within *institutions* rather than the *circulation* of news in *ecosystems*".

The Circulation of Meaning

Anderson (2010) addresses this neglect by ingeniously analysing how "a single cluster of facts travelled within an actually existing metropolitan news ecosystem" (290) by looking at the roles played by different actors/identities and—importantly—how the diffusion challenged and/or underpinned some of these. His study is in many ways much more complex than the many diffusion studies that it builds upon. Yet, it still mainly focuses on the diffusion of meaning in a (local) media ecology. This has long been a concern within the sociology of news. Park, whose study of communication and journalism was linked to the urban sociology of the Chicago School, noted:

> The extent to which news circulates, within a political unit or a political society, deter-
> mines the extent to which the members of such a society may be said to participate,
> not in its collective life—which is the more inclusive term—but in its political acts.
> (Park 1940, 677)

Following this, Anderson's study may be said to reveal the "political acts" of those local actors—some journalists, some not—involved in the diffusion of (contested) meanings.

Broadening the perspective of diffusion from a specific context, there have been a number of attempts to understand circulation as the construction of meaning distributed along the axes of temporality and/or spatiality. A great deal of this has been linked to the construction of meaning over distances, i.e. cross-cultural media consumption. Much of this has been about (global) popular culture. But news has not, for the most part, been seen as a commodity that traverses cultural boundaries and, therefore, has not been seen as content, whose circulation calls for (much) interpretation. There may be two overall reasons why the traditional circulation of journalism has not been seen in meaning-making terms: firstly, because of its association with local and/or national culture in which its circulation was more or less "instant"; and, secondly, because its commodity status has not been given much attention.

An important exception has been grounded in Marxist thinking where the circulation of journalism has been linked to commodification of/and meaning. Stuart Hall's "encoding, decoding" model (from the late 1970s) is an important attempt to conceive the production, distribution and consumption processes as constitutive and articulated moments in the circulation of meaning (or ideology)—although Hall applies the notion of circulation itself to only part of the larger communicative circuit. Yet, his main concern is to understand how the production of meaning and culture is temporally and spatially distributed. Although Hall's discussion is related to the production of television news in a very different media landscape, it is arguably still a good starting point for beginning to understand journalism as cultures of circulation within a contemporary setting.

Hall (1993) starts his essay thus: "Traditionally, mass-communication research has conceptualized the process of communication in terms of a circulation circuit or loop" (90). But such a view, he argues, neglects the movement or construction of meaning through the processes of "production, circulation, distribution/consumption [and] repro-duction" (91). Hall sees the movement of meaning through these processes as "sus-tained through the articulation of connected practices, each of which, however, retains its distinctiveness and has its own specific modality, its own forms and conditions of existence" (91). Here, the movement of the physical (the "sign-vehicle" in Hall's terms) is intimately linked to the (re-)construction of meaning; or, put differently, here circulation is arguably both a technological and hermeneutical process. Journalism is here seen as a part of circulatory processes that transform occurrences on the ground into discursive forms, which then are circulated, distributed, interpreted and transformed (again) into lived (ideological) life.

Hall's processes of meaning-making linked to circulation may be illustrated and understood through a couple of journalistic meta-texts that emerged from the Google search above. The first of these is "Jeremy Paxman's photograph of the decade", where Paxman in a "Series" on "The 10 photographs of the decade" (in *The Guardian* in 2010) discusses the photo in Figure 1, and says that that he has "chosen this picture of the toppling of a statue of the Iraqi dictator to remind us that not everything we saw in that war was what it appeared" (*The Guardian*, November 13, 2010). "The event seemed to be the moment Iraqis freed themselves from dictatorship", he continues, "[but] the hook on the left of the frame belongs to a US military recovery vehicle [and] the Baghdadis had been summoned by American loudspeaker". "[M]inutes earlier a US marine had clambered to the top of the statue and draped Saddam's head in a Stars and Stripes" but this did "not suit the political narrative. A horrified American psy-ops [psychological operations] colonel watching the coverage somewhere in cyberspace ordered the marine back up the ladder, to remove the US flag and replace it with an Iraqi one". What seems at stake in the Paxman text is an attempt to salvage journalistic autonomy by arguing that the mediated event was largely managed by the military and that journalists were not complicit in its making.

While Paxman's discussion of the photo can largely be seen as boundary work, Maass (2011) gives a detailed and nuanced account of the transformation of occurrences in Firdos Square into "sign-vehicles". Maass is a freelance journalist whose homepage is one of the 15 that comes up via the Google image search. The page that the search leads to describes a *New Yorker* story that has won a "mirror award", which is given "for stories that look into the role of the media". The article is called "The Toppling—How the Media Inflated a Minor Moment in a Long War" and appeared in the *The New Yorker* on January 10, 2011. Maass, who was present that day in Firdos Square, describes in detail how events unfolded and how this led to some of the specific and iconic images. Both Paxman and Maass' texts exemplify Zelizer's argument that an important part of journalism as "interpretive communities" consists of discourses focusing on key moments in the self-understanding of journalism. The easy availability of a vast field of layered journalistic texts both complicates and makes increasingly important Zelizer's "double-time" argument that "[j]ournalists constitute themselves not only as the objects of the accounts they give but as the subjects of other accounts that elaborate on their earlier reportage" (Zelizer 1993, 224).

Maass' detailed descriptions illustrate rather succinctly Hall's point that the "event must become a 'story' before it can become a *communicative event*" (Hall 1993, 92, emphasis in the original). What happened that day in Firdos Square was not a stage-managed event, says Maass, but rather a somewhat contingent coming together of people from different professional and national cultures, i.e. a battalion of US marines, a large group of international journalists and (fewer) Iraqi civilians. The commander of the battalion heading into Baghdad that day, Lieutenant Colonel Bryan McCoy, knew about the Palestine Hotel, where at "least two hundred" "foreign reporters could be found"; but he had no intention of going there. That he did was a result of surprisingly little opposition and the ensuing possibility of being sent there by his commander (presumably in order to prevent anything happening to the large contingent of foreign reporters). McCoy was, however (as Maass points out) "fully cognizant that he was about to move into an area where there were lots of journalists and there were going to be opportunities" (Maass 2011, 46). What unfolded grew out of the situation and the people there. "I realised this was a big deal", McCoy says, and continues:

> You've got all the press out there and everybody is liquored up on the moment. You have this Paris, 1944, feel. I remember thinking. The media is watching the Iraqis trying to topple this icon of Saddam Hussein. Let's give them a hand. (Maass 2011, 47)

In what followed, it was, says Maass, the "media, rather than the government, that created the victory myth" (49) in that the live coverage (CNN and Fox, among others) was a result of "editors and anchors" in the United States "[p]rimed for triumph … and ready to latch onto a symbol of … what victory would look like". What they saw from afar was "an aesthetically perfect representation of that preconception" (49). After this, Maass argues, a "virtual echo chamber developed: rather than encouraging reporters to find the news, editors urged them to report what was on TV" (50).[1] What Hall says about the transposition of events into the television sign is highly relevant here:

> [T]hough the production structures of television originate the television discourse, they do not constitute a closed system. They draw topics, treatments, agendas, events, personal, images of the audience, "definitions of the situation" from other sources and other discursive formations within the wider socio-cultural and political structure of which they are a differentiated part. (Hall 1993, 92)

What Hall here calls "images of audiences", "definitions of the situation" and "other discursive formations" is the "primed for triumph" that Maass talks about in the sense that people within the television apparatus "knew" what audiences were longing to see. "Thus", says Hall (1993, 92–93), "circulation and reception are, indeed, 'moments' of the production process in television and are reincorporated, via a number of skewed and structured 'feedbacks', into the production process itself". Such "skewed and structured feedbacks" have, one could argue, become more prevalent in a digital landscape.

What becomes apparent through the Firdos Square example seen through Hall's perspective of the "social relations of the communicative process" (93) is that journalism—at each step of the process—is woven deeply into culture and time. In this specific example, the coverage was a product of the interactions between military personnel, journalists and editors, and Iraqi civilians. These groups were all driven somehow by expectations of certain images to be circulated. With regard to the civilians, Maass points out that the "level of Iraqi enthusiasm appeared to ebb and flow according to the number of and interest of photographers who had gathered". "Would the Iraqis have done the same thing if the cameras hadn't been there?", Maass asks. This, of course, is a question that cannot be answered, and as such underlines the necessity of seeing journalism as interactions between different cultures both within and outside its institutional settings. What is clear, however, is that the journalists were bound together by a culture premised on circulation of specific forms both in the processes taking place that day on the square and in the ensuing processes partly revealed through the two pieces of meta-journalism described here. Zelizer argues that discourses making up the interpretive communities of journalism tend to "proliferate when addressing unresolved dimensions of everyday newswork" (Zelizer 1993, 224).

These unresolved dimensions are—one could argue—precisely the "abstraction[s], eval-uation[s], and constraint[s]", which, Lee and LiPuma (2002, 192) argue, are "created by the interactions between specific types of circulating forms [in this instance the imagery from Firdos Square] and the interpretive communities built around them. It is in these structured circulations that we [Lee and LiPuma] identify cultures of circulation".

Hall's notion of circulation is pointing in that direction through his focus on the various cracks and contingencies in the communicative circuit of television. But although his underlying premise, i.e. an industrial-like process centred on the commod-ity form, is still valid for parts of the communicative landscape of journalism, it does not quite account for adjacent and complimentary forms that have emerged. Using Hall's own terminology, one might say that the different "moments" linked (articulated) in the industrial processes have been interrupted by or interspersed with new and related cultures of circulation. The images at the centre of Hall's analysis—and exempli-fied by Firdos Square above—do not only pass through prescribed "moments" within an industrial-like process. A very concrete but illustrative example of this can be seen in the fact that not only commodified images were circulated from Firdos Square. The image of the toppling that appears on the Wikipedia entry on Firdos Square (the page containing image number seven in the Google search) is taken from an article on the site of the homepage of the US Department of Defense and is accompanied by the text in Figure 3.

What is prefigured here is the proliferation of images from various events that are circulated outside the established processes of news production. Some of the images on the Wikipedia entry on Firdos Square are attributed to Flickr and private individuals. Studies of circulation thus (partly) have to move away from the notion of circulation in the Marxist sense, i.e. a focus on the movement and understanding of the commodity form. The circulatory view embodied in, for instance, Hall's encoding, decoding model is an example here. Another is Fiske's notion of primary, secondary and tertiary texts (Fiske 1987). Both scholars take the commodity form as their primary text. However, too much analytical focus on the commodity form in terms of both economics and meaning may push aside some of the newer developments within or in relation to journalism.

Seen in relation to the processes conceptualized by Hall, this points to a certain de-industrialization in the sense that the "moments" discussed by Hall are no longer necessarily articulated in any predictable institutional order or context. Such a de-indus-trialization of information is, argue Chris Peters and Marcel Broserma, precisely what has escalated with the rise of new technological possibilities of accessing and circulat-ing media content. "This is", they say, "a tough challenge … because of the dominance of industrial logic in every thread of the industry and the profession" (Peters and Broserma 2013, 5). A part of this logic is intimately linked to temporality. The newspa-per as a "one-day best-seller" whose "obsolescence" created a daily "extraordinary mass

FIGURE 3
Wikipedia, May 10, 2013

ceremony" (Anderson 1991, 35) is being supplemented by a much more dispersed land-scape in which news stories are layered technologically, spatially and temporally. Such a landscape poses a problem, argues Barnhurst, for much (industrial) journalism, which,

> remains fixed in modernist time. Deadlines, scoops, exclusives and competition encour-age thinking of news as a time-value product with a short shelf life, but the new time regime involves a flow of change, along with the ever-present access to the archived past, with processes and networks as products. (Barnhurst 2013, 216)

The slice of imagery from Firdos Square is a good example of this. Increasingly, news is not only relevant on the day of publication but also is part of a baggage that is tacked along with subsequent stories. Many articles thus partly exhibit their own genealogy and as such present themselves as on-going media events. The temporal shift embod-ied in the move from chronicling to archiving constitutes a partial externalization or textualization of the layering of meaning that has always been part of the production of journalistic texts. In a digital landscape, various versions of a constantly updated text are spread and stored in a variety of settings. This is produced through circulation in a news landscape in which established cultures of journalism increasingly are drawn into close contact with other, complimentary and/or challenging, domains of circulation.

The Meaning of Circulation

The multifaceted build-up of a layered body of interconnected texts calls for a closer attention to circulation, which is—and has always been—a temporal process. An extended notion of circulation will have to be aligned much more closely with the (re-) production of cultures through circulation over time and space; and this is linked to the emergence of new cultures (and modes) of circulation that—to quote Hall again —can be seen as "other sources and other discursive formations within the wider socio-cultural and political structure of which [journalism is] a differentiated part" (Hall 1993, 92).

Tracing a specific photo from the example above may allow us to think more closely about how a journalistic item or form passes through and thus takes part in constituting various cultural contexts. A point of departure may thus be the photo in Figure 1 from the *International Herald Tribune* article that formed the somewhat ran-dom entry point into the sketchy mediated archaeology of the Firdos Square event. Tracing this specific image through the online service TinEye gives a very diverse list of websites containing this exact photo.[2] The specific pages containing this photo are spread geographically and temporally and are (mainly) made up of conventional news sites and various types of political sites and blogs—some of which are interlinked.

A good example is the article "John Pilger: Why Are Wars Not Being Reported Honestly?" from the *Guardian* (December 10, 2010). This article appears on a number of sites, for instance SHOAH—The Palestinian Holocaust.[3] The article was pasted here two days after its appearance on the *Guardian* site and referenced to Pilger and the *Guard-ian* but not linked directly. There is, however, a link to johnpilger.com. Most of these sites contain sharing possibilities of various sorts and some also show the number of shares. The Pilger article has, for instance, been shared on Facebook 2825 times and tweeted 116 times and is also accompanied by 163 comments (each of which also can be shared).

How this specific photo has ended up on all these sites is impossible to discover. We can simply state that it is there—and probably on a lot more sites since no searches on the internet are complete. What is certain, however, is that the copying, pasting, linking or sharing, or whatever tool was used in order to incorporate this photo, was a meaning-making act of circulation that helped constitute the specific culture of which it was or became a part. What, in this context, is important is thus not the meaning contained in the image itself but rather the processes that made this photo appear and thus be part of the constitution of cultures in many different contexts. From such a perspective "circulation and exchange" must be seen not simply as "processes that *transmit* meanings" but as "constitutive acts in themselves" within "*cultures of circulation*" (Lee and LiPuma 2002, 192, emphasis in the original).

As pointed out above, the act of pasting the Pilger story on the SHOAH site is an integral and constitutive act of maintaining the specific culture of circulation or community on that site, a site that is not journalism as such but which cannot be wholly separated from it either. Somehow, the culture related to this site and the culture of circulation of which Pilger is a part feed on each other. Such cultures are from this perspective, Lee and LiPuma continue, "created and animated by the cultural forms that circulate through them, including—critically—the abstract nature of the forms that underwrite and propel the process of circulation itself" (Lee and LiPuma 2002, 192).

The cultural forms referred to here would, in the example of the Firdos Square image, include both the objectified forms of the image, the accompanying texts, the attached sharing buttons and links *and* the related cultural abstract forms such as acts of sharing and reading and the cultural identities related to such acts. The point here is precisely that these different types of forms, both objectified and abstract, constitute each other *in and through circulation*. "[F]lows and forms are", say Gaonkar and Povinelli (2003, 387), "integrally related". Based on this, one may assert that journalism is constituted by flows of circulation, which from within its specific cultures (both institutional and non-institutional) are made up of interactions between "real" objectified means of circulation, e.g. the tools allowing the posting of a story on a newspaper's Facebook site or the counting of shares, and the conceptualizations of such acts in relation to what it means to be a journalist. And, seen from a different perspective, what linking to a story and liking mean for the users of journalism. And, not least, how such acts and conceptions make up interacting cultures of circulation.

Such processes call, in the words of Will Straw, for an analysis that "address[es] the conditions under which cultural forms occupy social space, interconnect and move in relation to each other" (Straw 2010, 23). The tracing and discussion of the Firdos Square imagery in this article could be seen as tiny steps towards such an analysis in the sense that it points at what Gaonkar and Povinelli (2003, 391) call "the proliferating co-presence of varied textual/cultural forms in all their mobility and mutability". Following from this, it must be stressed that journalism cannot, if it ever could, be understood based on a separation between production and consumption bridged by stable textual forms. A more appropriate analysis would thus mean following specific forms, like the Firdos Square imagery, across time and space in order to understand how such movements and related contexts interact and consequently constitute cultures of circulation and thus, ultimately, social meaning.

Studying such processes in real time is extremely difficult. Any attempt to trace such processes will inevitably be a re-tracing. And, as pointed out above, since such circulation processes constitute a possibly never-ending layering, there is no "natural" cut-off point at which any real-time tracing can argue to be complete. What we are left with are archaeologies of media events. These should, however, be more than merely focused on textual traces. Ideally, such studies should conduct observations in various and related cultures of circulation (as the Maass' "witness-article" from *The New Yorker* exemplifies). Such studies should not be detailed ethnographies of various cultures but rather an untangling of the constitutive cultural aspects of the various forms as they move across the communicational landscape.

In a certain sense, such a venture would come close to a materiality of journalism or a sociology of the objects of journalism (as developed in this special issue by Juliette De Maeyer and Florence Le Cam [2014]). Yet, the centre of a study of cultures of circulation would not be a specific materiality or object but rather the following of cultural forms "reproduced and copied across a range of media, genres and topics", as Lucaites and Hariman (2001, 37) say about the iconic image. One place to start would be with the "edges" of a range of cultural forms where edges are understood as that which "constitutes the interfaces of cultural artefacts with human beings and other forms, the surfaces which organize a form's mobility" (Straw 2010, 23). In the Firdos Square example, these are the various "handles" that allow people from different cultures to hurdle an image or text further on out of and into (new) cultures of circulation; to follow such trajectories would be something like following a space explorer capsule as it is propelled into the galaxy by the gravity of different planets. But whereas the capsule remains out of contact with that which moves it on, the meeting between an objectified form of journalism, e.g. an image, and a related culture of circulation alters and helps constitute the latter. Surfaces or edges are thus an integral part of the objectified and abstract forms of journalism and may in this be perceived as sharing, tweeting and alert buttons, links, likes, spaces of commentary, updates, etc., which again are intricately linked to the abstract forms, e.g. new journalist roles and reading positions.

Following the processes related to such edges and forms would be a conscious and important move beyond or—rather—across prevalent foci within journalism studies, namely media institutions, audiences, media texts and specific genres (often political news), which have often been framed—deductively and/or normatively—by theories of public spheres and/or democracy, visible, for instance, in the current occupation within journalism studies with questions of participation. Such a pre-occupation with journalism as a political resource has, however, often neglected the increasingly complex ways in which different cultural domains—politics, culture, work, leisure—are interwoven through media practices.

A perspective focusing on journalism as interrelated cultures of circulation is precisely premised on the argument that the institution of journalism cannot be understood in isolation from related cultures of circulation. This may to some extent always have been the case, but it also seems clear that the professional culture at the heart of the institution of journalism increasingly is drawn into much closer contact with other cultures of circulation. In this connection it is important to stress, with Zelizer (2008, 88), that "[s]eeing journalism as culture" is to regard acts within the landscape of journalism "as more than just the relay of a certain kind of information". And, very appropriately for the view of circulation proposed here, she expands further on:

When seen as culture, journalism grows in breadth: Variables that have traditionally kept certain aspects or kinds of journalism distinct—hard versus soft news, mainstream news versus tabloid, journalism's verbal reports versus the visual images they use—are repositioned as links across journalism's different tools, different conventions, and journalism's similarities with the non-journalistic world. (Zelizer 2008, 90)

Zelizer's notion of repositioning as links underlines the growing diversification of journalisms and their internal relations. One might also argue that this not only draws out "similarities with the non-journalistic world" but that this world is constitutive of the communicative landscape of journalism. If no "meaning is taken, there can be no consumption" as (Hall 1993, 91) argued—a point that is fundamental in his larger argument of circulation. Taking meaning and sharing have arguably always been part of the circulation of journalism. "It is", said Park (more than 70 years ago), "not the intrinsic importance of an event that makes it newsworthy. It is rather the fact that the event is so unusual that if published it will either startle, amuse, or otherwise excite the reader so that it will be remembered and repeated" (Park 1940, 669). Sharing is thus arguably an integral part of making meaning.

Audience communities and the conversations that take place within them are thus one of the cultures of circulation making up the wider communicative landscape of journalism. Bird (2011, 490) notes—based on a range of studies—"that culturally, news is not really about text—it is about process" and that the "rise of the internet and its multiple forms for ... sharing has greatly expanded and complicated this process". Following on from this, and bearing in mind that the *Reuters Institute Digital News Report 2013* states that "perhaps the biggest trend in this data is the growing importance of social discovery" (Newman and Levy 2013, 62), social media make up increasingly important cultures of circulation in the overall make-up of journalism.

Other related cultures of circulation could be termed alternative journalism (the SHOAH example above), user-generated content (exemplified by the non-professional photos discussed above) and, not least, corporate communication (e.g. the communicative efforts of the US military in the example above). These relations were traced by following imagery but are indicative of more general relations within journalism. Each of the related cultures identified above (and others, i.e. citizen journalism), as well as an increased re-use of content across institutions and platforms, push professional journalism away from what traditionally was conceived as a production culture and in the direction of what, with a contemporary term, could be called "curation", which refers to the growing activity of handling, filtering and circulating content emanating outside the sphere of professional journalism.

This increased interaction and its ensuing relations have been conceptualized in various ways; one of these is the notion of "network journalism". Drawing on various usages of this concept, Heinrich (2011) describes her "paradigm of network journalism" thus: "*Network journalism* ... stands for a model of changing connectivity modes and interaction patterns in today's global journalism sphere (61, emphasis in original). "This", she argues further on, "goes against the notion of strict one-way flow of information coming from a standard news source" and towards a more "complex system of information strings organized in a more 'chaotic way'" in which networks are "permeable" (63). This perspective indeed allows for a number of very productive insights. Yet, the overall focus on the network, although permeable and "chaotic", as "a *structural* concept" (61, emphasis in the original) may leave out domains that are only very weakly linked to what is already recognized as belonging to the journalistic sphere. Aronczyk and Craig (2012) precisely point towards the "ways in the metaphor of circulation can be used to trouble the problematic notion of network" (98) in the sense that this has a tendency to emphasize connectivity and order rather than "the kinds of interactions, situations and experiences that constitute the cultural forms" circulating through different social domains. This is a move away from "the hermeneutic tradition —the interpretation of meaning according to the model of the text" (94). A range of practices related to journalism has shifted their focus from texts to circulation. This is, however, challenging for many scholars in media and cultural studies.

ACKNOWLEDGEMENTS

I wish to thank Professor Will Straw (McGill University, Montreal) for pointing me in the direction of circulation and for insightful and constructive comments on and suggestions to earlier drafts of this article. I also wish to thank Associate Professor Steen Steensen (Oslo University, Oslo) for very valuable feedback both in person and in writing. Finally, I also wish to thank the unnamed reviewers for very relevant suggestions, not least in terms of literature.

NOTES

1. Maass refers to some interesting academic studies of the consequences of the "victory" coverage. This will not be developed here.
2. The online service TinEye (http://www.tineye.com) is "the first image search engine on the web to use image identification technology rather than keywords, metadata or watermarks. It is free to use for non-commercial searching". The image from the *International Herald Tribune* was searched through TinEye on May 16, 2013: http://www.tineye.com/search/54e79c4055944eb698c4cac15bf1310839158eed/?page=1&sort=score&order=desc.
3. See http://www.shoah.org.uk/2010/12/12/john-pilger-why-are-wars-not-being-reported-honestly/

REFERENCES

Anderson, Benedict. [1983] 1991. *Imagined Communities*. London: Verso.
Anderson, C. W. 2010. "Journalistic Networks and the Diffusion of Local News: The Brief, Happy News Life of the 'Francisville Four'." *Political Communication* 27 (3): 289–309.
Aronczyk, Melissa, and Ailsa Craig. 2012. "Introduction: Cultures of circulation." *Poetics* 40 (2): 93–100.
Barnhurst, Kevin. 2013. "'Trust me, I'm an Innovative Journalist', and other Fictions." In *Rethinking Journalism — Trust and Participation in a Transformed News Landscape*, edited by Chris Peters and Marcel Broersma, 210–220. London: Routledge.
Bird, Elizabeth. 2011. "Seeking the Audience for News — Response, News Talk as Cultural Phenomenon." In *The Handbook of Media Audiences*, edited by Virginia Nightingale, 489–508. Oxford: Blackwell.

De Maeyer, Juliette, and Florence Le Cam. 2014. "The Material Traces of Journalism: A Socio-historical Approach to Online Journalism." *Digital Journalism*. doi:10.1080/21670811.2014.928021.

Fiske, John. 1987. *Television Culture*. London: Routledge.

Gaonkar, D. P., and E. A. Povinelli. 2003. "Technologies of Public Forms: Circulation, Transfiguration, Recognition." *Public Culture* 15 (3): 385–398.

Goode, Luke. 2009. "Social News, Citizen Journalism and Democracy." *New Media & Society* 11 (8): 1287–1305.

Hall, Stuart. [1977] 1993. "Encoding/decoding." In *The Cultural Studies Reader*, edited by Simon During, 90–103. London: Routledge.

Heinrich, Ansgard. 2011. *Network Journalism — Journalistic Practice in Interactive Spheres*. London: Routledge.

Lee, Benjamin, and Edward LiPuma. 2002. "Cultures of Circulation: The Imaginations of Modernity." *Public Culture* 14 (1): 191–213.

Lucaites, John Louis, and Robert Hariman. 2001. "Visual Rhetoric, Photojournalism, and Democratic Public Culture." *Rhetoric Review* 20: 37–42.

Maass, Peter. 2011. "The Toppling — How the Media Inflated a Minor Moment in a Long War." *The New Yorker*, January 10.

Miller, James. 2012. "Mainstream Journalism As Anti-Vernacular Modernism." *Journalism Studies* 13 (1): 1–18.

Newman, Nic, and David A. L. Levy, eds. 2013. *Reuters Institute Digital News Report 2013 — Tracking the Future of News*. https://reutersinstitute.politics.ox.ac.uk.

Park, Robert E. 1929. "Urbanization as Measured by Newspaper Circulation." *The American Journal of Sociology* 35 (1): 60–79.

Park, Robert E. 1940. "News as a Form of Knowledge: A Chapter in the Sociology of Knowledge." *The American Journal of Sociology* 45 (5): 669–686.

Peters, Chris, and Marcel Broserma. 2013. "Introduction—Rethinking Journalism: The Structural Transformation of a Public Good." In *Rethinking Journalism — Trust and Participation in a Transformed News Landscape*, edited by C. Peters and M. Broersma, 1–12. London: Routledge.

Straw, Will. 2010. "The Circulatory Turn." In *The Wireless Spectrum: The Politics, Practices, and Poetics of Mobile Media*, edited by B. Crow, M. Longford, and K. Sawchuk, 17–28. Toronto: University of Toronto Press.

Ureta, Ainara L. 2011. "The Potential Of Web-only Feature Stories." *Journalism Studies* 12 (2): 188–204.

Valaskivi, Katja, and Johanna Sumiala. 2013. "Circulating Social Imaginaries: Theoretical and Methodological Reflections." *European Journal of Cultural Studies*, November 15, 2013.

Westlund, Oscar. 2013. "Mobile News — A Review and Model of Journalism in an Age of Mobile Media." *Digital Journalism* 1 (1): 6–26.

Zelizer, Barbie. 1993. "Journalists as Interpretive Communities." *Critical Studies in Mass Communication* 10: 219–237.

Zelizer, Barbie. 2008. "How Communication, Culture, and Critique Intersect in the Study of Journalism." *Communication, Culture & Critique* 1: 86–91.

PLACE-BASED KNOWLEDGE IN THE TWENTY-FIRST CENTURY
The creation of spatial journalism

Amy Schmitz Weiss

This study investigates how information and geographic space can be connected to a concept called place-based knowledge that can be applied within a journalistic framework of how we see journalism practice, news producers, consumers, and the news experience within this light. This connection of geographic space with place-based knowledge can form a unique concept called spatial journalism that is the main premise of this article. Future research directions are explored using this concept and implications of this approach are discussed for the future of the academy and profession.

Introduction

Digital technologies now allow news organizations to bring the news closer to the consumer than ever before—in the palm of their hand via the smartphone or tablet. In addition, these devices are embedded with geo-location or GPS capabilities (Farman 2012), opening a world of location-based activities for the on-the-go consumer. Nowadays, consumers are actively using location-based services for activities ranging from social networking to play (Sutko and de Souza e Silva 2011). They are also using their smartphones for other location-based services such as finding directions on a map, checking weather, finding local restaurants, going online for news about the community, and getting traffic information. Thus, the idea of location now takes on a different connotation for the individual in this digital era.

This study seeks to examine the traditions of location within journalism practice and the notions of geographic space and place in order to understand the evolution of location in today's digital media landscape to arrive at a unique juncture called spatial journalism.

Location-based Services—A Growing Industry

According to Gartner, location-based services is a growing industry. They predict revenue from such services will reach $13.5 billion in 2015 (Gartner 2012).

Location-based services are being incorporated into many aspects of digital life. As of January 2014 (Foursquare, n.d.), Foursquare had over 45 million users worldwide and over 5 billion check-ins with over a million businesses using their API (application programming interface) to develop their own "check-in" services. Twitter and Facebook now embed location into their mobile apps. Location is also becoming a part of online searches. Microsoft uses Foursquare for its Bing search engine results (Carr 2013). Google also offers location-based search results from its smartphone app. Recently, Yahoo was in business talks with Foursquare about possibly incorporating location data into their search tool (Carr 2013). The Google Maps app now enable users on the go to get real-time traffic information using Waze (Weiss 2013). Also, the launch of the latest iPhone includes embedded sensors to accommodate location-based services indoors (Epstein 2013).

All these uses of location-based services demonstrate that this kind of innovation is here to stay and its use will expand into many areas of digital life. Location-based services have the power to transform several industries, including the news industry.

The ability for news to be geo-located to your exact neighborhood, street corner or home address is not too far off to imagine. Many people might remember Adrian Holovaty's idea of Everyblock and its original premise of connecting readers to information at the city block level where it allowed users to search nearby public records, find articles based on location, and participate in a "geo-forum" about things near you (Holovaty 2012).

Holovaty's Everyblock did not reach its full potential as it was shut down in 2013 by MSNBC. However, there are other players trying to implement Holovaty's vision. CBC Hamilton in Canada is a media company that is currently experimenting with a geo-location model with news coverage in the Hamilton community. Launched in May 2012, they have a news website that has a local map on the homepage with pins on a map connected to specific news stories (Investigative News Network 2012).

CBC is the only organization currently experimenting with this format at the time of this study. The hesitancy by the overall news industry to use location-based services with news may be due to existing privacy and data security issues that remain in the discussion (Belicove 2012) about location-based services and content ownership. Many people remain concerned about the freedom that users have to opt-in and opt-out of such services and how much geo-located data companies have on such users when location is enabled.

Yet, despite these concerns, current trends and consumption habits show that a new form of location-based activity is occurring between the intersection of mobile, location-based services and news. A recent study found that 74 percent of smartphone users get location-based information (Zickhur 2013).

As for the academy, location can be considered a neglected unit of analysis when studying the field of journalism because it is assumed to be an automatic component of journalism practice by the sheer nature that most news has some location connected to it (e.g. news happening down the street, in another city, in the state or in another country).

Our understanding of location can also be understood by the deeper context and meaning that a location has that ties to a concept called place-based knowledge (Fisher 2012). Fisher states that place-based knowledge can entail the use of Geographical Information Systems (GIS)

> to embed all the knowledge relevant to a place in the myriad layers of information about it. And as we scroll over a place, we can select the pertinent layers and begin to see the relationships among disciplines and the connections among data. (Fisher 2012, 6)

Fisher presents this approach in a recent issue of ArcNews, a publication targeted to those who work in the field of GIS as practitioners and/or academics. He presents this concept as a way of showing how the details of information around us can be layered more effectively for consumption. He identifies that the arranging of knowledge may be best categorized by spatial phenomena.

However, knowing about the world around us by space alone may have its limitations when we consider those aspects that are space-less such as finite concepts (e.g. financial matters, health, etc.), emotions (e.g. depression, anger, happiness), or intangible assets (e.g. reputation, goodwill, intellectual property).

Yet, knowing about the world around us by spatial phenomena may make more sense when we consider the dimensions of timeliness. Timeliness is not only about what is happening now or in the past, but can also be tied to contextual elements such as historical spaces or moments (e.g. The Parthenon, JFK assassination, etc.) and it can also be tied to aspects of interconnectedness such as the sharing of a cultural tradition with others in a common space and place (e.g. parade, festival, etc.). This extension of timeliness to contextual elements and interconnectedness can be a bridge to the arrangement of our knowledge of the world around us as it relates to spatial phenomena.

Thus, this study seeks to build from Fisher's perspective and bring it into journalism practice to investigate how news and location can be connected to form a unique concept, which I call in this article, spatial journalism. This article addresses how spatial journalism helps to define the role and importance of location in today's digital media landscape.

Literature Review

The concept of spatial journalism derives from four research domains: journalism studies, mobile technologies, network theory, and media art via locative media. These four areas help to explain how location has been contextualized and how it can help bring together the different pieces of the puzzle concerning what spatial journalism is as well as its significance for the academy and journalism practice.

Journalism Studies

Location plays a significant role in journalism practice from the sense of what it means to report an event to deciding what news to cover to how the news consumer receives the news.

For as long as the journalism profession has existed, the location of where the news has happened has been an important part of what the journalist does (Tuchman 1978). For example, early nineteenth-century newspapers were based on where the town criers were located and the location of publishers became the central point for where information was exchanged (Tuchman 1978). Early muckrakers of the twentieth century conducted their news investigations based on the happenings at night court and its location (Tuchman 1978).

The traditions of location are connected to the basic aspects of the journalist's work in newsgathering and reporting. Reportage, the act or process of reporting the news, focuses on providing information to the public on events going on around them. Reportage allows an individual to have insight and knowledge about the world around them, take a break from the trivial aspects of their day, have a sense of reassurance, and to place the meaning of the world around them within a specific context (Carey 1987). Location can be tied to how reportage demonstrates the actions of the reporter and what information is gathered from where it takes place and how it is reported.

Location's use in journalism practice may also be considered as an organizing device for decision making by the reporter or editor via the concept of proximity—determining what news is by "how close the news is" based on what news is "nearby" or "close" to their audience.

For example, White's (1950) seminal study on the role of gatekeeping in the newsroom explained how an editor made the decision of what would go "in the gate and out of the gate." Those determinations were made by the editor's experiences, attitudes, and expectations, which also included location. Findings from this study showed that editorial decisions were tied to location in which the editor rejected wire stories that were "too far away," "out of area," or "too regional" for the intended audience (386).

In Galtung and Ruge's (1965) study of foreign news of four countries' crises, they identified that location can impact on how the news is covered and in what forms. Specifically, the distance of the location can impact on how the news is reported and how it is received and perceived by the audience. The further the news event's location is for an individual, the likelihood of its importance and understanding for the individual will be lessened.

This may be further explicated by the traditional values of what makes news worthy to cover[1] (Galtung and Ruge 1965, 70). However, these values may not be representative of values in the current media landscape. In their analysis, Harcup and O'Neill (2001) found that the Galtung and Ruge (1965) taxonomy was upheld but only captured big news events, crises, and did not capture daily news nor all types of news. Furthermore, they found that news values might communicate more how stories are covered versus why they are chosen in the first place.

Tuchman (1978) highlights that location and geography are central components in journalism but implied in the routine as part of the overall "news net." News creates and recreates social meanings as part of the news net. The news net makes three assumptions of the reader: that they are interested in occurrences at specific locations; concerned with activities of specific organizations; and interested in specific topics, out of which "geographic territoriality" is the most important (Tuchman 1978, 25).

This territory is marked by a boundary within the news organization of what news is deemed national or local by such editors. This determines which reporters or bureaus cover that news. In some cases, it can be hard to discern when a story may cross both a national and local focus, or it is hard to note the geographic boundary (Tuchman 1978, 26). Furthermore, this notion of territory can also be tied to the dependence of the publisher and their location, the location of the reporter, and the location of the source of the news item. Thus, location and geography can be considered a part of this news net and thus a construction of social meaning that is given to any news item.

Specific places and thus news stories can have greater meaning by how the journalist maps the meaning of their communities. The way in which they define news events, where they occur, and how they contextualize them dictates how the community understands what news happens around them in their community. "Journalists, in other words, produce a news geography, a representational space in which they situate their community and its people" (Gasher 2007, 299). Thus the tradition of location takes on a different meaning for journalism practice and the audience.

This may be further explicated by understanding location from a different perspective. The postmodern approach of "space" and "place" (Tuan 1977) has formed a unique area in scholarship where location has lived in other disciplines (e.g. geography, anthropology, theology, psychology, etc.) where studies have focused on how people interact with the concept of location. Space and place take on different social meanings. As such, a place is not a fixed matter of just a zipcode but something more fluid, "the first thing is to re-conceptualize place, specifically by conceiving of place as relational rather than stable and fixed" (Wilken 2008, 46).

The significance of location and this meaning of space and place can also be contextualized through the lens of community journalism and automated journalism in today's media landscape.

In recent years (Gillmor 2006; Singer et al. 2011), a larger focus has been placed on how journalism can better serve its publics by going micro instead of macro—going deeper into the community with "hyperlocal," "local," or community journalism efforts. This effort includes a focus on more narrow news coverage of particular areas in the community and the involvement of the news audience in a variety of ways from blogs to user-generated content. This has been demonstrated in a myriad of ways by several legacy media (e.g. *The New York Times*, *The Washington Post*, *Los Angeles Times*, etc.) and nonlegacy media (e.g. Baristanet, Outside.in, Patch by AOL, single-authored blogs, etc.) in recent years (Gordon and de Souza e Silva 2011). These efforts show that community journalism is not new, traditions extend back to Robert Parks' work with news and community formation in the early 1900s (Lowrey, Brozana, and Mackay 2008), but demonstrate that local remains very important today to the public—as bloggers have been at the forefront of getting local news to their audiences that is highly focused on location (whether that is a neighborhood, one city block, etc.), "blogs have raised the stakes of local coverage, because they have been able to converge the consumption of local information with the production of local information" (Gordon and de Souza e Silva 2011, 119).

It is important to note that location is not separate from community. A recent content analysis of mass communication scholarship on community journalism (Lowrey, Brozana, and Mackay 2008) highlighted that a majority of the studies defined community by its location. Community was defined by the concepts of towns, cities, and political districts, as well as where people meet and interact. The scholars concluded that community could tie to a negotiated shared meaning by its members and its geographical location. In return, community journalism helps to foster these concepts in both virtual and physical space. Thus, the extension of community journalism and its growing popularity and prominence has created a natural connection to the significance of location and journalism in today's media environment.

Furthermore, the development of automated journalism also plays a significant role for location and journalism today. Automated journalism is the act of having news content provided on the digital platform through specific computer algorithms that select and determine which news content appears on the platform and in which order (e.g. Google News). Automated journalism has become a popular and debated topic in the profession and the academy in recent years (Schroeder and Kralemann 2005) because of its possible impact on the journalistic profession. In relation to location, automated journalism can be a double-edged sword. Nowadays, computer algorithms have become sophisticated to the point where a user can enter in a location by zip-code, address, or place and it populates a list of relevant news content related to that query. This may prove helpful to news consumers seeking to find news by their address, but how does the computer algorithm define location? Does it take into consideration the cultural nuances and social meanings of a location for a news consumer? Automated journalism may provide a news feed of stories tied to a location but the relevance of the story may be lackluster if it is only querying datelines or street addresses in news content. As the digital platform and computer algorithms continue to develop, automated journalism poses an opportunity and a challenge for spatial journalism.

Today's digital media landscape embraces a new form of understanding space and place within the concept of augmented reality and mobile technologies that helps us to understand and relate to society in a new way (Wilken 2008). As mobile technologies such as the smartphone have become virtual appendages to our physical bodies, these devices have impacted the way we interact, communicate, and learn about the world around us as the ease and access of the mobile device has transformed how close we are to people, information, and places.

Mobile technologies cannot be overestimated for their influence on how place and space has been contextualized in this current timeframe (Gordon and de Souza e Silva 2011).

Mobile Technology Studies

In 2000, President Bill Clinton opened civilian access to GPS signals. This moment was instrumental because several companies saw the opportunity to use this to experiment with the possibilities of location with GPS devices and the mobile phone (Farman 2012, 19). Several experiments would lead to new innovations in the twenty-first century of how consumers would use their mobile phone for location-based services such as getting directions, for play (i.e. geocaching), and social networking (i.e. locative mobile social networking applications like Foursquare) (Farman 2012; Sutko and de Souza e Silva 2011).

Thus, the development of mobile technologies and location-based services nowadays plays an important role in today's society for helping consumers navigate their daily life but also how they make meaning of the places and spaces they travel through. de Souza e Silva (2004) states that mobile technologies are nomad technologies that create a hybrid form of space, "Nomadic technologies are mostly used for communication connected to mobility … Therefore, they become a part of our lives and also a part of our bodies" (de Souza e Silva 2004, 216).

As mobile and Web technologies advance, location-based services will become more pervasive in how people will understand and make meaning of the spaces in which they move, work, and play (Hardey 2007). Thus, there is a great need to examine and analyze the changes that location-based services have on society in a variety of contexts (Gordon and de Souza e Silva 2011). Sutko and de Souza e Silva (2011) state that location-based media studies are necessary to study at this juncture in communication scholarship because they help to extend existing theories of the virtual and real and reflect current communication phenomena of how individuals interact with each other and technology today.

The scholarship on location-based services is still fairly new. Studies thus far have examined the influence of geo-tagging and geo-location in various contexts, including social games (Licoppe and Inada 2006; de Souza e Silva and Sutko 2008; de Souza e Silva 2009), art displays in urban areas (Galloway and Ward 2006; Hemmet 2006; Hight 2006; Hudson and Zimmermann 2009; Levine 2006; Tuters and Varnelis 2006), and social networking (Humphreys 2007; Humphreys and Liao 2011). The impact of location-based services within the journalistic context has only been addressed in a handful of studies to date.

Nyre et al. (2012) developed a location-based news project called LocaNews that had two interfaces: one was a digital tool for people to access news on their smartphone, and the other a digital tool for the reporter to access via their smartphone in order to write the story and incorporate location into their story.

They tested the digital tool on 32 users in conjunction with a week-long event and observed the reporters and the public using the tool. Few people were able to understand how to view the news through this location format and the reporters had issues in categorizing and classifying news to a specific location. Nyre et al. (2012) had three versions of stories in the digital tool categorized by "here," "nearby," and "far" to tie to three aspects of proximity. Nyre et al. (2012) stated they had challenges in setting up criteria for the reporters to know which of the three categories to choose when marking the location for a story and for the readers to understand which category to view from depending on where they were. The researchers concluded that it was easy to build the digital tool but harder to change journalistic practice.

Another study (Schmitz Weiss 2013) identified the use of mobile phones for location-based services by young adults and how news organizations were utilizing location-based services in their news apps. Based on survey findings, the author found young adults were consuming news on their smartphones and there was a high use of location-based services including consumption of local news content through such services. Yet, in a content analysis of over 100 top news organizations' (television, radio, print) mobile apps, few were using geo-location features in their mobile apps and if they were, then they were mainly used for geo-locating traffic and weather. The study pointed out a gap between what news consumers are doing and using on their smartphones and what news organizations are able to provide when it comes to geo-located news content. Considering this gap, there are possibilities for the news industry to innovate and create new media products that provide location-based services in their news dissemination and distribution models that are more advanced than the traditional forms of organizing media audiences through market research, market analysis, and zoning.

Network Theory

Another research domain to be discussed is network theory and its connection with location through space and place.

Network theory is the study of the symmetric and asymmetric relations between objects (Newman, Barabasi, and Watts 2006). Network theory has for years influenced scholars to explore the interconnections among all kinds of phenomena, from the connections in human relations, in biology, in mathematics, and the internet (Barabasi and Albert 1999; Erdos and Renyi 1959; Milgram 1967; Newman, Barabasi, and Watts 2006; Pool and Kochen 1978; Watts and Strogatz 1998).

Network theory has also been explored within the mass communications realm from the lens of Castells' (2000) Network Society. His focus has been on the power of the network as it relates to information and the global society. Castells' research set a new path of scholarship about where the power of the network could be taken—within communications specifically. For Castells (2000), the future of society is based on an information-based economy where social action and organization are embraced and nurtured in a network that is open, dynamic, and ever-changing. Within this perspective, Castells identifies that space has a significant role in the overall social structure of society.

Castells (2000, 443) identifies that there is a space of flows with three layers: a circuit of electronic exchanges (e.g. mobile and Web technologies), nodes and hubs (e.g. the network links up with specific places with social, cultural, physical, and functional characteristics), and spatial organization of the dominant, managerial elites.

Places are not just physical locales but are areas that have meaning and characteristics that are unique to the people who live, work, and play there, "Not all places are socially interactive and spatially rich. It is precisely because their physical/symbolic qualities make them different that they are places" (Castells 2000, 457).

Nowadays, our focus on places has to go beyond just the street address or block to peel away the layers that give meaning to the street address or the block within its social, cultural, and functional nuances.

Our idea of place does not have to be exact, it can be relative. Famous social psychologist Stanley Milgram and researchers (Milgram et al. 1972) conducted a unique experiment with New Yorkers to see how they could identify pictures of specific places in boroughs in New York on a map. Of the 152 scenes shown to the respondents, most respondents got the scenes wrong. A majority plotted the scenes to the Manhattan borough instead of their actual borough. Milgram's study highlights the aspect of "relative recognizability" and that we make meaning of the neighborhoods we know and recognize. We come to know of the spaces around us not by a specific geographic coordinate but by the connections we have in the network to the social, cultural, relative understandings we have to places and where they are located.

This new logic of understanding location within the network must not be separated from the layers of information that are embedded within it and how that translates into specific meanings for the everyday citizen.

Locative Media

Lastly, the idea of location can be further understood by examining the research domain of locative media and how it helps to bring the layers of information and knowledge to a deeper level in society through various media forms.

Locative media is a term coined by Karlis Kalnins who hosted a research workshop with several scholars in 2003 in Latvia that focused on GPS, mapping, and location-aware technologies (Locative Media 2003). Locative media takes into consideration how different media forms (e.g. art, video, audio, etc.) can be tied to physical space but also be virtual and location-absent. Since 2003, locative media has become a unique and important area of research for several scholars in various disciplines. *Leonardo Electronic Almanac* devoted a special issue to the subject in 2004. Locative media projects have been mainly organized as annotative or phenomenological in scope (Tuters and Varnelis 2006).

One of the most well-known projects of locative media stems from media art: the MILK project from 2005 (Tuters and Varnelis 2006). Researchers traced the milk from a rural Lativan cow to a cheese vendor in the Netherlands through GPS technology. They visualized the path on a digital map and transformed it into an artistic exhibition. The power of the project was not just an exercise in art, but showed the power of locative technologies, digital media, the aspects of global trade and power in a globalized world.

Furthermore, locative media studies have examined the mediation of technology in current placemaking in artwork (Cornelio and Ardevol 2011), the impact of digital mapping via locative art (Hemmet 2006), the role and impact of sound (Behrendt 2012) tied to location, the impact of archaeology and the mapping of people and spaces over time (Galloway and Ward 2006), and the impact of online applications on geo-located communities (Hamilton 2009).

As this area of scholarship is still fairly young, there is more room for research and further investigation of locative media in various contexts. Tuters (n.d.) conceptualizes the potential of locative media in the future as one that facilitates "awareness" in how information is consumed from locative media.

Thus, the research in locative media provides another lens to see how location can be contextualized in the scholarship with new understanding of the places around us and its meaning.

Spatial Journalism

Taking the four research domains and their explication of location, we can now arrive at the concept of spatial journalism. First, it is important to define how we got here, and then discuss its significance as well as the future of this concept for journalism studies and digital journalism practice.

First, journalism studies show us how much location has been a part of practice, journalist's routines, and the consumer's behavior with the news. We can see that the unit of location has been subsumed into the scholarship without giving much recognition or importance to it. This lack of direct attention and focus on location in journalism can be a limitation to understanding the nuances of how journalism is defined, how it is performed by journalists on a daily basis, and how consumers take in the news they receive daily. Furthermore, it can also limit us in not seeing the weaknesses in journalism in how location isolates, separates, or segregates the way in which news is identified, covered, and consumed. Spatial journalism can provide a deeper lens to explore these nuances in the field by breaking apart location and bringing it forward as the main focus.

Second, the study of mobile technology is not separate or unknown to the field of journalism. In fact, studies (Nyre et al. 2012; Schmitz Weiss 2013) show that mobile technology is having a direct impact on the journalism field. As the mobile device becomes ubiquitous and easily accessible, the idea of mobile location becomes prominent, not just because of the device but also because of the individual now using the device. This brings the idea of location closer to the individual than ever before through location-based services—a person can now find a restaurant, search for a business while they are out and about—just by using their mobile device. Spatial journalism provides an opportunity to explore how these worlds of location-based services, mobile technology, and information can form a powerful union in understanding communication phenomena today. It can help to break down the components of what represents news and information for the individual, how they interact with it via the location-based service they are using, the kind of location they are identifying with, and how the mobile device brings it all together.

Third, network theory and its scholarship in the communication realm (Castells 2000) provides another unique perspective to understanding journalism, the news industry, and the news consumer today. In particular, it provides a unique bridge to the concepts of place and space. Place and space are both different and one in the same, but also related to location based on the meaning that the person places on it. The scholarship (Milgram et al. 1972; Tuan 1977; Wilken 2008) shows us that the idea of place and space within our networked global environment provides us an outlet to see exactly how location can be defined beyond just geographic coordinates or zip-code, it can take on a different meaning. Spatial journalism provides that bridge between finite and nontacit location.

Lastly, locative media scholarship (Behrendt 2012; Cornelio and Ardevol 2011; Galloway and Ward 2006; Hamilton 2009; Hemmet 2006; Tuters, n.d.; Tuters and Varnelis 2006) highlights how storytelling can occur through the ways in which individuals and groups assign meaning to location around the world and demonstrate them as art performance. It takes a unique approach to understanding how people define the meaning of location within a performing arts lens. Spatial journalism helps to broaden this approach of locative media and the possibilities of expanding our notions of what meaning making is as it relates to news content.

Drawing on these four research domains, spatial journalism can be defined as the kinds of information that incorporate a place, space, and/or location (physical, augmented, and virtual) into the process and practice of journalism. Location in this context can be either relative and/or an absolute location.

Spatial journalism is not limited to examining just the journalists in the newsroom and the practice, but can extend into all aspects of journalism, from content production to news consumption. For those in the academy, the study of journalism and its practice can be rich by examining it through the lens of spatial journalism, as detailed in Table 1.

In order to examine any of the areas outlined in Table 1, spatial journalism requires the following components when applied to any phenomena:

- information must be communicated across one or several channels (e.g. digital, mobile, etc.) to a group or public;

TABLE 1
Spatial journalism and areas of academic inquiry

Area of study	Operationalization of study
News consumption patterns and behaviors	Examine the places people choose to read about as well as why and how they locate that information
News content analysis via deeper layers of proximity and place	Examine the places presented in the news story for its context and meaning by the community
Mobile device use of location-based information and news	Examine the news consumer's uses of location-based news on the smartphone or tablet. Does the individual perform this action through search? Through an app?
News editorial decisions	Identify how communities are defined (not by zipcode or neighborhood) by journalists and the meaning of places that are decided newsworthy
Journalistic routines	Examine how reporters determine which places to cover as part of a daily beat, and how geography is defined and conceptualized in their daily work
Creation, production, curation, and aggregation of news content	Examine why spaces and places are covered in communities and how they shape the audience understandings of such locations
News story layers by attribution, facts, opinion, media type, and data	Examine the specific people, entities, places that are conceptualized in a news story and the meaning it carries

- information must be connected to its social meaning via a place, space, and/or location (physical, augmented, virtual); and
- information must be considered a form of journalism (e.g. text articles, websites, videos, graphics, multimedia pieces, blog posts, broadcasts/programs, print publications, tablet magazines, etc.).

The application of the concept and components of spatial journalism may thus be studied in a variety of current journalistic phenomenon. A concrete example is community journalism (Gordon and de Souza e Silva 2011) and using the spatial journalism approach to better understand the depth and breadth of how communities are being covered from within and outside the newsroom. Furthermore, it can help in operationalizing how "local" is defined and what those social meanings of "local" represent in relation to the spatializing of knowledge.

As for the profession, spatial journalism can help editors, reporters, designers, programmers, videographers, and others in the newsroom have a better understanding of the work they do and how they perform it. It can provide them a deeper lens to understand the communities they cover, not just by significant or prominent individuals, historical landmarks, or specific addresses, but the layers of meaning that make up the areas that they cover and where the public works, lives, and plays daily. It can showcase the successes of what the news organization is doing right and what they are doing wrong in regards to the kinds of issues or communities they are not addressing that are important to cover. It may also bring news audiences closer to news organizations as the news audience finds that the stories they read and consume are closer to identifying the world they know and want to know more about in the places and spaces they frequently visit.

Conclusions and Discussion

The tradition of location has had a unique spot in scholarship—whether that is in journalism studies, mobile technology, or locative media. But, now we can see the power of digital technologies (e.g. mobile devices) that enable location-based services to open a new form of discussion related to the power of location and information in a variety of contexts across a range of communication phenomenon. The convenience and access of mobile devices can enable and nurture new habits and patterns of how location can become a bigger part of an information-rich digital life (Deuze 2007).

Also, location plays a significant role in how communities function and how they see themselves. Mersey (2009) found that geography and the news resonates with the public and how they see and live in their own communities based on her survey of online newspaper readers. She found that readers had a strong geographic sense of their community, whether they were active online users or not.

Democracy can be geographically constructed (Mersey 2009) and can play a significant role in how a community operates by how the citizens make sense of the spaces and places around them that are governed for the people and by the people. That community is defined by a space and how people come to understand that space—if it is a series of blocks, a zipcode area, or a region that they identify by the places they frequent daily. Milgram and Jodelet (2010) identify that a city is a social fact, a collective representation of what is shared by the individuals who live there and how they make meaning of the streets, buildings, parks, and other places around them and use them daily in their lives. Thus, as the public interprets their surrounding world that is underlined by relative and absolute location, a strong link can also be formed with the democratic tradition and function of journalism.

We have to understand how location and the role of geography have significance for the democratic function of journalism. Can location communicate forms of more or less freedom as well as more or less equality of the coverage of communities that are covered? Spatial journalism can provide that lens to examine how the journalism profession, journalism practice, and news consumer's habits are being shaped in the digital media landscape as location takes on a different meaning and understanding. From the opposite perspective, spatial journalism can also identify the holes, gaps, and lack of attention given to communities that are underrepresented or not represented at all. It can highlight social and cultural issues tied to race, class, and socioeconomics. It can expose the issues and faults of a journalism practice that aims to serve a democratic function.

Geographic construction of democracy is not a novel concept but one that is sound in context, history, and time, thus highlighting the importance of the concept of spatial journalism in a democratic society.

Furthermore, as digital and mobile technologies are adopted into society and their uses expand into other aspects of daily life, one has to also be cognizant of the power of such technologies that incorporate their own cultural, political, and economic biases (Barreneche 2012; Castells 2000; Deuze 2007). Barreneche (2012) highlights the potential issues with using such tools (e.g. Google Places) and how these tools may be subject to specific interpretations of daily space around us.

Location can create different meanings of the spaces in which we live, work, and play, but location can also create distortions of reality (Zook and Graham 2007). For example, some places or locations may not be exactly marked to a particular set of coordinates on a digital map. Consider rural areas and places unseen or less known by popular travel. If these places are not visited or traveled through, do they not exist? Does their lack of recognition in the digital sphere on mobile devices through location-based services deny the reality of their actual importance and meaning to the people who do frequent those lesser-known locations or spaces? Does it make the journalism in these areas any less important?

These are important questions to address as the development of location progresses in the future. It also highlights the need for journalism scholars to examine how location and information are being interpreted, aggregated, curated, organized, and presented with the latest and upcoming digital mobile technologies in society.

Thus, spatial journalism provides the lens and framework through which to examine these aspects and how they influence communication phenomenon around the world and its impact on journalistic practice. Spatial journalism opens up new pathways for the academy and the profession to examine and understand the importance of location within a journalistic context and its impact on how we see ourselves and make sense of the world around us.

NOTE

1.   For example, frequency, threshold, absolute intensity, intensity increase, unambiguity, meaningfulness, cultural proximity, relevance, consonance, predictability, demand, unexpectedness, unpredictability, scarcity, continuity, composition, and reference to elite nations.

REFERENCES

Barabasi, Albert-Laszlo, and Reka Albert. 1999. "Emergence of Scaling in Random Networks." *Science* 286 (5439): 509–512.

Barreneche, Carlos. 2012. "Governing the Geocoded World: Environmentality and the Politics of Location Platforms." *Convergence: The International Journal of Research into New Media Technologies* 18 (3): 331–351.

Behrendt, Frauke. 2012. "The Sound of Locative Media." *Convergence: The International Journal of Research into New Media Technologies* 18 (3): 283–295.

Belicove, Mikal. 2012. "Privacy of Location-based Services on FCC's Radar." *Entrepreneur.com*, http://www.entrepreneur.com/blog/223940.

Carey, John. 1987. *The Faber Book of Reportage*. London: Faber and Faber.

Carr, Austin. 2013. "Why Yahoo And Apple Want Foursquare's Data." *Fast Company*, August 23. http://www.fastcompany.com/3016250/why-yahoo-and-apple-want-foursquares-data.

Castells, Manuel. 2000. *The Rise of the Network Society*. Malden, MA: Wiley-Blackwell.

Cornelio, Gemma, and Elisenda Ardevol. 2011. "Practices of Place-making Through Locative Media Artworks." *Communications* 36: 313–333.

Deuze, Mark. 2007. *Media Work*. Cambridge: Polity Press.

Epstein, Zach. 2013. "Apple's iPhone 5s Ushers in the Future of Indoor Location-based Services." *BGR*, September 13. http://bgr.com/2013/09/13/iphone-5s-m7-analysis-location-based-services/.

Erdos, Paul, and Alfred Renyi. 1959. "On Random Graphs." *Publicationes Mathematicae* 6: 290–297.

Farman, Jason. 2012. "Historicizing Mobile Media." In *The Mobile Media Reader*, edited by Noah Arceneaux and Anadam Kavoori, 9–22. New York, NY: Peter Lang.

Fisher, Thomas. 2012. "Place-based Knowledge in the Digital Age." *ArcNews* 34 (3): 1–6.

Foursquare. n.d. About Foursquare. *Foursquare.com*, https://foursquare.com/about.

Galloway, Anne, and Michael Ward. 2006. "Locative Media as Socialising and Spatialising Practices: Learning From Archaeology." *Leonardo Electronic Almanac* 14 (3): 12.

Galtung, Johan, and Mari Holmboe Ruge. 1965. "The Structure of Foreign News." *Journal of Peace Research* 2 (1): 64–91.

Gartner. 2012. "Gartner Highlights Top Consumer Mobile Applications and Services for Digital Marketing Leaders." *Gartner.com*, October 11. http://www.gartner.com/newsroom/id/2194115.

Gasher, Mike. 2007. "The View From Here: A News-flow Study of the On-Line Editions of Canada's National Newspapers." *Journalism Studies* 8 (2): 299–319.

Gillmor, Dan. 2006. *We the Media: Grassroots Journalism by the People, for the People*. Sebastopol, CA: O'Reilly Media.

Gordon, Eric and Adriana de Souza e Silva. 2011. *Net Locality*. Malden, MA: Wiley-Blackwell.

Hamilton, Jillian G. 2009. "Ourplace: The Convergence of Locative Media and Online Participatory Culture." *The Proceedings of OZCHI 2009* 23–27.

Harcup, Tony, and Deirdre O'Neill. 2001. "What is News? Galtung and Ruge Revisited." *Journalism Studies* 2 (2): 261–280.

Hardey, Michael. 2007. "The City in the Age of Web 2.0: A New Synergistic Relationship Between Place and People." *Information, Communication & Society* 10 (6): 867–884.

Hemmet, Drew. 2006. "Locative Media." *Leonardo Electronic Almanac* 14 (3–4): 5.

Hight, Jeremy. 2006. "Views From Above: Locative Narrative and the Landscape." *Leonardo Electronic Almanac* 14 (7–8): 1–9.

Holovaty, Adrian. 2012. "Onto the Next Chapter." *Holovaty.com*, August 15. http://www.holovaty.com/writing/goodbye-everyblock/.

Hudson, Dale, and Patricia Zimmermann. 2009. "Taking Things Apart: Locative Media, Migratory Archives, and Micropublics." *Afterimage* 36 (4): 15–19.

Humphreys, Lee. 2007. "Mobile Social Networks and Social Practice: A Case Study Of Dodgeball." *Journal of Computer-mediated Communication* 13 (1): 341–360.

Humphreys, Lee, and Tony Liao. 2011. "Mobile Geotagging: Reexamining Our Interactions With Urban Space." *Journal of Computer-mediated Communication* 16 (3): 407–423.

Investigative News Network. 2012. Case Study: CBC Hamilton. http://investigativenewsnetwork.org/guides/case-studies-of-nonprofit-news-organizations/case-study-cbc-hamilton/.

Levine, Paula. 2006. "Art and GPS." *Leonardo Electronic Almanac* 14 (3–4): 3.

Licoppe, Christian, and Yoriko Inada. 2006. "Emergent Uses of a Multiplayer Location-aware Mobile Game: The Interactional Consequences of Mediated Encounters." *Mobilities* 1 (1): 39–61.

Locative Media. 2003. "Location-based Workshop in Karosta." Latvia, http://locative.x-i.net/intro.html.

Lowrey, Wilson, Amanda Brozana, and Jenn B. Mackay. 2008. "Toward a Measure of Community Journalism." *Mass Communication and Society* 11: 275–299.

Mersey, Rachel Davis. 2009. "Online News Users' Sense of Community: Is Geography Dead?" *Journalism Practice* 3 (3): 347–360.

Milgram, Stanley. 1967. "The Small-world Problem." *Psychology Today* 1 (1): 61–67.

Milgram, Stanley, and Denise Jodelet. 2010. "Psychological Maps of Paris." In *The Individual in a Social World*. 3rd ed, edited by Tom Blass, 77–100. London: Pinter & Martin.

Milgram, Stanley, Judith Greenwald, Suzanne Kessler, Wendy McKenna, and Judith Waters. 1972. "A Psychological Map of New York City." *American Scientist* 60 (2): 194–200.

Newman, Mark, Albert-Laszlo Barabasi, and Duncan Watts, eds. 2006. *The Structure and Dynamics of Networks*. NJ: Princeton University Press.

Nyre, Lars, olveig Bjørnestad, Bjørnar Tessem, and Kjetil Vaage Øie. 2012. "Locative Journalism: Designing a Location-dependent News Medium for Smartphones." *Convergence: The International Journal of Research into New Media Technologies* 18 (3): 297–314.

Pool, Ithiel de Sola, and Manjked Kochen. 1978. "Contacts and Social Influence." *Social Networks* 1 (1): 5–51.

Schmitz Weiss, Amy. 2013. "Exploring News Apps and Location-based Services on the Smartphone." *Journalism & Mass Communication Quarterly* 90 (3): 435–456.

Schroeder, Roland, and Moritz Kralemann. 2005. "Journalism Ex Machina*/Google News, Germany and Its News Selection Processes." *Journalism Studies* 6 (2): 245–247.

Singer, Jane, Alfred Hermida, David Domingo, Ari Heinonen, Steve Paulussen, Thorsten Quandt, Zvi Reich, and Marina Vujnovic. 2011. *Participatory Journalism: Guarding Open Gates at Online Newspapers*. Malden, MA: Wiley-Blackwell.

de Souza e Silva, Adriana. 2004. "From Simulations to Hybrid Space, How Nomadic Technologies Change the Real." *Technoetic Arts: An International Journal of Speculative Research* 1 (3): 209–221.

de Souza e Silva, Adriana. 2009. "Hybrid Reality and Location-based Gaming: Redefining Mobility and Game Spaces in Urban Environments." *Simulation & Gaming* 40 (3): 404–424.

de Souza e Silva, Adriana and Daniel M. Sutko. 2008. "Playing Life And Living Play: How Hybrid Reality Games Reframe Space, Play, and the Ordinary." *Critical Studies in Media Communication* 25 (5): 447–465.

Sutko, Daniel M., and Adriana de Souza e Silva. 2011. "Location-aware Mobile Media and Urban Sociability." *New Media & Society* 13 (5): 807–823.

Tuan, Yi-Fu. 1977. *Space and Place: The Perspective of Experience*. Minneapolis, MN: University of Minnesota Press.

Tuchman, Gaye. 1978. *Making News: A Study in the Construction of Reality*. New York, NY: Free Press.

Tuters, Marc. n.d. "The Locative Utopia." http://www.itu.dk/~amie/Digital%20%E6stetik/Be fri_kunsten/Litteratur/locative_utopia_tuters.pdf.

Tuters, Marc, and Kazys Varnelis. 2006. "Beyond Locative Media: Giving Shape to the Internet of Things." *Leonardo Electronic Almanac* 39 (4): 357–363.

Watts, Duncan J., and Steven H. Strogatz. 1998. "Collective Dynamics of 'Small-world' Networks." *Nature* 393: 440–442.

Weiss, Todd. 2013. "Google Maps Mobile Users Can Now Get Waze Traffic Reports." *eWeek*, August 21. http://www.eweek.com/mobile/google-maps-mobile-users-can-now-get-waze-traffic-reports/#sthash.T92rf9wK.dpuf.

White, David Manning. 1950. "The 'Gate Keeper': A Case Study in the Selection of News." *Journalism Quarterly* 27: 383–390.

Wilken, Rowan. 2008. "Mobilizing Place: Mobile Media, Peripatetics, and the Renegotiation of Urban Places." *Journal of Urban Technology* 15 (3): 39–55.

Zickhur, Kathyrn. 2013. "Location-based Services." *Pew Internet & American Life Project*, September 12. http://pewinternet.org/Reports/2013/Location/Overview.aspx.

Zook, Matthew, and Mark Graham. 2007. "Mapping DigiPlace: Geocoded Internet Data and the Representation of Place." *Environment and Planning B: Planning and Design* 34: 466–482.

FROM GRAND NARRATIVES OF DEMOCRACY TO SMALL EXPECTATIONS OF PARTICIPATION
Audiences, citizenship, and interactive tools in digital journalism

Chris Peters and **Tamara Witschge**

This article critically examines the invocation of democracy in the discourse of audience participation in digital journalism. Rather than simply restate the familiar grand narratives that traditionally described journalism's function for democracy (information source, watchdog, public representative, mediation for political actors), we compare and contrast conceptualisations of the audience found within these and discuss how digital technologies impact these relationships. We consider how "participatory" transformations influence perceptions of news consumption and draw out analytic distinctions based on structures of participation and different levels of engagement. This article argues that the focus in digital journalism is not so much on citizen engagement but rather audience or user interaction; instead of participation through news, the focus is on participation in news. This demands we distinguish between minimalist and maximalist versions of participation through interactive tools, as there is a significant distinction between technologies that allow individuals to control and personalise content (basic digital control) and entire platforms that easily facilitate the storytelling and distribution of citizen journalism within public discourse (integrative structural participation). Furthermore, commercial interests tend to dominate the shaping of digital affordances, which can lead to individualistic rather than collective conceptualisations. This article concludes by considering what is gained as well as lost when grand visions of journalism's roles for democracy are appropriated or discarded in favour of a participation paradigm to conceptualise digital journalism.

Introduction

Democracy has long been a pivotal concept in analysing, evaluating, and critiquing journalism. Indeed, the coupling of the two is almost axiomatic; for centuries, especially in the Anglo-American world, a robust democracy has implied a free press, a "Fourth Estate more important far than they all" (Carlyle 1840), and still does to this day. Moreover, the industry traditionally asserts its institutional legitimacy and associated discourses of value based upon these classic democratic notions. It is a watchdog, a fourth estate, a representative of the people (McNair 2009). However, whereas the dominant, established discourses connecting journalism and democracy feature grand narratives and strong notions of democracy (and consequently high demands of journalism and high expectations of citizens), in the age of digital journalism the emphasis oftentimes seems to shy away from this to stress the interactional possibilities afforded by new media. In many articulations, the focus is not so much on *citizen* engagement but rather *audience* or *user* interaction; instead of theorising and empirically examining journalism's role for democracy (participation *through* news), the focus is on participation *in* news. Democracy does not so much feature as the main aim in this new wave of digital journalism, but is still an important part of the discourse surrounding it: democracy in journalism, rather than through it.

This has consequences for the institutional and societal position envisioned for journalism in a digital age and the associations we make with ideas of democracy, publics, and citizenship. Derivative concepts aligned with the idea of democracy, such as participation, interaction, and openness, are increasingly espoused by and coupled with mainstream professional journalism through its various user-based initiatives. However, the scope for participation that many of these opportunities provide is somewhat limited and their affordances are highly individualised. In this respect, allowing people more opportunities to interact with the "mass media" does not necessarily mean such practices translate to greater inclusivity or "thicker" forms of citizenship.

Conversely, rather than focus on changes in the "top down" mass media, many emphasise the emerging possibilities generated through new media initiatives. Niche journalism outlets are frequently posited as sites for more robust democratic notions such as civic empowerment and active citizenship. However, such initiatives exist largely at the margins, with far lesser reach than established news outlets, which does imply a fairly narrow "public" to which they are oriented. Accordingly, we must be wary of conceptualising the democratic efficacy of the changing media landscape in a manner that succumbs to a "reductionist discourse of novelty" that tends to privilege new media and laud the exceptional (Carpentier 2009, 408).

Whether one considers changes in established or emerging news outlets, one commonality is to situate the analytic centrality of transformations in terms of the institution and/or its technological initiatives. This way of thinking through the democratic possibilities of digital journalism follows a tendency in journalism studies to rely on "the audience" to justify the importance of change but to then subordinate it analytically to production, convergence, and content, and thus render it implicit (Madianou 2009). In this article, we focus on and attempt to clarify the discrepancy that arises from this decentring and address it by starting from the perspective of the audience. This double special issue of *Digital Journalism* and *Journalism Practice* looks to reassess theories on journalism and democracy in the current era, and we argue that an audience-centred, or at least audience-inclusive, perspective on the (democratic and societal) functions of journalism is crucial if we want theory that is not only internally consistent but also aligns with—and is testable against—people's lived experiences.[1]

The shift from a mass press to a more hybrid networked media ecology raises many questions for digital journalism in terms of the relationship between audiences and journalistic institutions. While by no means exhaustive or exclusive, we can posit that some combination of the following is likely (and to some extent in the latter cases, is already happening):

1. "Legacy" journalism outlets will somehow stabilise their increasingly precarious usage rates amongst audiences and/or strengthen cross-subsidy funding models to cement their standing as key societal institutions that safeguard democratic functions (such as informing audiences, acting as their representative conduit, and auditing the powerful for them).

2. New "niche" media outlets will take the place of older outlets, providing specialised democratic services, on an "as needed" basis, as part of more tailored and diversified media repertoires.
3. Media outlets claiming to do journalism in the classic democratic sense will be replaced by other forms of communication (direct address from governments and special interests, information curated and sourced by crowds, and so forth).

These scenarios form a forward-looking backdrop to the theoretical discussions entertained in this article. Underlying the question of significance in all of them is the question of how we view participation and the different ways we envision democracy and journalism's function within it through the eyes of the audience. More specifically, the political ramifications of such transformations are significant and demand specifying the particularities of the possible experiences of involvement that audiences have from the media they consume and engage with (Peters 2011). In this sense, the analytic aim of this article is to evaluate how the established political philosophies of journalism intertwine with the shifting particularities of journalism's audiences, both in terms of collective experience and individualised use, in an increasingly wired world.

We first discuss the traditional narratives that connect news to democracy, but rather than simply restate these familiar notions, we try to envision how the audience is conceptualised through such discourses. From here, we explore the ways new media technologies impact this relationship, and by association, the democratic functions of journalism. This leads to the next section of this article, in which we consider how "participatory" transformations impact how we view the practice of accessing politically and socially relevant information. This section draws out some initial analytic distinctions based on structures in which participation is embedded and the levels of engagement with digital journalism. The final section concludes by exploring how collective versus individualistic ways of conceptualising the democratic subject and the participatory tools made available to them potentially impacts journalistic purpose and production in a digital era.

The Grand Narratives of Journalism's Role for Democracy in the Digital Age

The roles attributed to journalism in most Western democracies are exceedingly familiar: we look to the news media to inform about issues of public concern; to function as a watchdog, monitor those in power; represent the public in political matters; and to mediate for political actors. While perhaps not in these specific terms, in the increasingly mediated landscape of the twentieth century these notions became familiar not only to scholars and journalists but also to the so-called "general public" itself (Hackett and Zhao 1998). The relationship is a prime example of a double hermeneutic: as the journalism industry and those who study it came to describe and configure its role in democracy, audiences came to engage with these definitions. This in turn shapes—and potentially changes—the roles journalism plays within society and our scientific understanding of it. Thus, it is instructive to review how four of the principal functions that journalism is attributed in democracy can be perceived in terms of their suggested relations to the audience, how people in turn may understand their position in this equation (cf. Loosen and Schmidt 2012), and how this may change in digital journalism. Interestingly, despite being the key stakeholder when it comes to journalism's democratic function, in many of these commonly understood roles, the relation with audiences is quite cursory and implicit. As Curran (2011, 3) points out: "Much theorising about the democratic role of the media is conceived solely in terms of serving the needs of the individual voter." This informing function is consequently a good place to start this review, as it is the most evident *sine qua non* of journalism's assumed benefit for the public.

The notion that journalism provides citizens with "information and commentary on contemporary affairs" (Schudson 2000, 58) is at the core of the discourse on journalism's central role in Western democracy and grounds much of its traditional rhetoric to audiences: "news should provide citizens with the basic information necessary to form and update opinions on all of the major issues of the day, including the performance of top public officials" (Zaller 2003, 110). Audiences here are typically assumed to be the aggregate of rationally engaged citizens (cf. Dahlberg 2011), selecting from a variety of news options to satisfy a need to stay informed. Even when practices are conceived of in lesser degrees than that of highly engaged, daily news consumption rituals, as with the notion of monitorial citizenship (Schudson 1998), or journalism functioning like a burglar alarm (Zaller 2003), the provision of quality information to citizens is core. Often cited as the most relevant function of the media, journalism is frequently faulted for not providing enough quantity or quality of coverage (e.g. Franklin 1997).

A second, related function is the view of journalism as a watchdog for society, which implies that journalists monitor and hold actors in power to account. Acting as a fourth estate, journalism is deemed to bring to light the wrongdoings and misdeeds of governmental actors, commercial businesses, and non-governmental organisations (NGOs). Central to this conceptualisation of journalism's role for society is then not the audience, apart from perhaps sourcing stories, but rather the journalist and the actors in power whose actions are monitored. It is only when a wrongdoing is reported that the audience comes into play as a "public", in terms of its reaction and resultant demands placed upon officials. In this regard, journalism serves somewhat of an auditing function on audiences' behalf; the mere fact that media are there to check and control actions and processes in society has a function in itself. On this function too, journalism has been critiqued: in capitalist media systems it can be seen to be so tangled up with commercial and/ or political interests that it is unable to act as an independent agent (e.g. McChesney 1999).

Third, news media are attributed an important role in representing the public in political matters: they are crucial in making the voice of the public heard. Here, the audience is central again, but this time as public subject to the media, as needing the media to talk for them. Having no means of publishing at the scale of mass media, journalism has been seen as the place for the public opinion to be formed, informing both political actors as well as other members of the public of their preferences, concerns, and opinions. This function may seem somewhat abstract to the audience; how, exactly do media make "them" heard and who are "they"? In this sense, the promotion of this function to audiences is largely rhetorical and intangible in a pre-participatory age. Again, major criticism exists as to the way in which journalists represent the public in that the public is seen to have limited control over its own mediated image and even less control over the ends for which this representation is deployed (Coleman and Ross 2010).

Finally, journalists mediate for political actors. News media are the main information source with regard to issues of public relevance and the "main vehicle of communication between the governors and the governed" (Strömbäck 2008, 230). This is a crucial part of understanding media's role in democracy during the age of mass media: for political actors to reach the public they go through (news) media. In theories on the mediatisation of institutional politics, we see that the focus is on the relation between political actors and journalistic media, and that the role of the audience is largely implicit (Witschge 2014). Building on agenda-setting theory, framing, and effect studies, the conceptualisation of the audience is largely passive. In this regard, media and politics may seem "distant" for audiences, as theories of public alienation from the political process and journalism's failure in this regard outline (e.g. Rosen 2006). In this theoretical perspective the public takes on a central role mainly as voters and as consumers of (political) information.

What all these conceptualisations of journalism *vis-à-vis* democracy hold in common is that they assume, at least in principal, that the public needs journalism even if it does not always actively engage with it. Minimally, it implies a threshold based on audiences consuming news from time to time and/or providing a justification for its financing. In an age of digital journalism, when these relationships and purposes are viewed from the perspective of audiences, and people potentially change their relationship with news itself, many fear that these democratic functions are destabilising (e.g. Mindich 2005). Ideas about journalism's role in society being under threat are far from unique to this era, and debates about its utility to audiences are not novel. Nonetheless, the vast proliferation of media options and outlets over the past few decades has made certain concerns quite tangible. Longitudinal surveys indicate that younger generations are turning away from news consumption as a common practice (e.g. Pew Research Center 2012) and established news habits for the population as a whole are slowly becoming de-ritualised, without any clear indication what will replace them (Broersma and Peters 2013). The question becomes: what significance will journalism continue to play for future generations?

Answering this is complicated further in a landscape where the interactional possibilities in terms of political communication change more broadly and digital tools make possible an increasingly participatory role for audiences, both within and outside news journalism. Each of the four functions previously outlined can now, in theory, be conducted by the public and political actors directly, without the intervention, or mediation, of journalists. News is now produced and distributed by a myriad of actors, not just those in the institutional domain of "mass media" journalism, and thus political and other societally relevant information is provided by journalistic as well as non-journalistic actors. The role of watchdog is similarly taken over or at least available to other actors, whether activists, NGOs, or members of the public themselves, for instance through the actions of whistleblowers and crowdsourced data sets. The third function discussed, that of representing the public, is maybe the most prominent example of the potential provided by digital tools: they allow the public to circumvent, or challenge, dominant institutional news media by distributing "more widely the capacity to tell important stories about oneself—to represent oneself as a social, and therefore potentially political, agent" (Couldry 2008, 386).

In this regard, one of the main changes is the erosion of the gatekeeping role that helped define the relation between politics and journalism in the era of mass communication (Schulz 2004). This gatekeeping function made news media a powerful actor in political communication and for democracy but the extent to which this pertains to the digital era has been questioned. New media are argued to lift the barriers of communication and consequently take away news media's monopoly on mass commun-ication and disable journalism's gatekeeping function (Hansen 2012). Political actors have the possibility to communicate directly to audiences without necessarily going through traditional media and new possibilities are widely available to the public to access, publish, and interact with information online.

In short, digital tools are argued to enable and encourage users "to participate in the creation and circulation of media" (Lewis 2012, 847) and this participation affects journalism's role (and that of the audience) in democracy. In this respect, the key changes—from the perspective of the audience or user—to the four positions above could be summarised as:

- *Information source*: Mass media move from being a primary way for audiences to be informed to one of many possibilities.
- *Watchdog*: News media still publish misdeeds, but whistleblowers augment traditional investigative journalism and citizens can increasingly publicise misconduct.
- *Public representative*: Citizens groups can unite and bypass journalism to communicate their issues directly as "publics".
- *Mediate for political actors*: Digital tools allow more unfettered access from politicians and other political actors to citizens and *vice versa*, circumventing journalism.

What these potentialities point to is a possible shift in the paradigm through which journalism is viewed by academics, spoken about by news organisations, and engaged with by audiences. We see that increasingly a "participation paradigm" rather than a "mass communication paradigm" is applied to conceptualise the institutional setting of journalism (cf. Livingstone 2013). Furthermore, the industry promotes this change in its rhetoric of purpose to audiences, emphasising a different set of practices for digital journalism and its consumption, and connecting the implementation of digital tools now available to the empowerment of audiences in the news production process. In this way of thinking and the initiatives being developed under it, we see that the idea of democracy shifts. There is a distinction between prominent conceptualisations of digital journalism, in which audiences are seen as active co-participants, invoked to argue that journalism is becoming democratised, and that of the former grand narratives, wherein audiences were mostly separate from journalism, which facilitated different democratic functions on its behalf.

Envisioning Participation in Digital Journalism

In recent literature on journalism, and within rhetoric emanating from the industry itself, an increasing emphasis is placed on embracing a move towards participation (e.g. Singer et al. 2011). Partially, this is a response geared towards potential economic benefit; in the age of Web 2.0 discouraging audience interaction may be seen as an isolating or losing proposition. However, while revenue generation may be part of the equation, there is an alternative discourse surrounding participation, which valorises it in terms of its democratising effect on media. In light of the focus of this article, we see that when the affordances of digital technologies are invoked, the focus is placed more squarely on journalism–audience interaction as opposed to a broader dialectic surrounding journalism's democratic function for citizens in society. Embracing participation, in this sense, potentially bestows a less meaningful role for journalism than was envisioned under the familiar grand narratives in the era of the mass press.

This refocusing is not unique to digital journalism studies, as recent scholarship has increasingly viewed media consumption in general in terms of such a "participation paradigm" (Livingstone 2013). This emphasises not only a lessening of barriers between the traditional mass media and the "people formerly known as the audience" (Rosen 2006), and the rise of more "networked" forms of mass communication (Cardoso 2008), but also stresses the contributory and creative potentialities of the digitised, Web 2.0 media landscape (Gauntlett 2011). Many such accounts are careful not to assert that all participation is uniform and there is a long history of delineating the notion, especially when it comes to the question of what constitutes political participation. Moreover, from a socio-cultural perspective, participation via the news media is but one of a far more dynamic series of interactions that constitute civic engagement.

However, given the societal importance attributed to the provision of a common, consistent source of information, and the role of journalism in providing frameworks of meaning, the particular domain of participation through journalism is one of central importance. Through its reach, journalism potentially allows the shaping of communities of interest, permitting participation both for more "passive", disengaged citizens (by way of providing information) as well as active, engaged citizens (by way of providing tools for direct participation). Yet despite the fact that both minimalist and maximalist forms of participation are theoretically possible through news media, they are not equally present in the digital domain. While a select group of media provide the platform for maximalist engagement in helping produce and shape meanings and perhaps even communication structures within society, these are not the dominant form.

What is needed are clearer distinctions, considering the specifics of participation in digital journalism, its means, and its ends. Instead of simply celebrating new media technologies for their potential for participation, we need to question what makes their use meaningful, both in terms of the experience of using them and in terms of their material integration within everyday life. While there are an ever-increasing number of ways for the public to be involved in the news process, there are a more limited number of discussions of the different affordances and structural differences of participation and— quite crucially—the consequences of participatory digital tools and the extent to which such opportunities are actually available equally to different social groups. It would be erroneous to treat the current possibilities for audience engagement in traditional news media, whether we refer to "most-read" lists, "have-your-say" invitations, audience polls, "comments" sections or "send-in-your-pictures" requests, as equally promising avenues for public participation.

Similarly, journalistic initiatives facilitated by digitalisation like Indymedia may provide a space outside traditional mainstream journalism for alternative voices, with much greater scope for distribution online. But to ignore the structural disadvantages that beset such organisations (lack of access, lack of material resources and infrastructure, lack of viable financing and tax advantages, lack of prominence versus more established outlets, lack of salaried employees with time to devote to its maintenance, and so forth) easily overstates their emancipatory potential (for a critical discussion of the potential for alternative media online, see Curran and Witschge (2010). In this respect, distinguishing between forms of participation and their implications allows us to make a more constructive assessment of current practices (see Figure 1). The operationalisation of interactive features and the structures within which they are integrated in this respect belie more robust notions of participation.

Expressed broadly, as Figure 1 notes, there is a significant distinction in the scope and degree of participation between technologies that allow individuals to control and personalise content (basic digital control) and entire platforms that easily facilitate the

Scope of participation	Minimal ⟶		Maximal
Visibility and presence of audience	As respondents to certain items only	As authors of texts in designated areas	As structural contributors throughout the platform
Hierarchical level of interaction	Reply-based audience response (i.e. polls), detached from journalistic interaction	Interaction-based with other audience members and/or journalists, limited impact on production (i.e. audience photos, tweets for breaking news)	Dialogue and consultation-based input in news production at an editorial level
Stage of production	Post-hoc, after news is presented as finished product	Real-time, during the (on-going) creation of a story	During the planning stages to co-design the news agenda, news angles and stories

FIGURE 1
Scope and degree of participation

storytelling and distribution of citizen journalism within public discourse (integrative structural participation).

This realisation points us towards the necessity of distinguishing the scope for which citizen-led contributions are welcomed. Is participation specific to a single story, across certain sections (i.e. "Comment is Free"), or a principle of the entire publication (a fully realised "public journalism")? This is an important aspect in terms of the possible entry points in the text itself and within processes of production. Whether individual audience members are interested in involvement or not, the idea of co-production, crowdsourcing, and co-creation speak to how *visible and present* the public is as author, not just as audience. News websites are typically sectioned off with audiences cordoned in specific places and moments where participation is made available.

This relates to a second crucial distinction, the organisational permeability and *hierarchical level* of participation, which is central to understanding power relations and the level at which connection is enabled. Are audiences able to reply only to institutional requests or is this extended to interaction with other members of the audience and journalists? To what extent can audience participation be extended to dialogue and structural consultation with the editorial department or even financial department? Participation is often equated with a greater equalising of the relationship between audiences and the mass media but the organisational level to which they are welcomed differentiates this sharply. Most participation remains outside the control of production and the editorial process as a whole remains a level quite impervious in most digital initiatives.

Finally, a consideration that often goes unexplored is the timing of participation, in terms of during what *stage of production* it is made available. Is it limited to *post hoc* responses, extended to real-time co-production (such as that witnessed with live-blogging), or integrated in pre-coverage organisational integration and story development? These different moments and phases of possible connection delimit the ability to set the day-to-day agenda of news organisations. While the rhetoric of participation appears to suggest an opening up of journalism and inclusion of audiences as key stakeholders to help fulfil the functions of journalism, the breadth of participatory opportunities may not be matched by a comparable depth.

If we look at actual journalistic practices—even in a digital age where participation is frequently emphasised as a panacea against journalism's perceived growing disconnect with audiences—at most outlets: the contribution of audiences is still distinctly and visibly separated from that of journalists and editors; power has not been transferred from the institution; and audience response is welcomed mostly after-the-fact as a possible citizen source or commenter. These distinctions highlight a main challenge that hinders meaningful participation being established on behalf of audiences, namely the divide between the private and public interests served by it. Meaningful participation, allowing for a more democratic distribution of the power to speak not only in the news but also within the newsroom, ideally leads to a more symbiotic relationship between news organisations and audiences and more diversity in media voices. A classic critique of media is that minority viewpoints have a hard time being heard, but if we extend this to the entire news production process, we might say that audiences as a whole traditionally exert little control. Day-to-day, this is likely unproblematic for most people. They are not journalists, have no historical basis for assuming they should help determine the news agenda, and likely are generally disinterested in having such expectations foisted upon them.

However, there is a large swathe of territory between demanding full participation and governance over journalism by audiences versus offering mere token participation. We should remember that media have an important role in voicing opinions and are needed to make "contemporary contests" visible (Couldry 2010, 148). As we see time and time again, the power for individuals to influence coverage when a group they are part of is suddenly thrust on to the front pages—from ethnic minorities during riots, to striking teachers, even to investment bankers—is demonstrated to be little. Many of the classic notions of primary definers setting the terms of debate and secondary definers only being allowed to respond still seem to hold true, even in the current "age of participation". Even with ever-increasing interactive possibilities in mainstream media, the public "does not control its own image" (Coleman and Ross 2010, 5).

News organisations are inevitably "embedded in networks of commercial and political power" (Couldry 2010, 148) and the way in which the public is allowed to participate is heavily shaped by these interests. In the most ardent, some might say instrumental, political economy assessment of the media system, audiences are viewed as nothing more than a market to sell to advertisers, and journalism is little more than a technology of capitalism that consolidates the public and renders it controllable. A different view of the role of audience, through an adapted field theory perspective, might view participation as a struggle which threatens journalism's status as the arbiter and key distributor of day-to-day public information in societies. Under this logic, public participation through online news does not escape the tendency that news media have to "create a public opinion that amplifies, or at least, does not challenge, their own power" (Hind 2010, 7).

This is relevant, as it raises questions over what new kinds of citizenship the currently available tools facilitate, if any at all? In terms of the four functions traditionally assigned to journalism, we see that the public is not equally attributed a role in fulfilling them, and mainstream journalists seek to maintain their gatekeeping role (Witschge 2013). As such, participatory tools are employed in a selective fashion, and journalism is a long way from allowing audiences to share information jointly, co-monitor those in power, represent themselves in public affairs, and get into contact with political actors directly. This may not be surprising, given the commercial pressures and the continued (self-) understanding of journalism as a separate profession. However, the rhetoric that connects these tools to democracy often suggests that a fundamental shift of power is occurring and invokes a stronger role for the audience than that with which it is currently furnished. On the whole, practices in mainstream journalism contradict expectations or presumptions that the "new digital environment has jolted traditional journalism out of its conservative complacency; [or that] news operations are much more responsive to their empowered and engaged audiences" (Bird 2009, 295).

Commercial considerations frequently weigh more heavily than any moral motivations in the new relationship between the professionals and the audience, such as creating a more democratic environment. Yet even outside the mainstream, the potentialities of Web 2.0 have been critiqued for the limited version of citizenship they afford. Fenton and Barassi (2011, 180) note that whereas alternative media were founded on a collective ethos and a collectively negotiated construction in response to perceived structural inequalities, the recent emphasis on using social media promotes individual agency and "self-centred forms of communication". These sorts of structural considerations should lead us to question paradigmatic assertions of the intrinsic value of participation from digital journalism initiatives—or at least to critique their assumed political efficacy on behalf of the audience.

Discussions on the value of participation are quite meaningless unless we strive to understand the utility of different participatory tools for audiences, which demands not only empirical research on the way they are experienced but also specificity on their different affordances and implications. While on the surface it may seem that technology is making it increasingly simple for individuals to integrate personalised news within every space and place of their daily lives, and news organisations are increasingly emphasising their capabilities around the convenience for audiences to interact (Peters 2012), this does not necessarily translate into more inclusive forms of participation. This is further problematised when we consider the dislocation of journalism for many people, the lack of integration of news in their everyday lives, and the segregation of participation in new virtual spaces in terms of the ability to participate equally (Shakuntala Banaji, personal communication, October 11, 2013). Understanding the lived materiality of technological developments means greater specificity about said efforts at interaction and inclusion. Such particularities of participation not only illustrate its potential shape, scale, and substance for audiences, it also, quite tellingly, clarifies the ways audiences themselves are conceived.

The Participatory Individual and the Democratic Collective in Digital Journalism

Classically, journalism is conceived of as an intermediary of sorts, a social institution that serves a number of bridging functions between the populace and the political process. In terms of its civic role, this means discussions typically distinguish some aspect of this relation, whether it is centred on journalism's function in competitive, deliberative, procedural, or participatory visions of democracy (Strömbäck 2005), or people's likely uses of journalism as they move from being conceived of as informed to monitorial citizens (Schudson 1998). Such discussions have often taken a normative and prescriptive stance in terms of how journalism can "best" serve the civic needs of the public, and this trend has continued when considering new digital initiatives. For instance, Nip (2006) looks more closely into how the second phase of public journalism could use participatory tools to strengthen democratic values in terms of deliberation, engagement, and community connection. While these sorts of accounts look to the nature of democracy imagined, the subjects within it, and the role of journalism envisioned, they tend to conceive of this relation in terms of the institution of journalism and the tools it makes available to audiences. The risk with such an approach is that it can fall prey to considering the instrumental means of digital initiatives as opposed to the "ends" with which people actually use them (cf. Dahlberg 2011).

The popular rhetoric increasingly emanating from journalistic institutions around the question of participation often emphasises such instrumental means, which parallels a proclivity observed in analyses of online journalism to focus on technological innovation (Steensen 2011). These types of institutional discourse, closely tied to marketing strategies, tend to privilege how digital tools facilitate *individuals'* possibilities to interact and exert greater control over shaping the information offered to them. As we noted in the first part of this article, traditional discourses of journalism tend to be framed *collectively* in terms of saying what journalism can do for people, what it offers citizens in democracy. But in discourses of participation, we frequently see emphasis placed on what individuals can do with journalism. For journalism studies scholars, this is an important caveat. When the tools of digital journalism are viewed primarily in terms of how people can possibly use them as opposed to the impact of their uses, there is a danger of making individualised interactional possibilities trumpet questions of communicative collectivity (cf. Livingstone 2003).

Rather than assuming the democratised nature of interactive journalism, we need to view journalism's role through the eyes of audiences and question the rhetoric surrounding digital tools. As Rebillar and Touboul (2010, 325) point out, in the "libertarian-liberal" model currently dominant, "views of the Web 2.0 associate liberty, autonomy and horizontality". But these are more often than not highly individualised notions of political engagement. Moreover, it is not clear if people want or even conceive of themselves in the more active senses embodied in the idea of user or "produser" (cf. Bruns 2006). Empirical studies of audiences and their changing experience with digital journalism—as opposed to the more common approach to study journalistic and editorial *perceptions* of what change means to audiences—tend to bear this out. Bergström's (2008) early study of online participation in Sweden found relatively little interest from audiences in terms of content creation. Furthermore, the (already politically and socially engaged) minority which did comment did so for reasons of leisure as opposed to democratic engagement. Similarly, Costera Meijer's (2013) multiple studies in the Dutch context note the existence of a widely different logic operating between what users value in terms of participation—being taken seriously as individuals and a collectivity with wisdom and expertise to offer—and the professional scepticism with which journalists traditionally view more "inclusive" initiatives. Such research points to the fact that audience-based studies tend to highlight areas of tension and resistance between their empirical findings and the common discourse about digital, active, participatory audiences and the possible impact this has on democracy.

Such considerations alert us to what Silverstone (1999, 2) referred to as "the general texture of experience", which is why it is important to study the coupling of journalism and democracy not just from the perspective of the institution and its rhetoric, but also from its audiences and their practices. By foregrounding experience, rather than declaring the democratic impact of prominent shifts and technological advancements based on journalistic (or academic) want or intention, it forces us to begin from the perspective of the audience. If we begin from the premise that all forms of possible interaction with journalism are not equal in terms of their ability or even intent to promote audience agency in the news production process, the natural corollary of this is that audiences likely experience their own agency differently, depending on the participatory nature of their actual involvement.

For these reasons, the use of democratic discourses in relation to participative journalism should be exercised cautiously. The logics that drive the introduction of digital tools may not warrant the use of grand conceptualisations of democracy and the audience practices and experiences that accompany them may also challenge such narratives. However, at the same time, we wish to emphasise here how a singular focus on participation can lead to overly cautious expectations. In this regard we are faced with a bit of a conundrum. We sympathise with the concern raised by some authors (see the 2013 special issue of *Journalism* guest edited by Josephi) that with the rapid changes witnessed in the media landscape over the past couple of decades, the journalism and democracy paradigm may be "too limiting and distorting a lens through which journalism can be viewed in the 21st century" (Josephi 2013, 445). There may indeed be much to be gained from retiring the concept of democracy for understanding contemporary journalistic practice (Nerone 2013; Zelizer 2013); considering alternative, possibly more relevant concepts to replace the central role of democracy as the framework to make sense of key shifts and changes.

However, as this article hopefully illustrates, simply replacing the "democracy paradigm" with a "participation paradigm" to analyse digital journalism carries some risks. It became clear that while the concept of democracy is invoked in digital journalism studies to frame discussions on participation, this conceptualisation is at a different level than the grand narratives that have traditionally stipulated journalism's functions for democracy. The danger when we speak mostly in terms of participation is potentially sacrificing much of journalism's collective function, to which traditional discourses of mass media were quite attuned. This is not to say that these grand narratives should necessarily be our guideline when reviewing journalism and/or participation in and through journalism: there are a variety of ways in which democracy can be constituted through acts of the public. However, it is important to distinguish between the participatory affordances, the lived experiences of audiences, and the implications for journalism's relevance and function in society.

A journalism that consistently heralds the ability for the audience to personalise and interact based around new technological tools may gradually promote individualistic interpretations that are anathema to the idea of journalism's traditional collective, public ethos. Collectivity is a crucial aspect not only of democracy, but dare we say, of society/public life. While digital tools may promote connection in a very literal sense, these are not the same forms of "public connection" emphasised under the old grand narratives (cf. Couldry, Livingstone, and Markham 2010). News organisations signal much to us about our preferred societal roles, civic possibilities, and democratic responsibilities, and what they advocate is potentially transforming in the digital age. Are audiences still envisaged as citizens who "are actively engaged in society and the making of history" or rather as consumers who "simply choose between the products on display" (Lewis, Inthorn, and Wahl-Jorgensen 2005, 5–6)? The technologies of digital journalism may appear to plug into an audience that is assumed to value both simultaneously, but the individualised nature of connecting, personalising, and choosing when to be "part of the conversation" is foregrounded. More interactivity, in this regard, should not be automatically equated with a greater role for citizens to perform democratic functions. Moreover, the focus on individualised forms of participation may mean that the collective functions of journalism are neglected. In this regard, there is a relationship—and potentially a paradox—between discourses of empowerment and participation (that for the most do not distinguish between different levels of agency) and the actual practices and affordances of technological tools. As journalism scholars we need to examine critically the minimal expectations and affordances of participatory tools as well as consider what may be lost with the increasingly individualistic interpretation of both journalism and participation. This would involve empirically examining the experiences of audiences as both users *and* citizens simultaneously, as the changes we have outlined do beg the question: what are the implications for democracy if what was once deemed a collective institution begins to envisage its audiences as individuals?

ACKNOWLEDGEMENTS

Our thanks to an anonymous reviewer as well as the guest editors of this special issue, Steen Steensen and Laura Ahva, for their helpful comments on an earlier draft.

NOTE

1. It is important to note that there is a difference between the "audience" as a discursive construct versus the audience as an empirically studied entity. In this article we look primarily at its discursive formulation in the rhetoric of journalism and democracy. Yet of course, these notions are not completely distinct and interact in a number of ways. As we discuss in the first section after the introduction, the established discourse about the societal function of journalism has been internalised by the public and shapes how people traditionally perceive news. However, as we note in the final section, empirical studies of audiences illustrate tensions between this rhetoric and the actual uses audiences make from journalism and their experiences of participatory and interactive tools.

REFERENCES

Bergström, Annika. 2008. "The Reluctant Audience: Online Participation in the Swedish Journalistic Context." *Westminster Papers in Communication and Culture* 5 (2): 60–80.

Bird, Elizabeth. 2009. "The Future of Journalism in the Digital Environment." *Journalism* 10 (3): 293–295. doi:10.1177/1464884909102583.

Broersma, Marcel, and Chris Peters. 2013. "Rethinking Journalism: The Structural Transformation of a Public Good." In *Rethinking Journalism: Trust and Participation in a Transformed News Landscape*, edited by Chris Peters and Marcel Broersma, 1–12. London: Routledge.

Bruns, Axel. 2006. "Towards Produsage: Futures for User-led Content Production." In *Cultural Attitudes towards Communication and Technology*, edited by Fay Sudweeks, Herbert Hrachovec, and Charles Ess, 275–284. Perth: Murdoch University.

Cardoso, Gustavo. 2008. "From Mass to Networked Communication: Communicational Models and the Informational Society." *International Journal of Communication* 2: 587–630.

Carlyle, Thomas. 1840. *On Heroes, Hero-Worship, and the Heroic in History*. http://www.gutenberg.org/files/1091/1091-h/1091-h.htm.

Carpentier, Nico. 2009. "Participation Is Not Enough: The Conditions of Possibility of Mediated Participatory Practices." *European Journal of Communication* 24 (4): 407–420. doi:10.1177/0267323109345682.

Coleman, Stephen, and Karen Ross. 2010. *The Media and the Public: "Them" and "Us" in Media Discourse*. Oxford: Wiley-Blackwell.

Costera Meijer, Irene. 2013. "Valuable Journalism: The Search for Quality from the Vantage Point of the User." *Journalism* 14 (6): 754–770. doi:10.1177/1464884912455899.

Couldry, Nick. 2008. "Mediatization or Mediation? Alternative Understandings of the Emergent Space of Digital Storytelling." *New Media & Society* 10 (3): 373–391. doi:10.1177/1461444808089414.

Couldry, Nick. 2010. *Why Voice Matters: Culture and Politics after Neoliberalism*. London: Sage.

Couldry, Nick, Sonia Livingstone, and Tim Markham. 2010. *Media Consumption and Public Engagement: Beyond the Presumption of Attention*. London: Palgrave Macmillan.

Curran, James. 2011. *Media and Democracy*. Oxon: Routledge.

Curran, James, and Tamara Witschge. 2010. "Liberal Dreams and the Internet." In *New Media, Old News: Journalism and Democracy in the Digital Age*, edited by Natalie Fenton, 102–118. London: Sage.

Dahlberg, Lincoln. 2011. "Re-constructing Digital Democracy: An Outline of Four 'Positions.'" *New Media & Society* 13 (6): 855–872. doi:10.1177/1461444810389569.

Fenton, Natalie, and Veronica Barassi. 2011. "Alternative Media and Social Networking Sites: The Politics of Individuation and Political Participation." *The Communication Review* 14 (3): 179–196. doi:10.1080/10714421.2011.597245.

Franklin, Bob. 1997. *Newszak and News Media*. London: Arnold.

Gauntlett, David. 2011. *Making Is Connecting*. London: Polity.

Hackett, Robert A., and Yuezhi Zhao. 1998. *Sustaining Democracy?: Journalism and the Politics of Objectivity*. London: Broadview Press.

Hansen, Ejvind. 2012. "Aporias of Digital Journalism." *Journalism* 14 (5): 678–694. doi:10.1177/1464884912453283.

Hind, Dan. 2010. *The Return of the Public*. London: Verso.

Josephi, Beate. 2013. "De-coupling Journalism and Democracy: Or How Much Democracy Does Journalism Need?" *Journalism* 14 (4): 441–445. doi:10.1177/1464884913489000.

Lewis, Justin, Sanna Inthorn, and Karin Wahl-Jorgensen. 2005. *Citizens or Consumers? What the Media Tell Us About Political Participation.* Buckingham: Open University Press.

Lewis, Seth. 2012. "The Tension between Professional Control and Open Participation." *Information, Communication & Society* 15 (6): 836–866. doi:10.1080/1369118X.2012.674150.

Livingstone, Sonia. 2003. "The Changing Nature of Audiences: From the Mass Audience to the Interactive Media User." In *The Blackwell Companion to Media Research*, edited by Angharad Valdivia, 337–359. Oxford: Blackwell.

Livingstone, Sonia. 2013. "The Participation Paradigm in Audience Research." *The Communication Review* 16 (1–2): 21–30. doi:10.1080/10714421.2013.757174.

Loosen, Wiebke, and Jan-Hinrik Schmidt. 2012. "(Re-)Discovering the Audience: The Relationship between Journalism and Audience in Networked Digital Media." *Information, Communication & Society* 15 (6): 867–887. doi:10.1080/1369118X.2012.665467.

Madianou, Mirca. 2009. "Audience Reception and News in Everyday Life." In *The Handbook of Journalism Studies*, edited by Karin Wahl-Jorgensen and Thomas Hanitzsch, 325–337. London: Routledge.

McChesney, Robert W. 1999. *Rich Media, Poor Democracy: Communication Politics in Dubious Times.* Chicago: University of Illinois Press.

McNair, Brian. 2009. "Journalism and Democracy." In *The Handbook of Journalism Studies*, edited by Karin Wahl-Jorgensen and Thomas Hanitzsch, 237–249. London: Routledge.

Mindich, David. 2005. *Tuned Out: Why Americans Under 40 Don't Follow the News.* Oxford: Oxford University Press.

Nerone, John. 2013. "The Historical Roots of the Normative Model of Journalism." *Journalism* 14 (4): 446–458. doi:10.1177/1464884912464177.

Nip, Joyce. 2006. "Exploring the Second Phase of Public Journalism." *Journalism Studies* 7 (2): 212–236. doi:10.1080/14616700500533528.

Peters, Chris. 2011. "Emotion Aside or Emotional Side? Crafting an 'Experience of Involvement' in the News." *Journalism: Theory, Practice and Criticism* 12 (3): 297–316. doi:10.1177/1464884910388224.

Peters, Chris. 2012. "Journalism to Go: The Changing Spaces of News Consumption." *Journalism Studies* 13 (5–6): 695–705. doi:10.1080/1461670X.2012.662405.

Pew Research Center. 2012. "Trends in News Consumption 1991–2012." http://www.people-press.org/files/legacy-pdf/2012NewsConsumptionReport.pdf.

Rebillar, Franck, and Annelise Touboul. 2010. "Promises Unfulfilled? 'Journalism 2.0', User Participation and Editorial Policy on Newspaper Websites." *Media, Culture & Society* 32 (2): 323–334. doi:10.1177/0163443709356142.

Rosen, Jay. 2006. "The People Formerly Known as the Audience." *PressThink.* http://archive.pressthink.org/2006/06/27/ppl_frmr.html.

Schudson, Michael. 1998. The Good Citizen. New York: Free Press.

Schudson, Michael. 2000. "The Domain of Journalism Studies around the Globe." *Journalism* 1 (1): 55–59. doi:10.1177/146488490000100110.

Schulz, Winfried. 2004. "Reconstructing Mediatization as an Analytical Concept." *European Journal of Communication* 19 (1): 87–101. doi:10.1177/0267323104040696.

Silverstone, Roger. 1999. *Why Study the Media?* London: Sage.

Singer, Jane B., David Domingo, Ari Heinonen, Alfred Hermida, Steve Paulussen, Thorsten Quandt, Zvi Reich, and Marina Vujnovic. 2011. *Participatory Journalism: Guarding Open Gates at Online Newspapers.* Chichester: John Wiley & Sons.

Steensen, Steen. 2011. "Online Journalism and the Promises of New Technology: A Critical Review and Look Ahead." *Journalism Studies* 12 (3): 311–327. doi:10.1080/1461670X.2010.501151.

Strömbäck, Jesper. 2005. "In Search of a Standard: Four Models of Democracy and Their Normative Implications for Journalism." *Journalism Studies* 6 (3): 331–345. doi:10.1080/14616700500131950.

Strömbäck, Jesper. 2008. "Four Phases of Mediatization: An Analysis of the Mediatization of Politics." *The International Journal of Press/Politics* 13 (3): 228–246. doi:10.1177/1940161208319097.

Witschge, Tamara. 2013. "Digital Participation in News Media: 'Minimalist' Views versus Meaningful Interaction." In *The Media, Political Participation and Empowerment*, edited by Richard Scullion, Roman Gerodimos, Daniel Jackson, and Darren Lilleker, 103–115. London: Routledge.

Witschge, Tamara. 2014. "Passive Accomplice or Active Disruptor: The Role of Audiences in the Mediatization of Politics." *Journalism Practice* 8 (3): 342–356. doi:10.1080/17512786.2014.889455.

Zaller, John. 2003. "A New Standard of News Quality: Burglar Alarms for the Monitorial Citizen." *Political Communication* 20 (2): 109–130. doi:10.1080/10584600390211136.

Zelizer, Barbie. 2013. "On the Shelf Life of Democracy in Journalism Scholarship." *Journalism* 14 (4): 459–473. doi:10.1177/1464884912464179.

WHEN NEWS IS EVERYWHERE
Understanding participation, cross-mediality and mobility in journalism from a radical user perspective

Ike Picone, Cédric Courtois, and Steve Paulussen

This article contends that not only journalism but also journalism studies can benefit from a stronger commitment to the public. While the bodies of literature on "popular journalism", "public journalism" and "citizen/participatory journalism" have, in different contexts and from different angles, made a strong case in favour of a public-oriented approach to journalism, it is remarkable how few of the empirical studies on journalism are based on user research. As the control of media institutions over the news process is in decline, we should take the "news audience" more seriously and try to improve our understanding of (changing) news use patterns. Besides this rather obvious theoretical point, there are also societal and methodological arguments for a more user-oriented take on the study of journalism. Starting from a reflection on the key trends in news use in the digital age—participation, cross-mediality and mobility—this article attempts to show the theoretical and societal relevance of a radical user perspective on journalism and journalism research alike. Furthermore, we look at new methodological opportunities for news user research and elaborate on our arguments by way of an empirical study on changing news practices. The study uses Q-sort methodology to expose the impact a medium's affordances can have on the way we experience news in a converged and mobile media environment. The article concludes by discussing what the benefits of a radical user perspective can be both for journalism studies as for journalism.

Introduction

In our current digital news environment, journalistic production is no longer the sole product of professional journalists as "members of various publics make journalism material that intersects, mixes and is distributed to a new heightened degree" (Russell 2011, 1). In this context, news users claim an ever-more important role in the way journalism is shaped. Picard (2010, 20) observes that behind the many shifts in the media sector today lies the fact that the "locus of control over the content [has shifted] from communicators to audiences" and continues stating that this "fundamental power shift in the public communication sphere ... requires all of us concerned with the broader needs of society to alter our ways of thinking about audiences, the role of media and society, and how we seek to develop informed and active citizens". The changing ways in which media are consumed should therefore be at the core of our understanding of journalism in the digital news environment.

Indeed, as we will argue in this paper, we need to fundamentally incorporate the perspective of the news user in journalism studies and do so by adopting a radical user approach in journalism studies. A radical user perspective should go beyond merely acknowledging the importance of the user within journalism studies, but should consider it to be an intrinsic part of the epistemology of journalism studies. Concretely, this implies rethinking the idea of the user on a conceptual, methodological and normative level.

First, on a conceptual level, we should be wary of approaching the user as an "imagined audience" (Hartley 1987). Our notions of the user should not be shaped by what we think or want the audience to be, but by what we know it to be (Gray 1999). An imagined user, be it theoretically, empirically or politically, will always serve "the needs of the imagining institution" (Hartley 1987, 125). If, as Picard (2010) suggests, we aim to alter our ways of thinking about audiences, we should make sure that new conceptualisations will be informed by how news is actually used, rather than by how journalists—or researchers for that matter—expect it to be. This implies that, as Peters (2012, 704) aptly puts it, "we must certainly begin to speak with audiences, as opposed to just about them".

Secondly, following from this first point, user research should be considered as a fundamental element of the methodological toolkit that journalism scholars dispose of to understand what the experience of journalism will be in the future. As a research field, journalism studies would benefit from both quantitative and qualitative user studies that are driven by journalistic concerns and focus on the relationship between user and news, rather than the readily available, but market-, media- or technology-oriented consumer insights.

Thirdly, if we acknowledge that, even more than was the case before, journalism is being shaped by the way audiences use news, we should not only incorporate the vision of the user in our understanding of what journalism *is*, but also in what it *should be*. This entails that the radical user perspective we put forward should allow for it to be positioned not as opposed to more political or democratic visions on the role of news in society, but as encompassing the notion of the democratic value of news. It is only by thinking about both at the same time that we can make useful progress in understanding news as the specific kind of valuable information it is. More focus on the user can lead to such understanding, as long as our conceptual and theoretical vision on the audience allows us to grasp the democratic value that users seek in their news use. Underlying this assumption is the belief that users do value news in more than merely functional or consumptive ways (cf. Costera Meijer 2013).

To make the case for a radical user perspective, we begin by critically examining audience-oriented perspectives in journalism studies so far. We will show how various authors have come to defend user-oriented approaches to journalism, but ultimately failed to integrate this user perspective in journalism research itself, as they merely reflected on rather than with the public. Subsequently, we discuss some of the key trends in news use and try to illustrate why these changes make the need for a radical audience turn in our thinking about journalism urgent. Thirdly, to elaborate on our arguments, we revisit a previous study (Courtois, Schrøder, and Kobbernagel, forthcoming) in order to illustrate the kind of nuanced insights that can be obtained when we allow news users to speak about journalism, rather than letting journalists speak about the public. We will also touch upon specific methodological issues raised by this study. Finally, we discuss the implications of our proposed perspective for future research and relate it to the normative dimension of journalism.

The User Perspective in Journalism Studies

Within the discipline of media and communication studies there is a long tradition of audience research (e.g. Nightingale 2011; Alasuutari 1999). Indeed, a good deal of knowledge has been acquired from research on the complex relationship between media and their audiences. On the one hand, effect and reception studies help us to understand how people are influenced by and engage with media content (Potter 2013; Livingstone 1998). On the other hand, the literature comprises a large number of quantitative and qualitative studies on the adoption of media and the various roles and functions they fulfil in people's daily lives (Schrøder 1999; Courtois 2012). The literature also documents how media use patterns have evolved with the emergence of digital media technologies that brought about a convergence or "liquification" of once discrete "established categories—such as sending and receiving, producing and consuming, being online or offline" (Deuze 2010, 2; Jenkins 2006).

Given the rich tradition of media audience research, it is remarkable how little attention is paid to it in the scholarly literature on journalism. As Bird (2011, 489) says, "[w]e know surprisingly little about audiences for news". The focus on the production side of the news process has left journalism scholarship somewhat ignorant of the fact that "the fate of 'the media' is indeed closely tied to the fate of 'the audience'" (Couldry 2011, 214). Considering that journalism's "first loyalty is to citizens", as solemnly stated by Kovach and Rosenstiel (2007), one might expect to find citizens at the core of journalism studies, but this is not the case. Journalism scholars still tend to regard the audience in similar ways as many media practitioners do: as a group of passive spectators consuming and processing the news *after* it is published (Hermida et al. 2011). This is not a new observation. Both journalism and journalism studies have been criticised before for this dominant notion of the public as a monolithic mass of passive consumers rather than a heterogeneous community of active citizens (see also Carpentier 2011).

The first move towards a more public-oriented approach to journalism was made at the beginning of the 1990s. Under the influence of the cultural turn in the social sciences (Fiske 1989), media scholars began urging a more qualitative and interpretive investigation of journalism that would take the public, and how people give meaning to (news) media, as the focal point of attention (Dahlgren and Sparks 1992). The application of popular culture perspectives to journalism gave rise to a significant body of literature on popular journalism, which challenged the political economy perspectives on the "tabloidisation" or "dumbing down" of the news. However, this resulted in polarised discussions between proponents and opponents of the popularisation of news, which, ironically enough, ultimately reinforced the "binary distinctions" which cultural studies scholars tried to dismiss (Harrington 2008, 268–269). Examples of such dichotomies are those of hard versus soft news, information versus entertainment, reason versus emotion, or consumer demands versus citizens' needs. The main problem with the political economy and cultural studies perspectives on popular journalism is that both discourses concentrate on the production and content of the news. In other words, they deal with the question of how journalists (should) perceive their public—as either active or passive, consumers or citizens, aware or unaware of what they "need to know", etc.—rather than with the question of how the public perceives and uses (popular) journalism. With regard to the latter question, some authors have already shown that from an audience perspective the theoretical distinction between quality and popular news proves insufficient to grasp the complexity of news users' behaviour (Costera Meijer 2007; Schrøder and Larsen 2010).

Another scholarly debate that emerged at the end of the twentieth century, parallel but not linked to the debate over popular news, was the one over "public journalism". The basic idea of "public journalism" was that in order to combat the crisis of the press (i.e. a declining audience and an increasing lack of public trust), journalism had to reconnect with citizens and try to re-emphasise its democratic role in society by involving the audience more actively in the news process (Rosen 1999). Despite its efforts to put the "public" (again) at the centre of "journalism", some critics, like Schudson (1998, 137), pointed out that the movement did ultimately not succeed in removing "the control over the news from journalists" in favour of the public.

With the rise of the internet, however, some authors believed that "public journalism" would enter a "second phase" (Nip 2006), in which the control over the news would become more balanced between journalists and users (Paulussen et al. 2007). The emergence of citizen journalism and the adoption of user-generated content in mainstream media have received much attention within journalism studies. A major conclusion that can be drawn from the literature on "participatory journalism" is that professional journalists are increasingly coming to terms with the idea of a more active and responsive public, without giving up their gatekeeping role (Singer et al. 2011). Nevertheless, the literature on "participatory journalism" can be criticised for being too much focused on the production side. While researchers applied methods of content analysis, newsroom ethnography and in-depth interviews to examine how (professional) journalists deal with user-generated content and audience participation in the news, very few studies paid attention to the users themselves (see Borger et al. 2013). One exception is a study by Wahl-Jorgensen, Williams, and Wardle (2010), who conducted a series of focus groups to examine audience views on the value of user contributions to the news. Their study shows that users differentiate between types of user-generated content to assess its authenticity and value: factual content such as amateur footage is, for instance, valued higher than audience comments. Further, a few studies have paid attention to users' motivations to participate in the news (see the section on 'Participation in News Use' below), but overall, the number of user studies on citizen and participatory journalism remains very scarce compared to the production studies.

In sum, journalism research primarily focuses on the production and content of the news rather than on its consumption and reception. Several authors have argued for a more public-oriented approach to journalism before, but most of them stopped short of integrating this user perspective in journalism *studies*. Even when the notion of the (inter) active user was introduced to journalism studies through monikers like "the produser" (Bruns 2008), "the people formerly known as the audience" (Rosen 2006) and many others, studies focusing on these "lead users of news participation" (Picone 2011) seemed coherent with studying changes and innovation in the news production process and its impact on traditional, professional forms of news production. While this was perhaps defensible in times when journalists were still in charge of the news process, it has become very hard in today's participatory and convergent media environment to conceptualise journalism "without" its public. Understanding news use patterns is critical to understanding contemporary journalism and the role it can play in a networked society. In the next section, we look at how these news use patterns are changing in a digital media context and what it implies for our conceptualisation of news audiences.

Key Trends in News Use

Change is a keyword in all reports published in the past decade on news consumption. Generally speaking, the fundamental change is that audiences are shifting from traditional to digital media platforms. If we take a closer look at the annual trend reports on (digital) news consumption, such as the Pew Research Center's "State of the News Media" reports in the United States (www.stateofthemedia.org), the "Digital News Reports" of The Reuters Institute for the Study of Journalism (RISJ, www.digitalnewsreport. org) or—specifically for Flanders (Belgium)—the iMinds Digimeter reports (www. digimeter.be), we can identify at least three key developments.

First of all, the latest reports emphasise the growth of news consumption via mobile devices, particularly tablet computers and smartphones. Not only does this render users more flexible to access the news whenever and wherever they want. The use of mobile devices also results in a further convergence of media practices, since people increasingly cross and mix multiple media as they continuously travel back and forth between social networking sites, aggregator sites, legacy media sites, and so on. The RISJ Digital News Report, based on a survey in six European countries, the United States, Brazil and Japan, reveals "continuing shifts in how, when, and where people access the news, with digital patterns becoming more entrenched—particularly amongst the younger half of the population. Audiences increasingly want news on any device, in any format, and at any time of day" (Newman and Levy 2013, 9). Next to the increased mobility and cross-mediality, a third fundamental shift in news use is that it is becoming more and more participatory—or "social"—in nature. Below, we will look a little deeper into each of these three trends. We start with a discussion on participation and then move on to reflect on the increased cross-mediality and mobility in news use.

Participation in News Use

According to Jenkins, Ford, and Green (2013, 2), we witness the emergence of "a more participatory model of culture, one which sees the public not as simply consumers of pre-constructed messages, but as people who are shaping, sharing, reframing, and remixing media content in ways which might not have been previously imagined". Although media scholars are sometimes inclined to overstate the internet "revolution", it is widely acknowledged that with the rise of digital online media, the news process has become more interactive and more open to users (Singer et al. 2011). In today's digital media environment, users have indeed many options to participate in the creation, sharing and interpretation of news, information and opinions. Former distinctions between producers and consumers have become more fluid and the relationship between them more equally balanced and horizontal (Bruns 2008; Castells 2007). The RISJ Digital News Report shows that, despite significant international differences, the number of digital media users who share news through their online social networks, like or rate news stories, or post occasional comments keeps growing (Newman and Levy 2013).

Nevertheless, some authors stay sceptical about the kind and quality of users' participation in the news process. According to Carpentier (2011), for instance, it is important to differentiate between "participation" and mere "interaction". The simple fact that digital technologies have increased possibilities for users to interact and engage with media content does not automatically mean that they are also motivated and empowered enough to become involved in the process of media production ("participation *in* media") or to employ media to increase their voice in public debate ("participation *through* media"). In other words, whilst in the digital age people *"can* interact and *can* create their own content ... which they could do only to a limited extent in an earlier era" (Jönsson and Örnebring 2011, 141), we must be careful of overstating the impact of this growing audience activity on journalism and on democracy in general.

Further research is needed to enhance our understanding of how and to what extent the growing user involvement in the news process is changing our notions of "news" (e.g. in terms of credibility, pluralism and value) and "the audience", and what this means for both the economic viability and the democratic role of journalism in the networked society. Again, these questions should be approached not only from a production perspective, but also, and especially, from the user's point of view. In this respect, we can refer to Mitchelstein and Boczkowski (2010), who propose an integrative research agenda that aims to bridge the gap between research focusing on media features (for instance, the participatory options on news sites) and studies on users' news-related social practices. Besides this, the authors also argue that online news consumption research would benefit from giving up the "artificial differentiation among print, broadcast, and online news consumption" (1088), which brings us to a second fundamental shift in news use.

Cross-mediality in News Use

In 2010, the annual State of the News Media report of the Pew Research Center stated that "the American news consumer is increasingly becoming a grazer, across both online and offline platforms. On a typical day, nearly half of Americans now get news from four to six different platforms—from online to television to print and more" (Pew Research Center 2010). Other studies confirm that users increasingly build their own personal repertoires of media channels through which they follow and access the news. In a digital news environment characterised by information abundance and convergence, users seem more and more likely to spread their news consumption over multiple platforms, hence creating their own "personal information space" (Deuze 2007, 30–33). As argued by Couldry, Livingstone, and Markham (2007, 190–191), "the particular constellation of media on which one individual draws may be quite different than another's". One could even argue that there are virtually as many media constellations as there are media users (Schrøder and Larsen 2010).

News use thus becomes extremely fragmented and personalised. The personalisation of people's media repertoires has, next to the expansion of available media, also been hastened by the dematerialisation of content from its physical form (Lister et al. 2003, 16). In other words, the traditionally tight relationship between a medium and its content sublimes: audiovisual content, for instance, is no longer exclusively related to the television set, but can also be consumed in different socio-spatial contexts through a wide range of other devices such as laptops, tablet computers or smartphones (Courtois, De Marez, and Verdegem 2013). More fundamentally, users' increased control over what content they want to use through which media channels implies that they become more demanding. In the digital age, people expect media content, and thus also the news, to be tailored to their personal needs and convenience. For journalism, then, the challenge is to understand, from an audience viewpoint, "how news and information creates value in [people's] lives" (Picard 2010, 20). Therefore, the fundamental question regarding news use in a cross-media environment is: what media do people deem "valuable" (Costera Meijer

2013) or "worthwhile" (Schrøder and Larsen 2010) enough to be included within the particular, personalised media repertoire on which they draw for their daily news?

Mobility in News Use

As said above, news is also becoming more mobile. The fact that people increasingly tend to consume journalism anywhere and anytime of day reminds Peters of the importance of spatiality in our daily experiences of journalism:

> News consumption is not just something we do, it is something we *do in a particular place* … if we "think spatially" about our own habits and perceptions of media use, including news consumption, we quickly realise that such practices help structure and give meaning to the social spaces of everyday life … Accordingly, if journalism is to succeed in the future, it is crucial we understand where—and through what media—audiences consume news. (Peters 2012, 698, emphasis in original)

While this engagement with "space" is largely absent in journalism scholarship, as Peters (2012) shows, we can, again, find relevant clues in media audience theory, particularly within the literature on the domestication of media (Livingstone 2003). Dahlgren (2001, 37) notices that in the 1990s, "the humanities and social sciences have become increasingly sensitive to the spatial dimensions of social and cultural processes: the where is catching up in importance with the what, the who, the why, and the how". Indeed, audience researchers began taking into account the spatial *context*—both in terms of "place" and "social space"—of media consumption. This strand of research, also referred to as the ethnographic turn in audience studies, can be considered a response to the media-centrism in audience research and an attempt to move "further away from the medium itself in search of the local sites of cultural meaning-making which shape people's orientation to the media" (Livingstone 2003, 344). Today, with digital media consumption becoming more and more mobile, these "local sites of cultural meaning-making" seem to be changing. Media practices that once were bound to take place at shared domestic spaces, like watching television, can now be experienced on the go, in the intimacy of one's own room or with friends, and so on (cf. Courtois, De Marez, and Verdegem 2013). As media use, including news use, becomes mobile and ubiquitous, we also need to become more aware of the "mobilities"—or the "where" and "when"—of people's media experiences: domestic and non-domestic; private and public; leisure- and work-related; sedentary, mobile and nomadic; isolated and connected, etc. (see also, in a broader context, Urry 2007 and Schmitz Weiss 2014).

Looking at Journalism from a Radical User Perspective: A Q-sort Study on Cross-media News Use

Our next step is to look at the insights generated by a previous study that adopts a user perspective. We concisely present one of our studies—a comparative news use study described in detail in Courtois, Schrøder, and Kobbernagel (forthcoming)—for which this perspective was applied, especially focusing on the assumptions, mechanics and the kind of knowledge the study generated. We will focus on the uniqueness of the discernments the approach has to offer and also elaborate on the new methodological possibilities it enables. By doing so, we try to shed light on the social use of news as a "situated action" (Suchman 1987) undertaken by news users. The study discussed here approaches user activity as a social practice embedded into users' everyday activities or, in other words, as an experience seen through the eyes of the news users themselves.

The study draws upon Q-methodology, which entails a hands-on method to approach audience members' personally constructed media repertoires. More specifically, it fully acknowledges the individualised, constructive practice of composing a personal diet, consisting of multiple types of news media. In today's media environment, users are increasingly confronted with the available access to various interacting platforms that stretch far beyond the traditional media silos of television, radio and print. Boundaries between media forms are blurring into non-existence. It is apparent that now, more than ever, audiences are confronted with a broad pallet of choices in composing a media diet, or repertoires (Hasebrink and Popp 2006). In fact, audiences have always been confronted with multiple options, albeit that the number of options has become virtually unlimited. As such, audiences are inherently crossing media, although media research does not necessarily include this notion in its conceptual and operational models. Of course, it remains relevant to study individual modes of media consumption, albeit that the overviewing picture is at least equally important (Schrøder 2011). Keeping this overview poses the fundamental challenge to media researchers of how to determine users' combinations of media outlets, and especially the reasons for these specific combinations. In this respect, we wish to point to an especially relevant line of mixed-method research we have been involved in, drawing on Q-methodology. In this particular case, we especially refer to a comparative research project of two compatible news use studies, performed in Denmark (2009, $N = 35$; Schrøder and Kobbernagel 2010) and Belgium's Northern region (2011, $N = 32$; Courtois, Schrøder, and Kobbernagel, forthcoming). The initial Danish study immediately followed a more classic survey approach that provoked a need for a more in-depth interaction with news consumers.

The Q framework, which perhaps needs some introduction, invites participants in the course of a semi-structured interview to map out and discuss their personal news media repertoires. This technique, described at length by McKeown and Thomas (1988), has gained considerable momentum in audience research in the past few years (Davis and Michelle 2011). In these particular news studies, a predefined set of 25 new media outlets were presented on cards that need to be sorted on a normally distributed grid, following a specific dimension, i.e. "plays a role in my life" versus "does not play a role in my life" (see Table 1 for the so-called Q-sample). This entails an operationalisation of the multi-dimensional notion of worthwhileness (Schrøder and Larsen 2010; Courtois, Schrøder, and Kobbernagel, forthcoming), which is a multi-dimensional concept that decomposes in factors including the worth of spending time and money, next to the participatory potential, technological appeal, public connection, enticing content, situational fit and normative pressures. During this exercise, participants are invited to think aloud, disclosing their personal constructions of individual news media, while arranging them in the broader perspective of a cross-medial landscape.

This results in a raw data matrix cross-tabulating participants and news media regarding the value the individual participants address to such an outlet. Next, methods of quantitative data reduction—usually principal component analysis—are applied to distil patterns from the raw data. It is these patterns that are of special interest. They reflect participants with a common set of preferred news media. The Q-task is preferably embedded in a larger interview that probes into daily practices and circumstances, the personal value addressed to news consumption and the specific incorporation of news

TABLE 1
The communal Q-sample items used in the Danish and Flemish study

Q sample items	
1. Prime-time Danish TV news	14. Local free weeklies
2. 24-hour TV news	15. Professional magazines
3. "Serious" current affairs programmes on Danish TV	16. Family and women's magazines
4. "Entertaining" current affairs programmes on Danish TV	17. Magazines about lifestyle, health, culture
5. News and current affairs on international TV channels	18. News on Danish newspapers' and TV channels' websites
6. Radio news (mornings before 9 am)	19. News on other Danish websites
7. Radio news (after 9 am)	20. Blogs with news on the internet
8. Radio current affairs	21. Social net media (Facebook, Twitter, YouTube, etc.)
9. National mainstream newspapers	22. News on international news media websites
10. National specialised newspapers	23. International news sites not produced by media
11. Free daily newspapers	24. Text-TV news
12. Tabloid newspapers	25. News on mobile phones and other handheld media
13. Local/regional dailies	

Source: Schrøder and Kobbernagel (2010).

media in everyday life. As such, the quantitatively derived patterns serve as guiding principles in further qualitative data analysis. In short, the Q news studies provide a glimpse into the dynamics and rationales for engaging with multiple news media, clarifying their interactions and (in)compatible appropriations. Moreover, due to the emphasis on the ability of participants to reflect aloud, and to share constructions of news media repertoires in everyday circumstances, it furnishes user-centred insight in the constructions of news media.

In the aforementioned Danish and Belgian studies, this led to seven and eight types of repertoires, respectively, both juxtaposing traditionally oriented and more new, online media-oriented patterns, next to apparent preferences for light, general and background-laden news types.

In the Danish study, the following types of news consumers were found: (1) *the traditional, versatile news consumers* with a preference for national newspapers, prime-time television news, morning radio news and online services; (2) *popular culture-oriented digital news consumers*, who are tied to Web services (i.e. social media and news sites); (3) *background-oriented digital news consumers* with a similar profile as the previous type, albeit with a disposition to indulge in serious current affairs programmes and international television news; (4) *the light newspaper readers* who are, in contrast to others, prone to engage with tabloid newspapers and free newspapers; (5) *the heavy newspaper readers* with a strong print tendency towards national newspapers, specialised newspapers, next to local weeklies and free newspapers; (6) *the news update addicts* who are tied to 24-hour news and text television updates; and (7) *the regional omnivorous news consumers* that, contrary to others, address high value to regional dailies, combined with a diverse remainder of news choices.

In the Flemish case, hybrid forms mixing traditional and online media emerged, next to the selective prominence of both social and mobile media. Still, the latter two are most likely attributable to the time lapse between the studies, during which both types of news sources have gained substantial ground. The distinguished news consumption repertoires are: (1) *the traditional mainstream consumers*, following the flow of morning radio news, tabloid newspaper and prime-time television news; (2) *the hybrid light news consumers*, combining news websites with magazines and prime-time television news; (3) *the traditional background news consumers* with a preference for traditional media forms such as newspapers, radio and television (i.e. current affairs programmes); (4) *the mobile, light news consumers* who predominantly draw on mobile applications, supplemented by free dailies and lifestyle magazines; (5) *the online, social background news consumer* tied to social media as news sources, extended by news website and prime-time television; (6) *the mobile mainstream news consumers*, who are again tied to mobile applications, yet combined with a higher preference for current affairs on television, text news and news website; (7) *the hybrid background news consumers*, inclined to consume national specialised newspapers, followed by news websites and current affairs programmes; and (8) *the online, social light news consumers* who focus on social media, combined with family and women's magazines' news websites.

As such Q reveals fine-grained, latent repertoire structures shared by participants that allow for further qualitative analysis. In this particular case, it evoked the rationales that turn to the routine nature of news outlet selections, fitting morning routines, haphazard news checking during the day, and more elaborate and deepening information during the evening. This largely feeds back to the original conceptual news worthwhileness dimensions. More specifically, participants emphasise their situations and their practical constraints (social, spatial, temporal, i.e. listening to the radio at work in a forklift, browsing a smartphone news app in between administrative tasks, watching the television news in the evening together with the family), quality assumptions and assessments of the contributions (i.e. specific newspaper titles), technological affordances and the supporting skills (i.e. the ability to operate devices proficiently and understand their dynamics). Very similar to digital ethnography, the Q-methodology allows for an understanding of practices as they are embedded in the specific context of the mundane. It offers to focus on actual practices and what they are worth for the participant, rather than engaging in normative debate about what practices are valuable (although social norm is likely to persist as a factor).

All things considered, the Q-based audience research has the benefit of transparent data collection and analysis. It entails a clear, almost standardised procedure to engage in this kind of research, thus even affording cross-national comparisons. Still, there are several caveats that have harvested substantial criticism, including the methodological assumption the predefined sorting grid is under pressure, as well as the issue of recruitment that tends to affect the results and the potential for generalising the diversity in patterns (Courtois, Schrøder, and Kobbernagel, forthcoming). The common prerequisite of Q-methodology imposing participants to sort the items (i.e. news media) on a Bell-shaped distributed grid, rather than a free sort, is often criticised. Moreover, the results and conclusions are highly dependent on the scope of news media that are included and how these forms are interpreted. Nevertheless, if the emphasis is put on Q as a tool to guide deepening qualitative analysis, focusing on patterns within a pool of participants, the merits are considerable.

Discussion and Conclusion

This paper has tried to make the case for a radical user perspective in journalism studies as a way to deepen our understanding of a factor becoming increasingly important in how journalism is shaped: the news users themselves. If indeed, as Carey (2007, 12) has stated, "the 'public' is the god term of journalism", then journalism studies should devote a particular attention to news users. We would like to conclude this article by addressing how this perspective cannot only be important for journalism studies, but by extension also for journalism as such.

Adopting a radical user perspective in journalism studies implies the acknowledgement of the fact that our thinking about and study of journalism cannot be fruitful if the news user is not taken into account on the conceptual, methodological and normative level. As argued in this article, the need to do so has only become more pressing since the advent of digital and mobile technologies and the changes they brought about in news use in terms of participation, cross-mediality and mobility. The increased adoption of content-producing or -distributing activities by large parts of the audience has introduced a "productive" dimension in our thinking about the audience (Picone 2011). A "consumptive" dimension should equally be introduced in our thinking about media and journalistic production. In the same way as we cannot understand how people experience journalism by merely looking at the way they consult news, we can no longer understand the ongoing changes in journalism by solely looking at professional practice in the newsroom.

Relating this back to the study presented, the empirical results may, for instance, show that staying informed about what happens still largely remains a routine activity tied to well-known forms of delivery, even if users have an abundant window media and source options at their disposal. Although substantial audience proportions are diversifying towards online media, many others stick to more traditional consumption patterns, emphasising the need for approaches—like Q—that are able to grasp this audience diversification. This implies that news stories, how well written and publicly relevant they may be, will always be articulated to the specific individuals' situation and possible socio-spatial constraints. Such insights offer more tangible ways for journalists to conceive possible new forms of telling stories to their audience while at the same time allow journalists and academics alike to break free from the often normative misconceptions about what kind of news people want and how they experience it in their daily life practices.

In relation to the latter sentence, we are convinced that a radical user perspective will also help journalism scholarship move further away from the all too normative dichotomy between quality and popular journalism. It is exactly by adopting a more nuanced conceptualisation of the user that we can understand that news use is not solely driven by popular demand and news users' expectations about journalism are much more complex and ambiguous than what is often assumed—even though, we would quickly add, not *too* complex and ambiguous to study. A news story can be very much worthwhile to people because of its civic value too. Similarly, when it comes to the often little added value of user contributions to the news, both journalists and news users might share the same frustration about the unused democratic potential of user-generated content. The general idea here is that journalistic and user interests are not bound to be oppositional, nor is the common ground between both necessarily limited to the offering and consumption of popular news (cf. Costera Meijer 2013). (Certain) journalists and (certain) news users may very well share a series of civic goals ranging from offering grounded information to trying to solve issues or achieve social change on certain topics.

In conclusion, we hope to have shown that it is useful to give both journalists and news users an equal place in our thinking about what journalism should be. In line with Mitchelstein and Boczkowski (2010), the proposed radical user perspective may contribute to a more integrated theory of journalism that overcomes the dichotomy between "productive" and "consumptive" approaches that continues to blur our further under-standing of what form journalism takes—and should take—in the digital age. As such, the user perspective put forward in this article is radical in means much more than in scope. The user perspective has found its way into journalism studies before, but has never come on equal terms with the content- or production-focused approaches. Hence, in order to achieve an integrated theory of journalism we appeal for a more intensive focus on the user, one that must result in providing journalism studies with the much needed concepts to grasp the social relevance as well as the socially and spatially more complex (mobile) news use.

Of course, the proposed perspective is not without issues. Jenkins, Ford, and Green (2013) notice that convergence has led to the circulation of cultural material being more participatory but at the same time messier. As "audiences are making their presence felt by actively shaping media flows" (2), these media flows become much more complex, intertwining private and public messages, professional and collaborative information production, interpersonal and mass-communication, etc. It is quite a dare to single out the social logics and cultural practices emerging in such a "messy" media environment. Still, exactly in understanding those logics and practices lies the answer on the role journalism can keep on playing in our society. This calls upon journalism studies to take these evolutions into account: as journalism will be shaped by the interaction of both news users and journalists, so should journalism studies engage in both production-oriented and user-oriented research.

REFERENCES

Alasuutari, Pertti, ed. 1999. *Rethinking the Media Audience*. London: Sage.

Bird, S. Elizabeth. 2011. "Seeking the Audience for News. Response, News Talk, and Everyday Practices." In *The Handbook of Media Audiences*, edited by Virginia Nightingale, 489–508. Malden, MA: Wiley-Blackwell.

Borger, Merel, Anita Van Hoof, Irene Costera Meijer, and José Sanders. 2013. "Constructing Participatory Journalism as a Scholarly Object. A Genealogical Analysis." *Digital Journalism* 1 (1): 117–134. doi:10.1080/21670811.2012.740267.

Bruns, Axel. 2008. *Blogs, Wikipedia, Second Life, and Beyond: From Production to Produsage*. New York: Peter Lang.

Carey, James W. 2007. "A Short History of Journalism for Journalists: A Proposal and Essay." *Harvard International Journal of Press/Politics* 12 (1): 3–16. doi:10.1177/1081180x06297603.

Carpentier, Nico. 2011. "New Configurations of the Audience? The Challenges of User-Generated Content for Audience Theory and Media Participation." In *The Handbook of Media Audiences*, edited by Virginia Nightingale, 191–212. Malden, MA: Wiley-Blackwell.

Castells, Manuel. 2007. "Communication, Power and Counter-power in the Network Society." *International Journal of Communication* 1: 238–266. Accessed February 4 2013. http://ijoc.org/index.php/ijoc/article/viewFile/46/35.

Costera Meijer, Irene. 2007. "The Paradox of Popularity. How Young People Experience the News." *Journalism Studies* 8 (1): 96–116. doi:10.1080/14616700601056874.

Costera Meijer, Irene. 2013. "Valuable Journalism: A Search for Quality from the Vantage Point of the User." *Journalism* 14 (6): 754–770. doi:10.1177/1464884912455899.

Couldry, Nick. 2011. "The Necessary Future of the Audience … and How to Research It." In *The Handbook of Media Audiences*, edited by Virginia Nightingale, 213–229. Malden, MA: Wiley-Blackwell.

Couldry, Nick, Sonia Livingstone, and Tim Markham. 2007. *Media Consumption and Public Engagement. Beyond the Presumption of Attention*. Basingstoke: Palgrave Macmillan.

Courtois, Cédric. 2012. "When Two Worlds Meet: An Inter-Paradigmatic Mixed Method Approach to Convergent Audiovisual Media Consumption." *Participations* 9 (2): 716–742.

Courtois, Cédric, Lieven De Marez, and Pieter Verdegem. 2013. "The Triple Articulation of Media Technologies in Audiovisual Media Consumption." *Television and New Media* 14 (5): 421–439. doi:10.1177/1527476412439106.

Courtois, Cédric, Kim C. Schrøder, and Christian Kobbernagel. forthcoming. "Exploring Land-scapes of News Consumption Cross-Nationally." In *Revitalising Audiences Research: Innovations in European Audience Research*, edited by Frauke Zeller, Cristina Ponte, and Brian O'Neill. London: Routledge.

Dahlgren, Peter. 2001. "The Public Sphere and the Net." In *Mediated Politics. Communication in the Future of Democracy*, edited by W. Lance Bennett and Robert M. Entman, 32–55. Cambridge: Cambridge University Press.

Dahlgren, Peter, and Collin Sparks, eds. 1992. *Journalism and Popular Culture*. London: Sage.

Davis, Charles, and Carolyn Michelle. 2011. "Q Methodology in Audience Research: Bridging the Qualitative/Quantitative 'Divide'?" *Participations* 8 (2): 559–593.

Deuze, Mark. 2007. *Media Work*. Cambridge: Polity Press.

Deuze, Mark. 2010. "Survival of the Mediated." *Journal of Cultural Science* 3 (2): 1–11. Accessed February 7 2013. http://cultural-science.org/journal/index.php/culturalscience/article/view/42/120.

Fiske, John. 1989. *Reading the Popular*. Boston, MA: Unwin Hyman.

Gray, Ann. 1999. "Audience and Reception Research in Retrospect. The Trouble with Audiences." In *Rethinking the Media Audience. The New Agenda*, edited by Pertti Alasuutari, 22–37. Tampere: Sage.

Hartley, John. 1987. "Invisible Fictions: Television Audiences, Paedocracy, Pleasure." *Textual Practice* 1: 121–138. doi:10.1080/09502368708582010.

Harrington, Stephen. 2008. "Popular News in the 21st Century. Time for a New Critical Approach?" *Journalism* 9 (3): 266–284. doi:10.1177/1464884907089008.

Hasebrink, Uwe, and Jutta Popp. 2006. "Media Repertoires as a Result of Selective Media Use: A Conceptual Approach to the Analysis of Patterns of Exposure." *Communications* 31: 369–387. doi:10.1515/COMMUN.2006.023.

Hermida, Alfred, David Domingo, Ari Heinonen, Steve Paulussen, Thorsten Quandt, Zvi Reich, Jane B. Singer, and Marina Vujnovic. 2011. "The Active Recipient: Participatory Journalism through the Lens of the Dewey-Lippmann Debate." *#ISOJ – The Official Journal of the International Symposium on Online Journalism* 1 (2): 129–152.

Jenkins, Henry. 2006. *Convergence Culture. Where Old and New Media Collide*. New York: New York University Press.

Jenkins, Henry, Sam Ford, and Joshua Green. 2013. *Spreadable Media: Creating Value and Meaning in a Networked Culture*. New York: New York University Press.

Jönsson, Anna Maria, and Henrik Örnebring. 2011. "User Generated Content and the News: Empowerment of Citizens or Interactive Illusion?" *Journalism Practice* 5 (2): 127–144. doi:10.1080/17512786.2010.501155.

Kovach, Bill, and Tom Rosenstiel. 2007. *The Elements of Journalism. What Newspeople Should Know and the Public Should Expect*. New York: Crown.

Lister, Martin, Jon Dovey, Seth Giddings, Iain Grant, and Kieran Kelly. 2003. *New Media: A Critical Introduction*. London: Routledge.

Livingstone, Sonia. 1998. "Relationships between Media and Audiences: Prospects for Audience Reception Studies." In *Media, Ritual and Identity*, edited by James Curran and Tamar Liebes, 237–255. London: Routledge.

Livingstone, Sonia. 2003. "The Changing Nature of Audiences: From the Mass Audience to the Interactive Media User." In *Companion to Media Studies*, edited by Angharad Valdivia, 337–359. Oxford: Blackwell.

McKeown, Bruce, and Dan Thomas. 1988. *Q Methodology*. Newbury Park: Sage.

Mitchelstein, Eugenia, and Pablo J. Boczkowski. 2010. "Online News Consumption Research: An Assessment of Past Work and an Agenda for the Future." *New Media & Society* 12 (7): 1085–1102. doi:10.1177/1461444809350193.

Newman, Nic, and David A. L. Levy, eds. 2013. *Reuters Institute Digital News Report 2013. Tracking the Future of News*. Oxford: The Reuters Institute for the Study of Journalism, Oxford University. Accessed June 24, 2013. http://media.digitalnewsreport.org/wp-content/uploads/2014/05/Reuters-Institute-Digital-News-Report-2013.pdf.

Nightingale, Virginia, ed. 2011. *The Handbook of Media Audiences*. Malden, MA: Wiley-Blackwell.

Nip, Joyce M. 2006. "Exploring the Second Phase of Public Journalism." *Journalism Studies* 7 (2): 212–236. doi:10.1080/14616700500533528.

Paulussen, Steve, Ari Heinonen, David Domingo, and Thorsten Quandt. 2007. "Doing It Together. Citizen Participation in the Professional News Making Process." *Observatorio (OBS*) Journal* 1 (3): 131–154. Accessed February 7, 2013. http://obs.obercom.pt/index.php/obs/article/download/148/107.

Peters, Chris. 2012. "Journalism To Go: The Changing Spaces of News Consumption." *Journalism Studies* 13 (5–6): 695–705. doi:10.1080/1461670X.2012.662405.

Pew Research Center. 2010. *The State of the News Media 2010: Online – Summary Essay*. Washington, DC: Pew Research Center's Project on the Excellence of Journalism. Accessed February 4 2013. http://stateofthemedia.org/2010/online-summary-essay/audience-behavior/.

Picard, Robert. 2010. *Value Creation and the Future of News Organizations: Why and How Journalism Must Change to Remain Relevant in the Twenty-First Century*. Lisbon: Media XXI.

Picone, Ike. 2011. "Produsage as a Form of Self-publication: A Qualitative Study of Casual News Produsage." *New Review of Hypermedia and Multimedia* 17 (1): 99–120. doi:10.1080/13614568.2011.552643.

Potter, W. James. 2013. *Media Effects*. London: Sage.

Rosen, Jay. 1999. *What Are Journalists For?* New Haven: Yale University Press.

Rosen, Jay. 2006. "The People Formerly Known as the Audience." *Pressthink*. Accessed February 5, 2013. http://archive.pressthink.org/2006/06/27/ppl_frmr.html.

Russell, Adrienne. 2011. *Networked: A Contemporary History of News in Transition*. Cambridge: Polity Press.

Schmitz Weiss, Amy. 2014. "Place-Based Knowledge in the Twenty-First Century." *Digital Journalism* 1–16. doi:10.1080/21670811.2014.928107.

Schrøder, Kim C. 1999. "The Best of Both Worlds? Media Audiences Research between Rival Paradigms." In *Rethinking the Media Audience*, edited by Pertti Alasuutari, 38–67. London: Sage.

Schrøder, Kim C. 2011. "Audiences are Inherently Cross-Media: Audience Studies and the Cross-Media Challenge." *Communication Management Quarterly* 18 (6): 5–27. Accessed June 24, 2013. http://www.fpn.bg.ac.rs/wp-content/uploads/CM18-Web.pdf.

Schrøder, Kim C., and Christian Kobbernagel. 2010. "Towards a Typology of Cross-Media News Consumption: A Qualitative-Quantitative Synthesis." *Northern Lights* 8 (1): 115–138. doi:10.1386/nl.8.115_1.

Schrøder, Kim C., and Bent S. Larsen. 2010. "The Shifting Cross-Media News Landscape. Challenges for News Producers." *Journalism Studies* 11 (4): 524–534. doi:10.1080/14616701003638392.

Schudson, Michael. 1998. "The Public Journalism Movement and Its Problems." In *The Politics of News. The News of Politics*, edited by Doris Graber, Denis McQuail, and Pippa Norris, 132–149. Washington, DC: CQ Press.

Singer, Jane B., Alfred Hermida, David Domingo, Ari Heinonen, Steve Paulussen, Thorsten Quandt, Zvi Reich, and Marina Vujnovic. 2011. *Participatory Journalism. Guarding Open Gates at Online Newspapers*. Malden, MA: Wiley-Blackwell.

Suchman, Lucille Alice. 1987. *Plans and Situated Actions: The Problem of Human-Machine Communication*. New York: Cambridge University Press.

Urry, John. 2007. *Mobilities*. Cambridge: Polity Press.

Wahl-Jorgensen, Karin, Andrew Williams, and Claire Wardle. 2010. "Audience Views on User-Generated Content: Exploring the Value of News from the Bottom Up." *Northern Lights* 8 (1): 177–184. doi:10.1386/nl.8.177_1.

THE RELEVANCE OF JOURNALISM
Studying news audiences in a digital era

Heikki Heikkilä and **Laura Ahva**

The media-saturated nature of everyday life is well acknowledged in current audience research, but the role of journalism for people living in this digitalised environment remains less clear. To provide a better understanding of the role of journalism and news in everyday life, this article states the case for combining two complementary analytical perspectives in cultural audience research that draw on the framework of practice theory. We need to focus on both interpersonal communication practices within social networks and on discursive practices and patterns of how people use the media. Empirically, this article draws on an extensive audience study conducted in Finland, whose findings provide a cause for moderate optimism regarding the sustaining relevance of journalism in people's everyday life in the digital era. Firstly, social networks—both offline and online—constitute a vital structure within which the output of journalism is rendered meaningful by users. Secondly, the discursive practices applied by the participants emphasise the importance of news as a central means of orientation to society and making sense of the political nature of the public world. However, much of this potential remains unknown to journalists because users' activities occur at a distance from journalism and political institutions, which poses a challenge to digital journalism.

Introduction

Our lived experience is, as Mark Deuze (2007, 13) writes, "framed by, mitigated through, and made immediate by pervasive and ubiquitous media". In this new human condition, he continues, key organising categories of modern life, such as distinctions between public and private, or mediated and non-mediated experiences, have lost their intrinsic, commonly held and consensual meaning. In the same vein, Klaus Bruhn Jensen (2010, 64) argues that media are so closely integrated in our natural and cultural environments that they may no longer be recognised as media.

In these circumstances, individuals may well render their ways of living with the media meaningful for themselves without specific analytical rigour, but this is hardly acceptable for those who work in or study the media. However, not all attempts to make sense of the digital world are equally commendable. One of the developments we find misleading pertains to how the concept of "the audience" in digital journalism is pulled in two opposite directions. On the one hand, audiences are labelled as things of the distant past in the changing media environment—as Jay Rosen's famous formulation about "people formerly known as the audience" suggests—and subsequently upgraded into a generative entity, "produsers" (Bruns 2008), carrying the capacity to take part in and change cultural production and the production of cultures (Jenkins 2006; Tapscott and Williams 2006). On the other hand, due to the technological affordances to monitor Web traffic and measure clicks, news audiences are being reduced to quantifiable aggregates: herds or masses rather than creative individuals or groups (Napoli 2011; Anderson 2011).

Even if these notions are not mutually exclusive, there is a risk that they promote a polarised understanding of the audience. As a media developer, it is not possible to give equal weight to both audience models without compromising consistent thought.

Within the news industry, these opposite notions of audiences tend to reproduce a classic division with regard to two styles of journalism: "serious" and "popular". An indirect defence of a news policy of "Different Strokes for Different Folks" for digital journalism may be read from, for instance, Tenenboim and Cohen's (2013) recent empirical analysis. They demonstrate that two mechanisms of audience participation—commenting and clicking—tend to adhere to different types of content and "generate different expressions of interest" on the part of users. Those who want to comment do so by directing themselves towards news on controversies in political and public affairs, while those merely preferring to check out what is going on will focus on news items on sensational events that arouse their curiosity (Tenenboim and Cohen 2013).

Tenenboim and Cohen are careful in emphasising that commenting and clicking draw on different expressions of interest, and these expressions do not refer to two distinct audience groups but rather to two modes of relating to online news media. This important stipulation, however, easily escapes the mindsets of professionals in digital newsrooms if their focus is on *who* is clicking or commenting on the news rather than identifying *what lies behind* the different expressions of interest. The idea of understanding audiences as "people out there" relies on the fact that it is so commonsensical to think that audiences are social beings or fixed target groups constituted of distinct demographic features regarding, for instance, age, gender and education.

What is peculiar for all discourses about the audience is that the referent always seems to stand for something "other", and thus someone has to speak on behalf of the audience (Ridell 2006, 233). Mosco and Kaye (2000, 35) argue that within the media industry this gesture is self-serving, given that the interest in knowing the size, composition and preferences of the audience has always been economically motivated. Thus, attempts to understand audiences imply a desire to gain control over recipients. Bearing this in mind, many audience researchers—who are also not immune to this tendency—suggest that we should be agnostic towards *any* attempts to speak on behalf of the audience, whether those stem from academia or the media industry (Carpentier, Schrøder, and Hallet 2014, 7). In trying to be sensitive about this tendency, we suggest that it is useful to turn attention away from audience profiles to audience practices, and hence to the tradition of cultural audience research.

As far as the digital journalism audience is concerned, it is noteworthy that discussions regarding the potential of user-generated content (UGC) and the merits of Web metrics have been either unaware of or unimpressed by cultural audience research. To some extent, this negligence stems from the fact that from the early 1980s until relatively recently, cultural audience researchers focused more on studying people's relation to television and/or entertainment than to news (Morley 1992). A shift of attention was set in motion in the early 2000s, as it became apparent that news continues to provide a common reference for citizens, and probably even more so in the conditions of "media manifold" than in the days of mass communication (Madianou 2009). Based on this observation, a number of audience studies have attempted to analyse how news draws people's attention to the public world (Couldry, Livingstone, and Markham 2007) and how their everyday talk is connected to their news use (Bird 2011).

In addition to the traditions of cultural audience research, many contemporary studies on media use share an interest in the concept of "practice" (Bräuchler and Postill 2010). Practice theory (Rouse 2006) understands practice as "a routinised way in which bodies are moved, objects are handled, subjects are treated, things are described and the world is understood" (Reckwitz 2002, 250). By studying practices, it is possible to understand how people's everyday lives become orderly and meaningful. Applying practice theory to media use thus proposes that to fully understand the role of media in daily life, the research must focus on the open-ended variety of things people say and do in relation to media (Couldry 2004, 121). This route may seem complicated and wide, but it offers a robust means of making sense of the regular, social and need-related role that the media play in people's lives without automatically placing the media at the centre of attention (Couldry 2012, 33–35).

In this article, we suggest that practice theory is useful for broadening our understanding of the relevance of journalism. We summarise the core findings and conceptualisations of an empirical audience study conducted in Finland between 2009 and 2012, and in doing this we also develop a cultural audience research framework that combines two complementary analytical perspectives of practices. We propose focusing on interpersonal communication practices in social networks that make up the everyday context for media consumption, and on discursive audience practices and patterns through which audiences relate to the media. We begin by describing our empirical research design and how it relates to the traditions of cultural audience research.

Beyond the Determinate Moments of Reception: The Framework of a Study

Many advocates of cultural audience research subscribe to two fundamental presumptions. Firstly, audiences are not understood as social beings, "unknown, but knowable sets of people" (Ang 1991, 2). Rather than focusing on *who* the audiences are, researchers aim to study *what people do* as audiences and how their varying modes of media-related behaviour may be distinguished from each other empirically and conceptually (Ridell 2006, 245; Couldry 2012, 35). Within this framework, the concept of "audience" is understood as a discursive construct produced by a particular analytical gaze, and therefore the outcomes of the analysis cannot be reduced to any particular demographic section of the population (Alasuutari 1999, 6).

Secondly, contemporary examples of cultural audience research share an ambition to move beyond the determinate moments of reception—a given act of reading, watching or clicking—to grasp the broader environment wherein people encounter media products (Spitulnik 2010, 107). For a long time, this environment was located at homes and loosely dubbed "everyday life", the seemingly authentic domain for individuals and families (Drotner 2000). In recent years, greater emphasis has been placed on the role that social networks play in the background of media use. This emphasis results partly from the digitisation of media, whereby the convergence of media platforms and the increased vertical and horizontal interaction between producers and recipients have directed scholarly attention to interpersonal communication practices. While social networks may be seen as products of the social media era or the "culture of connectivity" (van Dijck 2013), their significance as a distribution system of mediated messages and contexts for sense-making were already acknowledged within the Mass Communication Research tradition, most notably in Katz and Lazarsfeld's (1955) seminal study on *Personal Influence*. Today, the importance of social networks—both offline and online—in audience research is, as Livingstone (2006, 243) argues, "a starting point rather than a discovery".

In our empirical audience study,[1] we applied and developed these presumptions in two ways. Firstly, the 74 participants, whose various relationships to news and journalism were analysed over a period of one year, were not treated as representative of any specific demographic group (young/old, women/men, etc.) within the population. Rather, they were regarded as informants on a variety of discursive media-related practices wherein news and media become part of people's daily lives. Thus, we were not so much interested in the differences between the groups, but in the shared ways by which journalism becomes relevant for people. The participants repeatedly emphasised the importance of their social networks in how they discussed current affairs and news, which meant the overarching objective of the study was to learn more about *social networks* as an environment for news. While there seemed to be a gap between interpersonal discussions and determinate moments in the reception of news, our second objective was to theorise how people connect to news with regard to three specific discursive practices: (1) media *routines*, (2) *interpretation* and (3) *public action*. In the study, the concept of "social networks" pertains to relations forged in both face-to-face situations and online. Figure 1 summarises the way in which the theoretical input was developed into a research design.

The empirical material for the study was produced in co-operation with nine "audience groups" from different parts of Finland. Three of the groups were *work-based* (high school teachers, employees of a multicultural centre and civil servants working in a state-run bureau), two were *interest-based* (an association for home owners and a local association for the unemployed) and four were *leisure-based* (a book club, student theatre, choir and a network of old friends).[2] Each group convened approximately once a month over a period of a year to participate in focus group discussions that systematically addressed journalism from different viewpoints. Each session included an assignment for research-led teamwork followed by a discussion. In addition to the focus group meetings ($N = 77$), the entire empirical data set featured individual interviews ($N = 74$) and media

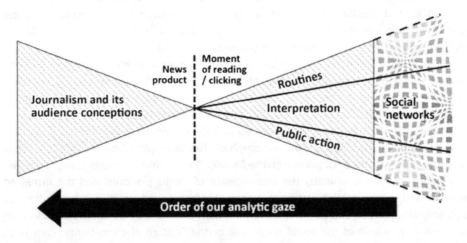

FIGURE 1
Theoretical framework for understanding the relevance of news

diaries (N = 49). All interviews were recorded and analysed qualitatively by the research team.

The rich empirical findings of the project have been reported in full in Finnish (Heikkilä et al. 2012). Rather than replicating empirical results in the present article, we wish to elaborate on observations with theoretical and conceptual significance to digital journalism that resonate with debates regarding "the audience", beyond the immediate cultural context of the study. We start with social networks, and then look into whether and how the participants connect to the news in their media-related practices. From the perspective of practice theory, the order of analysis moves from right to left (see Figure 1), which is deliberately contrary to the conventional view of information flow as directed from producers to recipients. In this way, news is analysed as a social process rather than a product (Bird 2011, 490).

Social Networks as a Context for Journalism

In their book *Personal Influence*, Katz and Lazarsfeld (1955) stress that social networks are important elements of the distribution systems of mass communication. Contrary to the then dominant two-step flow model, their study suggested that the mechanism did not rest on specific opinion leaders in a given community, but instead that meanings were discussed among various social networks depending on the topic and the interests of participants.

Recently, many audience researchers have emphasised the role of interpersonal communication with regard to news consumption in the same vein. For instance, Couldry, Livingstone, and Markham (2007, 116) note that news consumption intersects with "putting the world to rights" or "just having a good old moan" at homes, pubs and workplaces. This everyday talk about current affairs is central to how people connect to the public world (Couldry and Markham 2006, 252–253; Barnhurst 2011, 582). Schrøder and Phillips (2005, 187) point out that citizens have a desire for an overview of societal affairs in the media because they see it as a prerequisite for participation in different social communities. Barnhurst (1998, 215–216) observes that young people in particular make sense of media content and their emerging selves in social contexts. From the outset it appears that social networks as information delivery conduits are far more important to young people than traditional news media. This does not render news insignificant for the youth but rather points out that their impact is diffused through social networks. As Costera Meijer (2007, 105) observes, young people do not necessarily feel the need to watch the news, as they will learn about important developments through their social contacts.

Our study confirmed that the participants lived among an abundance of social networks. Even if their range and scope varied from one person to another, these social relations proved to be important sites of conversation about, and reception to, news. In understanding how social networks work with regard to news, we can make use of Granovetter's (1973, 1983) classic distinction between strong ties and weak ties.

Strong ties refer to relations that are frequently and directly available, allowing for regular opportunities for interaction. Strong ties are typically drawn between family members and their closest relatives, and are forged face-to-face rather than online. Not surprisingly, our participants explained that relationships with their family members—including the parents of children living elsewhere—mattered most, as these were the persons that participants wanted to care for and to whom they wished to devote as much time as possible. At the same time, it appeared that regular encounters between family members did not necessarily lend themselves to discussing current affairs or "politics". In terms of discussions, social networks with strong ties often focused on phatic communication, and remained relatively banal with regard to the public world.

For Granovetter, *weak ties* pertain to relations that are infrequent, loose, distant and not always readily available. Empirically, these weak ties refer to a variety of locations outside participants' homes: work places, participating in hobbies and informal encounters with friends or acquaintances. Weak ties are drawn both offline and online, but varying social networking sites clearly make it easier to form and maintain these relations. With regard to discussions, weak ties, too, tend to trigger transient conversations, but the participants also revealed that discussions with their peers often become serious. The list of topics tackled during coffee breaks, walks with the neighbour or meetings with friends were said to pertain to the varying effects of social and structural injustice, such as the "inadequate care for the elderly", "growing economic cleavages", "climate change" and "the power of the media". One participant in the teachers' group explained that her social network discussions tended to drift on to work pressures because those pressures are regarded as cultural: "The idea that we need to work harder and more efficiently is so widely spread that we want to talk about it whenever we get an opportunity."

Discussions within the networks tend to focus heavily on *concerns*. These were discussed more often by the networks defined by weak ties, where there is more flexibility for social interaction, but the issues discussed tended to pertain to the networks of strong ties, as the concerns stemmed from everyday worries about the wellbeing of the family members, friends and peers. This finding is compatible with other audience studies. In Denmark, Schrøder and Phillips (2007, 910) found that their audience groups held a reflexive detachment from politics, and argue that this "metadiscourse" enables people to critically analyse the dynamics of a political system. In her ethnographic study in the United States, Eliasoph (2000, 90) noted that even politically active people tended to avoid speaking up at public meetings and committees, and preferred to delve into political issues in private settings, such as Sunday lunches, which are clearly separated from the public domain. These observations point to a dual meaning of political discussions for social networks. On the one hand, those conversations are considered as enjoyable in their own right, and are applied as a feasible method for making sense of "how the political world stands" (Heikkilä et al. 2012, 225). On the other hand, people tend to perform their "deep citizenship" (Eliasoph 2000) in their everyday life because they find themselves distant from the institutions of power.

The network practices described above are clearly different from the ways in which audiences are polarised as either active generative producers or quantifiable consumers. The context of social networks appears fit for tackling large-scale social and political problems. In our study, it appeared that news stories were applied as reference points to discussions, when possible. However, this connection proved tenuous, mainly because the concerns the participants enjoyed talking about were often incompatible with the logic of news, wherein the issues are supposed to be clear-cut and limited in scope. If journalism aims to retain its relevance to readers' social network discussions, it should attempt to tap into a different sensibility about what is going on in the world. In the digital environment, newsrooms are more capable of tapping into the chains of sense-making through online discussions, social networking sites or microblogging. However, while half of our participants said they were active on Facebook, they strongly emphasised that they preferred discussing current affairs in an offline environment. The same finding emerged from a survey related to our study, which found that no less than 69 per cent of the respondents regularly discussed the news and current affairs face-to-face with other people, whereas only 2 per cent tended to do so in social networking sites or online discussion boards.[3]

Given the rapid changes in how people make use of the digital environment, the high discrepancy between offline and online discussions with regard to news may already be overestimated. Nonetheless, the results clearly demonstrate that not all social networks are digital, and neither are all discussions indicative of "public opinion" readily available on the internet. These findings suggest that more effort—both journalistic and academic— should be directed at understanding discussions in unorganised offline social networks, even if this remains problematic in practice.

Audiences' Media-related Discursive Practices

To take a step away from the realm of the social networks and closer to the media, we will now focus on three distinct discursive practices through which people relate to the media: routines, interpretation and public action. These three practices are neither mutually exclusive nor hierarchical, but as analytical constructions they enable us to examine these users' activities separately from each other. This is important for identifying possible patterns in media uses, which help in challenging excessively reduced images of news audiences (see Heikkilä et al. 2014).

Routines

From the perspective of routines, people treat media primarily as material objects, with the contents secondary (Silverstone 1994). This view was illustrated in our study through familiar accounts of how people listen to the radio during the working day "with just one ear", or set a news website as the home page of their browser to get regular updates without the trouble of browsing. In addition, social media (mostly Facebook in our case) is often checked routinely with the sole purpose of establishing whether anything new is happening, without any intention of submitting content. With regard to routines, digital technologies offer an unlimited supply of media that compete for public attention: the volume of media material has become essentially unlimited, and the convergent media environment allows people to move easily from one media product to the next (Webster 2011, 43). According to a national survey, Finns spend on average over 8.5 hours per day with the media. Even if much of the time living with the media tends to be "just routine", it brings structure to the daily lives of people. For example, one of the elderly participants described his days in the media diary with references to "radio moments" in the morning, "newspaper moments" at midday and evenings "with the television".

In our study, the participants described themselves as "poly-users", drawing connections to a number of media outlets and platforms in the course of their day-to-day lives: irrespective of their age, education and location, people enjoyed very good access to various outlets. While this rich supply allows for diverse media diets, in our data the strongest common denominator in the media routines was news monitoring. The number of platforms through which the participants accessed the news had multiplied in recent years, and the role of digital news had gradually increased. Nonetheless, in our study there were no signs of a zero-sum game with regard to news routines. In addition to online news, newspapers, prime-time news bulletins and teletext news proved to be important reference points of the mediated centre of society (Couldry 2003); a social imaginary that combines an idea of an organisational centre where public resources are allocated and a generative centre that explains the social world's functioning. While the legacy media provided the sole access point to this centre in the era of mass communication, in the current media landscape there are many media channels providing parallel access points.

The routine of news monitoring in daily media use proved to be so robust in our study that it lends support to an argument that the mass audience of journalism still exists in the digital environment. The mass audience, however, is no longer sustained by the scarcity of media output, nor is it controlled by the top-down communications managed by powerful media institutions. Rather, the mass-like audience is constituted by bottom-up media routines and brought together by news consumption. It seems obvious that mass-like uses of the media have not ceased to exist in the digital era, but the variety of instruments that enable such uses has expanded.

Due to their reliance on news, users seem resistant to the tendencies of audience fragmentation stemming from the multiplication of media interfaces. This line of thought is, however, far from organised or even self-reflexive. While our participants described their own media routines positively, they were at the same time concerned with whether "other people" would have such "healthy" media diets, and whether others were capable of resisting the seemingly addictive features of the digital media and its race for clicks. This contradiction demonstrates that the participants' self-understanding as audiences is not merely shaped by their own experiences, but also responds to other discourses of audiences, not least those held by the media industry.

Interpretation and Criticism

At some point in the process of news monitoring, users select particular news items for closer inspection. In this phase, recipients shift their attention from media as objects to media as texts (Silverstone 1994). At the core of this phase there are two practices enacted by readers or viewers: interpretation and criticism. In cultural audience research, interpretation is generally understood as a semiotic process, wherein readers identify a piece of text as news and while reading it they apply specific cultural frameworks for making sense of the claims presented. Interpretation encompasses both the explicit and implicit meanings of the text. A reader of a news item may well combine elements of what the news says *expressis verbis* and what it does *not* say or is taking for granted (Morley 1992, 76–77).

A standard tenet in journalism suggests that every newspaper report should answer the questions: What?, Who?, Where?, When? and Why?, and should do this in the first paragraph. This is, as a textbook for practical journalism from the 1920s suggests, "the first and greatest commandment in the matter of journalistic style, and the penalty for breaking it is the waste-basket and swift oblivion" (Shuman 1926, 60). Since then, a number of audience studies have questioned such straightforward functionalism in the relationship between news and its readers. It is argued, for instance, that the formal and official address found in the news has a tendency to subdue recipients' capacities to set the information of news into a broader context and their personal experiences (Coleman, Scott, and Morrison 2009; Madianou 2009).

According to Morley, members of the audience draw symbolic resources for interpretation from their particular social and cultural backgrounds. This premise found empirical resonance in his famous *The "Nationwide" Audience* study, wherein three types of ideal-typical readings—"dominant", "oppositional" and "negotiated"—found relative matches with the socio-economic statuses of audience groups (Morley 1980). While the design of our study differed from *The "Nationwide" Audience*, both historically and culturally, we acknowledged that a standard news item published in the Finnish daily newspaper *Helsingin Sanomat*[4] in April 2010 triggered a range of political readings in our audience groups. These readings were relatively compatible with the same ideal-typical categories (dominant–oppositional–negotiated), albeit their congruence with the socio-economic backgrounds of the participants remained vague.

This finding suggests that the semiotic tension between news producers and recipients still exists, and that political views are instrumental in the interpretation of news. In our study, those groups that interpreted the news item more politically (a dominant or oppositional reading) regarded the story as useful and also found pleasure in "decoding" its message. At the same time, those groups that adopted the negotiated reading were more doubtful of the relevance of the news item. For example, the student theatre group that typically expressed strong political opinions ended up with a negotiated reading and thus somewhat loose engagement with the sample story. One of the participants summarised: "OK, the story says that some people want to work when they are retired. So what? Should I have an opinion about this?"

The tendency to interpret news politically relates to the second activity involved in attentive news consumption: criticism. To begin with, users' willingness to criticise journalism does not mean that they would regard all journalism as "bad". Instead, the critical attitude emanates from the strong cultural resonance of news. Given that following the news is a common practice for many people, they are also aware of the standard norms of journalism and the generic rules about the presentation of news. While readers have their ideas about how journalism should be practised, these are not necessarily identical to those of journalists.

In terms of journalistic norms, the participants held conventional professional values in high regard. In their view, the news production should aim for topicality, relevance and neutrality. At the same time, they noted that news organisations seem to take a freehand approach to these values. The participants claimed that journalists often fail to justify why a given news report was published "now", and why it should be considered relevant by readers. The critical argument about the loosening of journalistic norms was connected with other changes participants observed in journalism. One of the most controversial was the widely promoted incentive for UGC, which appeared particularly confusing for some audience groups. "I don't like that kind of self-exposure", was the criticism of one participant.

Rather than dismissing the opportunities for participatory journalism altogether, this argument emphasises that interpretation and criticism allow audience members to conceive a comprehensive view on what is at stake in a given issue or piece of news as they wish, whereas while participating in production users are expected to complete an assignment set by newsrooms: "Have your say on this", "send your photo", etc. In this perspective, the public role facilitated by UGC comes with a price tag. "You can participate providing you would accept our (journalism's) rules". There may be, of course, a number of occasions when people have no objections to such regulations. However, given the relative autonomy invested in interpretation and criticism as audiences, people are not easily persuaded to leave their comfortable position at the receiving end of communication.

Contrary to what newsrooms tend to expect from "audiences", our participants showed that their interpretation and criticism easily drifted towards critical and politicised arguments, which may be bewildering to newsrooms. Many journalists and commentators have assumed that politically motivated—and sometimes uncivil—feedback stems from the anonymous user cultures of online discussion boards and social networking sites. Our analysis suggests there is not necessarily much new in this kind of audience response in its own right, but the new digital feedback tools have made it more audible and more difficult to ignore.

Public Action

The practice of media-related public agency is a third category through which users connect to news. In these moments, their focus is neither on the media as object nor as texts but on issues that call for resolution or at least a response from institutional decision-makers (cf. Dewey [1927] 1991). Our data provide limited evidence of situations where participants actually engaged in public action through journalism. Their media diaries disclosed that a few of them had submitted their views via the letters-to-the-editor and some had updated their hobby-related blogs. But rather than seizing such active momentum with regard to public problems presented in journalism, the participants mostly drew on their networks to rework these issues outside public attention. While these discussions seemed to help in analysing these issues, paradoxically, these redefinitions tended to render the issues *less* suitable for public action, since they were reworked into abstract notions, such as "security" or "commercialisation".

Even though mediated or journalism-related public agency was relatively rare in their everyday contexts, some participants were active in various local associations, sports or culture clubs, and charities. Given that these organisations were functionally rather specific and "down-to-earth" in their scope, their activities were neither especially dependent on media attention nor regarded as newsworthy or interesting by media organisations. This reminds of Dewey's ([1927] 1991, 123) analysis of the problems in discovering the public(s).

The invisibility of local public agency points to a general problem in political systems, known as a lack of effective *action contexts* where citizens' public discussion and agency might make a difference. Couldry, Livingstone, and Markham (2007, 121) note that this deficiency is not a question of discursive constraints, but rather pertains to the absence of practical platforms for articulating everyday talk into action. The problem lies in that neither national governments nor local councils provide them. While the facilitation of action contexts falls only indirectly to news media, this remit is sporadically embraced by particular reform movements in journalism (Romano 2010). Digital journalism clearly introduces new opportunities for this due to its capacity to foster participation and interaction. In the face of the current developmental stage of digital journalism, it seems the opportunities that online journalism is now offering—such as citizen photos—are not necessarily what publicly active people are looking for. Given that their interests often relate to broad and abstract concerns, it may be difficult to communicate such issues through the typical routes of UGC. It is difficult to suggest what would be a better means for making citizens' concerns more public thorough digital journalism. What seems clear, though, is that before digital journalists can invent better tools for public agency, they should learn more about the issues that motivate public action.

Conclusion

Despite the fact that a number of alternative rationalisations of the audience have been proposed recently, most of them reinforce the underlying assumption of the audience members as social beings. In this framework, journalists and media managers may easily get carried away with the logic of fragmentation and segmentation. Using this route, there is less likelihood of carving out a solid understanding of the "audience". The tendency towards the polarisation of what "the audience" stands for—a generative force of "produsers", on the one hand, and a free-floating herd attracted by "clicks", on the other—is unsatisfying, as neither seem able to capture the richness of the practices people use in living with the media.

An alternative to excessively reduced images of "audiences" is provided in this article by proposing a conceptual framework that draws on practice theory and cultural audience research. In our case, practice theory means an attempt to reverse the dominant framework of information flow in the field of journalism. To expose how the relevance of journalism is articulated by users, we started at social networks and worked our way towards the determinate moment of reception: the act of reading or "the click". This strategy was empirical, as the evidence of how people render news relevant to themselves was drawn from our participants. At the same time, this investigation was also theoretically informed, because the articulations were not readily available and had to be gleaned from the vast empirical data. In this analysis, traditions of cultural audience research were very helpful.

Empirically, our study provides moderately positive support for the fact that the relevance of news is not entirely lost in the current media landscape. These findings may be partly specific to the distinct media system and cultural context in Finland, which are often regarded as offering greater support to newspaper reading and public service media than those found in other parts of Europe (Hallin and Mancini 2004). At the same time, it is not outlandish to assume that social networks function similarly in other cultural settings, as sites for making sense of the world through the frame of concern. What is likely to be different are the issues discussed in interpersonal communication and the weight given to news in those conversations.

Our analysis of distinct practices of how people use the news is important, as it illustrates the different routes by which journalism becomes meaningful and relevant for people, and this analysis may be elaborated on a more conceptual level. For instance, by relating "news monitoring routines" to the concept of the "mass", "interpretation" to the concept of "audience", and "public action" to the concept of "public", the empirical observations of how people relate to news can be anchored to the broader context of communication and social theories (see Heikkilä et al. 2014).

The proposed theoretical framework seems useful for digital journalism for two reasons. Firstly, it helps to carve out a firm perspective on the current media environment. Media users' practices are not changing overnight, and a number of well-known routines and means of news consumption remain intact. Despite the fact that users' media diets are undoubtedly diverging, the news remains an important source for culturally shared meanings, and a central reference point for the worries that people address and express in interpersonal communication.

Secondly, this framework assists us in providing an antidote against excessively reduced or polarised images of news audiences. The set of three distinct practices in media consumption identified in the article suggests that people do not live in fixed target groups; instead, they cross over between varying news practices. Most of the time, they just monitor. At some point, they immerse themselves in interpretation and sometimes— at least potentially—they may take public action. While journalism proves to be useful in all these respects, it can always do better. The solutions for how journalism can improve itself are not merely based on practical choice, but require theoretical inquiry into the concept of "the audience".

Even if our focus in this article was on the user aspect of journalism (the right-hand side of Figure 1), we suggest that it would be fruitful to theorise the entire field of journalism as practice rather than as distinct and separate processes of production and reception. This is useful as it helps to compare the shifting ideas of the "audience" in both realms analytically, and to assess how they connect to each other. In line with Raetzsch (2014, in this special issue), we find it fruitful to regard journalism as a structure of public communication enacted in practices that are increasingly open for various actors. Thus, even if we started out with the idea and visualisation that journalistic production and audience experiences meet at the distinct moment of consumption, the framework of practice theory might help in widening that meeting point. It may help in uncovering more points of intersection between the practices of the two domains, for example, through identifying interdependencies in the routines, interpretations and agency of journalistic and civic agents, thus rendering the forms of digital journalism meaningful in both domains.

FUNDING

This work was supported by The Helsingin Sanomat Foundation [grant for a project: Towards Engaging Journalism].

NOTES

1. The study was conducted between 2009 and 2012. In addition to the authors of the article, the research team included Jaana Siljamäki (University of Jyväskylä, Finland) and Sanna Valtonen (University of Helsinki, Finland).
2. The group compositions were based on a self-organising principle. As a result, our sample was demographically over-represented by females (67 per cent women; 33 per cent men) and the middle-aged (50 per cent being 35–50 years). Socio-economically, most of the participants ranked at the average level or higher, while in two groups the level of income was lower than the average (student theatre, the unemployed).
3. The survey, encompassing 455 respondents from three different regions in Finland, was conducted in September 2010. The representative sample was drawn from people who subscribed to the biggest newspaper in their respective region.
4. The news item published on 19 April 2010 focused on the theme of working life, an issue initially identified as extremely relevant by all the groups. The article looked into the ramifications of a government policy that aims to facilitate and encourage pensioners'

return to work. The tone was supportive of the policy, as many of the sources quoted highlighted positive aspects of the policy.

REFERENCES

Alasuutari, Pertti. 1999. "Introduction: Three Phases of Reception Studies." In *Rethinking the Media Audience*, edited by Pertti Alasuutari, 1–21. London: Sage.

Anderson, C. W. 2011. "Between Creative and Quantified Audiences: Web Metrics and Changing Patterns of Newswork in Local US Newsrooms." *Journalism* 12 (5): 550–566. doi:10.1177/1464884911402451.

Ang, Ien. 1991. *Desperately Seeking Audience*. London: Routledge.

Barnhurst, Kevin. 1998. "Politics in the Fine Meshes: Young Citizens, Power and Media." *Media Culture & Society* 20 (2): 201–218. doi:10.1177/016344398020002003.

Barnhurst, Kevin. 2011. "The New 'Media Affect' and the Crisis of Representation for Political Communication." *The International Journal of Press/Politics* 16 (4): 573–593. doi:10.1177/1940161211415666.

Bird, S. Elizabeth. 2011. "Seeking the Audience for News: Response, News Talk, and Everyday Practices." In *The Handbook of Media Audiences*, edited by Virginia Nightingale, 489–508. Oxford: Blackwell.

Bräuchler, Birgit, and John Postill. 2010. *Theorising Media and Practice*. New York: Berghahn Books.

Bruns, Axel. 2008. *Blogs, Wikipedia, Second Life, and Beyond: From Production to Produsage*. New York: Peter Lang.

Carpentier, Nico, Kim Christian Schrøder, and Lawrie Hallet. 2014. "Audience/Society Transformations." In *Audience Transformations: Shifting Audience Positions in Late Modernity*, edited by Nico Carpentier, Kim Christian Schrøder, and Lawrie Hallet, 1–12. New York: Routledge.

Costera Meijer, Irene. 2007. "The Paradox of Popularity: How Young People Experience the News." *Journalism Studies* 8 (1): 96–116. doi:10.1080/14616700601056874.

Coleman, Stephen, Anthony Scott, and David Morrison. 2009. *Public Trust in the News: A Constructivist Study of the Social Life of the News*. Oxford: Reuters Institute for the Study of Journalism.

Couldry, Nick. 2003. *Media Rituals: A Critical Approach*. London: Routledge.

Couldry, Nick. 2004. "Theorizing Media as Practice." *Social Semiotics* 14 (2): 115–132. doi:10.1080/1035033042000238295.

Couldry, Nick. 2012. *Media, Society, World: Social Theory and Digital Media Practice*. Cambridge: Polity Press.

Couldry, Nick, Sonia Livingstone, and Tim Markham. 2007. *Media Consumption and Public Engagement: Beyond the Presumption of Attention*. New York: Palgrave Macmillan.

Couldry, Nick, and Tim Markham. 2006. "Public Connection through Media Consumption: Between Over-Socialization and De-Socialization? In *The Annals of the American Academy of Political and Social Science* 608: 251–269. doi:10.1177/0002716206292342.

Deuze, Mark. 2007. *Media Work*. Cambridge: Polity.

Dewey, John. [1927] 1991. *The Public and Its Problems*. Athens: Swallow Press/Ohio University Press.

Drotner, Kirsten. 2000. "Less is More: Media Ethnography and its Limits." In *Consuming Audiences? Production and Reception in Media Studies*, edited by Ingunn Hagen and Janet Wasko, 165–188. Cresskill, NJ: Hampton Press.

Eliasoph, Nina. 2000. "Where Can Americans Talk Politics: Civil Society, Intimacy, and the Case for Deep Citizenship." *The Communication Review* 41: 65–94. doi:10.1080/10714420009359462.

Granovetter, Mark. 1973. "The Strength of Weak Ties." *American Journal of Sociology* 78 (6): 1360–1380. doi:10.1086/225469.

Granovetter, Mark. 1983. "The Strength of Weak Ties: A Network Theory Revisited." *Sociological Theory* 1: 201–233. doi:10.2307/202051.

Hallin, Daniel, and Paolo Mancini. 2004. *Comparing Media Systems: Three Models of Media and Politics*. Cambridge: Cambridge University Press.

Heikkilä, Heikki, Laura Ahva, Jaana Siljamäki, and Sanna Valtonen. 2012. *Kelluva kiinnostavuus: Journalismin merkitys ihmisten sosiaalisissa verkostoissa* [The Floating Relevance: The Role of Journalism in the Everyday Social Networks]. Tampere: Vastapaino.

Heikkilä, Heikki, Laura Ahva, Jaana Siljamäki, and Sanna Valtonen. 2014. "The Mass, the Audience, and the Public: Questioning Pre-Conceptions of News Audiences". In *Public Media Management for the Twenty-First Century: Creativity, Innovation, and Interaction*, edited by Michal Glowacki and Lizzie Jackson, 161–179. New York: Routledge.

Jenkins, Henry. 2006. *Convergence Culture: Where Old and New Media Collide*. New York: New York University Press.

Jensen, Klaus Bruhn. 2010. *Media Convergence: The Three Degrees of Network, Mass, and Interpersonal Communication*. London: Routledge.

Katz, Elihu, and Paul Lazarsfeld. 1955. *Personal Influence: The Part Played by People on the Flow of Mass Communications*. New York: The Free Press.

Livingstone, Sonia. 2006. "The Influence of Personal Influence on the Study of Audiences." *The American Annals of Political and Social Science* 608: 233–250. doi:10.1177/000271620 6292325.

Madianou, Mirca. 2009. "Audience Reception and News in Everyday Life." In *Handbook of Journalism Studies*, edited by Karin Wahl-Jorgensen and Thomas Hanitzsch, 325–357. New York: Routledge.

Morley, David. 1980. *The "Nationwide" Audience*. London: BFI.

Morley, David. 1992. *Television, Audiences, and Cultural Studies*. London: Routledge.

Mosco, Vincent, and Lewis Kaye. 2000. "Questioning the Concept of Audience." In *Consuming Audiences? Production and Reception in Media Studies*, edited by Ingunn Hagen and Janet Wasko, 31–46. Cresskill, NJ: Hampton Press.

Napoli, Phillip. 2011. *Audience Evolution: New Technologies and the Transformation of the Media Audiences*. New York: Columbia University Press.

Raetzsch, Christop. 2014. "Innovation through Practice: Journalism as a Structure of Public Communication." *Journalism Practice* XX: XX–XX. doi:10.1080/17512786.2014.928466.

Reckwitz, Andreas. 2002. "Toward a Theory of Social Practices: A Development in Culturalist Theorizing." *European Journal of Social Theory* 5 (2): 243–263. doi:10.1177/13684310 222225432.

Ridell, Seija. 2006. "Yleisö [Audience]." In *Mediaa käsittämässä* [Understanding Media], edited by Seija Ridell, Pasi Väliaho, and Tanja Sihvonen, 233–257. Tampere: Vastapaino.

Romano, Angela. 2010. *International Journalism and Democracy: Civic Engagement Models from Around the World*. New York: Routledge.

Rouse, Joseph. 2006. "Practice Theory." In *Handbook of the Philosophy of Science, Vol 15: Philosophy of Anthropology and Sociology*, edited by Stephen Turner and Mark Risjord, 499–540. Amsterdam: Elsevier BV.

Schrøder, Kim Christian, and Louise Phillips. 2005. "The Everyday Construction of Mediated Citizenship: People's Use and Experience of News Media in Denmark." In *Cultural Dilemmas in Public Service Broadcasting*, edited by Gregory Lowe and Per Jauert, 179–197. Gothenburg: Nordicom.

Schrøder, Kim Christian, and Louise Phillips. 2007. "Complexifying Media Power: A Study of the Interplay Between Media and Audience Discourse on Politics." *Media, Culture & Society* 29 (6): 890–915.

Shuman, Edwin. 1926. *Practical Journalism: A Complete Manual of the Best Newspaper Methods*. New York: D. Appleton.

Silverstone, Roger. 1994. *Television and Everyday Life*. London: Routledge.

Spitulnik, Debra. 2010. "Thick Context, Deep Epistemology: A Mediation on Wide-Angle Lenses on Media, Knowledge Production and the Concept of Culture." In *Theorising Media and Practice*, edited by Birgit Bräuchler and John Postill, 105–126. New York: Berghahn Books.

Tapscott, Don, and Anthony Williams. 2006. *Wikinomics: How Mass Collaboration Changes Everything*. London: Atlantic Books.

Tenenboim, Ori, and Akiba A. Cohen. 2013. "What Prompts Users to Click and Comment: A Longitudinal Study of Online News." *Journalism*. doi:10.1177/1464884913513996.

Van Dijck, José. 2013. *Culture of Connectivity: A Critical History of Social Media*. Oxford: Oxford University Press.

Webster, James. 2011. "The Duality of Media: A Structural Theory of Public Attention." *Communication Theory* 21 (1): 43–66. doi:10.1111/j.1468-2885.2010.01375.x.

INNOVATION THROUGH PRACTICE
Journalism as a structure of public communication

Christoph Raetzsch

Practices of news selection, presentation and distribution have been transposed to the domain of audiences communicating through network media. Media practices of journalists and "media-oriented practices" of audiences (Couldry) make use of the network as a common resource, merging into a new form of "news-based communication." This new situation of public communication questions institutional approaches to journalism and the crisis it currently experiences. The paper proposes to regard journalism as a structure of public communication which is mutually enacted by journalists and audiences alike. Practice is outlined as a conceptual tool to study how social structures such as journalism can innovate. In practice, cultural schemas value resources of communication and endow actors with agency. As media of public communication are de-differentiated in digital contexts, practice offers a way to understand innovation as the gradual transposition of such schemas to new resources.

Introduction

In the digital environment, news is more popular than ever. Links are forwarded through email and posted on Facebook. Tweets alert us to new information online and blog postings and comments proliferate in specialized and general publics. Taken together, these forms of online communication emulate forms of news production that used to be an exclusive domain of journalism. Although many of these forms of news would not qualify as speaking to "a public" in general, they are still public because they can be accessed through links. In networked and digital public communication, every message is exactly one link apart. The difference between the institutional news communicators and the private tweeter, blogger or YouTuber is that the latter will have less visibility, less impact and thus less relevance for the wider debates in society. However, this difference in impact should not deter us from finding a new conceptual basis for defining journalism. This paper argues that journalism is too narrowly defined in terms of occupational routines, professional standards or institutional parameters.

In a cultural perspective, journalism is a structure of public communication between producers and audiences. If we take seriously that "media-oriented practices" of audiences (Couldry 2004, 119) can be likewise journalistic in kind, we can approach journalism as a structure of communication that implicates audiences in every issue of a newspaper or every airing of a news show. The same focus on an audience, though, is implicated in the tweet, the posting, the comment found online, rendering a process of public communication transparent without turning every member of the audience into a producer. The digital environment creates new opportunities to observe the complementarity of journalism and its audiences as links are tracked around the net. Defining journalism as a structure means that both audiences and producers need to provide resources to its continuation and need to find cultural schemas that endow these resources with meaning. The thesis of this paper is that the continued "enactment" of a structure called journalism takes place in media practices and in "media-oriented practices" alike. Both forms of practice sustain journalism as a social structure and it is in practice where innovation takes place. In practice, the traditions of old media and the potentials of new media are negotiated. As the connectivity of the internet has ushered in a crisis of so-called "legacy media," network media are still in a phase of experimentation concerning their social uses. Historically, we are now in a privileged position to observe the ongoing negotiation of the social meaning of journalistic media:

> [W]hen new media emerge in a society, their place is at first ill defined, and their ultimate meanings or functions are shaped over time by that society's existing habits of media use (which, of course, derive from experience with other, established media) … The "crisis" of a new medium will be resolved when the perceptions of the medium, as well as its practical uses, are somehow adapted to existing categories of public understanding about what that medium does for whom and why. (Gitelman and Pingree 2003, xii)

The present period of network media becoming firmly established on all levels of public and private communication exemplifies how both a crisis of legacy media and an uncertainty about the social uses of new media create an "ill defined" identity in public perception. From the perspective of practice, the routines that are inscribed in the usage of particular media of communication represent a model case for the concurrent stabilization and innovation of social structures. The aim is then to re-evaluate journalism itself under digital conditions as a structure of public communication that needs to be enacted by journalists and audiences alike to sustain its privileged role in public communication.

In order to outline the conceptual framework, this paper will first look at the resistance of journalistic practice to innovate in the present crisis. This resistance is explained in terms of the institutionalization of a particular commercial model of news production, in which the audience was rarely more than a news consumer. In a second part, we will look at "media-oriented practices" of audiences that emulate structural properties of institutionalized journalism. News-based communication is here introduced as a practice in which the positions of news consumer and news audience are more fluid. The third part presents an overview of sociological approaches to the study of practice, which can help us to understand practice as the domain of social action where structures are innovated to survive. The last part will underline why journalism as a structure of public communication does not obliterate the differences between institutional and individual producers of news. By highlighting the structural aspect of journalism, however, we can insist on the different cultural valuations that audiences and producers place on a given journalistic medium.

Innovating Journalism and the Resistance of Practice

Modern journalism distinguished itself from both the partisan press and business news media, like commercial advertisers, in the nineteenth century. In the United States, the market orientation of the penny press in the 1830s is commonly regarded as an important step toward endowing the press with financial independence from party founding (Schudson 1978; Mindich 1998). The disavowal of party interests allowed "journalists to become professional technicians, experts at gathering information and separating truths from half-truths." Journalists could step up to offer a "public service" independent of "particular communities or private interests" (Kaplan 2002, 192). The newspaper emerged as a commercial enterprise that had something to offer for everyone —it became an "omnibus press" (Baldasty 1992, 140). With its orientation toward an enlarged consumer market of news, journalism became organized in industrial dimensions, requiring vast resources to maintain its staff, its production facilities and its distribution networks. The newspaper was in this modern sense used for materially transporting graphically standardized information about contemporary affairs to audiences. Journalism became "the sense-making practice of modernity ... a product and promoter of modern life" (Hartley 1996, 33).

But more importantly, this practice of journalism became tied up with a particular organizational structure, in which the medium of modern journalism—the newspaper— was used not just to spread information, commentary, and news but also advertising. As Raymond Williams argued in *Keywords*, the media as corporate organizations of public communication acquired historically specific "material forms" based on a "primary practice" of human communication (Williams 1979, 203). The connection between news (as a daily resource for audiences) and advertising (as a daily communications channel for business) was thoroughly established in the practice of publishing newspapers. The news consumer became metonymically identified as an "informed citizen." Lance Bennett remarks that such an identification of news with democratic values is an "illusion" because "news must be 'sold' to the audience in the first place" before audiences are marketed to advertising clients (Bennett 2001, 4; see also Benson 2010; Turow 1997).

The functional connection between news as a prime journalistic genre, the industrial organization of journalism and the ascribed importance of an independent press for democracy has been articulated many times. It formed an unchallenged paradigm of journalism studies for a long time before being re-evaluated in the present. As soon as economic profit is taken out of the equation, news becomes mindless fodder rewritten from press releases and the public importance of journalism seems to evaporate. Calls for innovation in journalism depart typically from the diagnosis of its faltering business model to propose new ways of ensuring the continued production and patronage of high-profile journalism by audiences. Meyer, for example, proposes a "certification" of journalistic quality, through new skills like "filtering, refining, decorating and packaging information" that are needed by journalists in an information-saturated online environment. Instead of producing more information, journalists need to focus on "processing" information and making it understandable to their audiences (Meyer 2004, 230). Meyer wants to reform journalism within its institutional form. Similarly, Schudson and Downie (2009) as well as McChesney and Nichols (2010) advocate a model of "quality journalism" that is funded independently of market interests. What these analyses have in common is that they regard innovation only in terms of the established model of public communication that journalism has created over a period of more than 100 years. Typically, the introduction of digital and network technologies into that model concerns only modes of production and distribution, leaving intact the authority of "a centralized source with a particular vision of the news" (Uricchio 2006, 79).

This bias toward the productive side of journalism (organizations, corporations, journalists) fails to conceptualize audiences as agents which endow journalistic news with meaning. Although Anderson has shown that audience orientation has become "incorporated into the DNA of contemporary news work" (Anderson 2011, 529), this audience is the statistical product of data aggregation about the popularity of articles, traffic and access rates. Culturally, the "primary practices" of communication among members of audiences now also take place within the same digital and networked environment but not necessarily on the same sites as commercial journalism.

Pavlik (2013) acknowledges the problem of "audience fragmentation" as a reason for the dispersion of attention away from traditional news media, or what Broersma and Peters (2013, 8f.) call the "de-ritualization of news consumption." Pavlik regards innovation in journalism as a revival of "quality news content," although presented as a more "interactive news discourse" with audiences. He proposes that "reporting optimized for the digital, networked age" and "new management and organizational strategies" are necessary to continue journalism in the present. Not surprisingly, his normative principles of journalism remain anchored to "intelligence or research," "freedom of speech," "pursuit of truth" and "ethics" (Pavlik 2013, 183). Innovation, according to Pavlik, is primarily driven by economic and technological factors, in close analogy to the model proposed by Rogers on the "diffusion of innovations" (Rogers 2003). Pavlik is exemplary in his industry-focused approach to journalism in which audiences are now conceptualized as (gratuitous) co-producers of the content they consume. But he inadvertently points toward a very different dimension of innovation by citing Gabriel Tarde's (1903) classic *Laws of Imitation*. Although Pavlik leaves open in what way this classic might be helpful, *Laws of Imitation* offers an enigmatic but fitting formulation of how invention is linked to practice. Tarde writes that:

> every invention resolves itself into the timely intersection in one mind of a current of imitation with another current which reinforces it, or … which throws new light on some old idea … *that finds unhoped-for resources in some familiar practice.*
>
> (Tarde 1903, 43, emphasis added)

Every invention, according to Tarde, is an act of selection from other possibilities. Once a selection was made, certain alternatives no longer appear tenable, while other combinations of resources suddenly appear plausible. As a "current of imitation" finds new application in a different domain of activity ("timely intersection") or is applied to a new problem, this current of imitation is effectively transposed. Every selection contributes to an "irreversible" (Tarde 1903, 45) order of steps toward other selections. Tarde's "current of imitation" closely resembles what is often designated by the term practice: a regular, patterned or structured order of actions taken to achieve a particular aim. However, this regularity of practice needs the moment of transposition to account for innovation. What appears as a habitual practice in one domain may influence or innovate practices in another domain. In that sense then, practices are themselves "unhoped-for resources" because they encapsulate sequences of actions that can be applied to new contexts.

Transposing Practice: "News-based Communication"

In the digital environment, forms of news-based communication proliferate through emails, news feeds or blogs. What used to be a restricted genre of journalistic text has been transposed to become a new practice of interaction. News in this enlarged sense is no longer restricted to any particular content but merely organizes attention and interaction through the sequencing of its publication and distribution. In news-based communication, news includes a content dimension, an audience orientation and a temporal order, similar to Stephens' definition of news as "new information about a subject of some public interest that is shared with some portion of the public" (Stephens 1988, 9). In this definition, news is neither the product of specific actors creating news, such as journalists, nor is the content of news limited to any specific subject. By equating news only with new information about public affairs, the concept has become too limited to account for the continued patronage and popularity of news media themselves. What is far more interesting is how the concept of news now also structures interactions among audiences.

A number of scholars working on the connections between popular culture and journalism have emphasized how entertainment, or the "other news" (Langer 1998), has always been important to win acceptance among audiences for new media of journalism—from the penny and sensationalist press to television and online news (Dahlgren and Sparks 1992; Curran and Sparks 1991; Lünenborg 2005). Graham Meikle argues that "news is not just a product, it is also a complex of practices" such as practices of production, distribution and reception. These practices are given particular forms in journalism but they are at the same time general enough to apply equally well to what audiences do with widely circulated news. Meikle continues that "the practices of journalism are, self-evidently, what journalists do; but the practices of news include things in which we all participate—story-telling and argument; reading, viewing, listening and discussing" (Meikle 2009, 18). In news-based communication, the "primary practices" of communication are sustained by media technologies that place a premium on what changes in a given network by journaling, indexing and aggregating previous (ex-) changes. Such communication is more interactive in the sense that each exchange takes place within the same medium, which according to Rafaeli (2009, 27), marks a high level of "medium transparency" to each user. News in such an interactive context is a continuous updating of an ongoing social process. Accordingly, Nick Couldry has asked: "What if social networking sites induce a shift in our sense of what news is—from public politics to social flow...?" (Couldry 2012, 23). In a convergent media environment, news becomes defined in terms of its topical relevance in a given sequence of interactions between a limited number of participants.

As practices of news-based communication begin to involve the same digital resources that journalists use in their day-to-day work—search engines, graphic editors, storage devices and networking platforms—news becomes a form of de-differentiated information. This is an effect of digital information, which exists as pure data on the level of computing but that is not socially meaningful. Digital technology disrupts social contexts by converting information that has distinct spheres of circulation into a homogeneous, commutable format. As Luciano Floridi points out, data in computers is represented as binary data (1/0; on/off) to the system while being semantically meaningful (as letter, word, command) to a user. Binary data encoding thus has the advantage that it allows for a machine that "manipulate[s] data in ways which we find meaningful" (Floridi 2010, 28f.). While the machine level remains obscure to most users of digital technology, the universality of digital code allows the establishment of new relations between types of information. Benkler argues that "information is both input and output of its own production process" (Benkler 2006, 37), it is transformed and recombined only to serve as new input for further operations. Information is "non-rival," meaning that it cannot be used up as a resource for further conversions (Benkler 2002, 404). The de-differentiation of information as data has a powerful cultural effect: it obliterates social, geographical or media-specific spheres of circulation and presents all information within the same communications space. The blog as a personalized, network medium can be regarded as a way to reconnect bits of data into socially meaningful information.

Instead of defining news in terms of a particular content or as the product of a particular routine of production, news begins to mark the transgression of a threshold between information shared in small circles or private networks to become an object of public debate. Gaye Tuchman wrote that "news imparts to occurrences their public character" (Tuchman 1978, 3). What was once the privileged domain of journalists and their media has now been transposed to users of digital media connected in a global network. Every linked website is equally public although not all are equally visible. Communicating an experience of immersion in many different news sources can thus be a way to impose structure on a chaotic field of conflicting views, opinions and information. Such practices of publication and communication "[contribute] to even more complex practices of narrating one's life through news or orienting oneself to a public world through news consumption" (Couldry 2012, 53). Links to news from elsewhere on the Web serve not only as reference but also as a form of interaction that activates common reference points among small networks of individuals. John Kelly has stressed that "online clusters form around issues of shared concern" (Kelly 2008, 37). Circulating news in a limited network is not structurally different from the same practice employed in mainstream media.

The challenge is to explain theoretically the transposition of practices to news-based communication without insisting on dichotomies of professional/amateurs, producers/consumers, or between journalists and their audiences. The lesson to be drawn from the widespread transposition of practices of public communication to the domain of news-based communication is to question the privileged role of journalism itself. Moving "beyond the audience" (Bird 2010a, 2010b) as a theoretical construct, the insistence on practice highlights how audiences are central to enacting and innovating a structure like journalism. To resolve this seeming antagonism of enacting and innovating social structures, it is useful to revisit some core concepts of practice theory as it has developed in the last 30 years in sociology and cultural studies.

Innovation Through Practice?

James Carey was one of the most prominent advocates for the cultural study of journalism, who was interested in "meaning … as a constituting activity whereby humans interactively endow an elastic though resistant world with enough coherence and order to support their purposes." Carey underlined that "communication is at once a structure of human experience—activity, process, practice—an ensemble of expressive forms, and a *structured and structuring set of social relations*" (Carey 1989, 84–86, emphasis added). This paradoxical formulation establishes a core tenet of practice theory: social actors are enabled and constrained through social structures and it is in practice that agency and constraint are negotiated. Practice is both structured action as it unfolds and a structuring pattern for subsequent actions. The more frequently some action is practiced, the more it establishes its own routine, becomes a habit, an unquestioned, self-evident pattern of action. Like common sense, practice is "one of the oldest suburbs of human culture" (Geertz 1992, 225). But practice achieves its apparent stability only through permanent innovation, through minute variations of a pattern that remains recognizable throughout. Social structures can only continue to exist over time if they are stabilized and innovated through practice.

In this sense, practice implies regularity and change at the same time: "the concept of practice inherently combines a capacity to account for both reproduction and innovation" (Warde 2005, 140). Beyond the common notion of practice as something that is merely done, a core dimension of practice is its reflexivity, a contradictory oscillation between change and stability. The "practice turn" in sociology (Schatzki, Knorr-Cetina, and von Savigny 2001) has prepared the ground for studying practices as that dimension of social life, where stability and change are reflexively connected. Because practices are "routine activities ... notable for their unconscious, automatic, un-thought character" (Swidler 2001, 74), they are often hard to make explicit and resist rationalization. At the same time, practices can serve as routinized actions that become applicable to new contexts precisely because their individual elements are embodied, learned through repetition and require little reflection as they are executed. In culture and social life, "a practice represents a pattern which can be filled out by a multitude of single and often unique actions reproducing the practice" (Reckwitz 2002, 250).

Practice theories pay attention to the way social action is structured from the perspective of those acting. Deriving their inspiration from anthropology, ethnology and sociology, practice-based approaches to social order revise structuralist and textualist methods of understanding society. As William Sewell argues, structuralism had "abstracted a realm of pure signification out from the complex messiness of social life and sought to specify its internal coherence and deep logic" (Sewell 2005, 161). In favor of "logic" or "coherence", structuralism excluded the "messiness" of social life by ignoring the often contradictory motivations of individual actors and the uneven access to and valuation of resources for specific social practices. Practice as a form of structured action does not imply that an underlying rationality serves as a generating motif of actions. The concept rather places great emphasis on the contingencies of actions and the conflicting cultural presuppositions that go into rationalizing an action as it unfolds.

On a very general level, Raymond Williams can count as a theorist of practice and its role for cultural innovation. He was acutely aware of the almost unresolvable tension between his own attempt to formulate a theory of culture as a "whole way of life" (Williams 1963) and the multitude of cultural practices that he had to exclude in the name of consistency. But these practices were nonetheless part of a culture. In his works we encounter phrases like "in practice" as cautious reminders of the diverging ways in which culture manifests itself. The non-institutionalized practices of "ordinary life," for Williams, represent a form of culture, which is always outside dominant cultural orders, outside of the national discourses and debates formulated in the media and the arts. What exists as a practice among individuals may resist theoretical appreciation, but it is still meaningful in limited circles. The domain of practice is central to the cultural struggles between dominant, residual and emergent cultural elements that Williams invokes to explain cultural change (Williams 1977, 122f.). Eager to formulate an inclusive concept of culture that does not exclude "the ordinary," Williams writes that *no dominant culture ever in reality includes or exhausts all human practice* (125, italics in original). Williams points out that the domain of practice is inexhaustible for its potential to innovate cultural forms. Culture itself, as Stuart Hall explains, is regarded as a *praxis* that is composed of all social practices: "Culture is not a practice ... It is threaded through all social practices, and is the sum of their inter-relationship" (Hall 1996, 34). As societies change, individual experiences may question practices and vice versa; culture thus represents a "process" that is instantiated by a historically varying "set of practices" (Hall 1997, 2). The heterogeneity of practice, in Williams's view of culture, serves as a potential of resistance to dominant cultural orders.

In Pierre Bourdieu's *Outline of a Theory of Practice* (1977), we encounter practice as a generative scheme of social structure. For Bourdieu, practices sustain social structures in time and are in turn enabled by such structures. The aim of Bourdieu is to "restore to practice its practical truth" (8) by assuming in his description of practice the viewpoint of the actors he is studying. He underlines that practices are "defined by the fact that their temporal structure, direction, and rhythm are constitutive of their meaning" (9), which entails that they cannot be classed in simple dichotomies. Central to Bourdieu's notion of practice is the acquired habitus of actors, which "enabl[es] agents to generate an infinity of practices adapted to endlessly changing situations, without those schemes ever being constituted as explicit principles" (16). Practices are structured and structuring modes of perception and action, learned through repetition. In the long run, practices account for the stability of social structures and their existence over time. Despite this seeming reflexivity of practices, Bourdieu overdetermines habitus somewhat tautologically as "structured structure," describing it as the result of formative conditions, and "structuring structure," where it generates a multitude of seemingly disparate practices (72). Due to this hermetic formulation, Bourdieu's theory of practice retains a certain "an agent-proof quality" (Sewell 1992, 15). Structure and practice seem inescapably intertwined and account primarily for the stability of a society, similar to the inclusiveness of Williams' view on culture. What is lacking from these early theorists of culture is a notion of how structure, practice and agency can account for change and innovation.

Such a concept of agency and structure is developed by the social-historian William Sewell, who argues: "Structures shape people's practices, but it is also people's practices that constitute (and reproduce) structures. In this view of things, human agency and structure, far from being *opposed*, in fact, *presuppose* each other" (Sewell 1992, 4, original emphasis). The "recursive enactment of structures" (6) contributes to the stability of society over time, yet this enactment is at the same time a potential source of agency and innovation for individuals. One source of innovation for actors is that they can generalize and transpose cultural "schemas" that "can be actualized in a potentially broad and unpredetermined range of situations" (8). Schemas are forms of cultural knowledge about social situations that implicitly guide courses of action because they have been learned through repetition. The second component of Sewell's model of structure and agency are material (non-human) or human resources that actors have at their disposal. In social interactions non-human resources like technologies or tools are tied to cultural schemas which determine their "value and social power" (12). Material resources are not empowering by themselves but become powerful in their valuation for particular purposes in interaction.

Sewell argues that there are four reasons why structures can innovate while being reproduced: (1) The "multiplicity of structures" implies that many different social structures interfere and overlap with each other, of which some are more dominant or are valued differently than others. (2) Because social actors are "capable of applying a wide range of different and even incompatible schemas and have access to heterogeneous arrays of resources" schemas are generalizable and transposable. A schema may emerge in one structure and find application in another structure. Such a schema can also value a resource for new purposes. Agency crucially "entail[s] the capacity to transpose and extend schemas to new contexts," writes Sewell. New practices result from such transpositions of schemas to new contexts. (3) If schemas can be transposed to different contexts, the effect is that resources may accumulate in unpredictable ways. (4) The unpredictability of resources becoming available for new practices has the consequence that resources themselves become valued differently by actors. The differing ways in which resources become meaningful for actors and the transposability of schemas lead to an intersection of structures, where structures may address and empower social agents in different ways. Sewell summarizes that "structures, then, are sets of mutually sustaining schemas and resources that empower and constrain social action" (Sewell 1992, 16–19). The emphasis on the enactment of structures in part explains why structures (as schema and resource) can go out of fashion and why others persist over time. Structures which continue to renew their resources and continue to be valued in practice endure over time. Their renewed enactment is effectively a transposition of cultural schemas to new circumstances which endows new actors with agency. Sewell contends that "structures empower agents differentially" (21) because actors differ in their ability to transpose schemas to new resources or re-evaluate existing resources in new ways.

Sewell's model of how social structures can innovate can be applied to resolve the seeming antagonism between journalistic practices in the narrow sense and "media-oriented practices" in the wider sense. As the network becomes a resource of both public and private communication, its cultural valuation through schemas remains distinct. In journalism, digital media can be valued for their ease of access both in terms of the production and distribution of news. News production continues as a practice, although its resources now are transposed to the digital domain. Among audiences, the same resources may be valued for purposes of "self-communication" (Castells 2007), for gathering information or for sharing opinions among a limited sphere of acquaintances. The differing levels of agency that individuals can exert depend in no small part on their ability to find new schemas for resources that may have emerged in some other domain of social life. A news item can be a contribution to a wider public debate or it may be part of an interactive, news-based discourse in a limited public. On the level of practice, such differences can be explained in terms of the cultural schemas that are invoked to value a given resource for particular communicative purposes. Because many media potentially allow public participation by design, the concentration on practice can foreground how such potentials are individually adopted and appropriated.

Journalism as a Structure of Public Communication

In this view of practice, journalism can be conceived as a structure of public communication which is enacted in historically distinct journalistic practices. While those practices vary largely depending on historical circumstances, they all instantiate a structure of public communication which is identified as journalism in the long run. By renewing resources for its continued production and placing varying emphases on the cultural value of its product, journalism constantly innovates itself. Individual practices here stand in the same relation to a social structure as the individual issue of a newspaper, for example, is related to all others preceding and following it. While the human and non-human resources that go into the preparation of a single issue may vary from day to day, the sequence of issues creates a tradition, a newspaper style, a preferred audience. In short, it creates durable social structures that are being revived every day:

> Each issue of a periodical responds to a particular moment, orienting content towards the perceived interests of its readers, while restating its underlying identity. In this way, the abstract identity of the periodical, imperfectly manifested in each individual issue, is a negotiated, consensual structure into which new content could be assimilated as a version of the familiar. (Mussell 2012)

Jim Mussell here points out that the "perceived interests" of audiences are an integral element in journalistic communication which contribute to the "consensual structure" established between periodicals and their readers. The same can be said of journalism renewing ties to its audiences on a regular basis through conventionalizing its "performative discourse" as authoritative statement about the world (Broersma 2013, 33). Likewise, some practices have contributed more to the institutionalized form of journalism than others. The practice of publishing daily news in close proximity to events (topicality) and not as a random selection of reprints is an example here. The codification of practices of journalistic objectivity in the early twentieth century was equally important for the institutionalization of journalism. These practices exemplify how a structure of public communication like journalism needs to adapt to a changing technological, cultural and social environment, especially because the journalistic field is "permanently subject to trial by market" (Bourdieu 1998, 71). The cultural schemas journalism employs to legitimize its own practices need to relate in meaningful ways to audiences seeking resources of agency in practices which are media-oriented but which need not be media-centric. In journalism, what is published in a topical fashion crucially involves addressing and renewing an audience on a regular basis. Journalistic media serve an "anchoring" function for other social practices as Nick Couldry argues: "media ... anchor other practices through the 'authoritative' representations and enactments of key terms and categories they provide." Media as institutionalized public actors operate on the "fundamental categorical distinction between what is 'in' the media and what is not 'in' the media" (Couldry 2004, 122–128).

As outlined above, news as a journalistic genre marks the passing of a threshold between semi-private and public networks of circulation. What appears "in" the media is assumed to have relevance for a wider public, which is the audience of journalism. The same threshold, though, is passed when a blog post, tweet or online comment addresses itself to a potentially unlimited public. From a structural similarity between such practices and journalistic practices, we cannot draw the conclusion that both are valued as sustaining structures of public communication in the same way. What we can conclude, however, is that practices of news-based communication are becoming inscribed in other social practices beyond journalistic media themselves.

By placing the emphasis on social structure, journalism can be seen in its mutual implication of media, topical content and audiences. Both producers and audiences need resources to (re)produce a structure called journalism. These resources need to be valued in any form to become socially meaningful. A newspaper can serve as an advertisement for local business or theaters, or it can serve a political crusade against perceived ills in society. It can serve audiences to feel embedded in the social fabric of society, chronicle the passing of events, or offer tables of stock prices, weather forecasts, amusing content, and so on. Both sides of the structure value journalistic media by different cultural schemas. Without an audience valuing journalism as a daily resource of information (or entertainment, or political discourse), such a resource ceases to be socially relevant. The cultural crisis of journalism is that journalistic practices no longer distinguish a sphere of limited circulation in a digital environment, but are transposed to other domains of social life. The adoption of practices of public communication among members of audiences signals that journalism itself needs to be empirically and historically re-evaluated as a structure of public communication. A practice-based approach to innovation could highlight how the change in journalistic practices within journalism is itself the product of a similar recombination of resources and cultural schemas that are actualized in given crisis situations. As journalism historian John Nerone argued: "[A] medium is essentially a relationship or a combination of relationships, it is not a thing in itself" (Nerone 1989, 5). In each of these relationships certain patterns are discernible as forms of practice, which may be "messy" and change over time but which are not arbitrary.

REFERENCES

Anderson, Christopher W. 2011. "Deliberative, Agonistic, and Algorithmic Audiences: Journalism's Vision of its Public in an Age of Audience Transparency." *International Journal of Communication* 5: 529–547.

Baldasty, Gerald J. 1992. *The Commercialization of News in the Nineteenth Century*. Madison, WI: University of Wisconsin Press.

Benkler, Yochai. 2002. "Coase's Penguin, or, Linux and 'The Nature of the Firm.'" *The Yale Law Journal* 112 (3): 369–446. doi:10.2307/1562247.

Benkler, Yochai. 2006. *The Wealth of Networks: How Social Production Transforms Markets and Freedom*. New Haven: Yale University Press.

Bennett, W. Lance. 2001. *News: The Politics of Illusion*. New York: Longman.

Benson, Rodney. 2010. "Futures of the News: International Considerations and Further Reflections." In *New Media, Old News: Journalism & Democracy in the Digital Age*, edited by Natalie Fenton, 187–200. London: Sage.

Bird, Elizabeth. 2010a. "From Fan Practice to Mediated Moments: The Value of Practice Theory in the Understanding of Media Audiences." In *Theorising Media and Practice*, edited by Birgit Bräuchler and John Postill, 85–104. New York: Berghahn.

Bird, Elizabeth. 2010b. "News Practices in Everyday Life: Beyond Audience Response." In *Routledge Companion to News and Journalism*, edited by Stuart Allan, 417–427. London: Routledge.

Bourdieu, Pierre. 1977. *Outline of a Theory of Practice*. Translated by Richard Nice. Cambridge: Cambridge University Press.

Bourdieu, Pierre. 1998. *On Television*. Translated by Priscilla Parkhurst Ferguson. New York: New Press.

Broersma, Marcel. 2013. "A Refractured Paradigm: Journalism, Hoaxes and the Challenge of Trust." In *Rethinking Journalism: Trust and Participation in a Transformed News Landscape*, edited by Marcel Broersma and Chris Peters, 28–44. London: Routledge.

Broersma, Marcel, and Chris Peters. 2013. "Introduction: Rethinking Journalism. The Structural Transformation of a Public Good." In *Rethinking Journalism: Trust and Participation in a Transformed News Landscape*, edited by Marcel Broersma and Chris Peters, 1–12. London: Routledge.

Carey, James W. 1989. *Communication as Culture: Essays on Media and Society*. Boston, MA: Unwin Hyman.

Castells, Manuel. 2007. "Communication, Power and Counter-power in the Network Society." *International Journal of Communication* 1 (1): 238–266.

Couldry, Nick. 2004. "Theorising Media as Practice." *Social Semiotics* 14 (2): 115–132. doi:10.1080/1035033042000238295.

Couldry, Nick. 2012. *Media, Society, World: Social Theory and Digital Media Practice*. Cambridge: Polity.

Curran, James, and Colin Sparks. 1991. "Press and Popular Culture." *Media, Culture and Society* 13 (2): 215–237. doi:10.1177/016344391013002006.

Dahlgren, Peter, and Colin Sparks, eds. 1992. *Journalism and Popular Culture*. London: Sage.

Floridi, Luciano. 2010. *Information: A Very Short Introduction*. Oxford: Oxford University Press.

Geertz, Clifford. 1992. "Common Sense as a Cultural System." *The Antioch Review* 50 (1/2): 221–241. doi:10.2307/4612512.

Gitelman, Lisa, and Geoffrey B. Pingree, eds. 2003. *New Media, 1740-1915*. Cambridge, MA: MIT Press.

Hall, Stuart. 1996. "Cultural Studies: Two Paradigms." In *What is Cultural Studies? A Reader*, edited by John Storey, 31–48. London: Arnold.

Hall, Stuart, ed. 1997. *Representation: Cultural Representations and Signifying Practices*. London: Sage.

Hartley, John. 1996. *Popular Reality. Journalism, Modernity, Popular Culture*. London: Arnold.

Kaplan, Richard L. 2002. *Politics and the American Press. The Rise of Objectivity, 1865-1920*. Cambridge: Cambridge University Press.

Kelly, John. 2008. "Mapping the Blogosphere: Offering a Guide to Journalism's Future." *Nieman Reports* 62 (4): 37–39.

Langer, John. 1998. *Tabloid Television. Popular Journalism and the "Other News"*. London: Routledge.

Lünenborg, Margreth. 2005. *Journalismus als kultureller Prozess. Zur Bedeutung von Journalismus in der Mediengesellschaft. Ein Entwurf* [Journalism as a Cultural Process: On the Meaning of Journalism in Media Society]. Wiesbaden: VS Verlag für Sozialwissenschaften.

McChesney, Robert W., and John Nichols. 2010. *The Death and Life of American Journalism: The Media Revolution that Will Begin the World Again*. New York: Nation Books.

Meikle, Graham. 2009. *Interpreting News*. Basingstoke: Palgrave Macmillan.

Meyer, Philip. 2004. *The Vanishing Newspaper: Saving Journalism in the Information Age*. Columbia, MO: University of Missouri Press.

Mindich, David T. Z. 1998. *Just the Facts: How "Objectivity" Came to Define American Journalism*. New York: New York University Press.

Mussell, Jim. 2012. "The Matter with Media." *jimmussell.com*, December 18. Accessed July 21, 2014. http://jimmussell.com/2012/12/18/the-matter-with-media/.

Nerone, John. 1989. *The Culture of the Press in the Early Republic. Cincinnati, 1783-1848*. New York: Garland.

Pavlik, John V. 2013. "Innovation and the Future of Journalism." *Digital Journalism* 1 (2): 181–193. doi:10.1080/21670811.2012.756666.

Rafaeli, Sheizaf. 2009. "Interactivity: From New Media to Communication." In *New Media*, edited by Leah A. Lievrouw and Sonia Livingstone, 22–41. Vol. 3. Los Angeles, CA: Sage.

Reckwitz, Andreas. 2002. "Toward a Theory of Social Practices: A Development in Culturalist Theorizing." *European Journal of Social Theory* 5 (2): 243–263. doi:10.1177/13684310222225432.

Rogers, Everett. 2003. *Diffusion of Innovations*. New York: Free Press.

Schatzki, Theodore R., Karin Knorr-Cetina, and Eike von Savigny, eds. 2001. *The Practice Turn in Contemporary Theory*. London: Routledge.

Schudson, Michael. 1978. *Discovering the News: A Social History of American Newspapers*. New York: Basic Books.

Schudson, Michael, and Leonard Downie Jr. 2009. "The Reconstruction of American Journalism." *Columbia Journalism Review*. Accessed July 21, 2014. http://www.cjr.org/reconstruction/the_reconstruction_of_american.php.

Sewell Jr., William H. 1992. "A Theory of Structure: Duality, Agency, and Transformation." *The American Journal of Sociology* 98 (1): 1–29. doi:10.1086/229967.

Sewell Jr., William H. 2005. "The Concept(s) of Culture." In *Logics of History. Social Theory and Social Transformation*, 152–174. Chicago: University of Chicago Press.

Stephens, Mitchell. 1988. *A History of News: From the Drum to the Satellite*. New York: Viking.

Swidler, Ann. 2001. "What Anchors Cultural Practices." In *The Practice Turn in Contemporary Theory*, edited by Theodore R. Schatzki, Karin Knorr-Cetina, and Eike von Savigny, 74–92. London: Routledge.

Tarde, Gabriel. 1903. *The Laws of Imitation*. Translated by E. Clews Parsons. New York: Henry Holt.

Tuchman, Gaye. 1978. *Making News: A Study in the Construction of Reality*. New York: Free Press.

Turow, Joseph. 1997. *Breaking up America: Advertisers and the New Media World*. Chicago: University of Chicago Press.

Uricchio, William. 2006. "Convergence and Diffusion: The Struggle to Re-define Media Practice at the Dawn of the 21st Century." In *Media Cultures*, edited by William Uricchio and Susanne Kinnebrock, 61–87. Heidelberg: Winter.

Warde, Alan. 2005. "Consumption and Theories of Practice." *Journal of Consumer Culture* 5 (2): 131–153. doi:10.1177/1469540505053090.

Williams, Raymond. 1963. *Culture and Society 1780–1950*. London: Penguin.

Williams, Raymond. 1977. *Marxism and Literature*. Oxford: Oxford University Press.

Williams, Raymond. 1979. *Keywords: A Vocabulary of Culture and Society*. London: Fontana, Croom Helm.

POLITICIANS AS MEDIA PRODUCERS
Current trajectories in the relation between journalists and politicians in the age of social media

Mattias Ekman and **Andreas Widholm**

The emergence of social media raises new questions concerning the relationship between journalists and politicians and between news media and politics. The increasingly complex media milieu, in which the boundaries between media producers and audiences become partly dissolved, calls for new theoretical approaches in the study of journalism. This article reassesses central theoretical arguments about the relationship between journalism, sources, politics and democracy. Drawing on a pilot study of the printed press, it explores the increased social media use among politicians in Sweden and its implications for political journalism. The article suggests that power relations between journalism and politics can be fruitfully explored from the perspective of mediatized interdependency, a perspective that acknowledges that journalists and politicians have become both actors and sources through mutual interaction in online spaces. Furthermore, it argues that social media use has expanded journalism's interest in the private life of politicians, thereby contributing to a de-politicization of politics.

Introduction

A key trajectory in the relationship between news media institutions and political institutions is related to the changing practices of media production. The interconnections between journalists and politicians have been increasingly complex after the rise of political communication on and through social media platforms. Political actors, previously positioned outside the realm of media institutions, have now incorporated social media such as Twitter, Facebook and blogs into their daily communication strategies. Politicians use Twitter and Facebook as communicative platforms, both in relation to private users (citizens, audiences), and in order to influence and network with news media professionals (e.g. Larsson and Moe 2012). Thus, journalists are now facing politicians in a multimodal communication environment, which means that they cannot solely rely on traditional journalistic methods such as interviewing political actors or attending press conferences, etc. Simultaneously, journalists are also incorporating social media use in their daily work routines. A recent study shows that Twitter is the fastest growing social media platform deployed by journalists in Sweden (Lindqvist 2013). In 2013, 68 per cent of all Swedish journalists used Twitter in their profession compared to 48 per cent in 2011, thus making Twitter-use equal to Facebook-use. On the other hand, the number of journalists that used Facebook in their profession declined to 68 per cent in 2013 from 77 per cent in 2011 (Lindqvist 2013). If this trend continues, it means that Twitter soon will be the biggest social media platform used by Swedish journalists in their work practices. This trend is also evident in other countries. In the United Kingdom, 97 per cent of business journalists use social media regularly for their work, with Twitter being the most popular platform used by 70 per cent (Cision 2012).

Considering the specific character of online social media, both politicians and journalists become increasingly dependent on factors that pertain to certain communicative processes of social media use and practices. Furthermore, this implies that if all institutions are to some extent media institutions (e.g. Altheide and Snow 1991), it calls for both theoretical and empirical clarity when addressing processes and events that seem to rely on the meta-process of mediatization (cf. Strömbäck 2011a) or the overall media logic (Altheide and Snow 1979). Therefore, there is a need to reassess some theoretical perspectives on journalism practices and on the relationship between news media, politics, audiences and democracy. Whereas previous studies of Twitter have scrutinized, among other things, the dissemination and discussion of news topics (Bruns and Burgess 2012), journalistic practices in relation to Twitter (Lasorsa, Lewis, and Holton 2012, 30), news coverage of Twitter as a technological phenomenon (Arceneaux and Schmitz Weiss 2010) and how Twitter is deployed during election campaigns (Larsson and Moe 2012), this article explores some of the theoretical implications that emerge concerning the changing relationship between politicians and news journalism reflecting the emergence of social media use.

The article begins with a review of central theoretical arguments concerning the power relations between journalism and sources. These are then discussed in relation to the new forms of interaction that take place between journalists and politicians in online environments, where the concept of "mediatized interdependency" is introduced. The following sections set the focus on social media logics and how the interrelationship between journalists and politics on Twitter actualize new questions concerning personification and celebrity politics. Drawing on a pilot study of the printed press, the article explores the increased social media use among politicians in Sweden and its impact on political news journalism. In the final section, the article discusses both the problems and benefits of the new media environment for journalism's role in democracy.

Sources, Journalists and Power

Sources are a key ingredient in all forms of professional journalism. As a cornerstone in journalistic work, sources provide information, background and broader contexts that journalists draw upon in the construction of journalistic texts. Political journalism would be unthinkable without established relations with political institutions and, traditionally, the same has been said about political institutions and their relationship with news media. In fact, politicians' ability to communicate their agenda is to a great extent governed by their relationship with journalists and media institutions. It is against this background that we also need to understand one of the most classic questions of journalistic research, namely who has the upper hand in the source–reporter relationship. Before we go into a couple of empirical examples of how social media, and especially the use of Twitter, has changed the dynamics between reporters and sources, it is important to reflect briefly on the historical context of research on sources and news media. Basically, three strands of research can be seen here. First, there are those who centre on journalism's central role regarding the selection and framing of social phenomena, arguing that journalists have acquired an informational power position that few other actors in society can match. The classical works on "media logic" (Altheide and Snow 1979, 1991; Hernes 1978) and some of the more recent works on "mediatization" (Strömbäck 2011a) represent a position that centres on the media's ability to influence the behaviours and modes of communication of other social institutions. Although the concept of mediatization comes in several versions, most scholars who use the term tend to underline that, for example, political institutions need to adapt their strategies and operations so that they fit the logic of the media. In some of the classical analyses of journalistic production practices, we find analogous arguments about journalism's power in society. Tuchman's (1973) contention that news work can be understood in terms of a "routinization of the unexpected" indirectly underlined that sources need to adapt their strategies in both time and space, packaging information subsidies in a media-friendly manner in order to have a chance to pass journalism's gatekeeping function. Recent studies have argued that these relations prevail in the digital era. Journalists may be served with an extensive amount of information by external sources, but they still decide how this information is turned into news through the practices of journalism (Reich 2008; Broersma, den Herder, and Schohaus 2013). Thus, journalists hold the power of selecting, processing and distributing information according to a set of rules that are generally inaccessible to members of the public (Quandt 2011).

A second type of research sets the focus on professional sources and effective strategies for managing the news. A bearing argument is that journalists generally reproduce rather than challenge political agendas and frames of understanding. The reporter–source relationship has been a contested issue in media research for several decades. As indicated above, there are also several reasons why we need to problematize the notion that mediatization works in favour of journalistic institutions. The fact that journalism is governed by rules and conventions that have consequences for the operations of other social institutions does not necessarily mean that sources are "dominated" by the news media. The increased *awareness* of journalism's *modus operandi* also opens up for effective strategies of news management, reflected in the vast resources spent on public relations by political institutions (Strömbäck 2011b; Davis 2002). More recent studies of structural transformations in the media industry have suggested that sources have strengthened their grip in the source–journalist relationship due to a long list of factors. The shift to digital distribution has caused severe problems for most media companies, which are still leaning on traditional newspaper business models. Downsized news desks and multi-skilled journalists rather than special reporters (Witschge and Nygren 2009) together with a growing dependence on externally produced materials are some of the consequences often brought to define journalism in the digital era. In such a situation, information subsidies become increasingly significant raw materials for news production (Lewis, Williams, and Franklin 2008), and so do the "primary definers" (Hall et al. [1978] 2013) who serve as journalism's main informants. Journalists can still be "internal" gatekeepers, but without resources for critical scrutiny, fact checking and investigative reporting, the "power" of journalism is reduced to headlining and choice of angle.

The rise of social media has had several implications for the interrelationship between journalist and politics. As journalism no longer can claim monopoly over public information, there is also much that indicates that information providers that are located outside the traditional news institutions increasingly challenge journalistic constructions through alternative forms of communication, not least through social media platforms.

A third type of research that focuses on journalism and sources in terms of interaction are therefore particularly helpful here, as the question of influence becomes increasingly complex and difficult to determine. Berkowitz (2009) conceptualizes the relationship between journalists and sources in terms of negotiation, where both parties hope to achieve their goals and strengthen their statuses through mutual interaction. In this process of "give and take", sources strive for both public influence and personal recognition in the same way as journalists are driven by the ambition to produce stories that become appraised both internally in the news organization and externally by the general public. In order for this relationship to be effective, it is important that both parties feel that they gain from it. Thus, according to this view, neither sources nor journalists have the upper hand since the relationship is built on a mutual recognition of interests. In a similar manner, Broersma, den Herder, and Schohaus (2013) talk about the source–reporter relationship as a struggle, where sources decide what *could* be published while journalists eventually decide what *will* be published. In addition, they argue that this interdependency is important for the constant reproduction of journalistic norms. Personal relationships between politicians and reporters are usually considered problematic in the journalistic profession, while professional contacts that give "access" to important information is considered both valuable and necessary. An integral part of journalism's professional ideology is to acknowledge constantly the fact that sources are both biased and partial. For example, the basic journalistic principle of validating a story with at least two independent sources is indicative of how this acknowledgement is applied in the daily work. According to Deuze (2007), most journalists see their work as a *public service*, meaning that they want to produce valid and legitimate information as a service to society using professional codes of *ethics*. In order to uphold this ambition, they commonly accept established principles of *objectivity* (to be fair, neutral, impartial, etc.) as well as principles of *autonomy* (to keep a proper distance and independence to the actual "objects" of news reporting). The power of news journalism—the capability to produce information that is perceived as true by its public—lies to a great extent in its ability to establish legitimacy through the adoption of such an ideology (Ekecrantz and Olsson 1994).

Mediatized Interdependency

In the context of new media technologies, and especially considering the role of social media, there are several reasons why we need to approach the interrelationship between sources and journalism from a fresh analytical lens. It is, of course, worth noticing that much of the research above is still valid. There is an urgent need, however, to develop theories on journalistic sources in ways which make them applicable in a media landscape characterized by an increasing expansion of various forms of media technologies and practices. We suggest that power relations between journalists and political actors are most fruitfully explored from the perspective of *mediatized interdependency* where both parties are reliant on each other in order to get their work done properly. Previous research seldom takes into account the fact that sources to an increasing extent are active media producers themselves (through practices that are increasingly similar to those used by journalists). Twitter and blogs, tools that are used extensively by politicians, are dynamic and fast-changing sources that are very different from traditional journalistic raw materials such as press releases or the type of information that "comes alive" through face-to-face interaction during an interview or at a press conference.

A brief overview of Twitter use among political journalists and politicians reveals a vast flow of information being disseminated on the platform by both parties. Sixty-eight per cent of all Swedish journalists use Twitter professionally (Lindqvist 2013) and according to a recent survey made by an online news outlet, more than 200 members (57 per cent) of the Swedish MPs are active on Twitter (Adolfsson 2013). Twitter is a fast and effective distribution channel for political information, and as Broersma and Graham note, "searching for quotes on Twitter has developed into an established journalistic routine, while the inclusion of tweets in news discourse has become an established textual convention" (Broersma and Graham 2013, 451). The struggle is, however, no longer so much about what "could" be published, but about an on-going discursive struggle that takes place in the digital public space. Political actors often make official statements through Twitter, where they "correct" publications they consider problematic. When doing so, they become media producers themselves who, in turn, use *journalism* as a source and vehicle for promoting their own agenda. Consequently, media logic in the digital era is not restricted to the ground principles of journalistic work, but to a much broader set of *opportunities*, available to political and commercial institutions in society as well as to the broader public. Hjarvard (2008) has touched upon this development, distinguishing between, on the one hand, *media logic*, which is the institutional and technological *modus operandi* of the media, and on the other hand, *mediatization*, which is the process whereby society becomes submitted to, or dependent on, this logic. Mediatization can thus be seen as a process that changes the modes of interaction between various social and cultural institutions as a consequence of the media's major role and influence in society. This means, on the one hand, that the media become integrated into the functions and operations of societal institutions, but also, on the other hand, that interaction within and between institutions to a greater extent is performed through the interaction with a medium (Hjarvard 2008, 111). As noted by Kammer (2013), mediatization can be conceived of as a process that draws together societal institutions in a mutually influencing and moulding relationship. The fact that journalists and politicians have become both "media actors" and "media sources" give evidence to the new type of interdependency that this development entails.

The negotiation of meaning between journalists and politicians is, for example, an activity that to an increasing extent takes place in public, and Twitter provides an important space for such interactions. Göran Hägglund (@goranhagglund), party leader of the Christian Democrats and current minister for Health and Social Affairs in Sweden, can be taken as an interesting example of this new mediatized interdependency. Through his Twitter account, Hägglund provides links to news articles he finds interesting and that support his party's policies on a variety of issues. However, he also actively contests interpretations offered by journalists and analysts, seen for example on 30 September 2013, when he confronted Carl Melin (@carlmelin), "Chief pollster" at the Swedish PR company United Minds, and political analyst at *Aftonbladet*, Sweden's largest tabloid. Melin had criticized the Christian Democrats' new policy on a coming Swedish NATO membership, resulting in a Twitter conversation where Hägglund called Melin a "social democratic demagogue". Hägglund also tweets extensively about his favourite hockey team, HV71, accentuating a more private side of online political communication. In fact, being private is a thinkable key to success for a politician on Twitter. Other examples of such "personal" forms of political communication can be detected in the practices of image-blogging on platforms such as Instagram. Several high-ranking Swedish politicians use their Instagram accounts as a way of disseminating visual snapshots of their daily life, a type of communication that has no or a weak connection to traditional politics. Instead, this form of political communication is more about the construction of symbolic values, reflected in the way politicians portray themselves as "ordinary" hard-working citizens, concerned and dedicated parents, culturally engaged, and so forth.

Another interesting example of the blurring boundaries between the personal and professional aspects of political communication was highlighted by the *New York Times*. In the article, Sweden's foreign minister, Carl Bildt, was interviewed together with the US ambassador to Russia, Michael A. McFaul. Bildt's style on Twitter appears in the news article as a mix of life and work, "one moment tweeting about Syria and the next gently complaining about the long line for takeoff at the Istanbul airport". McFaul, one of Bildt's followers, says in the same article that he is "learning where the lines are" between private and personal forms of communication: "any time there is something personal or something with a photo or video it gets much more pick up or retweets than a statement on Syria" (Freeland 2012).

Besides being a new, potentially rich, source of information for journalists, social media becomes a space where they can publicly address politicians directly and indirectly in real-time. When politicians respond to journalists on Twitter, their comments become mediated to the greater audience of online users. Twitter is a platform where rapid public conversation takes centre stage, but in order to gain public status (followers, re-tweets, etc.) and uphold professional prestige, both journalists and politicians have become increasingly dependent on each other. During September 2013, Niklas Svensson (@niklassvensson), political news reporter on Sweden's second largest tabloid, *Expressen*, published over 30 tweets tagging Swedish foreign minister Carl Bildt's Twitter account (@carlbildt), and during the same month the same reporter re-tweeted eight tweets from the foreign minister. The two *users* also engaged in short discussions over political matters, resulting in a total of nearly 50 tweets on the reporter's Twitter account mentioning the Swedish foreign minister in September alone. The specific practice of tweeting implies that both journalistic and political messages are shaped by specific media logics constituted by the characteristics of Twitter—short and witty messages that ultimately strive for large public attention. This communicative interaction both reflects and increases the ongoing transformation from "traditional journalistic 'objectivity' to the 'subjectivity' of bloggers, social networking and adversarial journalism" (Wheeler 2013, 18–19), prevailing in social media communication. Since Twitter accounts of political journalists tend to be semi-attached to the publisher- or broadcaster-employer,[1] reporters are inclined to be both more personal and more subjective on their social media outlets, compared to the publications in their respective news medium. These "ambient" forms of journalism (e.g. Hermida 2010; Bruns 2010) reflect the increasingly blurred boundaries between the professional and the personal in news practices, and between journalists, political actors and the audience. Political news journalism on Twitter also seems to be about marketing individual news reporters in order to enhance personal careers, but also to boost the publishers' or broadcasters' image and profile. So, it is not only politicians that use social media in order to profile themselves, but also journalists. Social media can be used as platforms where specific political journalists are promoted as celebrities in the same fashion as anchors and reporters have been promoted on television over the past decades (e.g. Hamilton 2004, 161).

Politicians' Tweets as News Sources

The extent to which politicians' social media use transforms the practices and content of news can be approached from various angles and in order to substantiate the theoretical discussion, the findings from a pilot study are presented here.[2] The pilot study is heuristic in the sense that it provides a first analytic step towards assessing the theoretical concept of mediatized interdependency. The study examines the impact of politicians' Twitter-use on news content, looking at the way tweets are used as sources, what news topics they are part of and what parties receive most attention. The study also looks at the extent to which the articles pertain to personal or political dimensions of the tweeter. Furthermore, the article examines if the tweets are framed in negative, positive or neutral terms. The analysis deliberately deals with the relation between tweets and print news rather than online news, since this can reveal if social media use has any effect on more traditional political news reporting outside online communication. The sample is based on news stories published in the printed Swedish press during 2012. The material was collected using the database "Retriever", Sweden's largest online press archive, and we chose to include eight newspapers: *Aftonbladet, Expressen, Dagens Nyheter, Svenska Dagbladet, Sydsvenskan, Östgöta Correspondenten, Dagens Industri* and *Göteborgsposten*. We limited the sample to articles that contained the word "Twitter" together with one or several of the political parties represented in the Swedish parliament. The material was narrowed down to articles where political Twitter messages were explicitly cited or referred to in the text. This resulted in 86 news articles, of which the majority was published in the two tabloids *Aftonbladet* and *Expressen*. The relatively small sample of 86 articles made it possible to navigate the material more qualitatively. For example, the part of the analysis dealing with the particular framing of the tweet (using the values *positive, neutral* and *negative*) demanded more attention from the coder, which was manageable due to the sample size (i.e. the coding implied a more qualitative approach). Furthermore, it was also possible to re-assess the material in order to get some more qualitative insights on specific news events that included tweets as sources (e.g. the news articles dealing with Twitter-generated scandals and the articles using tweets from the Swedish foreign minister as sources).

The Swedish political landscape is divided into two major blocs. A centre-right constellation of four parties including the Center Party, the Liberals, the Moderate Party and the Christian Democrats has held power since 2006. Prior to the 2010 election, the Left Party, the Social Democrats and the Green Party co-operated as a united political alternative, but after failing in the same election, that strategy was abandoned. Although informal co-operation still exists, the three challenging parties are now developing separate political agendas. The right-wing populist party Sweden Democrats constitutes a third political force in Sweden. The party managed to get seats in the Swedish parliament for the first time in 2010, drawing on anti-immigration policies and highly conservative ideals similar to the populist right-wing tendencies that have been consolidated in other European countries. An important question is thus to what extent this landscape is reflected in the way Twitter messages are used as explicit news sources.

The Moderate Party received most of the attention during the period with 38 mentioned tweets or 44 per cent of all articles. The Social Democrats and the Sweden Democrats reached 16 tweets or nearly 19 per cent each, followed by the Center Party and the Christian Democrats, which stayed at 7 per cent each. Neither the Left Party, nor the Liberals or the Green Party, reached more than 2 per cent in total during the studied period. On a more general level, these figures reflect the power constellation in Swedish politics, as the Moderate Party to the right and the Social Democrats to the left are the largest parties on each side of the political spectrum. However, the uneven distribution, and especially the high figures for the Sweden Democrats, suggests that there are other factors that seem to be at work here. The pilot study indicates that there are two specific factors that appear to have an impact on why politicians' tweets are used as news sources—negativity and personification.

When addressing the modality variable *attitude*, we measure the news article's specific attitude towards the tweet. Since this part of the coding implied a more qualitative dimension, the values used were *positive*, *neutral* and *negative*. These values measure when the tweet is referred to (or framed) in *positive*, *neutral* or *negative* terms by the main author of the text (i.e. the journalist). The result reveals that an important factor for news impact seems to be *negativity*. Fifty-five per cent of all news articles framed the politician's tweet in negative terms (34 per cent were neutral and only 12 per cent were positive). If we look more specifically at the distribution between the political parties, we see, for example, that the Moderates as well as the Sweden Democrats received extensive negative coverage while other parties seemed to face a milder treatment during the period. The reasons for these figures can be explained by both thematic and producer-oriented factors. Sweden's foreign minister, Carl Bildt (a member of the Moderate Party), is very active and well established on social media platforms (which points to frequency and professionalism as important factors). He often uses his blog and Twitter account to comment on political currents, trying to establish his own agenda without journalistic interventions. Bildt's influence on journalistic content can be seen in the figures for foreign policy (10 per cent in total, of which all articles dealt with messages communicated by him).

The importance of negativity is also highly visible in the high figures for scandals (14 per cent) and in news on migration (11 per cent), both displayed in Figure 1. The Sweden Democrats as well as the Moderate Party had representatives that were involved

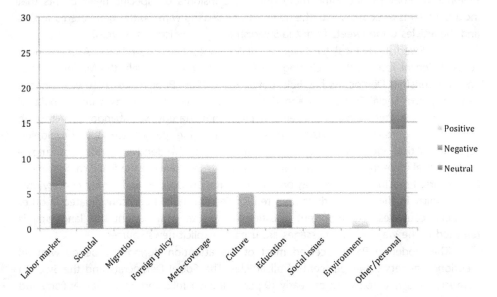

FIGURE 1
News topics in relation to positive, negative or neutral framing of the tweet by the Swedish press (%)

in scandals pertaining to allegations of racism during the studied period. In November, Swedish tabloid *Expressen* published controversial videos of three representatives of the Sweden Democrats in the city centre of Stockholm. The party tried to parry a huge wave of criticism by using Twitter, but as suggested by our figures, that was hardly a successful strategy as the tweets were framed in exclusively negative terms. The Moderate Party, on the other hand, was involved in a "Twitter Scandal" after one of the party representatives had expressed racist comments on his micro-blog. While the former example illustrates that Twitter does not necessarily increase the influence on news media, the latter also shows that the level of professionalism is highly important to succeed. Without a carefully chiselled communication strategy, politicians become easy targets for journalists. However, that is not to say that political communication through Twitter must be "serious" and carefully planned in advance. On the contrary, one of the most striking results from our study is the extensive coverage devoted to tweets that offer insights into the private and personal sphere of politicians. This is also a type of communication that receives a predominantly neutral or positive response from journalists.

The second factor that seems to affect the impact of tweets as sources in the news is connected to *personification*. Twenty-six per cent of all articles, using tweets as sources, relate to the personal aspects of the politician rather than to "conventional" political news topics. The category personal/other is by far the most common one in the sample (see Figure 1). The result indicates that more trivial topics (e.g. when politicians comment on everyday life) seem to generate news impact. News reporting focuses on both the professional and personal/private aspects of politicians, hence reflecting the increased blurring of the private and professional in politics at large (Wodak 2011).

As illustrated in Figure 1, Twitter seems to increase the personalization of politics in news reporting. Furthermore, when journalists produce news about political tweets, they are often doing so by focusing on negativity, conflicts and scandals. As journalism still leans on professional ideals and pre-established working routines and news values, there is not much that indicates a radical change in the relationship between print news media and politics in terms of power. However, the results indicate that the communicative practices among journalists and politicians inherit a dimension of interdependency that takes increasingly mediatized forms. The personalization of politics is not only the result of commercialized news values or market-driven journalistic priorities. It is also a consequence of more personalized forms of communication among politicians. Being personal is both a way of increasing the possibility of journalistic publicity and a good chance to establish personal political brands in the public debate (cf. Mancini 2011). Needless to say, the personal dimension is also widely visible in the modes of conversation that take place between journalists and politicians on Twitter. In contrast to traditional interviews, where journalists commonly want to mark a sense of distance by being objective and impartial, Twitter has made subjective and confrontational forms of interaction increasingly common. Mediatized interdependency does not necessarily involve more "matey" relations, as it also constitutes a new ground for the marking of professional identities and ultimately also for the reproduction and development of social agency (cf. Kammer 2013).

Since one of the normative cornerstones of journalism in democratic societies has to do with its ability to provide citizens with information that ultimately guides them in political matters (e.g. Rosenstiel and Kovach 2001), it becomes necessary to reflect upon the development of political news in relation to politicians' communication on social media. The rise of online communication and social media has sparked many hopeful comments about an amplified political engagement among citizens (e.g. Castells 2009), more horizontal information flows (e.g. Keane 2009), digital democracy (e.g. Dahlberg 2001), a more diversified media landscape, and so forth. However, social media also tend to speed up other less desirable aspects within contemporary news media–politics relations. The study of politicians' tweets as news sources discloses that Twitter unquestionably contributes to the ongoing process of increased personalization of politics, foremost by mediating the personal and private realm of politicians' lives. Two important factors that pertain to the specific character of social media use within the process of unfolding and constructing political news, such as scandals or other unforeseeable events, is the dynamics of spatial–temporal proximity (to the driving factors of the event) and the velocity (the ability to provide updated information). Both of these are important mechanisms in accelerating the de-politicization of political news. This also adheres to traditional forms of media logic such as intensification and personalization (Hernes 1978; Altheide and Snow 1979).

The situational and communicative aspects of political tweeting seem to increase the entertainment aspects of political news reporting. Both scandalization and personalization can be understood as drivers in reifying political journalism, as part of the market logic of news production. In relation to tweets as sources, the news focus tends to shift from political issues to the personal and private realms of individual politicians. The emergence of politicians' social media use (or at least parts of it) therefore relates to what Mancini (2011) defines as the "commodification of politics", and what Wheeler (2013) calls "celebrity politics"—the construction of highly individualized and branded politicians. Since "high-end users" on Twitter tend to be already-established actors that belong to an elite in the public debate, for example politicians and news journalists (Larsson and Moe 2012, 741), social media constitute an arena where both political messages and identities become increasingly marketized (e.g. Wodak 2011; Wheeler 2013). This also means that politicians' communication on Twitter contributes to a process where politics becomes increasingly de-politicized. A previous study reveals that politicians' micro-blogging focuses on disseminating information rather than dialogue with other users (Larsson and Moe 2012). The communicative function of micro-blogging entails explicit aspects of image-making and branding of individual politicians (e.g. Wheeler 2013). It facilitates slogan-friendly communication and privileges reified and simple messages. The two tendencies observed seem to have a reciprocal relation to each other—news reporting focuses on the personal/private aspects of politicians, and politician-users tend to emphasize the personal/private realms of their professional identity while communicating on social media. Hence, both actors are contributing to the increased blurring of the private and professional in politics.

News media actors and political journalists encounter a vast amount of communicated content emanating from high-end politicians that reaches far outside the realm of traditional politics, but that nevertheless makes it into the news from time to time. So, the "commercialization of news" (cf. McManus 2009; Schudson 2003) also feeds from the overall "commercialization of politics", and social media add to, and speed up, the general tendencies advanced by televised politics. The processes of commercialization in news media and politics, respectively, are highly interrelated, and one visible output of increased marketization of political public life is the emergence of "celebrity politics" (Wheeler 2013). When politicians become celebrities they tend to rely on various factors related to news media, with the most notable one being staged performance on television (e.g. van Zoonen 2005). These performances (most often) make the private life of politicians the centre of interest (Sennett 1976, 284). Politicians' social media use seems to have similar consequences.

The growing media interest in the private life of politicians (cf. Wodak 2011), and the general orientation towards personalization and individualization in political news reporting, appear to be key components in contemporary society (cf. Crouch 2004). The digitalization of news media increases the marketization processes through emergent interpersonal and intrapersonal communication practices. The infrastructure of social media platforms such as Twitter privileges individualized communication and therefore it also reinforces these tendencies in both news media and political communication.

However, social media practices are still in an early and evolving stage, and there are also other, more positive, tendencies worth highlighting here. Social media such as Twitter and Facebook engage citizen-users in new forms of multi-communication practices relating to both news journalists and politicians. This implies that certain processes of news journalism become more transparent and increasingly dependent on the trust of audience-users (Lasorsa, Lewis, and Holton 2012). The interactivity with users and the emergence of user-generated content can harvest new forms of contra-flows. Since the communication between journalists and politicians becomes (partly) more visible in public, audiences can engage in and possibly add to the processes of news production in new and more diversified ways. Thus, social media can thereby contribute to a more engaged public and enable new forms of accountability.

Final Reflections

In recent years, media scholars have devoted a great deal of energy on Twitter as a publication platform and as a journalistic tool for information gathering. Few studies, however, have turned a critical spotlight on how tweets are used as news sources and what distinctive functions they play in news discourse. The examples discussed in this article are all indicative of the mediatized interaction that takes place in and through online public spaces such as Twitter, which also comes with new forms of interdependency between journalists and politicians. The pilot study also reveals that Twitter seems to strengthen processes of personalization and "celebritization" in political journalism. In order to understand the generative factors behind this development, we have to concentrate the analysis on the discursive connections and the mediatized intersection of interests between journalists and politicians that take place on new media platforms. With a more palpable "social" orientation of journalism and political communication comes an increased interest in the personal and the private. However, much more research is needed before we can draw precise conclusions regarding the consequences of this development. That includes, for example, specific case studies on prominent political actors and their ability to manage the news in specific directions. Further studies are also needed that deal more specifically with questions of discursive interaction and the way mediatized interdependency is manifested through digitalized forms of conversation. For example, analysing the public discursive "struggle" between journalists and politicians on social media platforms such as Twitter could be one way to further assess the concept of mediatized interdependency.

There are also other potential consequences of increased social media use by politicians that point in other directions. While this article has focused on new interrelationships, social media may also strangle the social interaction between journalists and sources. As journalism has lost its former information monopoly, politicians can now increasingly rely on their own media production. Digital communication through social media is fast, accessible to anyone and easy to use, without any costs for journalistic institutions that are set under hard economic pressures. Communicating through blogs and social media can thus be used as a way of taking control over public discourse, where politicians can avoid tough questions and the critical scrutiny that they may entail. That can lead potentially to a breakdown of established source–journalist relations and to a decline of "the negotiation-through-conversation" that has characterized journalism for centuries (Broersma and Graham 2013). Furthermore, that would include implications regarding the power balance between journalism and sources, not in favour of journalists, as many mediatization scholars have argued, but in favour of sources.

NOTES

1. Several journalists run their Twitter accounts more or less independently from the routines at their news outlet.
2. The authors wish to thank Erik Hedenvind for coding assistance.

REFERENCES

Adolfsson, Viktor. 2013. "Top-politicians': 'Twitter Is a Duck Pond.'" *Nyheter24*, May 16. Accessed January 9, 2014. http://nyheter24.se/nyheter/politik/745987-toppolitikerna-twitter-ar-en-ankdamm.
Altheide, David L., and Robert P. Snow. 1979. *Media Logic*. London: Sage.
Altheide, David L., and Robert P. Snow. 1991. *Media Worlds in the Postjournalism Era*. New York: Walter de Gruyter.
Arceneaux, Noah, and Amy Schmitz Weiss. 2010. "Seems Stupid Until You Try It: Press Coverage of Twitter, 2006-9." *New Media and Society* 12 (8): 1262–1279. doi:10.1177/1461444809360773.
Berkowitz, Daniel A. 2009. "Reporters and Their Sources." In *The Handbook of Journalism Studies*, edited by Karin Wahl-Jorgensen and Thomas Hanitzsch, 102–115. New York: Routledge.
Broersma, Marcel, Bas den Herder, and Birte Schohaus. 2013. "A Question of Power." *Journalism* 7 (4): 388–395.
Broersma, Marcel, and Todd Graham. 2013. "Twitter as a News Source: How Dutch and British Newspapers used Tweets in Their News Coverage, 2007–2011." *Journalism Practice* 7 (4): 446–464. doi:10.1080/17512786.2013.802481.
Bruns, Axel. 2010. "Oblique Strategies for Ambient Journalism." *Media-Culture Journal* 13: (2). Accessed January 9, 2014. http://www.journal.media-culture.org.au/index.php/mcjournal/article/viewArticle/230.
Bruns, Axel, and Jean Burgess. 2012. "Researching News Discussion on Twitter: New Methodologies." *Journalism Studies* 13 (5–6): 801–814. doi:10.1080/1461670X.2012.664428.
Castells, Manuel. 2009. *Communication Power*. Oxford: Oxford University Press.

Cision. 2012. *2011 Social Journalism Study: Perceptions and Use of Social Media among Journalists in the UK*. Accessed January 9, 2014. http://www.cision.com/uk/pr-white-papers/uk-social-journalism-survey-2012/.

Crouch, Colin. 2004. *Post-democracy*. London: Polity Press.

Dahlberg, Lincoln. 2001. "The Internet and Democratic Discourse: Exploring the Prospects of Online Deliberative Forums Extending the Public Sphere." *Information, Communication and Society* 4 (4): 615–633. doi:10.1080/13691180110097030.

Davis, Aeron. 2002. *Public Relations Democracy: Politics, Public Relations and the Mass Media in Britain*. Manchester: Manchester University Press.

Deuze, Mark. 2007. *Media Work*. Cambridge: Polity Press.

Ekecrantz, Jan, and Tom Olsson. 1994. *Det redigerade samhället: Om journalistikens, beskrivningsmaktens och det informerade förnuftets historia* [The Edited Society: On Journalism's Power to Describe and a History of Informed Intelligence]. Stockholm: Carlsson.

Freeland, Chrystia. 2012. "Blending Governance and Twitter." *New York Times*, April 5. Accessed January 9, 2014. http://www.nytimes.com/2012/04/06/us/06iht-letter06.html?_r=0.

Hall, Stuart, Chas Critcher, Tony Jefferson, John Clarke, and Brian Roberts. [1978] 2013. *Policing the Crisis: Mugging, the State and Law and Order*. 2nd ed. Basingstoke: Palgrave Macmillan.

Hamilton, James T. 2004. *All the News That's Fit to Sell: How the Market Transforms Information into News*. Princeton: Princeton University Press.

Hermida, Alfred. 2010. "Twittering the News: The Emergence of Ambient Journalism." *Journalism Practice* 4 (3): 297–308. doi:10.1080/17512781003640703.

Hernes, Gudmund. 1978. "Det mediavridde samfunn [The Media-twisted Society]." In *Forhandlingsekonomi og Blandningsadministrasjon* [Negotiation, Economy and Mixed Administration], edited by Gudmund Hernes, 181–195. Oslo: Universitetsforlaget.

Hjarvard, Stig. 2008. "The Mediatization of Society." *Nordicom Review* 29 (2): 105–134.

Kammer, Aske. 2013. "The Mediatization of Journalism." *MedieKultur. Journal of Media and Communication Research* 29 (54): 141–158.

Keane, John. 2009. *The Life and Death of Democracy*. New York: Simon and Schuster.

Larsson, Anders O., and Hallvard Moe. 2012. "Studying Political Microblogging: Twitter Users in the 2010 Swedish Election Campaign." *New Media and Society* 14 (5): 729–747. doi:10.1177/1461444811422894.

Lasorsa, Dominic L., Seth C. Lewis, and Avery E. Holton. 2012. "Normalizing Twitter." *Journalism Studies* 13 (1): 19–36. doi:10.1080/1461670X.2011.571825.

Lewis, Justin, Andrew Williams, and Bob Franklin. 2008. "A Compromised Fourth Estate? UK News Journalism, Public Relations and News Sources." *Journalism Studies* 9 (1): 1–20. doi:10.1080/14616700701767974.

Lindqvist, Håkan. 2013. "Increasing Twitter Use among Journalists." *Journalisten*, September 27. http://www.journalisten.se/nyheter/Twitter-okar-bland-journalister.

Mancini, Paolo. 2011. *Between Commodification and Lifestyle Politics: Does Silvio Berlusconi Provide a New Model of Politics for the Twenty-first Century?* Oxford: Reuters Institute for the Study of Journalism, University of Oxford.

McManus, John H. 2009. "The Commercialization of News." In *The Handbook of Journalism Studies*, edited by Karin Wahl- Jorgensen and Thomas Hanitzsch, 218–232. London: Routledge.

Quandt, Thorsten. 2011. "Understanding a New Phenomenon: The Significance of Participatory Journalism." In *Participatory Journalism: Guarding Open Gates at Online Newspapers*, edited by Jane B. Singer, David Domingo, Ari Heinonen, Alfred Hermida, Steve Paulussen,

Thorsten Quandt, Zvi Reich, and Marina Vujnovic, 155–176. Chichester: John Wiley and Sons.

Reich, Zvi. 2008. "How Citizens Create News Stories: The 'News Access' Problem Reversed." *Journalism Studies* 9 (5): 739–758. doi:10.1080/14616700802207748.

Rosenstiel, Tom, and Bill Kovach. 2001. *The Elements of Journalism: What News People Should Know and the Public Should Expect.* New York: Crown.

Schudson, Michael. 2003. *The Sociology of News.* New York: W.W. Norton.

Sennett, Richard. 1976. *The Fall of Public Man.* New York: W.W. Norton.

Strömbäck, Jesper. 2011a. "Mediatization and Perceptions of the Media's Political Influence." *Journalism Studies* 12 (4): 423–439. doi:10.1080/1461670X.2010.523583.

Strömbäck, Jesper. 2011b. *Lobbyismens problem och möjligheter: Perspektiv från dem som både lobbar och har blivit lobbade* [The Problems and Possibilities of Lobbyism: Perspectives from Lobbyists and Those Being Targeted by Lobbyists]. Stockholm: Precis.

Tuchman, Gaye. 1973. "Making News by Doing Work: Routinizing the Unexpected." *American Journal of Sociology* 79 (1): 110–131. doi:10.1086/225510.

van Zoonen, Lizbeth. 2005. *Entertaining the Citizen: When Politics and Popular Culture Converge.* Lanham: Rowman and Littlefield.

Wheeler, Mark. 2013. *Celebrity Politics.* London: Polity Press.

Witschge, Tamara, and Gunnar Nygren. 2009. "Journalism: A Profession under Pressure?" *Journal of Media Business Studies* 6 (1): 37–59.

Wodak, Ruth. 2011. "Disenchantment with Politics and the Salience of Images." In *Images in Use*, edited by Matteo Stocchetti and Karin Kukkonen, 69–88. Amsterdam: John Benjamins.

GATEKEEPING IN A DIGITAL ERA
Principles, practices and technological platforms

Peter Bro and **Filip Wallberg**

The original concept of gatekeeping within journalism was based on a particular research method, a particular sub-profession within the news media, and a particular—now extinct— technological platform. This article describes and discusses what has happened to the function of gatekeeping as new technologies have developed, and it suggests that three models of gatekeeping are present in the digital era. The first model is based on a process of information, the second model is based on a process of communication, and the third and last model is based on a process of elimination, where the function of gatekeeping is taken over by people outside the newsrooms. All three models have been part of the history of journalism from the very beginning, but their importance for news reporters and the news media have changed with the invention of new technological means, methods and tools. This reassessment of the principles, practices and new technological platforms for gatekeeping concludes by discussing the ways in which our models of journalism can affect not only researchers but also news reporters and audiences.

Introduction

"It's a new language", said Ernest Hemingway, when he started working as a cable correspondent in Europe in the 1920s. Here, in countries like France and Italy, he became familiar with what researchers have termed "the stripped-down language used to file stories for overseas transmission" (Hochfelder 2013, 44). Hemingway himself expressed the changes in language in another, more metaphorically laden form that predated his change of career from news reporter to literary writer: "[N]o fat, no adjectives, no adverbs— nothing but blood and bones and muscle. It's great", he later described (cited in Meyers 1984, 94) the form of what was at that time often referred to as "cablese".

Hemingway was not the only news reporter who became fascinated with the form and focus of cablese. A fascination he brought with him into his new line of work. "I was getting too fascinated with the lingo of the cable", he later explained (cited in Steffens 1931, 142), and one has only to read a little of the later Nobel Prize-winning writer to recognize the source of inspiration for the prose in his books. The same fascination for electro-magnetic telegraphy is, however, also shared by many journalism researchers, who for decades have taken principles and practices associated with electro-magnetic telegraphy as their starting point.

For some researchers, this classic form of telegraphy—that was based on a pivotal scientific discovery in 1820 of the previously unknown relation between magnetism and electricity—came to influence not only news reporters' use of semantics and syntax, such as Hemingway himself came to experience. The new technology, that in the words of some historians has marked a "climatic moment in the widespread communication revolution" (Howe 2007, 1) since it meant that messages could be transmitted rather than transported physically, might also have changed the underlying structure of news reporting altogther, according to some researchers.

The telegraph led to a fundamental change in news, James Carey has written, and he and other researchers have described how the fear of an unstable technology prompted news reporters to send the most important part of a news story first (Carey and Sims 1976; Carey [1983] 1989; Allan 2004). The result was shorter, more condensed writing and the pre-eminence of a new practice—the inverted news triangle. In the minds of some researchers telegraphy also promoted new principles (Emery and Emery 1996), since the wire services generated "'objective' news, news that could be used by papers of any political stripe" (Carey [1983] 1989, 210).

Some of these claims about the effects of electro-magnetic telegraphy on the principles and practices of journalism have since been challenged by other researchers (see e.g. Schudson 2001). But in the past, researchers have not only tried to explain the form and focus of journalism, but also the function and influencing factors by way of this particular technological platform. In few places and research publications does that come across more clearly than in the case of the concept of gatekeeping.

When the concept of gatekeeping was originally introduced within journalism studies, it was employed to describe a process where a wire editor received telegrams from the wire services. From these telegrams the wire editor, known as Mr. Gates in David Manning White's (1950) seminal study, selected what to publish. This capacity to select and reject content for publication has become a popular way of portraying the function of news reporters. In time, however, telegraphy has been succeeded by new technologies, and they have inspired new practices and principles when it comes to producing, publishing and distributing news stories.

This is a technological development that challenges us to revisit, reassess and rethink the process of gatekeeping in a digital era. Particularly, since the insights from White's study still "exert a powerful guiding effect", as Stephen Reese (2007, 31) has written, in determining both researchers', news reporters' and audiences' understanding of journalism. For even if some news organizations might still employ personnel who perform a function similar to Mr. Gates, this article describes and discusses how new technologies and new ideologies within the profession are transforming the practice of gatekeeping—inside and outside newsrooms.

By taking its starting point from this first study of journalisic gatekeeping, this article describes and discusses what has happened to the function and influencing factors of gatekeeping in a digital era. This reassessment leads to the development of a new framework for understanding what to include and exclude in the news media, and on what values the selections and rejections of gatekeepers in the digital era are based.

The Original Concept of Gatekeeping

"Even as the body of theoretical concepts of the nature of mass communication was evolving, an important notion was being overlooked", David Manning White (1964, 160) explained several years after his initial article about gatekeeping had been published. White was the first to conduct an explicit study of gatekeeping within the news media, but he was originally inspired by what he termed "a germinal suggestion from an important study" (160) by the sociologist Kurt Lewin. Lewin (1943) had coined the concept to describe those people and professions that affected the flow of transportation within the food industry.

Lewin (1947, 145) later suggested that the transportation of other products, such as news items, could be studied in a similar way, and as a former journalist White quickly picked up on the idea. His application of the concept proved to be a great success in terms of the number of people, both inside and outside academia, who became inspired by it and have come to employ it. The concept has since been termed a "classic" (Reese and Ballinger 2001, 641) and "a household term in journalism scholarship" (Zelizer 2004, 53), and the concept has even transcended the boundaries of university campuses and become a household name among news reporters and news consumers.

The popularization of the concept of gatekeeping might at first seem paradoxical in light of the criticism that followed after White's original study of a wire editor from a local newspaper. Years before the study, Mr. Gates had—as White later omitted—actually been employed by White himself as an adjunct instructor. Knowing about this prior work relation might help explain the wire editor's strenuous effort throughout a week in February 1949, where he meticulously noted the background for his "choices" and "discards" (White 1950, 383). White's study of the notes and the published content let him to conclude that eight news items were rejected for everyone selected.

Based on observations, content analysis and an interview with Mr. Gates, White (1950, 390) concluded that the wire editor's decision about what to include and exclude in the next morning's newspaper was based on the gatekeeper's "own set of experiences, attitudes and expectations to the communication of what 'news' really is". This conclusion about the function and influencing factors of content in the news media has since been referred to and discussed in hundreds of publications.

Later, researchers have studied the selection processes made by other wire editors (see e.g. Gieber [1956] 1964), and some have even repeated the original gatekeeper study with the exact same wire editor as White used a few decades later to see if Mr. Gates' choices and the reason he would give for them had changed (Snider 1967). The short version of the conclusion: Mr. Gates had not in any significant way changed his views about what to select and reject. But this line of research has not ended with the retirement of Mr. Gates. Other researchers have since looked into other types of gatekeepers in the news media.

Among these are studies of reporters rather than editors (Whitney and Becker 1982), female gatekeepers (Bleske 1991), photographers (Bissell 2000), gatekeepers from radio stations (Bass 1969), from TV stations (Harmon 1989) and from online news media (Singer 2001; Singer et al. 2011). Furthermore, the research field has been concerned with the different processes and criteria used for selection and construction of the final news products. Among these is Galtung and Ruge's (1965) "The Structure of Foreign News" that became a starting point for a new line of research about those news values that influence the selections of news.

Many of these subsequent gatekeeper studies have highlighted the conceptual inspiration and importance of White's original study, even if White was not the first scholar who wrote with an insider's perspective on the selection process in the news media. "[W] ithout standardization, without stereotypes, without routine judgments, without a fairly ruthless disregard of subtlety, the editor would soon die of excitement", Walter Lippmann (1922, 123) wrote decades earlier as part of his critique of the content in the news media. But White's work has become a key reference and prompted many new studies.

Gatekeeping as a Process of Information

Tectonic technological shifts have marked the news media in recent decades, according to some researchers (Anderson, Bell, and Shirky 2012), and the tributes to White have increasingly included criticism of the way his study was designed and depended upon a particular technology. "Classic studies", as Reese and Ballinger (2001, 642) have observed, "capture the imagination", but they "may not be the most advanced in either theory or method". This criticism is certainly valid in the case of White's study, which was based on a restricted research design, an analysis of a particular sub-profession and the importance of a particular technological platform.

Research in recent years has shown that this dependency on telegraphy has become more problematic, particularly since many new transmission technologies have supplanted this electro-magnetically based technology that was invented in the early nineteenth century. Some have even argued that the concept has become irrelevant. The role of the news media as "gatekeeper has gone", a former BBC director has proclaimed (cf. Allan 2006, 169), while others have noted that "[t]he challenge is for scholars to think creatively about applying the theory to a changing world", where some have "predicted that the idea of gatekeeping is dead" (Shoemaker and Vos 2009, 130).

But rather than being irrelevant, the concept of gatekeeping seems to have been used to encompass an increased variety of different principles and practices in journalism, and when one reviews the literature about gatekeeping and relates it to contemporary journalism, three models of gatekeeping stand out. Such "models cannot capture all of the complex interrelationships involved in the media. Models, by definition, are meant to simplify, highlight, suggest and organize", as Reese (2007, 31) has written, and these three distinct, but interconnected models cannot encompass all the ways in which gatekeeping takes place in different journalistic contexts. But they can help to describe and discuss how a particular type of gatekeeper and gatekeeping has developed over time: the "final" gatekeeper, who determines what news stories readers, listeners and viewers receive.

The first model is closely linked to the original gatekeeping concept, as it focuses on a linear process of information transmission. White knew that news production involved several gatekeepers, but in his original study he was primarily interested in one type of gatekeeper. The wire editor in White's (1950) mind was the "last" (384) and the "terminal" gate (390), since his decisions had a direct impact on what was published in the newspapers. White was therefore well aware that there were several other places in the news production process where news passed through gates: "From reporter to rewrite man, through bureau chief to 'state' file editors at various press associations' offices, the process of choosing and discarding is continuously taking place" (White 1950, 384).

But even if White refers to a complex process that includes several "steps in the chain from event to reader"—to paraphrase Galtung and Ruge (1965, 71)—his article describes a linear process of information distribution that passes through a particular and sequenced set of phases and places. This is a process that closely resembles the transportation processes that White's original source of inspiration, Kurt Lewin (1947), had described, when he some years prior to White's study attempted to determine the "channels", "flows", "key positions" and "gatekeepers" when it came to the transportation of food from producers to consumers.

"Food comes to the family table through certain 'channels'", Lewin wrote (1947, 144), and his field studies within this societal sector let him distinguish between a "buying channel" and a "gardening channel" where the food within each of the channels proceeds in certain steps. Lewin summarized his findings in a multilayered figure entitled "channels through which food reaches the family table" (147, 149), and it illustrates a one-way process where food is transported by way of different channels, like the garden or grocery store, but where all items flow towards the "table".

White's article from 1950 does not include any illustrations, but he does describe a similar one-way process in which news is picked up at key positions, passes through different channels and ultimately reaches the tables, where readers await the newspaper. In White's paper, key positions are places like "congress", "channels" are formed by wire services, and "gatekeepers" are reporters and editors like Mr. Gates. In effect, White thus describes gatekeeping as a process of information ranging from news sources to news audiences, where journalists in the words of Axel Bruns (2005, 11) "control the gates through which content is released to their audience".

What White (1950, 384) described as a daily "avalanche" from the wire services, such as United Press and Associated Press, has not vanished in news organizations even though the technological platform has changed. Many news media still publish news to their readers, listeners and viewers by way of a one-way linear process, where persons inside the newsrooms are charged with the function of selecting or rejecting news stories for publication. In the twenty-first century, this process of gatekeeping has even been prompted by the fact that "digital storage and transmission has massively expanded space and time available for media content", as Axel Bruns (2005, 13) has noted.

But not only has a new generation of gatekeepers in the news media found more available space for the publication of their news with the rise of digital platforms. Digital technologies have also been introduced that can automatically select, reject and even generate some rudimentary type of news stories on their own by way of statistical information, stock phrases and pre-conceptualized views of what constitute a news story (see e.g. van Dalen 2012). This automated content can help the traditional news media to satisfy the needs of the general audience which consumes more news than before, through a greater number of media platforms, at increasingly various points throughout the day (Newman 2013).

Gatekeeping as a Process of Communication

To portray the current principles and practices of gatekeeping solely as a process where information is transmitted in a linear process, however, fails to account for the many ways news finds its way to audiences. This is a point made by several researchers. The main criticism of White's conclusions about the function of the gatekeeper has in this context been that his particular research design and choice of data offer only a simplistic understanding of the function of gatekeeping in a digital era. A simplistic function where gatekeepers are left with decisions about what is "in or out" (Reese and Ballinger 2001, 647), as if gatekeeping is "a single stage in isolation from other factors" (Wanta 2009) and "as a process heavily influenced by individuals" (Shoemaker and Vos 2009, 33).

The general criticism has been that with the choice as his research object, White leaves out many of the complexities that other people employed in the news media experience when it comes to the relationship with their news sources and audiences. White's interest in a particular sub-profession means that he never really addresses the complex process that involves multiple and succeeding acts of selection as part of the news production (Shoemaker 1991). This is a complex process that White might have noticed if he had followed the production processes elsewhere at Mr. Gates' workplace, but which has been highlighted even more by new technological and ideological developments.

One of the chroniclers of the changing ideologies of journalism, Tanni Haas, has described a development from a journalism-as-information to a journalism-of-communication (Haas 2007) that began in the last decades of the twentieth century. One of the results was what Michael Schudson (1999, 118) has called "the best organized social movement inside journalism in the history of the American press". This movement also spread to countries across the Atlantic. Under names such as *public journalism* and *civic journalism*, news reporters and editors, researchers and lecturers started experimenting with new norms and forms of journalism, where citizens were approached as active participants in the media "rather than victims and spectators" (Rosen 1999).

The proponents of this movement attempted to change traditional journalism, which was thought of as "disconnected", "detached" and "disinterested", and sought to have the news reporters actively help "reconnect" private citizens with decision-makers. At times these attempts to foster communication rather than simply relay information were done in very practical ways, like bringing questions from private citizens to press conferences with politicians. As later research has shown, the principles behind a journalism-of-communication have little news value in media history (Haas 2007). But new technologies have helped news reporters and the news media operationalize these principles into a concrete journalistic practice.

These technological changes have led some researchers to term telegraphy "the Victorian Internet" (Standage 1998). A term that simultaneously testifies to the importance of the electro-magnetic telegraphy in the past, while at the same time reflects the rise, reach and relevance of a new technological infrastructure in the present. This continual development of new communicative infrastructures, from telegraphy over telephony to the internet, has from invention to invention prompted new possibilities—and problems— for the ways in which gatekeepers in the news media can interact with sources and audiences (see e.g. Deuze 2003; Allan 2006; Jones and Salter 2012).

These possibilities have, in the often cited words of Jay Rosen (2006, 1), "busted open the system of gates and gatekeepers". In time, these new digital means, methods and tools have affected the people who function as gatekeepers and the ways in which the main actors in White's study are connected: news sources, reporters and audiences. The second model of gatekeeping can, in this context, be described as a non-linear communication process where news reporters can connect both with citizens and authoritative decision-makers as news sources, after which representatives from both parties can be approached as news audiences.

This communicative turn in the ways in which journalists can function as gatekeepers has inspired a number of new concepts among researchers. Researchers have attempted to develop their own concepts to describe more adequately the new ways in which some news reporters, sources and audiences can interact by way of the many new technologies that have proliferated in the nineteenth and twentieth centuries.

These descriptions includes labels, concepts and catchphrases like "the people formerly known as the audience" (Rosen 2006), "participatory journalism" (Allan 2006; Singer et al. 2011), "interactive journalism", "gatewatching" (Bruns 2005), "mutualisation", journalism as a "conversation" rather than a "lecture" (Gillmor 2006) and "produsers", a concept where the former users also become producers of news-related content (Bruns 2005). All these notions mark a distinctive difference from the view of gatekeeping in the news media as a mere distributive process of information along the lines Lewin had delineated and which White later became inspired by.

Gatekeeping as a Process of Gradual Elimination

The new labels, concepts and catchphrases describe many different but intercon-nected aspects of the changing processes of gatekeeping in a digital era. In these processes, where gatekeeping is based on the notion of communication rather than information, news reporters pro-actively collect or re-actively receive input from both private citizens and authoritative decision-makers, and when their news stories are finally published, people outside the newsrooms might also help—or hinder—the final distribution. As mentioned, new means, methods and tools associated with the internet have namely given people outside the newsrooms a distributive capacity in the news process.

This development can potentially prompt a shift in terms of who functions as the "last" and "terminal" gatekeeper, and a growing number of studies have described the ways in which people outside the newsrooms occupy an increasingly influential gatekeeper position for news (see e.g. Foster 2012, 44; Newman 2013). This development naturally challenges the role of news reporters as gatekeepers, since new technological platforms now have enabled people outside the newsroom to become both producers, publishers and distributers of news themselves, and according to some researchers it has also challenged the importance of the traditional news media altogether.

"The old business model required media companies to act as gatekeepers to information. This is traditionally how they made their money. The internet, on the other hand, promoted the elimination of the middle man. The right to be a gatekeeper was partially revoked when the news product went online", write Janet Jones and Lee Salter (2012, 45). Axel Bruns has noted that the process of digitization has changed the condition for gatekeeping altogether. News organizations can no longer monopolize the means for the publication and distribution of news.

The development has started to bring a third model to light, where the traditional news media might be gradually eliminated as the prime intermediary between private citizens and authoritative decision-makers (see Figure 1). This is a model—or in Michael Schudson's words a "world"—where "governments, businesses, lobbyists, candidates, churches, and social movements deliver information directly to citizens" (Schudson 1995, 1); a model where the news media might still cover the actions and attitudes of other people, but where still fewer

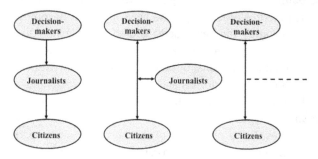

FIGURE 1
Gatekeeping based on information, communication and gradual elimination

readers, listeners and viewers pay any attention, since they themselves can produce, publish and distribute news of their own. By way of social media, private citizens can namely communicate directly with each other and with decision-makers in political parties, companies and organizations, who in turn use their own portals and platforms to communicate directly with each other and larger audiences. The effect of this third model of gatekeeping, where the news media might be gradually eliminated as an intermediary between the former news sources and audiences in the first and second models of gatekeeping, has been described at length—even in book length—in these past years by several and often severely concerned researchers.

Under titles such as *Post-industrial Journalism* (Anderson, Bell, and Shirky 2012), *Can Journalism Survive?* (Ryfe 2012), *Will the Last Reporter Please Turn Out the Lights* (McChesney and Picard 2011) and "Farewell to Journalism?" (McChesney 2012), scholars have discussed the impact of new technologies that have empowered news sources and news audiences to a point where persons and organizations outside the newsrooms no longer necessarily need the news media to mediate between them. This development is associated with the digital era that challenges and calls on researchers to rethink the process of gatekeeping in the news media altogether.

To sum up, reviewing research literature about the practices and principles of gatekeeping among what White referred to as the "terminal" and "final" gatekeepers and relating it to current practices seem to point to the existence of three distinct, but partly interconnected, models. These models are ideal types in the sense that they capture and incorporate key features of the ways in which news reporters and the news media are helped—and hindered—in their work as gatekeepers in a digital era. New principles, practices and technological platforms associated with the digital era have namely brought new potentials and problems to light.

The first of these ideal-type models is based on a one-way linear process of information, where news stories pass through a number of gates from news sources to a news audience, whereas the second model of gatekeeping is based on a non-linear process of communication. In this second model, news reporters connect with people outside the newsrooms who can be approached as news sources, members of an audience and as potential news reporters, and who can relay material and help report new stories themselves by way of their own platforms.

In this sense, audiences can also "contribute to the perseverance" of the traditional news media by way of social media and other portals and platforms (Jones and Salter 2012, 33), since persons and organizations outside the news organizations can help publish and distribute the work of news reporters. These new digital portals and platforms, however, also pose potential problems for the news media, as becomes clear in the third model. Here, gatekeeping by the news media is gradually eliminated and replaced by a new generation of "last" and "terminal" gatekeepers—from outside the newsroom—who prompt political, commercial, personal or other more narrow interests.

In this third model, private citizens and authoritative decision-makers communicate directly with and among one another by way of the means, methods and platforms associated with various types of social media, search engines and other new digitally based media companies. These new types of media companies have, over the past few years, grown to the extent that in several instances they have even surpassed traditional news media organizations in terms of revenues, the number of employers, and the number of users and audiences.

The Influencing Factors of Gatekeeping

White's interest in how the gatekeepers function runs parallel to his interest in why gatekeepers operate as they do. "Our purpose for this study was to determine some preliminary ideas as to why this particular wire editor selected or rejected the news stories", he adds later in his article (White 1950, 384). Following the calculations and descriptions about how much of the approximately 12,400 inches of news stories from the wire services was used, and a breakdown of the received and selected material into various categories, White ends his original study by looking into the reasons Mr. Gates has given for rejecting and selecting each of the received news stories.

The "highly subjective" views by Mr. Gates included a prejudice "against a publicity-seeking minority with headquarters in Rome" and a general fondness for human-interest stories and "stories well-wrapped up and tailored to suit our needs" (White 1950, 390). The importance of subjective selection criteria—and other forces, factors and influences on the function of gatekeepers—has been much discussed in a particular strand of the gatekeeper studies that followed. And some of these studies about the influencing factors have in time become classics in their own right. Less than two years after White's original article in *Journalism Quarterly*, Walter Gieber ([1956] 1964) published the results of a study in which he had investigated the work flows of 16 wire editors from different types of news organizations. The title of his article, "News is What Newspapermen Make It", tells the main story.

Gieber found that editors had no "perception of their audience" ([1956] 1964, 174). The gatekeeper is mainly "preoccupied with the mechanical pressures of his work rather than the social meaning and the impact of his work", Gieber wrote. This "strait jacket of mechanical details" (175) relates directly to Mr. Gates' comment on issues being "well-wrapped up and tailored to suit our needs". Gieber did several subsequent studies—among both editors and reporters—that strengthened his understanding that various types of gatekeepers in the news organizations in general were more concerned about practical matters rather than principle aspects of how the news would and could affect readers.

The title of Warren Breed's (1955) "Social Control in the News Room" is no less telling, and even though there is no direct mention of White's study, it concerns itself with the same focus in terms of the factors that influence news reporters and editors. Breed, who had worked as a news reporter himself, described a process of "newsroom socialization" that constrains reporters and makes them orient themselves toward the inside workings of the newsroom. While Mr. Gates talked about news stories that were "slanted to conform to our editorial politics", Breed found, in the words of Barbie Zelizer, that "the publisher set policy and the reporters followed it" (2004, 53).

Many other studies, inspired directly or indirectly by White's study, have since followed, and some have prompted new concepts that have gained notoriety both inside and outside academia. Most prominent among these might very well be Johan Galtung and Marie Ruge's (1965) study of the criteria—what White termed "standards of taste"— that can help explain what gatekeepers select and reject.

This body of scholarly work that concerns itself less with the effects of news reporting and more with what affects news reporters themselves has helped our understanding of the often complex interplay of factors, forces and influences that can affect the actions and attitudes of various gatekeepers in the news media. But in light of the ways in which the process of gatekeeping is developing by way of new technologies and ideologies, we also need to re-assess the influencing factors on these news ways of gatekeeping. For as Deirdre O'Neill and tony Harcup (2009) have noted in a review of the literature about news values, definitions are and should not be fixed.

"Many lists of news values have been drawn up, and news values can change over time, from place to place, and between different sectors of the news media", write O'Neill and Harcup (2009, 171), after having given examples of the pre-eminence of particular news values, ranging from the time of the original gatekeeper study to more recent developments, where news reporters attempt to prompt a more collaborative, construct-ive, participatory and user-generated approach to the world outside the newsrooms. Researchers have in the past decades shown that the process of gatekeeping based on communication rather than information is accompanied—or prompted by—a new set of values.

Researchers have in past years started to document some of the ways in which the news media are "learning how to adapt to a more collaborative media environment in which journalists share the creation and dissemination of the news with users", as Alfred Hermida (2011, 179) has summed up developments from a cross-national study about participatory journalism at an online newspaper. This scholarly work also includes an interest in how people outside the newsrooms not only play a part in the production of news stories, but also in the selection and rejection in terms of what should be distributed.

For in our digital era, the "final" and "terminal" gatekeeper White was originally interested in is increasingly a friend, member of the family or someone else familiar (see e.g. Newman 2013). As research has shown, these gatekeepers outside the newsrooms might have their own conceptions about what news to select and reject before they publish and distribute it by way of the new communicative infrastructures made possible by the internet. And recently researchers have looked into the values that determine what people outside the news media pass along by way of Twitter and Facebook (Bro and Wallberg 2014).

The increasingly varied ways in which news stories are channelled to audiences (Newman 2013; Singer et al. 2011) challenge researchers to study the influencing factors among a new generation of gatekeepers in a digital era. But these new gateways do not only include new persons. Popularity engines, portals and platforms based on a set of predefined values integrated in computer algorithms are also becoming more important as the final gatekeeper. "Researchers must quickly turn to understanding the complexity of programming in order to develop a better understanding of emergent patterns of gatekeeping", Axel Bruns (2005, 119) has suggested, while Shoemaker and Vos (2009, 130) have prompted researchers "to adapt research methodology that keeps pace".

Models for Future Research in Gatekeeping

The historical importance of telegraphy is still visible and audible in the twenty-first century. Some news organizations still take their name after this technology that was developed in its electro-magnetic form in the nineteenth century, and many news organizations still publish news items referred to as "telegrams". And according to some researchers, even some of the basic practices and principles of journalism—such as the inverted news triangle and the objectivity norm—have directly or indirectly been affected by telegraphy. A point several individual writers, like Hemingway, have testified to.

But it is high time to reassess, rethink and remodel the concept of gatekeeping at a moment in history where the empirical basis on which the original study was made has vanished, even if we should place proper value on the important results this study generated. For the fact that White's study was based on journalistic principles, practices and a platform that seems somewhat outdated in a digital era does not render his work or the later studies useless. Even today some of the best-known models of the function of journalism and the forces that affect journalists are based on and inspired by "The 'Gate Keeper': A Case Study in the Selection of News" (White 1950).

As scholars like Stephen Reese and James Carey have reminded us, however, we should continuously rethink the potential usefulness of the models on which we base our understanding of the world. Models are not only "symbols of", but also "symbols for" that can affect the ways in which we orient us and navigate in the world (Carey [1975] 1989, 28), and in this context some models are surely more meaningful than others. This warning seems particularly prudent in the case of gatekeeping that has transcended the realm of research and has become a popular concept among not only researchers and reporters but also sources and audiences.

In a time when many news organizations on both sides of the Atlantic are challenged and news reporters are laid off—a point that might partly be explained by the new types of gatekeepers in the digital era—there is a need to model the function of journalism and its influencing factors in new ways that are more in line with current problems and potentials. This will not only strengthen a scholarly understanding of the current situation, but might also prompt awareness among persons outside the universities.

Such an active approach also falls in line with the original work on which the gatekeeper study was based. Kurt Lewin originally conceived the concept as part of a research project, where he attempted to help solve specific problems. Lewin was one of the early proponents of a more active research—"Research that produces nothing but books will not suffice", he claimed (Lewin 1947, 150).

The question of the proper role for researchers is also a relevant issue within journalism studies in general and our understanding of the processes of gatekeeping in particular. It "is not clear that our theorizing contributes enough to the resolution or even the common understanding" of the troubles we are facing today, as one of the proponents of a more participatory journalism Jay Rosen (1994, 363) has written. He and other researchers have therefore in recent years pointed to the need for not only a more "public journalism", but also a more "public scholarship" (Rosen 1995, 34), where a "third language" can be developed, shared and practised.

The purpose of such a third language is to mediate between news reporters and researchers so that both professions might work better together. In this context, the three models of gatekeeping can hopefully inspire news reporters, editors and owners of traditional news organizations to think more about what hinders and helps their work in a digital era, and how they might explain their own work to people outside the newsrooms. These are people who seem to become more and more critical of the news work that is done in traditional news organizations.

But the three models can hopefully also inspire and prompt new research into the function and influencing factors of journalism in a digital era. For even though these three models cannot capture all of the complex interrelations involved in gatekeeping—to paraphrase Reese—they can help highlight, inspire and suggest future research into the ways in which gatekeeping has evolved over space and time. In different news media, nations and media systems and in different centuries, decades and generations of gatekeepers, one model might take precedence over the others even if all them might very well co-exist and complement one another across different news media.

Indeed, the third model that has been brought to light by new technological developments in some ways seems to mark a return to the days of the party press, where newspapers were organized on the basis of political, commercial or other interests which news reporters and editors of that time were required to promote actively in their news work. Today, these types of media are sometimes referred to under names such as "branded media" or "custom media", but as was the case with the party press or the commercial press, these media are established to strengthen relations between companies and consumers, organizations and members, and political parties and voters.

At best, this and other future models of gatekeeping will thus not only help researchers and scholars clarify differences between the function and influencing factors of journalism in different contexts, they might also help us to understand the commonalities between different periods, platforms and even professions, such as researchers and news reporters.

REFERENCES

Allan, Stuart. 2004. *News Culture*. London: Open University Press.

Allan, Stuart. 2006. *Online News*. London: Open University Press.

Anderson, C. W., Emily Bell, and Clay Shirky. 2012. *Post-Industrial Journalism: Adapting to the Present*. New York: Columbia University, Tow Center for Digital Journalism.

Bass, Abraham. 1969. "Refining the 'Gatekeeper' Concept: A UN Radio Case Study." *Journalism and Mass Communication Quarterly* 46 (1): 69–72. doi:10.1177/107769906904600110.

Bissell, Kimberly. 2000. "A Return to 'Mr. Gates': Photography and Objectivity." *Newspaper Research Journal* 21 (3): 81–93.

Bleske, Glen. 1991. "Ms. Gates Take Over: An Update Version of a 1949 Case Study." *Newspaper Research Journal* 12 (4): 88–97.

Breed, Warren. 1955. "Social Control in the Newsroom: A Functional Analysis." *Social Forces* 33 (4): 326–335. doi:10.2307/2573002.

Bro, Peter, and Filip Wallberg. 2014. "Digitial Gatekeeping: News Media Versus Social Media." *Digital Journalism*. doi:10.1080/21670811.2014.895507.

Bruns, Axel. 2005. *Gatewatching: Collaborative Online News Production*. New York: Peter Lang.

Carey, James. [1975] 1989. "A Cultural Approach to Communication." In *Communication as Culture*, edited by James W. Carey, 13–36. New York: Routledge.

Carey, James. [1983] 1989. "Technology and Ideology: The Case of the Telegraph." In *Communication as Culture*, edited by James W. Carey, 201–230. New York: Routledge.

Carey, James, and Norman Sims. 1976. "The Telegraph and the News Report." Paper presented at the Annual meeting of the Association for Education in Journalism, Maryland August.

Deuze, Mark. 2003. "The Web and Its Journalisms: Considering the Consequences of Different Types of Newsmedia Online." *New Media & Society* 5 (2): 203–230. doi:10.1177/1461444803005002004.

Emery, Michael, and Edwin Emery. 1996. *The Press and America: An Interpretive History of the Mass Media*. Boston, MA: Allyn & Bacon.

Foster, Robin. 2012. *News Plurality in a Digital World*. Oxford: RISJ.

Galtung, Johan, and Marie Ruge. 1965. "The Structure of Foreign News." *Journal of Peace Research* 2 (1): 64–91. doi:10.1177/002234336500200104.

Gillmor, Dan. 2006. *We the Media*. Sebastopol, CA: O'Reilly.

Gieber, Walter. [1956] 1964. "News is What Newspapermen Make It." In *People, Society and Mass Communication*, edited by Lewis A. Dexter and David M. White, 173–182. New York: Free Press.

Haas, Tanni. 2007. *The Pursuit of Public Journalism: Theory, Practice, and Criticism*. New York: Routledge.

Harmon, Mark. 1989. "Mr. Gates Goes Electronic: The What and Why Questions in Local TV News." *Journalism & Mass Communication Quarterly* 66 (4): 857–863. doi:10.1177/107769908906600412.

Hermida, Alfred. 2011. "Fluid Spaces, Fluid Journalism." In *Participatory Journalism*, edited by Jane B. Singer, Alfred Hermida, David Domingo, Ari Heinonen, Steve Paulussen, Thorsten Quandt, Zvi Reich, and Marina Vujnovic, 177–191. Oxford: Wiley-Blackwell.

Hochfelder, David. 2013. *The Telegraph in America, 1832–1920*. Baltimore, MD: Johns Hopkins University Press.

Howe, Daniel. 2007. *What Hath God Wrought: The Transformation of America, 1815–1848*. Oxford: Oxford University Press.

Jones, Janet, and Lee Salter. 2012. *Digital Journalism*. London: Sage.

Lewin, Kurt. 1943. "Forces behind Food Habits and Methods of Change." *Bulletin of the National Research Council* 108: 35–65.

Lewin, Kurt. 1947. "Frontiers in Group Dynamics II: Channels of Group Life." *Human Relations* 1 (2): 143–153. doi:10.1177/001872674700100201.

Lippmann, Walter. 1922. *Public Opinion*. New York: Macmillan.

McChesney, Robert. 2012. "Farewell to Journalism?" *Journalism Practice* 6 (5–6): 614–626. doi:10.1080/17512786.2012.683273.

McChesney, Robert, and Viktor Picard. 2011. *Will the Last Reporter Please Turn Out the Lights: The Collapse of Journalism and What Can Be Done to Fix It*. New York: The New Press.

Meyers, Jeffrey. 1984. *Hemmingway: A Biography*. New York: Harper & Row.

Newman, Nic, ed. 2013. *Reuters Institute Digital News Report 2013*. Reuters Institute for the Study of Journalism, Oxford: University of Oxford.

O'Neill, Deirdre, and Tony Harcup. 2009. "News Values and Selectivity." In *The Handbook of Journalism Studies*, edited by Karin Wahl-Jorgensen and Thomas Hanitzsch, 161–173. New York: Routledge.

Reese, Stephen. 2007. "Journalism Research and the Hierarchy of Influences Model: A Global Perspective." *Brazilian Journalism Research* 3 (2): 29–42.

Reese, Stephen, and Jane Ballinger. 2001. "The Roots of a Sociology of News: Remembering Mr. Gates and Social Control in the Newsroom." *Journalism & Mass Communication Quarterly* 78 (4): 641–658. doi:10.1177/107769900107800402.

Rosen, Jay. 1994. "Making Things More Public: On the Political Responsibility of the Media Intellectual." *Critical Studies in Mass Communication* 11 (4): 363–388.

Rosen, Jay. 1995. "Public Journalism: A Case of Public Scholarship." *Change* 27 (3): 34–38. doi:10.1080/00091383.1995.10544661.

Rosen, Jay. 1999. *What Are Journalist For?* New Haven: Yale University Press.

Rosen, Jay. 2006. "Web Users Open the Gates." *Washington Post*, June 19.

Ryfe, David. 2012. *Can Journalism Survive? An Inside Look at American Newsrooms*. Cambridge: Polity Press.

Schudson, Michael. 1995. *The Power of News*. Cambridge, MA: Harvard University Press.

Schudson, Michael. 1999. "What Public Journalism Knows about Journalism but Doesn't Know About 'Public.'" In *The Idea of Public Journalism*, edited by Theodore Glasser, 118–133. New York: Guildford Press.

Schudson, Michael. 2001. "The Objectivity Norm in American Journalism." *Journalism* 2 (2): 149–150. doi:10.1177/146488490100200201.

Shoemaker, Pamela. 1991. *Communication Concepts 3: Gatekeeping*. Newbury Park, CA: Sage.

Shoemaker, Pamela, and Tim Vos. 2009. *Gatekeeping Theory*. New York: Routledge.

Singer, Jane. 2001. "The Metro Wide Web: Changes in Newspapers' Gatekeeping Role Online." *Journalism and Mass Communication Quarterly* 78 (1): 65–80. doi:10.1177/107769900107800 105.

Singer, Jane, Alfred Hermida, David Domingo, Ari Heinonen, Steve Paulussen, Thorsten Quandt, Zvi Reich, and Mariana Vujnovic. 2011. *Participatory Journalism: Guarding Open Gates at Online Newspapers*. Oxford: Wiley-Blackwell.

Snider, Paul. 1967. "'Mr. Gates' Revisited: A 1966 Version of the 1949 Case Study." *Journalism Quarterly* 44 (3): 419–427. doi:10.1177/107769906704400301.

Standage, Tom. 1998. *The Victorian Internet*. New York: Berkley Books.

Steffens, Lincoln. 1931. *The Autobiography of Lincoln Steffens*. New York: Harcourt, Brace.

Van Dalen, Arjen. 2012. "The Algorithms Behind the Headlines." *Journalism Practice* 6 (5–6): 648–658. doi:10.1080/17512786.2012.667268.

Wanta, Wayne. 2009. "Gatekeeping." In *The International Encyclopedia of Communication*, edited by Wolfgang Donsbach. London: Blackwell. doi:10.1111/b.9781405131995.2008.x.

White, David Manning. 1950. "The 'Gate Keeper': A Case Study in the Selection of News." *Journalism Quarterly* 27: 383–390.

White, David Manning. 1964. "Introduction to the Gatekeeper." In *People, Society, and Mass Communication*, edited by Lewis Anthony Dexter and David Manning White, 160–161. New York: Macmillan.

Whitney, Charles, and Lee B. Becker. 1982. "Keeping the Gates for Gatekeepers: The Effects of Wire News." *Journalism Quarterly* 82 (5): 60–65. doi:10.1177/107769908205900109.

Zelizer, Barbie. 2004. *Taking Journalism Seriously*. London: Sage.

CHARTING THEORETICAL DIRECTIONS FOR EXAMINING AFRICAN JOURNALISM IN THE "DIGITAL ERA"

Hayes Mawindi Mabweazara

This essay provides a metatheoretical framework for understanding the complexities surrounding African journalism in the era of interactive digital technologies. It argues for the continued relevance of traditional theoretical paradigms, and submits that radical calls to develop new theories as well as to de-Westernise contemporary journalism studies through exclusively deploying "home-grown" concepts such as ubuntuism *are not necessarily always viable. Rather, there is more to gain from appropriating traditional theories and identifying possible synergies between the "old", predominantly Western approaches, and the "new digital phenomena", and weaving out of that dialogue, approaches that are not radically different but are in tune with the uniqueness of African experiences. This approach, as the study argues, is particularly important given that journalism (including its appropriation of new technologies) always takes on the form and colouring of the social structure in which it operates. The study thus draws on social constructivist approaches to technology and the sociology of journalism, as well as an array of theoretical concerns from African journalism scholarship to offer a possible direction for a conceptual framework that can help us to capture the complex imbrications between new digital technologies and journalism practice in Africa.*

Introduction: Setting the Context

The purpose of this essay is to provide a metatheoretical[1] framework for illuminating our understanding of how African journalists are adapting to the new "digital era". The proposed framework is *metatheoretical* in that it draws on an array of theoretical perspectives, published literature, as well as the author's own impressions of the underlying assumptions which drive debates on the new media and journalism practice in Africa. As Hjørland (1998, 607) notes "metatheories are broader and less specific than theories. They are more or less conscious or unconscious assumptions behind theoretical, empirical and practical work ... and are often part of interdisciplinary trends".

While general scholarship has advanced beyond the one-sided euphoric approaches to new digital technologies, characteristic of the 1990s, there remains a lack of meaningful theorisation of how digital technologies are impacting on various social practices, including journalism practice in Africa (Mabweazara 2010a). For this reason, the bulk of the theoretical insights have mostly emerged from Western scholarship. The empirical lacuna in African journalism research has given space to utopian and speculative arguments on how new digital technologies are (re)defining African journalism practice (Mabweazara, Mudhai, and Whittaker 2014). Yet, even when theories and empirical studies developed in the West might appear to be wholly applicable to the African context, "a closer look shows significant differences requiring nuanced theorising and research" (Atton and Mabweazara 2011, 668), especially given that much of the research is "conducted in splendid oblivion of conditions in [Africa]" (Berger 2000, 90).

This study emphasises the continued relevance of traditional—predominantly Western theoretical approaches—in attempts to understand the connections between journalism and new digital technologies in Africa. It argues that "old" approaches to both *journalism* and *technology* provide relevant conceptual frames for understanding how journalists in Africa are appropriating new digital technologies. Contrary to calls by a number of African media academics to reject Western theoretical paradigms and concepts by foregrounding "home-grown" approaches derived from African cultural belief systems and experiences such as the concept of *ubuntu* (Tomaselli 2003; Ngomba 2012), the study submits that such "ethnocentric" stances are not always necessarily valuable. While they point to the defining and patently germane features of African cultural experiences that have implications for the practice of journalism, they are, however, not without weaknesses especially when deployed in isolation. The notion of *ubuntu* in particular, seen by many as a "cultural mindset" that encapsulates what it means to be human in Africa, particularly that "[a] person is a person through other people" (Shaw 2009, 493), and one is *human because, he belongs, participates and shares* (Murithi in Obonyo 2011), has dominated scholarly accounts that advocate "de-Westernising" African journalism studies.

Such radical approaches, however, overlook a number of factors, including the very fact that journalism as an *institutional* practice has a long history in Western scholarship, especially the United States and the United Kingdom. As de Beer (2010, 213) observes, the "knowledge colonialism" and publishing hegemony by Western countries have defining implications for journalism theory and research. This dominance has meant that Western scholarship, "largely set international paradigms and research trends" (215). Second, newsmaking practices in Africa continue to be influenced, and measured, against the backdrop of Western professional values and standards. Likewise, African journalists continue to seek examples of "best practices", training and education from Western countries. Mabweazara (2011, 62), for example, highlights how the internet facilitates Zimbabwean journalists' "continued reliance on Western journalistic forms" as a standard measure of their own practices—they "have become entrapped in the Northern 'way of doing things'" (de Beer 2010, 213). This view supports Peter Golding's 1970s study of the then Nigerian Broadcasting Corporation, in which he observed that "none of the few newspapers and magazines lying around the newsroom were African; they were all European, especially British" (cited in Ibelema 2008, 37).

Thus, while Africa is indeed unique, with its own nuances and defining commun-ication characteristics, it has nonetheless borrowed extensively the bulk of its *institutio-nalised* communication practices, including journalism, from the West. We, therefore, need to tread carefully and avoid reifying and essentialising African experiences by blindly locking ourselves in the specificities of locale as to lose sight of essential insights from "outside" intellectual traditions and experiences. However, in deploying established Western theoretical insights, as the study contends, we need to critically situate, adapt and possibly modify, the theories to suit African realities, which as Mano (2004, 18) puts it, are "complex and multifaceted and resist any attempts to simplify them". Similarly, Paterson (2014, 259–260, emphasis added) notes that African journalists operate in multifaceted conditions "where news production is sometimes strikingly similar to what might be seen in any global news hub … and, conversely, *sometimes distant from Northern norms in terms of its goals and methods*". Thus, African journalism research must be empirically rooted "in African realities and not in Western fantasies" (Nyamnjoh 1999, 15), and we must acknowledge that journalists there do their job under immensely varied circumstances offered by continent.

Highlighting some of the conditions, Kupe (2004) observes that African journalists operate in conditions starkly differing from those in the Global North. They work with significantly fewer resources and are poorly paid. They also broadly operate in multi-cultural countries that are at various stages of constituting themselves as nations in a globalising world. In addition, most African journalists are beset by: lack of appropriate skills; the prohibitive costs and inequitable access to relevant technologies; job instability; legal and regulatory challenges; complex political contexts; and poor telecommunications infrastructure, all of which coalesce to shape and constrain their adoption and appropriation of new digital technologies (Obijiofor and Hanusch 2011; Kperogi 2012).

We should, therefore, emphasise sensitivity to *context*—using established Western theories with close attention to the uniqueness of the conditions in which African journalists operate. As Tomaselli (2003, 429) advises us, we should be investing our energies on engaging with "international scholarly literature and intellectual debates from African perspectives", connecting our local indigenous knowledge with international systems of communication in order to come up with "a more integrated, conceptually holistic [approach] which studies glocalization (the local in relation to the global)" (438). This approach, as Ngomba (2012, 166) contends, calls for "the circumnavigation of mainstream Afrocentric discourses of de-Westernisation [and] selecting useful existing 'Western theories' [for use in research], in a way that offers contextually relevant extensions of such theories".

Against this backdrop, this study draws on *social constructivist approaches* to technology and the *sociology of journalism*, as well as an array of theoretical insights from African journalism and media scholarship to offer a direction for conceptualising a framework for examining how African journalists are adapting to an era permeated by digital technologies. It avers that to do so effectively, "we must put journalists into some critical and analytical context and … question the social relations within which they operate" (Mabweazara 2010b, 12). The study thus extends Francis Nyamnjoh's argument that "[all] [m]eaningful theorization has to be contextualized" and no theorization takes place in a void (cited in Wasserman 2009, 283).

It has to be stated from the outset, however, that the enormity and complexity of Africa makes a detailed account of the application of theory and concepts in every country impossible in the space available here. One must, therefore, avoid the "reductive assumption that African countries, and the myriad array of cultures, religions and languages, can be prescriptively reduced to homogenous sets of continent-wide social and cultural [practices]" (Obijiofor and Hanusch 2011, 53). In the same way, the diversity of Africa's 54 countries makes it difficult for African concepts such as *ubuntuism* to "*travel the length [and breadth] of the continent*" (Mano 2010, 11, emphasis added) homogenously. Nevertheless, the argument advanced here is about the continued relevance of traditional theory, which is qualitatively generalizable across a range of African countries despite the obvious socio-cultural differences on the continent. I submit that in order to make sense of digital technologies in the context of journalism, we must rid ourselves of reductionist attitudes and look at the intersections between new technologies and journalism as continuous with and embedded in situated socio-economic, cultural and political networks (Mabweazara 2010b).

Revitalising Social Constructivist Approaches to Technology and the Sociology of News

Towards Non-reductionist Approaches to Technologies

Although the late 1990s saw a shift from radical "technist" approaches to moderate constructivist perspectives by new technology researchers, technological determinism has continued to implicitly inform current research into African journalism. The trend has mainly been to celebrate uncritically (or disapprove of) the "impact" of new technologies on journalism practice without necessarily reflecting on the situated nature of their influences on journalistic practice, especially the localised political, economic, cultural and social circumstances in which the technologies are assimilated and appropriated. As Nyamnjoh (2005, 9) points out, "it is regrettable that scholarly focus has been rather on what ICTs *do to* Africans, instead of what Africans *do with* ICTs" (emphasis original).

The theoretical interjection proposed here departs from these technicist approaches and demonstrates that obsession with the "technicist" workings of digital technologies that exclusively privilege technology simply will not take our understanding of how journalists in Africa are adapting to the era of digital technologies far enough. We cannot take for granted that new technologies "will change journalism [in Africa] immediately and dramatically" (Paterson 2008, 1).

Although proponents of technological determinism argue for the new technologies' ability to enhance journalistic potential, the technologies must be viewed in relation to the multidimensional factors that shape and constrain the use of technologies by those with only limited access and ability to use them effectively, a scenario broadly prevalent in most sub-Saharan African countries (see Nyamnjoh 2005; Berger 2005). As Castells (2001, 247) explains, the differential use of new technologies in most economically developing countries is related, among other things, "to the kind of content that users can find on the Internet, and to the difficulty for people without sufficient education, knowledge and skills to appropriate the technology for their own interests and values".

This understanding is broadly rooted in the antithesis of technological determinism —*social constructivist* approaches to technology—which take into account localised social and cultural realities that shape and constrain the deployment and appropriation of technologies in specific contexts. The approaches draw on a broad range of academic traditions with different theoretical frameworks. However, taken together, they share a critical approach towards technological determinism and argue that it is much better to see technologies as social and cultural forms instead of autonomous forces acting on society for good or ill (Lievrouw 2002).

A central adage for their research, as Bijker (1995, 6), puts it, is that "one should never take the meaning of a technical artefact or technological system as residing in the technology itself, instead one must study how technologies are shaped and acquire their meanings in the heterogeneity of social interactions". Social factors are not merely incidental to the nature and direction of technology deployment; they are intimately tied to it (Woolgar 1996). Thus, the use of new technologies should be seen as constrained or enhanced by a broader range of social, economic and cultural factors.

One version of the arguments proffered by social constructivists views technology as embodying the various social factors involved in its design and development. In this way of thinking, technology is regarded as a "frozen assemblage" of the practices, assumptions, beliefs, language, and other factors involved in its design and manufacture (Woolgar 1996). According to Woolgar, this perspective offers significant new understandings of the "impact" of technology as it suggests that the social relations which are built into the technology have implications on how it is subsequently used. Users of technology thus confront and respond to the social relations embodied within it.

To illustrate the "interpretive flexibility" of technology and the wide variety of possible uses, Woolgar posits that it is useful to refer to technology as a "text". When construed as a *text*, "technology is to be understood as a manufactured entity, designed and produced within a particular social and organisational context" (Woolgar 1996, 92). This metaphor foregrounds questions about the extent to which the character of this socially constructed technology influences its use. It highlights that the character and capacity of texts are nothing but the "attributes" (93) given to them by their users within a specific socio-cultural context. Confronted with texts, the user will draw upon any available social resources to make comprehensible the task of making sense of the text.

It is important, however, to point out that while acknowledging the significance of insights brought forth by social constructivists (mainly that technology is inseparable from its social context), we must guard against uncritically lapsing into simplistic "social determinism", as some aspects of social constructivism do. This would yield a narrow or distorted understanding in much the same way as technological determinism (Dahlberg 2004). As Marx (1997) warns, we must be careful not to take the social constructivists' claims for "indeterminacy" too far, as this may lead to an understanding of technology so general and vague that it becomes almost completely vacuous and resistant to valid description. Such an understanding, according to Dahlberg (2004), would mean that we are unable to say anything of any real interest or value about a technology or about technology in general.

To locate this constructivist approach in the context of journalism, it is important to turn to the theoretical traditions and roots of journalism as an academic field of study. As Zelizer (2004) argues, these roots are to be located in sociology, which has long existed as the background setting for evolving journalism scholarship.

Newswork Through the Lenses of the "Sociology of Journalism"

Although the body of theory known as the *sociology of journalism* has a long and winding history that draws on a number of distinct theoretical approaches, it has generally been defined as concerned with the ways in which news organisations manage the processes through which information is gathered and transformed into news. It traces and attempts to organise into coherent schemata the pressures that encourage journalists to follow familiar and repetitive patterns of newsmaking. Emerging mostly from Anglo-American scholarship, it engages directly with the questions of what constitutes news and what factors shape it, and broadly argues that news is a social product shaped by the interactions among media professionals, media organisations and society (Schudson 2005).

Tuchman (1978) observes that the sociology of newsmaking originates from the epistemological principles of phenomenology, symbolic interactionism and ethnomethodology, which broadly argue that reality is a social construction mediated by processes that can be identified and analysed. Taking a different perspective, Reese and Ballinger (2001, 642) locate the origins of the sociology of journalism in the "gatekeeper theory" postulated by David Manning White (1950) in his seminal work: "The Gate Keeper: A Case Study in the Selection of News" and Warren Breed's (1955) "Social Control in the Newsroom". In applying the gatekeeper metaphor to journalism, White saw news selection as operating on the basis of choices made by *individual editors* acting as gatekeepers who subjectively classify items by deciding what counts as news (Reese and Ballinger 2001). He examined the personal reasons given by a newspaper editor for rejecting potential news items. On the other hand, Breed's study foregrounded the sociological concept of "social control" (Zelizer 2004, 53) in journalism. Recognising that no society could exist without social control, he noted that journalists' actions were bound within the policy set by the publisher.

Other researchers, however, explored a wider range of possibilities beyond the constricted role of individual gatekeepers. In the 1970s, several sociologists focused on institutional routines and organisational cultures, reflecting an increasing prominence of institutionalist and neo-institutionalist theories of organisational behaviour which empha- sised the need to look beyond the qualities of particular individuals as the preceding studies had done (Tuchman 1978; Zelizer 2004). Journalists' operations were thus viewed as constricted by organisational demands and expectations.

In the same vein, researchers sought to deconstruct the myth of media "objectivity" by showing that there are structural factors, including political influence, that make the media over-represent the official versions of events, thereby obscuring social reality instead of revealing it (Tuchman 1978; Schudson 2005). The consensus point among scholars was the understanding that news production is a highly regulated and routine process shaped by organisational pressures as well as the wider social setting, which encourage the routinisation and standardisation of news journalism. This illustrated the interface between human agency and social structure.

In addition to the above, some scholars have foregrounded professional journalistic values as key factors that determine the news outcome. They argue that professional values legitimise and neutralise the personal biases and working routines of journalists through a positioning characterised by detachment from the society represented in the news and by a striving for authoritativeness in the news (Schudson 2005). The concept of "objectivity" and the routines it shapes are viewed as mechanisms meant to neutralise the personal ideologies of journalists and ease their adaptation to the editorial bias of a given medium. News sources have also been seen as playing a key role in news production routines. Media sociologists argue that reporters are confronted by a plurality of sources of information located at different places at varying times, and requiring different means to access them. For McNair (1998), a focus on sources is seen as the best way (or perhaps the only one) to connect the study of journalism to the larger society.

The foregoing discussion can broadly be categorised under what Schudson (2005) refers to as the *social organisational* approaches to news, which focus more on the "internal" workings of news production—"institutional" and "professional" factors that shape newsgathering. However, a stringent focus on the "internal" workings of news production overlooks the relationships between news production and the broader routines of everyday life, especially "the culturally mediating nature of news"—the "diverse ways in which 'culture' variously conditions and shapes patterns and forms [of news production]" (Cottle 2000, 438), beyond the confines of the news institutions. These *cultural* factors "transcend the structures of ownership or patterns of work relations" (Schudson 2005, 187) by pointing to the fact that "journalists live and work within an encompassing social and cultural context that powerfully and implicitly informs their attempts to make sense of the world" (Ettema, Whitney, and Wackman 1997, 44). Journalists are thus dependent on preconceived categories of culture, which constitute "the unquestioned and generally unnoticed background assumptions through which news is gathered and within which it is framed" (Schudson 2005, 189).

It is important, however, to highlight that the sociology of journalism, like most theories, is not without weaknesses; it has, for instance, been criticised for its failure to consider the influences of new technologies, as well as changes in social and political processes to news production routines. However, its diverse traditions provide valuable insights into various factors that influence the operations of journalists as well as shape the news outcome. These factors chime with the *social constructivist* approaches to technology and thus provide a base upon which we can develop an approach for illuminating our understanding of how journalists (in Africa) are adjusting to an era pervasively mediated by new digital technologies.

Charting a Theoretical Direction for Exploring Journalism in the Digital Era

In order to fully appreciate and understand news production processes in the age of digital technologies, we need an analytical framework that can help us capture the nuances of the "social relations" within which journalism is generally practised. This approach should acknowledge "the complexity of the social context of news production" and, as discussed above, avoid "the reductionistic idea of fixing newsmaking at one point along a circuit of interactions without examining the circuit as a whole" (Mabweazara 2010b, 22). Such a framework is available in synergising aspects of the social constructivist critique of technology and the sociology of journalism.

Thus, the appropriation of technology in the context of journalism should be viewed as part of a complex social and institutional matrix, which stretches across a wide range of socio-cultural factors, as well as factors "internal" to the defining professional imperatives of journalism. This calls for a non-reductionist approach that is sensitive to the complex connections between multiple elements at play in the context in which journalism is practised (Marx 1997). Such a "multiple-determinations" approach, as Dahlberg (2004) puts it, recognises that each determining factor is itself embedded within, and constituted by, a system of *interlinked* processes and factors. The connections in these processes and factors are in no way linear or fixed, nor are they of equal influence. The nature of the processes and relationships involved in the appropriation of new technologies by journalists should thus be seen as "open and not restricted to any particular determining factor" (Mabweazara 2010b, 22). This is particularly important in the light of the fact that the practice of journalism itself is, as we have seen above, a culmination of a multiplicity of socio-cultural and organisational factors which make themselves known in news institutions in the form of economic, bureaucratic and professional normative pressures, all of which shape and constrain the autonomy of journalists (Schudson 2005).

As Ettema, Whitney, and Wackman (1997) note, the analysis of news production must be pursued on several levels of analysis, and the activities at each level should be seen as interpenetrating and difficult to disentangle. As Figure 1 attempts to show, we need to be alert and sensitive to the multi-dimensional elements of determinism that coalesce to shape and constrain the use of new technologies by journalists. Of critical importance is the fact that, although journalists aspire to autonomy and personal independence—and most have it to varying degrees—they can never be entirely "free" from the circumstances within which their work is organised, regulated and consumed (McNair 1998). It is equally important to note that the factors impacting on journalists' adoption and appropriation of new technologies are neither mutually exclusive nor exhaustive. In other words, "journalists are subject to pressures from proprietors; political factors; professional imperatives; social organisational and cultural factors; personal factors [and] the economy" (Mabweazara 2010b, 23), among other factors, often all at the same time. At times, the pressure from one direction may contradict that from another, intersecting "in the context of discursive struggles and contestations from a wide variety of competing perspectives" (24).

What is important is maintaining a degree of flexibility that helps to provide insights into ways of exploring how journalists in specific socio-cultural contexts use new technologies. This approach could be extended further to incorporate the metaphor of the *text* discussed earlier, which reinforces the multi-dimensional nature of factors shaping the use of new technologies by journalists. Given that technology is embedded within socio-cultural contexts, as social constructivists argue, it is proper to think of it as having an "interpretive flexibility" while at the same time, like all texts, containing "preferred readings" open to various uses (Woolgar 1996, 92). This brings to the fore the question of the extent to which the character of the technology influences its use by journalists in specific contexts. It further points to the inter-textual connections between technologies and journalists, thus foregrounding the fact that the appropriation of technologies in newsmaking contexts should be seen as dependent on a multiplicity of factors which border around the "interpretive repertoires" of the journalists concerned.

Overall, although the collective strength assigned to *social constructivist* approaches to technology and the *sociology of journalism* above is essentially a product of Western scholarship, and based on practices and experiences in the West, their collective strength is *"transnationally transposable"* (Ngomba 2012, 175) and applicable to the African context. Together, they provide precious indicators that can help to us to map out the analytic categories that capture African realities and thus facilitate a critical exploration of the complex imbrications of technology and contemporary journalism practice on the continent. Pulling together these established theoretical approaches and "relocating" them to the African context has the potential to enlighten our understanding of how journalists on the continent are appropriating new digital technologies against the backdrop of the mediating socio-cultural context—the *specificities of their locale*—as discussed below.

Transposing "Established Theoretical Lenses" to the African Context

Although, as noted earlier, a number of leading African journalism and media scholars have called for radical Afrocentric approaches to de-Westernise journalism studies, in this section I propose a "moderate heuristic approach" that emphasises deploying the collective insights of relevant Western theoretical understandings (*social constructivist* approaches to technology and the *sociology of journalism*, in this case) while at the same time "foregrounding the realities or contexts in which African journalists operate" (Mabweazara 2014, 5). To use Ngomba's (2012, 166) words, I propose a framework that "circumnavigates" radical Afrocentric discourses of de-Westernisation by accommodating (and in some cases modifying) Western theoretical approaches in ways that offer "contextually relevant extensions of [the] theories" to help frame and deepen our understanding of how new digital technologies are impacting on traditional journalism in Africa. This flexible approach, as I discuss below, enables us to look at African journalism in its diverse contexts: "its culture, institutions and the broader communication environment" (Mabweazara 2010b, 25), and weave out of that mosaic (Obonyo 2011) insights into how the use of new digital technologies is shaped by the multiple contexts in which journalists on the continent operate.

This sensitivity to *context* helps to define African journalism in the digital era as well as position it in "the universals that are [often] deaf-and-dumb to the particularities of journalism in and on Africa" (Wasserman 2009, 287). It allows us to see the appropriation of new digital technologies by journalists as a multifaceted experience that can be evaluated against the backdrop of local context factors, partly summed up in Figure 1. As Obeng-Quaidoo (1986) contends, socio-cultural, political and economic aspects are central to any attempt to understand African journalism. This connects to the sociology of journalism as well as work in the sociology of technology, which sustains a view of *technology as thoroughly socially shaped* (Hine 2001). The approach further reinforces the social constructivist view that in any attempt to understand the social influences of technologies, the starting point should not be a particular technological field but the particular social context in which the technologies are adopted and deployed (Bijker 1995; Woolgar 1996).

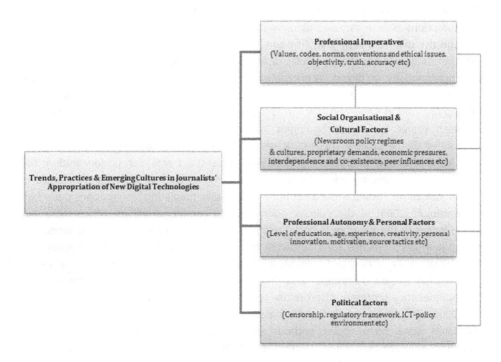

FIGURE 1
Factors shaping journalists' appropriation of new technologies (adapted from Mabweazara 2010b, 23)

An understanding of the structural and functional deficiencies associated with the *digital divide*, often defining African journalism as being in deficit "as regards the emerging global information order" (Berger 2005, 1), offers a critical conceptual point of departure. The well-documented challenges facing most African newsrooms, predominantly offer a "default explanatory framework" (Mabweazara 2014, 2) for the assessment of new technology adoption and appropriation in African journalism. As Obijiofor and Hanusch (2011, 193) observe, questions of limited access to new technologies, slow "technological diffusions", as well as limited training opportunities in various sub-Saharan African newsrooms, have a negative impact on journalists' "knowledge and understanding of how to [effectively] use technology in their job". Writing from a West African context, Kperogi (2012, 451) similarly avers that due to "low technological development and [general] unease with Internet technology", Nigerian newspapers are still largely "stuck in the mindset and production practices of pre-Internet newspapers". Likewise, Berger observes that new technology use in Southern Africa "is integrated unevenly into newsrooms, and there are major variations across the region in regard to problems of access. This, and the lack of proper training constrain the use of technologies to their fullest" (Berger 2005, 10).

While these contextual challenges cannot be overlooked, it is equally important to examine how they are mitigated by localised appropriations of technology. In particular, the intricacies embedded in practices connected to *local cultural factors* "give credibility to additional theoretical ways" of assessing how African journalists are adjusting to the era of digital technologies (Berger 2005, 1). The notion of *ubuntu*, in particular, has recurrently emerged as an overarching cultural compass for understanding what "Africaness" means (Tomaselli 2003; Shaw 2009; Ngomba 2012). Granted a blind adoption of this concept and its assumptions of "a unitary and binding [African] cultural authenticity" (Banda 2009, 235) runs the risk of essentialising or, "[freezing] the continent in time" (Obonyo 2011, 8), it, nonetheless, illuminates the intricacies of African cultural life, which have implications for the appropriations of digital technologies in newsmaking contexts. In other terms, it constitutes the "unquestioned and generally unnoticed" filter through which technologies are appropriated in news construction (Schudson 2005, 189). This is particularly so, if, as discussed earlier, we see technologies as "social texts" (Woolgar 1996), shaped and constrained by the broader social structure in which they are adopted and appropriated.

As a concept, *ubuntuism* provides an essential frame for understanding the complexities surrounding adoption practices as well as uses of digital technologies in African journalism. It directs our attention to "culturally mediating" foundations described by Nyamnjoh (2005) as the cultural orientation to communal values, which focus our critical lenses to the contingent social relationships and worldviews by which aspects of African journalism practice are maintained and defined. Nyamnjoh (2005) highlights how the innovative use of new technologies in Africa generally hinges on local cultural values of *solidarity*, *interconnectedness* and *interdependence*; "individuals and the cultural communities they represent often refuse to celebrate victimhood" (Nyamnjoh in Wasserman 2009, 291). These values make it possible for people to access the internet (and its associated digital technologies) without necessarily being directly connected. In many situations, as Nyamnjoh (2005) further contends, it suffices for an individual to be connected in order for whole groups and communities to benefit. Using the example of the mobile phone, he writes about the phenomenon of "single-owner–multiple-user" in

West Africa, where most mobile phone owners tend to serve as "points-of-presence" (Nyamnjoh 2004, 54) that link their community with others paying or simply passing through them to make calls to relatives, friends within or outside the country. Consequently, while internet connectivity and mobile phone ownership in Africa are significantly lower than in the economically developed regions of the North, Africa's cultural values of sociality, interconnectedness, interdependence and conviviality make it possible for others to access the opportunities associated with these technologies without necessarily being connected or owning the technologies themselves (Nyamnjoh 2005).

A number of scholars have demonstrated how this broader *cultural* characteristic permeates experiences in African journalism by highlighting how journalists operating in new technology-impoverished newsrooms yield benefits from the technologies through sharing the limited and largely dated resources available (see Berger 2005). Citing examples from selected Southern African newsrooms, Berger (2005, 9) writes: "even as regards unwired computers, in many cases journalists queue to share these rather than have personal workstations". Similarly, Mabweazara (2010a, 217) highlights how most journalists in Zimbabwean newsrooms described their first mobile phone experience as a "shared one with colleagues in the newsrooms". This scenario demonstrates how African journalists, like their fellow citizens, contest structural constraints to seek inclusion in the digital era (Wasserman 2009). Thus, the localised amenability "to conviviality, interdependence and negotiation" play a key role in mitigating "histories of deprivation [and] debasement" (Nyamnjoh 2004, 54). An understanding of these *cultural* dynamics is therefore central to any attempt to closely examine how African journalists negotiate their way around new digital technologies. It helps to avoid uncritically limiting explanations to the obvious and well-known contextual challenges facing most African newsrooms.

It is important to restate, however, that while the socio-economic pressures connected to the *digital divide* and the cultural orientation to communal values associated with *ubuntuism* suggest a homogenous African landscape with a collective singular identity, this is far from it; the continent is culturally, politically and economically fragmented, and "*ubuntuism* [itself] exists in various forms" (Mano 2010, 12). As Obonyo (2011, 4, emphasis added) aptly puts it, "There are many Africans, *both fitting stereotyping but simultaneously defying uniform description*". For Obonyo, North Africa is more closely aligned to the Middle East than to the wider Africa. "It engages less in scholarship terms with the rest of the continent" (2). Consequently, conversations about Africa invariably consider Africa south of the Sahara. But even here disparities informed by "language and colonial experiences make it somewhat of a challenge to make sweeping statements" (2). There are wide discrepancies between Francophone, Anglophone and Lusophone Africa and, indeed, within each of these regions.

In terms of the political economy of news organisations, the scene in Africa is equally diverse. It stretches from the well-developed and technologically advanced beacons of journalistic excellence in South Africa and parts of East Africa to the "still fledgling media operations" in much of the continent (Hyden, Leslie, and Ogundimu 2007, vii), especially in sub-Saharan Africa where the news media are largely unable to report effectively due to lack of resources and the constraining impact of political interference. South Africa, in particular, stands apart from the rest of English-speaking Africa; its media infrastructure is predominantly well-funded, with excellent newsroom infrastructure hence "markedly different from the rest of the continent" (Obonyo 2011, 2). As Verweij and van

Noort (2014, 100) observe, "post-independence South Africa shares a number of characteristics with Western countries: such as their organisation of the media and standards of journalism practice". "No other country on [the] continent has such a well-developed and sophisticated market infrastructure. What is happening there … has no direct parallel elsewhere in sub-Saharan Africa" (Hyden and Leslie 2007, 19). However, the active participation of the general public in digital media "is different because of the social deprivation of the bulk of its citizens, a challenge directly connected to South Africa's apartheid past" (Verweij and van Noort 2014, 100).

The scenario above points to the need for a more broadly encompassing approach that takes into account the wider complexities of the socio-cultural context in which African journalists operate. This calls for a normative pluralism that straddles the line between cultural relativism and absolutism. In that pluralism, as partly captured in the factors outlined in Figure 1, "it is possible to hold together both shared norms and values" which are "understood, interpreted, and/or applied in diverse ways … that reflect distinct values and norms of diverse cultures" (Ess 2009, 54, emphasis original). This form of pluralism allows for a shared understanding that avoids the trap of homogenising practices by ignoring or obliterating important and localised cultural differences that define our identities as a people and as professionals. The broadened approach would enliven critical notions like ubuntuism to the "interpenetrated cultural realities of African countries", thus transforming its "politico-cultural praxis" (Banda 2009, 236) into a more realistic "tool" that is sensitive to "relevant non-cultural dimensions that can complete our understanding" (Ngomba 2012, 169) of the complex connections between new technologies and journalism practice in Africa.

As Figure 1 attempts to show—in a more generic sense—some of these relevant non-cultural dimensions would include, among other factors, the intricacies of the political environment in which African journalists operate, including localised struggles for democracy and human rights, all of which shape and constrain the appropriations of new digital technologies. Obonyo (2011, 5) reminds us that "Africa does not provide a clear picture that is easy to diagnose. The continent has … some of the better politically managed constitutions and at the other end of the spectrum some of the most restrictive" and unfavourable for digital media. Skjerdal (2014, 89), for example, highlights how Ethiopia's semi-authoritarian regime has instituted "numerous measures that serve to restrict rather than encourage a vibrant online sphere". Similarly, Moyo (2009, 60) writes about the curtailment of "basic civil and political liberties such as the freedom of expression, opinion, association, and information" in Zimbabwe. These constraints not only result in "self-censorship" but also engender localised "innovations that borrow from and build on global developments" (Mudhai 2014, 123). In considering the non-cultural factors noted above, we also need not lose sight of the creative domestication of individual agency (Nyamnjoh 2005) in the appropriation of new technologies. As indicated in Figure 1, individual journalists equally have a propensity to shape and influence practices through bringing on board personal experiences, their educational background, personal motivations, etc.

Therefore, in seeking to understand how journalists on the African continent are adapting to the new digital era, we should not overlook the varied contextual influences "which [sometimes] lie outside journalism itself" (Conboy 2013, 149), but significantly influence the appropriations of new digital technologies. Thus, an assessment of the intersections between journalism and technology on the continent "needs insight from both the practice of journalism *as well as a general awareness of broader cultural trends and how technology forms part of [this context]*" (Conboy 2013, 149, emphasis added). In this sense, the use of new technologies by journalists in Africa should be seen as "a multifaceted experience" (Mabweazara 2010b, 25), shaped and constrained by multiple interconnected factors, which border around bureaucratically organised activities within newsrooms (or professional contexts), and the broader social structure outside journalism itself (Conboy 2013).

Conclusion

This study has proposed a metatheoretical approach for examining African journalism in the digital era. The framework views the appropriation of new digital technologies by journalists as socially shaped, a position sustained by the collective strength of insights drawn from social *constructivist approaches* to technology and the *sociology of journalism*. As argued above, these two broad theories offer the most promising basis for the development of a framework that can help us to reflect on African journalism practice in the digital era. Collectively, they provide a wide-ranging research setting that enables us to see the adoption and use of new digital technologies by African journalists as shaped by multiple elements within the social structure in which their professional routines unfold. The paper, therefore, demonstrates that established (predominantly Western) theoretical perspectives retain their relevance in providing frames for understanding and reflecting on how African journalists are adjusting to the era of new digital technologies. Thus, the application and appropriateness of a theory should be based on its relevance rather than its geographical or socio-cultural origins. As Ngomba (2012, 177) puts it: "where 'Western' theories appear relevant and promising … African scholars should neither shy away from using them, nor be apologetic when using them critically", even as they seek to de-Westernise accounts as well as realign connections with Western scholarship. In this light, we do not necessarily need to substitute or replace existing theory as "[t]he African condition is not a birthmark; it is not exclusive to Africa" (Nyamnjoh in Wasserman 2009, 287).

However, in deploying established theories, we need not lose sight of the fact that meaningful theorisation has to be contextualised by paying particular attention to the specificity of the context in which one seeks to understand the connections between new digital technologies and journalism practice. This "social shaping" approach offers prospects of moving beyond reductive approaches to technology towards nuanced and pragmatic approaches to understanding how journalists in Africa use new technologies. As researchers, we should therefore strive towards highlighting the *significance of locale*, as well as illustrating the agency and creativity exhibited by journalists (and their newsrooms). As Allan reminds us, we should delve into "the lived materialities of reportorial forms, practices and epistemologies, showing us wherein lie the challenges—as well as the remarkable potentials" (Allan 2014, x) for African journalism as it evolves under the influences of digital platforms. It is hoped that the theoretical posture mapped above will provide a crucial point of departure for further scholarly conceptualisations of how African journalism is adjusting to the era of new digital technologies.

NOTE

1. As a metatheoretical study, this paper is not anchored in its own primary empirical data; rather it draws on previous studies, including my own research and observations—both empirical and theoretical. In particular, the paper is informed by insights from my doctoral research (Mabweazara 2010a), and further develops an argument I make in Mabweazara (2010b) by amplifying the fact that *African* theoretical and conceptual paradigms such as *ubuntu* are not mutually exclusive from established *Western* theoretical perspectives. Thus, African experiences, and indeed, the unique socio-cultural characteristics of the continent can be examined effectively using an amalgam of established concepts and theories pulled from both worlds. Our primary challenge, in taking this approach, however, is to ensure that we do not lose sight of the contingent nature of experiences in Africa.

REFERENCES

Allan, Stuart. 2014. "Foreword." In *Online Journalism in Africa: Trends, Practices and Emerging Cultures*, edited by Hayes M. Mabweazara, Okoth F. Mudhai, and Jason Whittaker, ix–x. London: Routledge.

Atton, Chris, and Hayes M. Mabweazara. 2011. "New Media and Journalism Practice in Africa: An Agenda for Research." *Journalism: Theory, Practice & Criticism* 12 (6): 667–673. doi:10.1177/1464884911405467.

Banda, Fackson. 2009. "Kasoma's Afriethics: A Reappraisal." *International Communication Gazette* 71 (4): 227–242. doi:10.1177/1748048509102179.

Berger, Guy. 2000. "Grave New World? Democratic Journalism Enters the Global Twenty-First Century." *Journalism Studies* 1 (1): 81–99. doi:10.1080/146167000361186.

Berger, Guy. 2005. "Powering African Newsrooms: Theorising How Southern African Journalists make use of ICTs for Newsgathering." In *Doing Digital Journalism: How Southern African Newsgatherers Are Using ICTs*, edited by Guy Berger, 1–14. Grahamstown: High Way Africa.

Bijker, Wiebe E. 1995. *Of Bicycles, Bakelite and Bulbs: Towards a Theory of Socio-technical Change*. Cambridge, MA: MIT Press.

Breed, Warren. 1955. "Social Control in the Newsroom: A Functional Analysis." *Social Forces* 33 (4): 326–335. doi:10.2307/2573002.

Castells, Manuel. 2001. *The Internet Galaxy: Reflections on the Internet, Business, and Society*. Oxford: University Press.

Conboy, Martin. 2013. *Journalism Studies: The Basics*. London: Routledge.

Cottle, Simon. 2000. "Rethinking News Access." *Journalism Studies* 1 (3): 427–448. doi:10.1080/14616700050081768.

Dahlberg, Lincoln. 2004. "Internet Research Tracings: Towards Non-Reductionist Methodology." *Journal of Computer Mediated Communication* 9 (3). Accessed June 14, 2006. http://jcmc.indiana.edu/vol9/issue3/dahlberg.html.

de Beer, Arnold S. 2010. "Looking for Journalism Education Scholarship in Some Unusual Places: The Case of Africa." *Communicatio* 26 (2): 213–226. doi:10.1080/02500167.2010.485367.

Ess, Charles. 2009. *Digital Media Ethics*. Polity: Cambridge.

Ettema, James S., Charles D. Whitney, and Daniel B. Wackman. 1997. "Professional Mass Communicators." In *Social Meanings of News: A Textual Reader*, edited by Daniel Berkowitz, 31–50. London: Sage.

Hine, Christine. 2001. *Virtual Ethnography*. London: Sage.

Hjørland, Birger. 1998. "Theory and Metatheory of Information Science: A New Interpretation." *Journal of Documentation* 54 (5): 606–621. doi:10.1108/EUM0000000007183.

Hyden, Goran, and Michael Leslie. 2007. "Communications and Democratisation in Africa." In *Media and Democracy in Africa*, edited by Goran Hyden, Michael Leslie, and Folu F. Ogundimu, 1–27. New Brunswick, NJ: Transaction.

Hyden, Goran, Michael Leslie, and Folu F. Ogundimu. 2007. "Preface." In *Media and Democracy in Africa*, edited by Goran Hyden, Michael Leslie, and Folu F. Ogundimu, vii–ix. New Brunswick, NJ: Transaction.

Ibelema, Minabere. 2008. *The African Press, Civic Cynicism, and Democracy*. New York: Pelgrave Mcmillan.

Kperogi, Farooq A. 2012. "The Evolution and Challenges of Online Journalism in Nigeria." In *The Handbook of Global Online Journalism*, edited by Eugenia Siapera and Andreas Veglis, 445–461. Oxford: Wiley-Blackwell.

Kupe, Tawana. 2004. "An Agenda for Researching African Media and Communication Contexts." *Ecquid Novi: South African Journal for Journalism Research* 25 (2): 353–356. doi:10.3368/ajs.25.2.353.

Lievrouw, Leah A. 2002. "Determination and Contingency in New Media Development: Diffusion of Innovations and Social Shaping of Technology Perspectives." In *The Handbook of New Media*, edited by Leah A. Lievrouw and Sonia Livingstone, 183–199. London: Sage.

Mabweazara, Hayes M. 2010a. "New Technologies and Mainstream Journalism Practices in Zimbabwe: An Ethnographic Study." PhD thesis, Edinburgh Napier University.

Mabweazara, Hayes M. 2010b. "'New' Technologies and Journalism Practice in Africa: Towards a Critical Sociological Approach." In *The Citizen in Communication: Re-visiting Traditional, New and Community Media Practices in South Africa*, edited by Nathalie Hyde-Clarke, 11–30. Cape Town: Juta.

Mabweazara, Hayes M. 2011. "The Internet in the Print Newsroom: Trends, Practices and Emerging Cultures in Zimbabwe." In *Making Online News: Newsroom Ethnographies in the Second Decade of Internet Journalism*, edited by David Domingo and Chris Paterson, 57–69. New York: Peter Lang.

Mabweazara, Hayes M. 2014. "'Digital Technologies and the Evolving African Newsroom': Towards an African Digital Journalism Epistemology." *Digital Journalism* 2 (1): 2–11. doi:10.1080/21670811.2013.850195.

Mabweazara, Hayes M., Okoth F. Mudhai, and Jason Whittaker, eds. 2014. *Online Journalism in Africa: Trends, Practices and Emerging Cultures*. London: Routledge.

Mano, Winston. 2004. "African National Radio and Everyday Life: A Case Study of Radio Zimbabwe and Its Listeners." PhD thesis, University of Westminster.

Mano, Winston. 2010. "Communication: An African Perspective." In *Rethinking Communication: Keywords in Communication Research*, edited by Stuart Allan, 11–13. Cresskill, NJ: Hampton Press.

Marx, Leo. 1997. "Technology: The Emergence of a Hazardous Concept." *Social Research* 64 (3): 965–988.

McNair, Brian. 1998. *The Sociology of Journalism*. London: Arnold.

Moyo, Last. 2009. "Repression, Propaganda, and Digital Resistance: New Media and Democracy in Zimbabwe." In *African Media and the Digital Public Sphere*, edited by Okoth F. Mudhai, Wisdom J. Tettey, and Fackson Banda, 57–71. New York: Palgrave Macmillan.

Mudhai, Okoth F. 2014. "Immediacy and Openness in a Digital Africa: Networked-Convergent Journalisms in Kenya." In *Online Journalism in Africa: Trends, Practices and Emerging Cultures*, edited by Hayes M. Mabweazara, Fred O. Mudhai, and Jason Whittaker, 123–140. London: Routledge.

Ngomba, Teke. 2012. "Circumnavigating de-Westernisation: Theoretical Reflexivities in Researching Political Communication in Africa." *Communicatio* 38 (2): 164–180. doi:10.1080/02500167.2012.717346.

Nyamnjoh, Francis B. 1999. "African Cultural Studies, Cultural Studies in Africa: How to Make a Useful Difference." *Critical Arts: A Journal of Cultural Studies in Africa* 13 (1): 15–39.

Nyamnjoh, Francis B. 2004. "Globalisation, Boundaries and Livelihoods: Perspectives on Africa." *Identity, Culture and Politics* 5 (1&2): 37–59.

Nyamnjoh, Francis B. 2005. *Africa's Media: Democracy and the Politics of Belonging*. London: Zed Books.

Obeng-Quaidoo, Isaac. 1986. "A Proposal for New Communication Research Methodologies in Africa." *Africa Media Review* 1 (1): 89–98.

Obijiofor, Levi, and Folker Hanusch. 2011. *Journalism across Cultures: An Introduction*. New York: Palgrave Macmillan.

Obonyo, Levi. 2011. "Towards a Theory of Communication for Africa: The Challenges for Emerging Democracies." *Communicatio* 37 (1): 1–20. doi:10.1080/02500167.2011.563822.

Paterson, Chris. 2008. "Introduction: Why Ethnography?" In *Making Online News: An Ethnography of New Media Production*, edited by Chris Paterson and David Domingo, 1–11. New York: Peter Lang.

Paterson, Chris. 2014. "Epilogue." In *Online Journalism in Africa: Trends, Practices and Emerging Cultures*, edited by Hayes M. Mabweazara, Okoth F. Mudhai, and Jason Whittaker, 259–261. London: Routledge.

Reese, Stephen, and Jane Ballinger. 2001. "The Roots of a Sociology of News: Remembering Mr. Gates and Social Control in the Newsroom." *Journalism & Mass Communication Quarterly* 78 (4): 641–658. doi:10.1177/107769900107800402.

Schudson, Michael. 2005. "Four Approaches to the Sociology of News." In *Mass Media and Society*, edited by James Curran and Michael Gurevitch, 171–197. London: Arnold.

Shaw, Ibrahim S. 2009. "Towards an African Journalism Model: A Critical Historical Perspective." *International Communication Gazette* 71 (6): 491–510. doi:10.1177/1748048509339792.

Skjerdal, Terje S. 2014. "Online Journalism under Pressure: An Ethiopian Account." In *Online Journalism in Africa: Trends, Practices and Emerging Cultures*, edited by Hayes M. Mabweazara, Fred O. Mudhai, and Jason Whittaker, 89–103. London: Routledge.

Tomaselli, Keyan G. 2003. "'Our Culture' Vs. 'Foreign Culture': An Essay on Ontological and Professional Issues in African Journalism." *International Communication Gazette* 65 (6): 427–441. doi:10.1177/0016549203065006001.

Tuchman, Gaye.1978. *Making News: A Study in the Construction of Reality*. London: Free Press.

Verweij, Peter, and Elvira van Noort. 2014. "Journalists' Twitter Networks, Public Debates and Relationships in South Africa." *Digital Journalism* 2 (1): 98–114. doi:10.1080/21670811.2013.850573.

Wasserman, Herman. 2009. "Extending the Theoretical Cloth to Make Room for African Experience: An Interview with Francis Nyamnjoh." *Journalism Studies* 10 (2): 281–293. doi:10.1080/14616700802678237.

White, David Manning. 1950. "The 'Gate Keeper': A Case Study in the Selection of News." *Journalism Quarterly* 27 (4): 383–390.

Woolgar, Steve. 1996. "Technologies as Cultural Artefacts." In *Information and Communication Technologies: Visions and Realities*, edited by William H. Dutton, 87–102. Oxford: Oxford University Press.

Zelizer, Barbie. 2004. *Taking Journalism Seriously: News and the Academy*. London: Sage.

Index

INDEX

For Product Safety Concerns and Information please contact our EU
representative GPSR@taylorandfrancis.com
Taylor & Francis Verlag GmbH, Kaufingerstraße 24, 80331 München, Germany